365.9

966788

CULTURES OF CONFINEMENT

FRANK DIKÖTTER AND IAN BROWN
editors

Cultures of Confinement

*A History of the Prison in Africa,
Asia and Latin America*

Cornell University Press
Ithaca, New York

Originally published in the United Kingdom by C. Hurst & Co. (Publishers) Ltd., London

Printed in India

First published in the United States of America in 2007 by Cornell University Press

Librarians: Library of Congress Cataloging-in-Publication Data are available.

ISBN   978-0-8014-4630-6

Cloth printing   10 9 8 7 6 5 4 3 2 1

CONTENTS

ILLUSTRATIONS

ACKNOWLEDGEMENTS

The project 'Cultures of Confinement', from which this volume has evolved, received its initial financial support from the Research Committee of the School of Oriental and African Studies (SOAS) for the organisation of an exploratory workshop. The project was then financed for three years by the Arts and Humanities Research Council (AHRC), which made possible the employment of a research fellow and a research assistant, and the organisation of two further workshops. We are extremely grateful to both SOAS and the AHRC for their generous financial support. We also wish to acknowledge the contributions of David Rothman and Peter Zinoman to the preliminary workshop, where the basic approach to the project was hammered out. And finally we are delighted to thank James Warren, for the flawless organisation of the meetings and, in particular, for his preparation of the final manuscript for the publishers.

Frank Dikötter and Ian Brown
School of Oriental and African Studies
November 2006

CONTRIBUTORS

CARLOS AGUIRRE is Associate Professor of History at the University of Oregon. He is the author of several books and articles about crime, punishment and slavery in Peru and Latin America including, most recently, *The Criminals of Lima and their Worlds: The prison experience*, Durham, NC: Duke University Press, 2005, and *Breve Historia de la Esclavitud en el Perú*, Lima: Fondo Editorial del Congreso del Perú, 2005.

CLARE ANDERSON is Senior Lecturer in the School of Historical Studies, University of Leicester. Her research has focused on nineteenth-century prisons and penal settlements across the Indian Ocean world. She is the author of *Convicts in the Indian Ocean: Transportation from South Asia to Mauritius, 1815–53*, Basingstoke: Macmillan, 2000, and *Legible Bodies: Race, criminality and colonialism in South Asia*, Oxford: Berg, 2004.

DAVID ARNOLD is Professor of Asian and Global History at Warwick University, and was formerly Professor of South Asian History at the School of Oriental and African Studies, London. In addition to several essays on crime, the police and prisons in colonial India, his published work includes *Colonizing the Body: State medicine and epidemic disease in nineteenth-century India*, Berkeley, CA: University of California Press, 1993, and *The Tropics and the Travelling Gaze*, Seattle, WA: University of Washington Press, 2006.

FLORENCE BERNAULT teaches African History at the University of Wisconsin-Madison. Her publications include *Démocraties ambigües en Afrique centrale*, Paris: Karthala, 1996, *Enfermement, prison et châtiments en Afrique, XIXe–XXe siècles*, Paris: Karthala, 1999, translated into English as *A History of Prisons and Confinement in Africa*, Portsmouth: Heinemann, 2003.

IAN BROWN is Professor of the Economic History of South East Asia at the School of Oriental and African Studies, London. His principal publications include *The Elite and the Economy in Siam c. 1890–1920*, Singapore: Oxford University Press, 1988, *Economic Change in South-East Asia, c. 1830–1980*, Kuala Lumpur: Oxford University Press, 1997, and *A Colonial Economy in Crisis: Burma's rice cultivators and the world depression of the 1930s*, London: RoutledgeCurzon, 2005.

FRANK DIKÖTTER is Professor of the Modern History of China at the School of Oriental and African Studies, London. He is the author of a series of micro-studies which trace the contingent ways in which ideas, objects and institutions acquire global dimensions and were selectively appropriated in modern China. These include, among others, *The Discourse of Race in Modern China*, Stanford University Press, 1992 and *Crime, Punishment and the Prison in Modern China*, New York: Columbia University Press, 2002.

ANTHONY GORMAN is Lecturer in Modern Middle Eastern History, in the School of Literature, Languages and Cultures at the University of Edinburgh. He was formerly a Research Associate in the Department of History at the School of Oriental and African Studies, London. He is the author of *Historians, State and Politics in Twentieth-Century Egypt: Contesting the nation*, London: RoutledgeCur-zon, 2003 and a number of articles on the political and commercial activities of the resident foreign presence in modern Egypt.

INTRODUCTION

Frank Dikötter

THE PRISON IN THE WORLD

Prisons, it seems, are on the increase everywhere, from Britain to China, as ever larger proportions of humanity find themselves behind bars, doing time for crime. Such was the extent to which the twentieth century was marked by the incarceration of vast masses of people that Alain Besançon characterised the period as 'the century of concentration camps'. Over the course of the last two centuries the use of confinement has spread across the face of the world to become almost everywhere a major form of punishment, alongside fines, probation, community service and the death sentence, as countries differing widely in political ideology and cultural background have replaced a variety of existing modes of punishment with the custodial sentence. The actual rates of incarceration have varied over the course of the last century, but the trend is upwards, as new prisons continue to be built and prison populations swell, in the Americas, Europe, Asia and the Middle East. However, we know precious little about the history of the prison in global perspective. Rather than interpreting its popularity everywhere as the predictable result of 'globalisation', this book underlines the fact that the prison—like all institutions—was never simply imposed or copied, but was reinvented and transformed by a host of local factors, its success being dependent on its flexibility. Complex cultural negotiations took place in encounters between different parts of the world, and rather than assigning a passive role to Latin America, Asia and Africa, this volume points out the acts of resistance or appropriation which altered the social practices associated with confinement. The prison, in short, was understood in culturally specific ways and reinvented by a variety of local contexts examined here for the first time in global perspective.

Where confinement existed before the advent of modernity—in the guise of galleys in the Mediterranean, *oubliettes* in France or houses of correction in

1

England—it was used alongside many other forms of punishment. Punishment was characterised by a multiplicity of measures including whipping, the pillory and the gallows in England, or exile, penal servitude and beating in China. Variety characterised pre-modern penal regimes, as a whole range of punishments were meted out by courts in France, England, India, China or Japan. Each crime committed was deemed unique in its circumstances, dependent largely but not solely on the social status of both offender and victim, and a corresponding punishment was selected from a multiplicity of penalties. Moreover, where confinement figured in the judicial process, it was not necessarily or exclusively associated with punishment. In the local gaols of imperial China and France, suspects awaiting trial as well as witnesses were detained during the criminal investigation and the trial, which could last several months. In eighteenth-century England large numbers of debtors were held in gaol: their incarceration was not a measure of punishment but a means of securing a person until the debt was paid in a conflict between two private citizens. Imprisonment, in imperial China and *ancien régime* France, was not thought of as a punishment in itself, and time spent in gaol during trial was not treated as part of the penalty. Only during the nineteenth and twentieth centuries would the prison gradually become the principal sanction: while the death sentence and the levying of fines survived, most forms of bodily punishment were abolished in favour of the deprivation of liberty. The specific timing of the appearance of the custodial sentence across the globe varied, as the following chapters show, but by 1820 the movement in favour of penal reform was well established in parts of Europe and the United States, while most of the world witnessed the emergence of modern penitentiaries—either on paper or on the ground—in the second half of the nineteenth century. Whatever the chronology of their appearance, uniformity characterised modern penal regimes, as an exact measure of liberty was taken away for each category of offence: time was traded for crime. A shift from non-custodial to custodial punishment entailed a transformation of the meaning of spaces of confinement: where the traditional gaol held suspects awaiting trial, the modern prison became in time a therapeutic space for the reformation of convicted offenders.

If prisons are very much modern, penologists today often agree that they have not lived up to their promise, although a viable alternative has yet to be proposed: we seem to be stuck with the prison. Four missions have generally been proposed for the prison, namely retribution, incapacitation, deterrence and rehabilitation. Retribution was decried by most prison reformers as a 'populist' and reprehensible impulse: instead restitution has generally been emphasised by penal philosophy since the late eighteenth century. Incapacitation and deterrence, on the other hand, were rarely portrayed as adequate goals in themselves. Correction through segregation was thus the key notion which distinguished the modern prison from previous spaces of confinement. Reformation has been the most powerfully seductive idea espoused by modern penology, although the history of prisons, if it demonstrates anything, shows how they have generally failed to rehabilitate prisoners. Prisons from the very beginning resisted their supporters' intended purposes, generating wretched institutional conditions where humanitarian goals were heralded. The road to hell is paved with good intentions, and the great expectations placed on the capacity of prisons to perform often contradictory goals (how is punishment compatible with reformation?) stand in contrast to the climate of violence within its walls. A chasm separates proclaimed intentions from actual practices. Monuments of order on paper turned into squalid places of human suffering within walls of bricks and mortar. Envisaged as a haven for repentance—'a machine to grind rogues honest', according to Jeremy Bentham—prison is often no more than an enclave of violence, producing caged misery at worst, enforced lethargy at best. Contrary to the workhouse or the lunatic asylum, the prison, in the eyes of its critics, is an invention of modernity that has yet to be dismantled: prisons do not reform criminals, do not reduce reoffending rates and do not address the social problems conducive to crime.[1] If anything, they produce violence and generate crime by meeting harm with harm.[2]

It is precisely the singular resilience of this contested institution that makes a history of the prison so urgent. It is not just another trendy topic of cultural history claiming a global dimension, nor one more unremarkable aspect of a staid history of state institutions, but an inquiry into the formation of an incarcerating society in which we all live. A first step towards a global history of the prison is to recognise that élites around the world were generally fascinated by the penitentiary ideal and eager to embrace it, rather than compelled by dark forces of imperialism to adopt it. The prison epitomised the dreams of state officials and local authorities in Latin America, while confinement was praised as a viable alternative to banishment by the first Qing envoys to Europe who visited Pentonville Prison in the 1860s. In colonial contexts, prisons were part and parcel of the 'civilising mission' of colonisers, as existing penal practices, which were often based on physical punishment, were viewed as 'barbaric' and 'uncivilised'. Yet

---

[1]   Thomas Mathiesen, *Prison on Trial*, Winchester: Waterside Press, 2000.

[2]   Philip Priestley, *Victorian Prison Lives: English prison biography, 1830–1914*, London: Methuen, 1985, p. xiii.

postcolonial regimes more often than not consolidated rather than dismantled the prison for their own purposes.

A monument to modernity, the prison was admired by social and political élites around the world from Paris to Rio de Janeiro and Auburn to Tokyo. In England and France changing sensibilities towards pain, new representations of bodily integrity, humanitarian values heralded by Enlightenment thinkers, utilitarian ideas about punishment as a corrective measure, growing dissatisfaction with existing legal penalties and revulsion at the conditions of existing gaols combined towards the end of the eighteenth century to create a new conception of the prison as a total institution in which the criminal could be reformed into a viable citizen.[3] While commitment to social improvement and faith in the malleability of human nature pervaded early debates, the single most important factor in the emergence of the prison was the political revolutions of the late eighteenth and mid-nineteenth centuries. During the French revolution the fall of the Bastille symbolised the defeat of an entire *ancien régime* of punishment perceived as cruel and arbitrary. A post-revolutionary mode of governance, in which legitimacy was vested in the nation rather than in a king, based its authority to punish on a code of law. Moreover, as the social hierarchies specific to traditional regimes were theoretically swept away by a new ideology of equality and fraternity, the state proclaimed a duty of care over its subjects: criminals were part of a new political order and should be punished in a humane way before being returned to the social body. The idea of the prison—producer of obedient and honest citizens for a moral community based on the rule of law—paralleled the rise of the modern state and the extension of political rights. Russia opted for rehabilitation over corporal punishment during the era of Great Reforms, undertaking to redeem the nation's criminals in a new prison system, while prison reform was welcomed by the Tanzimat reformers in the Ottoman Empire. These global developments were dynamically interrelated: portraying their mission as a fight against barbarism and inhumanity, prison reformers around the world operated within a comparative framework in which prison reform was seen as an indicator of a country's progress. The dungeon stood as an embarrassing reminder of backwardness, while the prison epitomised civilisation. Corporal punishment, arbitrary justice and corrupt gaols were remnants of an old world order, while

---

[3]   There are some excellent essays in Norbert Finzsch and Robert Jütte (eds), *Institutions of Confinement: Hospitals, asylums, and prisons in Western Europe and North America, 1500–1950*, Cambridge University Press, 1996. On the importance of changing sensibilities, which started as early as the sixteenth century, see Pieter Spierenburg, *The Spectacle of Suffering: Executions and the evolution of repression*, Cambridge University Press, 1984.

reformed judicial systems, legal codes and modern prisons were indicative of a new political order. As Patricia O'Brien has argued for Europe, the moral consensus and shared political culture of punishment which appeared across the old continent, from France to Russia, was made possible by a new rationale of state sovereignty: at the very core of the political agenda of the modern state was the need to devise new ways of punishing subjects no longer bound by traditional restraints, an impetus which could be found across the globe as old orders collapsed to make place for new modes of governance which invoked 'the people' and 'the nation' rather than 'estates' or 'classes'.[4] Where the prison was posited as a symbol of modernity rather than an index of democracy, as in the case of Latin America, 'cruel and humiliating' punishments were nonetheless denounced by prison reformers, even as confinement continued to produce social exclusion.[5]

The ideas of Beccaria, Bentham, Locke, Montesquieu and other philosophers were appropriated across borders, as modernising élites dispersed around the globe identified with and shared in the Enlightenment concepts of law and government. This led to interesting shifts in meaning, for instance the 'Confucian' understanding attributed in China to the 'Christian' notion of repentance which so much preoccupied penologists. With the rise of evolutionary theories in the last third of the nineteenth century, the prison became one of the most discussed indicators of a country's capacity to endure in an international struggle for survival. Where modern states proclaimed their duty to provide adequate social protection for all their citizens and construct a united national community— building hospitals, schools and prisons—they also acted within a global frame of reference in which emulation and competition led to ever shifting standards, innovations and expectations: modernising élites in Peru, Russia or China posed as vanguards of a new world order indispensable in helping their country to 'catch up', while colonial rulers in Africa and Asia were keen to escape from the alleged 'backwardness' of indigenous practices. The prison was a prestige symbol that exerted fascination around the world, as governments enthusiastically invested vast amounts of money in cells and walls—often well beyond their financial

[4] Patricia O'Brien, 'Prison Reform in France and Other European Countries in the Nineteenth Century' in Norbert Finzsch and Robert Jütte (eds), *Institutions of Confinement: Hospitals, asylums, and prisons in Western Europe and North America, 1500–1950*, Cambridge University Press, 1996, pp. 298–9.

[5] Ricardo D. Salvatore and Carlos Aguirre, 'The Birth of the Penitentiary in Latin America: Toward an interpretive social history of prisons' in Ricardo D. Salvatore and Carlos Aguirre (eds), *The Birth of the Penitentiary in Latin America: Essays on criminology, prison reform, and social control, 1830–1940*, Austin, TX: University of Texas Press, 1996, p. 24.

capacities—in order to join the privileged group of 'advanced nations'. In London, Pentonville Prison opened its doors in 1842, the most expensive and technologically developed building in the capital apart from Parliament. Similar prestige prisons would appear in the world's capitals, from Lima and St Petersburg to Tokyo and Beijing.

While so far I have used the term 'failure of the prison' without any qualification, David Garland has underlined how such a condemnation runs the risk of portraying punishment as a means to an end. A teleological conception of a complex social institution like the prison can lead to impoverished historical understanding.[6] Most institutions like the prison or the guillotine are social artefacts which cannot be wholly explained in terms of mere instrumental purposes. They embody wider cultural meanings which can be unravelled only by careful historical contextualisation: these cultural meanings are explored comparatively in this volume. A comparative approach to the history of the prison thus highlights the extent to which common knowledge is appropriated and transformed by very distinct local styles of expression dependent on the political, economic, social and cultural variables of particular institutions and social groups. As ideas move across borders, they are adjusted to specific local conditions: inculturation, rather than acculturation, characterises a modernity that is inflected in a multiplicity of ways by different élites. The emergence of the prison in Latin America, Russia, Japan, China or India cannot be interpreted as a belated replication of a European model—and even less as a uniform imposition by 'world capitalism' or 'cultural imperialism'—so much as a local appropriation of global ideas. As internationally circulated discourses and practices of punishment intersected locally with concrete ideological and political configurations, they engendered new varieties of incarceration: underneath an overarching rationale based on the idea of humane and reformative punishment, the prison was multivalent, capable of being adopted in a variety of mutually incompatible environments, ranging from the *bagne* in Vietnam, the cellular prison in China or the concentration camps in South Africa. Confinement, in short, acquired specific cultural and social dimensions which help to explain its extraordinary resilience across the globe.

In China, for instance, the abolition of physical punishment and the adoption of the custodial sentence in the early twentieth century is generally interpreted as the result of a colonial encounter which forced the Qing to adopt a modern judicial system in order to obtain the abrogation of extraterritoriality: China had

---

[6]   David Garland, *Punishment and Modern Society: A study in social theory*, Oxford: Clarendon, 1990, p. 19.

to show foreign powers that it could treat its prisoners 'humanely'. A 'pre-history' of the prison, however, reveals a more complex story. As constant demographic growth led to deteriorating social and economic conditions in the eighteenth century, the Qing responded to rising crime rates by expanding the existing system of banishment. As exile grew, the existing gaols that provided overnight accommodation became seriously overcrowded, generating a discontent with the legal order which was expressed in organised trends of thought. When the first Qing envoys to Europe visited Pentonville Prison in the 1860s they were full of admiration: confinement appeared to be a viable alternative to banishment, as prisons, it seemed, could induce repentance (*huiguo*) and self-renewal (*zixin*). The prison was widely perceived by reformers as a 'modern' tool capable of implementing 'traditional' values: the idea of reformation in confinement—abandoned in Britain and the United States by the end of the nineteenth century—was at the heart of the prison reform movement in twentieth-century China.

Even colonial practices could be significantly inflected or altered by local élites. In India, for instance, proposals for penal reform between 1830 and 1920 were often rejected by colonial officers as impractical or inexpedient, and major aspects of contemporary penological thought in Britain were abandoned, showing that the 'British model' was never simply imported into the colonies. Not only was caste and religion allowed to affect prison management, as social hierarchies outside the prison walls were replicated inside its cells, but the entire emphasis on moral reform and basic education was all but abandoned. In some parts of the world, for example in India, the Netherlands East Indies and French Indochina, the prison also became a vector in local opposition to colonial rule. In a context of rising nationalism, the colonial regime saw imprisonment as an effective means of taking nationalist opponents out of circulation: it expressed little interest in their reformation and rehabilitation. Political prisoners, on the other hand, took confinement as an opportunity to develop oppositional networks and alliances, to learn the techniques of agitation and revolution, and to advance political education: for many a nationalist leader, time spent in prison reinforced their anti-colonial credentials and conferred status in the nationalist struggle.

The colonial context, while it varied from place to place and significantly altered over time, was different in two further respects. In some parts of the colonial world, for example in Burma, the prison administration, far from enthusiastically seeking to import new penological practices wholesale, came to harbour serious reservations about the effectiveness of the prison in reforming the criminal. They began instead to explore alternative approaches to the treatment of the convict that did not involve long-term confinement, and that were adjusted to the distinctive economic and social circumstances of their territory. In other parts of the colonial world, notably in Vietnam, a contrasting dynamic was at work. French prison officials may have maintained faith in the principle of the prison but argued that it would not be effective in the reform of 'native' criminals.[7] Nor was 'the colonial state' a homogeneous entity: in the case of Hong Kong, for instance, a harsh and punitive approach towards convicts from mainland China was widely supported by both European and Chinese communities, which had to be confronted repeatedly by reform-minded governors and by the Colonial Office, as it explicitly forbade any legislation 'whereby persons of African or Asiatic birth may be subjected to any disabilities or restrictions to which persons of European birth are not also subjected.'[8] The colonial state, in short, could participate in the spread of a vision of the person as a rational, responsible and equal individual—native or otherwise.

One of the results of these global variations is highly variable rates of incarceration. While the numbers of prisoners over the world are extremely difficult to gauge, even rough estimates compiled by the Howard League for Penal Reform on the basis of detailed prison statistics in 1936 show significant disparities: some of the lowest rates appeared in China (20 per 100,000 according to my own estimates), Ireland (19.4), Great Britain (29.9) and Chile (19.7), while most European, African and Asian countries varied from 50 to 150 per 100,000. The exceptions included Estonia (275), Finland (231), Southern Rhodesia (234), Sierra Leone (386), South Africa (232), Honduras (220) and Paraguay (258).[9] Needless to say, these figures were often gross underestimates, while many countries, for instance the Soviet Union, yielded no reliable statistics at all. Yet however problematic they may be, the numbers indicate both the global nature of incarceration and the disparate nature of its use. As the Howard League underlined in its report, there had never been a time when so many people were shut up, leading to overcrowding, unsanitary conditions, bullying, humiliation and even torture. Designed to replace 'feudal' and 'cruel' forms of physical punishment that were deemed to be incompatible with a modern mode of governance, the custodial sentence around the globe produced its own set of problems that to this day penologists have not been able to solve, even as the incarceration rates have grown far beyond those of 1936.

[7] Peter Zinoman, *The Colonial Bastille*, Berkeley, CA: University of California Press, 2001, pp. 16–17.

[8] Frank Dikötter, '"A Paradise for Rascals": Colonialism, punishment and the prison in Hong Kong (1841–1898)', *Crime, History and Societies*, 8, 1 (summer 2004), pp. 49–63.

[9] Howard League for Penal Reform, *The Prisoner Population of the World*, London: Howard League for Penal Reform, 1936, kindly provided by Tony Gorman.

THE WORLD IN THE PRISON

Too many of Foucault's admirers have uncritically accepted the French philosopher's vision of the prison as the perfect realisation of the modern state. Archival evidence, which allows us to move away from official rhetoric and lofty ideals towards the messy realities of incarceration, on the contrary highlights the limits of the state. As Carlos Aguirre has pointed out in a recent book on the prisoners of Lima, the constant lack of financial resources, poor strategies of personnel recruitment, lack of control over prison guards, and widespread corruption inside the penal system meant the authorities who operated the prisons had widespread discretion in dealing with inmates and were often detached from the main goals of penal reform formulated by the state.[10] Moreover, as David Garland notes, for theorists such as Weber or Foucault, punishment was a mere key to unlocking wider historical processes such as 'rationalisation' or the nature of 'modernity': frequently absent from ambitious explanatory schemes about the prison are the prisoners themselves.

To this we might add that however helpful the writings of Foucault, Marx, Durkheim or Elias may be in their single-minded pursuit of an explanatory theme—and authors of this volume predictably vary in their uses of these theorists—their work is unequivocally about Europe. One possible way of researching a global history of the prison might be to offer evidence from Asia and Africa which explicitly questions the views of European thinkers—would it not be for the fact that such an approach would still be Eurocentric, transforming the rest of the world into a laboratory for the testing of theories spun in Europe.

At the centre of our concerns are not only grand theories and imposing designs but also the guards and prisoners on the ground. Just as the continued use of coercion by guards created penal realities which had little to do with ambitious plans on paper, prisoners were never the passive subjects of a great 'disciplinary project' or a 'civilising process'. As this volume shows, a comparative history of confinement which puts prison life back into the picture not only tells us much about the agency of ordinary people supposed to be captives, but also illustrates how and why prison fails to be redemptive. As David Arnold notes in his chapter, prisoners were seldom entirely compliant, and in the long history of the colonial prison there were many ways in which prisoners evaded or resisted the

---

[10] Carlos Aguirre, *The Criminals of Lima and Their Worlds: The prison experience, 1850–1935*, Durham, NC: Duke University Press, 2005, pp. 143–55.

restrictions the prison authorities sought to impose upon them. Emile Durkheim observed long ago that the core problem of the prison as a form of discipline resides in the lack of inclination on the part of the majority of prisoners to participate in the process of 'reformation'. In other institutional situations such as the school or the factory, the individual must to some extent share the goals of the disciplinary process if discipline is to be effective. By robbing prisoners of self-respect, so central to self-discipline, the prison did not produce 'disciplined subjects' but hardened recidivists.

Inmate resistance, moreover, was often grounded in alternative cultures which had little to do with penal rhetoric. As Patricia O'Brien has shown in a pioneering study of prisons in France published a quarter of a century ago, prison subcultures offered alternative languages—some literally incomprehensible to outsiders, as in the case of argot—as well as forms of identity which shaped oppositional strategies.[11] Rather than being transformed by the penal system into industrious citizens, prisoners often deepened their criminal identifications thanks to the existence of inmate subcultures, prison having the opposite effect to its intended outcomes. While the study of subcultures is notoriously difficult, in particular in parts of the world where archives tend to be far more patchy than in France or England, the creation in prison of organised resistance is evident among political prisoners in most parts of Asia. In republican China and in colonial Vietnam, for instance, political prisoners were able to form networks, recruit new party members and obtain economic advantages by organising hunger strikes. After Mao Zedong started the Long March, the prisoners who turned their cells into studies to catch up on the latest learning could be better off than the southern guerrillas left behind to fight government troops: the Communist Party was strengthened rather than weakened by incarceration.[12]

However, a narrow focus on the formation of oppositional strategies by political prisoners would result in a biased interpretation of prison life. Such an account also runs the risk of unwittingly colluding with communist states which tend to discredit previous regimes by granting their political prisoners an importance which is blown out of all proportion, for instance by transforming them into martyrs of the revolutionary cause.[13] Moreover, beyond confronta-

---

[11] Patricia O'Brien, *The Promise of Punishment: Prisons in nineteenth-century France*, Princeton University Press, 1982.

[12] Frank Dikötter, *Crime, Punishment and the Prison in Modern China*, New York: Columbia University Press, 2002; Zinoman, *The Colonial Bastille*.

[13] This point is also made about Soviet historiography by Bruce F. Adams, *The Politics of Punishment: Prison reform in Russia, 1863–1917*, DeKalb, IL: Northern Illinois University Press, 1996,

tional forms of interaction with guards, the majority of prisoners—in China, Vietnam, India or Africa—were ordinary people with little inclination to identify with underground parties and with limited scope for collective bargaining with prison authorities or powerful inmates. Carlos Aguirre emphasises that open challenges in the shape of riots, escapes or strikes were relatively rare, as most prisoners aimed to maintain a tacit compromise with the authorities in order to prevent major eruptions of violence and unrest. Accommodation rather than open confrontation was a more fruitful strategy, as inmates took advantage of the many flaws which inevitably characterised a prison system which suffered from inadequate resources, insufficient personnel and widespread corruption. The type of order which emerged from the daily negotiations and transactions between prisoners and guards has been called the 'customary order' by Aguirre, a notion which captures how compromises between a variety of agents on the ground transformed the penitentiary project into something quite different from that envisaged by penal reformers. The customary order aimed at the maintenance of a fragile balance of power, as guards were keen to operate the prisons with the minimum disruption possible by granting prisoners small concessions and privileges: a mixture of tolerance and control, abuse and negotiation rather than coercion and despotism thus marked the widespread illegal and informal relationships between inmates and staff.[14]

This leads us to another important observation: as we move away from the serene panopticon we find that the boundaries of most prisons were porous, as guards colluded with prisoners, ideas and objects (paper and drugs) moved in and out of confinement, and, more generally, religious, social, ethnic and gender hierarchies were replicated inside the prison, undermining the very notion of penal equality to produce social exclusion. The exclusionary practices which marked the customary order inside most prisons worldwide were not merely relics from a traditional order to be eliminated by the advent of a modern penitentiary. Rather, they were consolidated and reinforced by the actual workings of daily life behind bars. Many historians have written about the prison in society, but we also need a history of society in the prison. Society colonised the prison and undermined discipline to a much greater extent than discipline ever managed to move out of the prison to regiment society. Prison is thus a microcosm which reflects society, making it a crucial topic for historical study, all the more as such a 'history from below' may be much more difficult in other contexts in which

---

pp. 5–7, but ignored in the methodology used by Zinoman, *The Colonial Bastille*.

[14] Aguirre, *The Criminals of Lima and Their Worlds*, pp. 143–55.

primary sources are less abundant. The colonial hierarchy found in British India
was strengthened in prison, while the authoritarian tradition of Peruvian society was exacerbated by the customary order created in Lima's penitentiary. In
China the gap between literate élites and ordinary farmers was deepened by the
experience of incarceration, while any study on the penitentiary project in the
United States will be confronted with entrenched racialised divisions. Already
in the early nineteenth century, Benjamin Constant feared the 'obscure dictatorship' exercised by guards over inmates.[15] But as the following chapters illustrate, equally arbitrary forms of oppression were used by powerful prisoners over
weaker ones, as the social hierarchies found outside the prison, whether based
on gender, ethnicity, religion, class or region, were reinforced by a customary
order inside the penitentiary in which those at the bottom of the social scale
had everything to fear—whether from the power of cell bosses or the tyranny of
influential guards. And where states did succeed, against all odds, to build more
centralised and better policed prisons, it has generally been to maintain social
inequalities and politically repressive regimes rather than to help and reform the
alleged criminal.

Finally, we should briefly mention the limits of the volume. The inclusion of
every country in every part of the world outside Europe and the United States
would not only have been an impossible task, given the state of current research
and the limits of the length of the volume, but also an undesirable goal. The aim
is not to provide an encyclopaedia of the history of the prison in Asia, Africa
and South America, but to provide a sufficiently diverse set of historical backgrounds to raise fruitful questions about the global nature of the penitentiary
project. Research on the Middle East, for instance, is still patchy, and it would
have been unfeasible to mention every single country: a far more effective strategy is to focus on one or two case studies while invoking examples from other
parts of the region to highlight distinct areas of discontinuity. The chapter on the
Middle East, as well as the one on South East Asia, thus offer a great amount of
original research which is not available elsewhere. In the case of East Asia, one
in-depth chapter on China seems more helpful than a superficial overview of the
entire region, especially as the available scholarship on the history of the prison
in that country now permits a detailed case-study. Further chapters on Korea or

[15] Jacques-Guy Petit, *Ces peines obscures. La prison pénale en France (1780–1875)*, Paris: Fayard, 1990,
p. 545.

Japan might have delighted specialists of the region but overwhelmed the more general reader and diluted the overall impact of the volume. We seek depth of analysis rather than extent of coverage. However, annotated bibliographies at the end of each chapter provide a guide to further reading. The sheer diversity of cultures and languages in Asia and Africa rules out thematic chapters, and each of the chapters in this volume instead takes up a number of themes, from political prisoners to architectural history and the imprisonment of women, to create an overarching sense of integration and comparability. Our hope is that the volume will generate sufficient interest in the global dimensions of the prison to prompt other researchers to take its story further.

PRISONS AND PRISONERS IN MODERNISING LATIN AMERICA (1800-1940)

Carlos Aguirre[1]

Prisons are many things at the same time: institutions embodying state power and authority; arenas of conflict, negotiation and resistance; spaces for the creation of subaltern forms of socialisation and culture; powerful symbols of modernity (or lack thereof); cultural artefacts representing the contradictions and tensions afflicting societies; economic enterprises aimed at manufacturing both commodities and workers; centres for the production of different forms of knowledge about the lower classes of society; and, last but not least, places where large segments of the human population live parts of their lives, shape their worldviews, and engage in negotiations and interactions with other individuals and state authorities in a constant struggle to survive. We study prisons for what they tell us about themselves—their designs, their functioning, their place in society—but also about their residents, about those exercising authority over them (the state, penal experts and others) and about the social arrangements they reflect, reproduce or subvert.

Writing the history of prisons in modern Latin America is not an easy endeavour, since it must encompass a number of countries with quite different sociopolitical processes, patterns of economic development, racial/ethnic make-ups and experiments with punishment and incarceration that have to do with the

[1] I would like to thank all the participants in the 'Cultures of Confinement' workshops (London, June and December 2005) for their encouragement, criticism and suggestions, and especially Frank Dikötter for the original invitation to be part of this project and for his valuable feedback on earlier versions of this chapter. I would also like to recognise my debt to Ricardo Salvatore (Universidad Torcuato di Tella, Buenos Aires), in dialogue and collaboration with whom many of my ideas about prisons in Latin America have been shaped over the years.

divergent adaptation of foreign doctrines, the development of internal ideological and political debates, and subaltern forms of agency and resistance. The difficulties faced by such an enterprise are even greater if we consider the relatively undeveloped state of the historiography on prisons in the region. This chapter, which builds upon a host of recently published monographs and edited volumes,[2] summarises the connections between the history of prisons and the evolution of Latin American societies from 1800 to 1940. The main goal is to offer a rough outline of some of the main contours of this history, focusing on the relationship between the design and functioning of prisons, the institutional forms of punishment being implemented, the forms of coping and resistance that prisoners adopted, and the specific forms of state-society relation that prison regimes reflect and reveal.

One caveat is in order at the start of this chapter. The term 'modern' will be frequently applied when referring to Latin American societies and prisons during the period under study. By that, two different things are meant. First, it is merely a chronological label, since the 'modern' period in Latin America is almost always considered to be the one that followed the end of colonial times (for most of the region except Cuba and Puerto Rico) around the second decade of the nineteenth century. Thus, according to this view, colonialism was necessarily pre-modern, and modernity a condition, or a possibility, associated exclusively with independent nation-states. For the sake of simplicity this usage of the term 'modern' will be maintained when referring to post-independence Latin America. Second, the term reflects the goals, hopes and self-image of Latin American élites and prison reformers. Modernity was their ultimate goal as well as the

---

[2] A short list must include Fernando Picó, *El día menos pensado: Historia de los presidiarios en Puerto Rico, 1793–1993*, Río Piedras: Ediciones Huracán, 1994; Ricardo D. Salvatore and Carlos Aguirre (eds), *The Birth of the Penitentiary in Latin America: Essays on criminology, prison reform, and social control, 1830–1940*, Austin, TX: University of Texas Press, 1996; Antonio Padilla Arroyo, *De Belem a Lecumberri: Pensamiento social y penal en el México decimonónico*, Mexico City: Archivo General de la Nación, 2001; Peter M. Beattie, *The Tribute of Blood: Army, honor, race, and nation in Brazil, 1864–1945*, Durham, NC: Duke University Press, 2001; Ricardo D. Salvatore, Carlos Aguirre and Gilbert M. Joseph (eds), *Crime and Punishment in Latin America: Law and society since colonial times*, Durham, NC: Duke University Press, 2001; Marco Antonio León León, *Encierro y corrección: La configuración de un sistema de prisiones en Chile (1800–1911)*, Santiago: Universidad Central de Chile, 2003; Marcos Fernández Labbé, *Prisión común, imaginario social e identidad social, 1870–1920*, Santiago: Editorial Andrés Bello, 2003; Lila Caimari, *Apenas un delincuente: Crimen, castigo y cultura en la Argentina, 1880–1955*, Buenos Aires: Siglo XXI, 2004; Carlos Aguirre, *The Criminals of Lima and Their Worlds: The prison experience, 1850–1935*, Durham, NC: Duke University Press, 2005; Ernesto Bohoslavsky and María Silvia Di Liscia (eds), *Instituciones y formas de control social en América Latina, 1840–1940. Una revision*, Buenos Aires: Prometeo Libros, 2006.

measure of their successes and failures. To be modern, or at least to offer the appearance of being so, was the almost universal aspiration of Latin American élites, and prisons (i.e. modern prisons) came to be imagined as part of that project. Thus it may seem legitimate to assess the evolution of prisons against those goals and objectives, i.e., against the aspirations to 'modernity' that the Latin American élites so proudly proclaimed.

PUNISHMENT AND PRISONS FROM COLONIAL TIMES TO THE NEW NATION-STATES

For most countries in the region, independence from colonialism was attained during the period from 1810 to 1825.[3] After the expulsion of Spanish and Portuguese colonial powers, those newly-independent countries started a protracted and complicated process of state- and nation-formation that, in most cases, was shaped by a continuous counterpoint between the imported ideals of republicanism, liberalism and the rule of law, and the realities of racist, authoritarian and exclusionary social structures. European colonialism was replaced by socio-political and legal structures that reinforced the exclusion of large sectors of the indigenous and black populations. In the name of individual liberal rights the Creole élites that captured state power deprived Indians and blacks of even the small, but not unimportant, windows of legal protection accorded them by paternalistic colonial legislation and practices. Profoundly hierarchical societies continued to exist under the legal façade of a republic of citizens. The permanence of slavery and other forms of labour, racial and social control—peonage, Indian tribute, forced military conscription and vagrancy laws, to name but a few—flagrantly contradicted the system of equality before the law and universal citizenship promised by most Spanish-American constitutions.[4] Within this context prisons played an important, albeit not necessarily central, role in the implementation of mechanisms of social, labour and racial control in the post-independence era.

During the colonial period prisons and gaols were not institutional spaces that administrators, visitors, travellers or inmates could praise for their organisation, security, hygiene or positive effects on their residents. They were not, in fact, overly important in the punitive schemes being implemented by colonial

---

[3] The only exceptions were Cuba and Puerto Rico, where Spanish colonialism ended in 1898.

[4] Florencia Mallon, 'Indian Communities, Political Cultures and the State in Latin America', *Journal of Latin American Studies*, 24 (1992), pp. 35–55; Brooke Larson, *Trials of Nation Making: Liberalism, race, and ethnicity in the Andes, 1810–1910*, Cambridge University Press, 2004.

authorities. In most cases they were simply places of detention for suspects being tried or for condemned criminals awaiting the execution of their sentences. Colonial forms of punishment and social control did not count prisons as one of their main conduits. Punishment, in fact, was more commonly applied through various other mechanisms typical of *ancien régime* societies, such as public executions, branding, whipping, public works or banishment. Housed in rather fetid and insecure buildings, most colonial gaols did not even keep records of inmates, dates of entry and release, or categories of crimes and sentences. Various types of gaols coexisted within a rather loose assortment of institutions of confinement: inquisition and municipal gaols, military and police stations, religious shelters for destitute women and private detention centres such as bakeries and textile sweatshops—where slaves and criminals were secluded and subjected to forced labour—or private gaols in rural *haciendas* and plantations, where unruly workers were punished. Penal islands such as Juan Fernández in Chile, San Juan de Ulúa in Mexico or San Lorenzo in Peru, or *presidios* (military barracks) located in frontier areas, were also used to detain and punish criminals deemed extremely dangerous. While some capital cities—Mexico City, Lima, Buenos Aires or Rio de Janeiro—could show some degree of organisation in the logistics of incarceration (with written bylaws and regular *visitas de cárcel* or gaol inspections performed by colonial authorities), imprisonment during the colonial period was a social practice regulated by custom, not the law, and aimed at simply warehousing detainees without implementing any institutional regime of punishment seeking to reform criminals.[5]

During the wars of independence and their immediate aftermath, criticism of colonial prison conditions was voiced by a few independent leaders that pointed to them as evidence of the horrors of colonialism. General José de San Martín, for instance, the 'liberator' of Argentina, Chile and Peru, visited Lima's gaols shortly after proclaiming the independence of Peru and was appalled by what he saw. He ordered the release of some inmates and shortly after enacted legislation aimed

[5] For studies about the various forms of punishment in colonial Latin America, see Patricia Aufderheide, 'Order and Violence: Social deviance and social control in Brazil, 1780–1840', PhD dissertation, University of Minnesota, 1976; William Taylor, *Drinking, Homicide, and Rebellion in Colonial Mexican Villages*, Stanford University Press, 1979, pp. 97–106; Gabriel Haslip-Viera, *Crime and Punishment in Late Colonial Mexico, 1692–1810*, Albuquerque, NM: University of New Mexico Press, 1999; Alberto Flores Galindo, *Aristocracia y plebe: Estructura de clases y sociedad colonial, Lima, 1760–1830*, Lima: Mosca Azul Editores, 1984; Marco Antonio León León, 'Justicia, ceremonia y sacrificio: Una aproximación a las ejecuciones públicas en el Chile colonial', *Notas Históricas y Geográficas*, Universidad de Playa Ancha, Chile, 11 (2000), pp. 89–122; León León, *Encierro y corrección*, vol. I, pp. 53–125.

at ameliorating prison conditions. More important, and echoing ongoing penal reforms in Europe, he announced his decision to transform those places, where 'men were buried, got desperate, and died during the old regime', into spaces where inmates could be 'converted, through moderate and useful work, from immoral and vicious men into industrious and honest citizens.'[6] However, attitudes like this were rather uncommon and prison conditions rarely attracted the attention of post-independence state-makers. Some promised to correct those atrocities by enacting legislation aimed at implementing more humane and secure conditions of imprisonment. The rhetoric of liberalism, republicanism, and the rule of law held by the leaders of these newly-independent nations was always neutralised by discourses and practices that emphasised the need to control unruly and undeserving masses through harsh mechanisms of punishment. Extrajudicial forms of punishment, as well as traditional legally-sanctioned punitive practices such as public works, executions, whipping and banishment, continued to be used for decades after the end of the colonial period.[7] Serious financial shortages and constant political turmoil prevented most states from embarking on meaningful institutional reforms. States were simply too weak and fragile, and the élites too convinced of the unworthiness of the effort, to even imagine that widespread support would exist for any initiative towards the reform of prisons. Still, echoes of penal debates in Europe and North America began to be heard in Latin America and new ideas about prisons and punishment began to circulate around the 1830s.

By the beginning of the nineteenth century the penitentiary had been embraced as the state-of-the-art institutional model of incarceration in Europe and North America. A setting that combined an *ad hoc* architectural plan, a highly regimented routine of work and instruction, constant surveillance, purportedly humane treatment and religions instruction, the penitentiary captured the imagination of a small group of Latin American state-makers eager to imitate metropolitan societal models as a way of both embracing 'modernity' and trying 'successful' mechanisms of control over the undisciplined masses. From at least the 1830s public debates began to show the awareness among Latin American enlightened commentators of ongoing penal reforms in Europe and North

---

[6] Quoted in Carlos Aguirre, 'The Lima Penitentiary and the Modernization of Criminal Justice in Nineteenth-Century Peru' in Salvatore and Aguirre (eds), *The Birth of the Penitentiary*, p. 50.

[7] Carlos Aguirre, 'Violencia, castigo y control social: esclavos y panaderías en Lima, siglo XIX', *Pasado y Presente* (Lima), 1 (1988); Ricardo D. Salvatore, 'Death and Liberalism: Capital punishment after the fall of Rosas' in Salvatore, Aguirre and Joseph (eds), *Crime and Punishment*, pp. 308–41; León León, *Encierro y corrección*, vol. II, chapter 4.

America.[8] As with other aspects of Latin American societies, these interventions usually pointed to the sharp contrast between what they saw (and were ashamed of) in their own countries and the 'successes' of 'civilised' nations in the implementation of social policies, in this case, the elimination of crime and the creation of modern prison regimes. Still we have to notice that this fascination with European and North American models of punishment was not universal, and that even if for many state-makers it sounded like a good idea, they were not eager to invest financial or political capital in the building of (quite expensive) institutions that, they thought, would not necessarily do a better job than the traditional and informal forms of punishment being widely used. Enlightened critics of existing forms of punishment—whipping, stocks, public works, private gaols and illegal executions—were few, and their voices were lost in the midst of other, more pressing challenges such as internal fragmentation, political dissent, economic backwardness and foreign wars. In fact traditional forms of punishment were usually considered more fitting to the kinds of peoples they were intended to punish: uncivilised and barbarous masses, not active and enlightened citizens. Debates about the implementation of the jury system, for instance, reflected the profound distrust that Latin American élites felt for their rural, non-white, and illiterate masses, almost always regarded (even by well-intentioned liberal reformers) as barbarous, ignorant and incapable of becoming 'civilised'.

Nonetheless, by the middle of the nineteenth century several modern penitentiaries were built. Their construction was an attempt to accomplish various goals: to expand state intervention in social control efforts, to project an image of modernity usually conceived as the adoption of foreign models, to get rid of shocking and offensive forms of punishment, to offer urban élites a greater sense of security, and to improve the chances of transforming criminals into law-abiding citizens. However, the appearance of these penitentiaries does not necessarily mean those goals were a priority for political and social élites. In fact the construction of modern penitentiaries was the exception, not the rule, and their fate would provide additional evidence of their rather marginal place within the overall mechanisms of control and punishment.

The earliest project to build a penitentiary in Latin America was the 'House of Correction' in Rio de Janeiro, whose construction started in 1834 but was completed only in 1850. The time it took to complete the project reveals a great

---

[8] Aguirre, 'The Lima Penitentiary', pp. 53–4; León León, *Encierro y corrección*, vol. II, chapter 3; Ricardo D. Salvatore and Carlos Aguirre, 'The Birth of the Penitentiary in Latin America: Toward an interpretive social history of prisons' in Salvatore and Aguirre, *The Birth of the Penitentiary*, pp. 1–43.

deal about the financial and political obstacles faced by early prison reformers.[9] Construction of the penitentiary of Santiago de Chile started in 1844, closely following the Philadelphia cellular model; it first accepted inmates in 1847, but would begin operating at full scale only in 1856.[10] The Peruvian government started to build a penitentiary in Lima in 1856 that was completed and began to function in 1862, this time following the Auburn or 'congregate' blueprint.[11] Two more penitentiaries were built in the following decade: the Quito penitentiary (Ecuador) was completed in 1874 and the Buenos Aires penitentiary (Argentina) in 1877. A few elements are worth emphasising in this first wave of prison reform in Latin America. First, the design and bylaws of these penitentiaries invariably followed the model of similar North American institutions, namely the penitentiaries of Auburn and Philadelphia. Several Latin American reformers, like their European counterparts such as Alexis de Tocqueville, toured US prisons and were involved in the design and building of penitentiaries in their own countries. This group includes Mariano Felipe Paz Soldán from Peru, Francisco Solano Astaburuaga from Chile and Mucio Valdovinos from Mexico. These penitentiaries were built using blueprints inspired by, but not rigorously modelled after, Jeremy Bentham's 'panopticon'. Instead of the circular pavilion with an observatory tower in the centre, which would allow the constant and total surveillance of all inmates that Bentham had planned, these buildings consisted of lengthy rectangular pavilions with cell rows on both sides, emanating from a central point 'like radii from a common centre'.[12] Second, the construction of these penitentiaries, although publicised as a major turning point in each state's efforts to both control crime and reform prisoners, was not followed by the implementation of similar changes in the rest of each country's prison systems. For many decades, in fact, each of those penitentiaries would be the only such modern penal institution in an otherwise 'pre-modern' or unreformed archipelago of institutions of confinement. Therefore their impact was exceedingly small despite the high hopes that reformers had placed in them. Since each of

---

[9]   Marcos Bretas, 'What the Eyes Can't See: Stories from Rio de Janeiro's prisons' in Salvatore and Aguirre (eds), *The Birth of the Penitentiary*, p. 104.

[10] León León, *Encierro y corrección*, vol. II, p. 429.

[11] Aguirre, 'The Lima Penitentiary', pp. 61–3.

[12] That is how Mariano Felipe Paz Soldán described the Lima penitentiary. Quoted in Aguirre, 'The Lima Penitentiary', p. 61. Benjamín Vicuña Mackenna described the Santiago penitentiary in similar terms: 'seven radii isolated from the building that depart from a common center.' Quoted in León León, *Encierro y corrección*, vol. II, p. 436. Probably the only Latin American prison to be built following Bentham's blueprint was the 'Presidio Modelo' in the Cuban Island of Pinos; its first circular pavilion opened in 1928.

these institutions hosted only a few hundred inmates, between 300 and 500 in average, the impact of the penitentiary reform over the entire inmate population was rather limited. Third, these early Latin American penitentiaries confronted serious and recurrent financial and administrative obstacles. They were invariably and severely criticised for not delivering on their promises of hygiene, humanitarianism and efficiency to combat crime and regenerate prisoners. Lack of resources was paramount, overcrowding marred the experiments from the very beginning, and the mixing of prisoners of different ages, legal conditions, degrees of dangerousness and even sexes became standard practice. Abuse against inmates betrayed the promises of humanitarian treatment, and economic shortages prevented prison authorities from delivering adequate food, health care, education and employment to the inmate populations. While they offered more secure conditions of incarceration, enforced daily routines on inmates, and exercised a degree of control over prisoners that was virtually unimaginable in non-reformed gaols and prisons, they still came short of their builders' promises.

One critical aspect of these penitentiaries was the implementation of labour regimes that, following the original blueprint, were seen as both conducive to the inmates' regeneration and a source of revenues to help finance the huge costs of maintaining such institutions. Prison work was not absent in non-reformed gaols and prisons, but it was usually performed on an *ad hoc* and informal basis. Penitentiaries were explicitly designed to include work as a central component of the prison therapy. Shoemaking, carpentry, printing and other workshops were set up, either under the direct control of prison authorities or run by private concessionaries. Penitentiary work became, in fact, one of the most distinctive aspects of daily life inside these reformed prisons, and many inmates welcomed the opportunity to earn some money, while authorities and private entrepreneurs profited from it. Thus it also became a central component in the negotiation of prison rules and the boundaries of power between and among inmates and prison guards and authorities.

At the heart of the penitentiary ideal, as developed in Europe and North America, was the notion that criminals were indeed reformable, that society had a debt with them (recognising the responsibility of social factors behind the commission of crimes), and that reforming criminals was the best way of integrating them to society as law-abiding and hard-working citizens. Moreover, penitentiaries were imagined in the Western world as intrinsic to a liberal and capitalist order. Prison time was thought of not only as a way of paying back to society for the commission of a crime, but as a means to instil certain values congruent with the liberal and capitalist order. As several authors have argued, modern forms of punishment played a key role in the development of liberal-democratic regimes: the penitentiary was, paradoxically, a central component of the system of freedom and democracy implemented in Western societies since the early nineteenth century.[13] In the rhetoric of Latin American prison reformers, the penitentiary would occupy a similar place in the process of building liberal-democratic societies; they seem to have believed that they could become 'laboratories of virtue' in which the unruly masses would be trained to become law-abiding citizens of their modern republics. But those hopes were shattered by the prevalence of societal models that drastically diverged from those ideals. Not only did these penitentiaries fail to deliver on their promise of humane treatment; they were in fact used to substantiate a social order in which the political and social exclusion of large sectors of the population was one of its cornerstones. As such, the early penitentiaries in Latin America came to symbolise the ambiguities and limitations of nineteenth-century liberal projects.

Liberalism in Latin America, we must recall, was the hegemonic ideology of Creole/*mestizo* states that, in countries such as Mexico or Peru, sustained quite authoritarian and exclusionary socio-political regimes and deprived the majority of their indigenous and rural populations from basic citizenship rights.[14] In countries such as Chile or Argentina the practices and rights associated with political liberalism (freedom of press, voting rights, equality before the law and the like) were restricted to the populations living in urban settings, while the implementation of brutal forms of economic and social exclusion resulted in the extermination of indigenous populations in the southern territories. In Brazil the permanence of both slavery and the monarchy precluded by definition the implementation of punitive regimes aimed at crafting virtuous citizens. In all these cases, highly stratified social and racial regimes served as the background in which penitentiary reform was tried. The potential beneficiaries of such reform were usually seen as inherently inferior, barbarous and irreformable, not as future law-abiding citizens with equal rights to their social superiors. What attracted state-makers to the penitentiary model was not the penitentiary's promise of reforming criminals through humanitarian means, but its much more tangible and feasible objective of strengthening existing mechanisms of control and

[13] See especially Thomas L. Dumm, *Democracy and Punishment: Disciplinary origins of the United States*, Madison, WI: University of Wisconsin Press, 1987; and Michael Meranze, *Laboratories of Virtue: Punishment, revolution, and authority in Philadelphia, 1760–1835*, Chapel Hill, NC: University of North Carolina Press, 1996.

[14] Mallon, 'Indian Communities', pp. 44–6.

confinement. That was, in fact, the way state-makers usually conceived the 'modernity' of their social projects.[15]

Although they were costly endeavours and, at least among certain circles, were embraced as major social achievements, let us not forget that the above-mentioned cases of early penitentiary building were the exception within a socially-sanctioned web of traditional punitive methods. Besides these modern penitentiaries existed a network of 'pre-modern' gaols and private institutions (including religious ones) that hosted many more inmates and where the continuities with ancient, pre-enlightened forms of punishment were pervasive. Of equal importance is the fact that existing legal provisions and practices represented serious obstacles to the implementation of modern forms of punishment. Due process was certainly a chimera, the lower classes lacked the protection of the law, their access to legal representation was quite deficient, corruption and abuse were rampant in all instances of the process (from police arrest to incarceration), and a huge part of these countries' prison networks remained unregulated by the state and usually even out of its sight. The private and arbitrary exercise of justice and punishment remained, well into the second half of the nineteenth century, an essential component of the societal mechanisms of social control.

BEYOND THE PENITENTIARY MODEL

Although the penitentiary model continued to attract the interest of policy makers in these and other countries for decades to come—Mexico, for instance, would inaugurate its first penitentiary only in 1900, and Cuba would do the same in the 1920s—a combination of pragmatic resignation and pessimism prevailed in the attitudes of penal reformers and state-makers during the final decades of the nineteenth century. Given the 'failures' of the existing prisons to impose any degree of discipline over their inmates, most commentators demanded not more humane but rather harsher punitive schemes. There was always a cluster of academic writers (physicians, lawyers, criminologists) that criticised the state of prisons and suggested reforms, but there was very little impetus on the part of state-makers to embark on costly and massive reform efforts. The introduction of new foreign penal and criminological doctrines after the 1870s—the reformatory model, positivist criminology—generated legal and scholarly debates and an extensive literature, but very little change or improvement in the prison systems

[15] Salvatore and Aguirre, 'The Birth of the Penitentiary', p. 17; Alberto Flores Galindo, *La tradición autoritaria: Violencia y democracia en el Perú*, Lima: Aprodeh/SUR, 1999.

of these countries. Legislation was usually passed to allow for the construction of new facilities or to improve the existing ones, but in most cases those projects were not implemented. The resort to traditional forms of punishment was extensive, as denounced by scores of scandalised commentators such as foreign visitors, journalists and also prisoners themselves. It is a tedious exercise to read descriptions of such infamous gaols as Guadalupe in Lima, Belem in Mexico City, or the Cárcel Pública in Santiago de Chile, where overcrowding, unhealthy conditions and despotism were compounded by state indifference towards the inmate population.[16]

Within this context the prison system operated as another institutional setting in which the eagerness of the élites to embrace 'modernity' was compounded (and subverted) by their determination to maintain archaic forms of social, racial and labour control. On the one hand it could be said that prisons merely attended the need to warehouse suspects and criminals in order to provide the decent classes of society a certain measure of security; on the other hand prisons reproduced and reinforced the authoritarian and exclusionary nature of these societies, thus becoming pieces of a larger scheme aimed at maintaining the social order. While this is certainly true, the place of the prison within the larger social projects being implemented in Latin America (authoritarian liberalism, integration into the world market, development of export economies, reinforcement of the exclusion of Indians and blacks, and the promotion of European immigration to 'whiten' the population) was indeed relatively marginal. Why would that be the case? Because the élites and the states they controlled had at their disposal other mechanisms for ensuring the reproduction of the social order. Incarceration was a relatively unimportant component of the economics of power in most Latin American countries during the second half of the nineteenth century, as illustrated by the cases of Mexico and Brazil.

Mexico had reached an important degree of political stability by the middle of the nineteenth century, at least in comparison with the chaotic decades of the post independence period, thanks to a series of liberal administrations that moved forward the concomitant processes of secularisation, institutional building, economic development, and the extension of civic rights to sizable segments of its population. At the same time, though, this very process of liberal state consolidation opened the way to the continuation and strengthening of forms of economic exploitation and labour control (debt peonage, land deprivation,

---

[16] Aguirre, *The Criminals of Lima*, pp. 101–4; Padilla Arroyo, *De Belem a Lecumberri*, pp. 203–74; León León, *Encierro y corrección*, vol. II, chapter 7.

servitude) that affected large sectors of the rural and indigenous populations. After 1876 the liberal political order was shattered by the imposition of a long-term dictatorship led by General Porfirio Díaz that lasted until 1911. However, liberal economic provisions—the destruction of communal land, the opening of Mexico to foreign investment, and the developing of the export sector, among others—were forcefully maintained and even strengthened, this time coupled with the implementation of brutal social- and labour-control policies that targeted the indigenous and rural populations. Increased rural policing, for instance, helped consolidate a system of quasi-feudal servitude in which labour and personal control were exercised by the landlord classes almost without limit.[17] While the *Porfiriato* proclaimed its modernity by embarking on the construction of railroads in the countryside and boulevards and theatres in Mexico City, it also worked to consolidate *ancien régime* social and labour structures. Within this context there was very little impetus to advance the cause of prison reform. During most of the nineteenth century, in fact, the Mexican prison system—symbolised by the infamous Belem gaol in Mexico City—remained as rotten and iniquitous as it had been during the colonial times.[18] Instead of striving for a reformed prison system, the Mexican élites resorted to quite oppressive punitive mechanisms such as the transportation of *rateros* (petty thieves) to the Valle Nacional (National Valley) in the state of Oaxaca, where they were contracted out to landowners, and from where, according to witnesses, they would never return.[19] The dramatic expansion of the system of debt peonage, with its economic and punitive ingredients, exemplifies the links between the Porfirian modernisation project and the use of 'pre-modern' forms of social and labour control such as servitude, enganche and transportation.

[17] Friedrich Katz, *La servidumbre agraria en México en la época porfiriana*, Mexico City: Secretaría de Educación Pública, 1976; Paul Vanderwood, *Disorder and Progress: Bandits, police, and Mexican development*, Wilmington, DE: Scholarly Resources, 1992.

[18] Padilla Arroyo, *De Belem a Lecumberri*, pp. 218–29; Laurence J. Rohlfes, 'Police and Penal Correction in Mexico City, 1876–1911: A study of order and progress in Porfirian Mexico', PhD thesis, Tulane University, 1983, pp. 204–11.

[19] Rohlfes, 'Police and Penal Correction', pp. 256–63. The verses included in a leaflet entitled 'Tristísimas lamentaciones de un enganchado' ('Saddest lamentations of an indentured worker'), accompanied by an engraving by famous artist José Guadalupe Posada, stated that it was better to be in the Belem gaol, 'eating beef broth and gamusa with coffee', than at the Valle Nacional, a testimony to the horrors of the latter as a destination for criminals. Reproduced in Patrick Frank, *Posada's Broadsheets: Mexican popular imagery, 1880–1910*, Albuquerque, NM: University of New Mexico Press, 1998, p. 44.

Brazil, on the other hand, had attained independence from Portugal in 1822 through a skilful negotiation of social and political options that resulted in the maintenance of both the monarchy and slavery as the cornerstones of Brazilian society. Although liberal-minded reformers had been able to implement an array of policies aimed at creating a modern system of justice, those projects were bound to have little impact in a society organised along drastic socio-legal (free *vs* slave) and racial (white *vs* black) hierarchical lines. Policing and punitive methods, as many scholars have emphasised, were geared first and foremost to guarantee the maintenance of the social, labour and racial order of which slavery was the essential factor. Patterns of policing and arrest in coffee and sugar production areas reflected the need to guarantee the supply of the labour force and the social control of the slave and free black population. Prisons and punishment were used, in this context, mainly as channels to promote the continuation of export-oriented, slave-based labour.[20] A Brazilian prison reformer blamed 'slavocracy' (the slave-owning élite) for the slow pace of prison reform in Bahia, where the private correction of slaves and other workers was the preferred punitive method for both authorities and slave owners.[21]

As slavery, and thus the private exercise of power, began to decline and social control issues became more pressing, the relatively undeveloped conditions of the Brazilian prison system made it necessary for the state to seek other alternatives to deal with the growing number of offenders, provide a minimum of security to the urban propertied classes, and impose strict mechanisms of social control over the freed black population. The solution was to use the army as a massive institution of social control. The army, in fact, became the single largest penal institution in Brazil during most of the second half of the nineteenth century. Thousands of poor, mostly black suspects were forcefully drafted into the army through impressment as a means of punishment for allegedly being in violation of the law (although, as is evident, no judicial authority had convicted them and the suspects had had no right to contest those allegations); in other cases judges 'legally' sent petty offenders to serve in the army. 'Brazil's underdeveloped penal system led administrators to depend on the army as an institution of penal justice', states Peter Beattie, adding that 'the Brazilian army's size, its share of national budgets, and its pre-eminent role in the management of

---

[20]   Thomas Holloway, *Policing Rio de Janeiro*, Stanford University Press, 1993; Martha K. Huggins, *From Slavery to Vagrancy in Brazil: Crime and social control in the Third World*, New Brunswick, NJ: Rutgers University Press, 1985.

[21]   Quoted in Salvatore and Aguirre, 'The Birth of the Penitentiary', p. 16.

government-legitimated violence made it the primary institutional bridge between the State and the "criminal" underworld.'[22] While, at its highest, the entire prison system housed about 10,000 individuals, the army enlisted between 8,000 and 12,000 men and adolescents that had been considered 'criminal'. At the very least the army was responsible for about the same number of 'criminals' as the entire Brazilian penal system. No wonder the Brazilian élites and state builders showed little enthusiasm for developing a network of reformed carceral institutions. A social structure in which first slavery and then *coronelismo* (bossism) were the dominant forms of power was not conducive to the embracing of prison reform packages predicated on quite different social arrangements.[23]

PRISONS AND OTHER CENTRES OF CONFINEMENT FOR WOMEN

Perhaps the only true penal innovation implemented in Latin American countries during the second half of the nineteenth century was the opening of female-only prisons and houses of correction. Female inmates had usually been secluded in male-dominated gaols and prisons, which created obvious complications for administrators and generated a number of abuses and problems for female inmates. The initiative to create centres of detention for women usually came not from state officials or prison reformers, but from philanthropic and religious groups. The Sisters of the Good Shepherd, a congregation that had been active in the administration of prisons in France, Canada and other countries, began to administer houses of correction for women in cities such as Santiago de Chile (1857), Lima (1871) and Buenos Aires (1880) with the enthusiastic support of the respective governments, eager to alleviate some of the tensions existing within prisons and to free themselves from the responsibilities of building and administering female-only institutions of confinement. Prevailing notions about how to 'treat' women were also behind these decisions: according to standard interpretations, criminal women needed less of a militaristic structure and more of a loving, maternal environment to be regenerated. Female criminals, as Lila Caimari suggests, 'were perceived as occasional criminals, victims of their own moral weaknesses, which were most likely the result of irrationality and lack of intelligence.'[24] It is revealing that mid-nineteenth-century debates on prison reform

[22] Beattie, *The Tribute of Blood*, pp. 135–6.

[23] Ricardo D. Salvatore, 'Penitentiaries, Visions of Class, and Export Economies: Brazil and Argentina compared' in Salvatore and Aguirre (eds), *The Birth of the Penitentiary*, pp. 194–223.

[24] Lila Caimari, 'Whose Criminals are These? Church, state, and Patronatos and the rehabilitation of female convicts (Buenos Aires, 1890–1940)', *The Americas*, 54, 2 (October 1997), p. 190; see

that led to the building of penitentiaries, or those on criminality as informed by positivist doctrines after 1870, did not take the issues of female criminality and female imprisonment seriously. The usually low numbers of female criminals and inmates seem to have convinced prison reformers and criminologists that there was no need for concern in that regard.

The state generally took a 'hands-off' approach regarding these and other institutions of confinement for women. They functioned as semi-autonomous entities not subject to state regulation or monitoring and clearly violated the law by allowing the seclusion of women (wives, daughters or servants) without a judicial mandate. Despite intermittent protests—from the victims of these detentions, some of their relatives or independent observers—most of these institutions of confinement continued to operate on the margins of the legal carceral system. These institutions, that we could generically call 'houses of deposit', included not only prisons for indicted or convicted women, but also correctional facilities that hosted the wives, daughters, sisters and servants of upper- and middle-class men who wanted to punish, or give a warning to, allegedly wayward women and adolescent girls.[25] Strict hierarchical rules permeated the relationship between nuns and inmates in these institutions, and there was always a tendency on the part of the Sisters to try to prevent these inmates from going back to the 'world' to face all kinds of risks and challenges. The notion that the 'female character' was weaker than that of men, and the idea that women needed protection against mundane temptations and threats, were pervasive among both state and religious authorities.

Prisons and houses of correction for women followed the house-convent model: inmates were purportedly treated as wayward sisters needing not harsh punishment but loving care and good examples. Praying and menial work were conceived as fundamental in the process of regeneration for female offenders. Inmates were put to work in trades 'proper' to their sex (sewing, laundering,

---

also María Soledad Zárate, 'Vicious Women, Virtuous Women: The female delinquent and the Santiago de Chile Correctional House, 1860–1900' in Salvatore and Aguirre (eds), *The Birth of the Penitentiary*, pp. 78–100; and María José Correa Gómez, 'Demandas penitenciarias: Discusión y reforma de las cárceles de mujeres en Chile (1930–1950)', *Historia* (Santiago de Chile), 38, 1 (2005), pp. 9–30; Carlos Aguirre, 'Mujeres delincuentes, prácticas penales, y servidumbre doméstica en Lima, 1862–1930' in Scarlett O'Phelan *et al.* (comp.), *Familia y Vida Cotidiana en América Latina, Siglos XVIII–XX*, Lima: IFEA/Instituto Riva Agüero/Pontificia Universidad Católica, 2003, pp. 203–26.

[25] Aguirre, 'Mujeres delincuentes'; Kristin Ruggiero, '"Houses of Deposit" and the Exclusion of Women in Turn-of-the-Century Argentina' in Carolyn Strange and Alison Bashford (eds), *Isolation: Places and practices of exclusion*, New York: Routledge, 2003, pp. 119–32.

handicrafts and cooking) and, when feasible, were released to work as domestic servants in the houses of decent, upper-class families, so as to complete their 're-generation' under the close surveillance of their employers.[26]

Although there were voices opposed to the state yielding its authority in favour of religious orders, most female inmates served their prison times under the surveillance and spiritual and moral guidance of religious sisters. Beginning in the 1920s the state gradually began to exercise greater authority over female prisoners, but sometimes even these state-run prisons for women were put under the administration of religious orders. The discussion as to 'whose criminals are these' would continue way into the second half of the twentieth century.

THE ERA OF SCIENTIFIC PENOLOGY

Around the turn of the twentieth century some important developments in prison design, administration and functioning took place in several countries in Latin America, all of them in one way or another resulting from the increased incorporation of the region into the international economy and the strong, albeit still ambiguous, move towards capitalist modernisation. By the end of the nineteenth century the last Spanish colonies (Cuba and Puerto Rico) had attained their independence (only to become territories under US control, though), the last slave societies (Cuba and Brazil) had abolished slavery, and export economies were flourishing almost everywhere, from Mexico and Central America to Chile and Argentina, with several visible effects on patterns of economic development, labour relations, urbanisation and both internal and international migration. Latin American élites were more optimistic than ever about the potential for transforming their societies into modern and civilised countries, but they still had to deal with a perceived major hindrance: the presence of large segments of the population living outside the law, unwilling to accept the invitation to behave in 'civilised' ways, and not quite integrated into the export-oriented and capitalist economic boom. As it happened, most of them were also dark-skinned, which added to the anxieties of Europeanised élites in whose imaginations only a 'whiter' population could in fact bring their countries into civilisation. What to do with these populations—whether or not they would or should be included as part of the national community—was the central question that intellectuals and state-makers debated as the nineteenth century wound down.[27]

---

[26] Aguirre, 'Mujeres delincuentes', pp. 219–20.

[27] For a sample of studies about these debates in different countries of Latin America see Tulio Halperin Donghi (ed.), *Sarmiento: Author of a nation*, Berkeley, CA: University of California Press,

Criminology as a new field of scientific inquiry began to flourish in most countries of Latin America precisely at that conjuncture, around the 1880s, promising to yield both explanations and solutions to criminal behaviour, but also critically addressing, as Robert Buffington among others has convincingly argued for the case of Mexico, central questions of nationhood and citizenship.[28] Lombrosian notions about the 'born criminal' were amply discussed and generally dismissed, but other tenets of positivist criminology—the connections between crime and race, inheritance and mental illness, for example—were more favourably received by late-nineteenth-century Latin American criminologists. As several studies have demonstrated, the way in which criminologists merged race and crime in their analysis of social deviance both reflected and reproduced the long-held notion that non-white groups were more likely to act criminally and were more difficult to reform than the white (or whiter) populations.[29]

One of the most common formulations proposed by Latin American criminologists—again, borrowing from similar debates in Europe—was the so-called 'social question', a pressing social predicament resulting from the combination of urban criminality, disease, poverty and political and social unrest that threatened, in the perception of élite observers, the integrity of the nation and the continuation of economic growth. These perceived threats brought to the forefront debates about crime, social disorder and punishment that were generally informed by positivism—recently imported from Europe and widely adopted among intellectual, legal and scientific circles in most Latin American countries—which attracted the sympathies of the majority of penal reformers and state-makers. Positivism, in fact, was used to propose and sustain quite different socio-political regimes, which speaks about its ambiguities and adaptability. Regimes as diverse as the *Porfiriato* in Mexico (1876–1911), the *Oncenio* of Augusto Leguía in Peru

---

1994; Mónica Quijada *et al.*, *Homogeneidad y Nación. Con un estudio de caso: Argentina, siglos XIX y XX*, Madrid: Consejo Superior de Investigaciones Científicas, 2000; Mark Thurner, *From Two Republics to One Divided: Contradictions of post-colonial nationmaking in Andean Peru*, Durham, NC: Duke University Press, 1997; Florencia Mallon, *Peasant and Nation: The making of postcolonial Mexico and Peru*, Berkeley, CA: University of California Press, 1995; Ada Ferrer, *Insurgent Cuba: Race, nation, and revolution*, Chapel Hill, NC: University of North Carolina Press, 1999; and Larson, *Trials of Nation-making*.

28   Robert Buffington, *Criminal and Citizen in Modern Mexico*, Lincoln, NE: University of Nebraska Press, 2000.

29   Salvatore, 'Penitentiaries', pp. 204–5; Carlos Aguirre, 'Crime, Race, and Morals: The development of criminology in Peru (1890–1930)', *Crime, History, Societies*, 2, 2 (1998), pp. 73–90; Buffington, *Criminal and Citizen*, chapter 7; Pablo Piccato, *City of Suspects: Crime in Mexico City, 1900–1931*, Durham, NC: Duke University Press, 2001, p. 58.

(1919–30), the restricted parliamentary democracies of early-twentieth-century Argentina and Chile, the pro-US dictatorship of Gerardo Machado in Cuba and even the post-revolutionary Mexican state, each borrowed heavily from positivism in their approach to government, population management, education, the promotion of different forms of racialised policies and efforts at crime control.[30] State policies informed by positivism shared the same impulse towards searching for scientific solutions to social problems, a deep-seated confidence in the superiority of Western societal models and, more ambiguous, a belief in the hierarchical nature of racial divisions. Legal codes began to incorporate the tenets of penal positivism—indeterminate sentence, the notion of dangerousness, the individualised treatment of the criminal—even if they were not always immediately translated into judicial practice.[31] Medical language and forms of diagnosis began to be widely used in both academic debates and state practices—including not only the criminal justice system, but also education, health and military reform, to name but a few areas of state intervention—to the extent that some scholars have spoken about the emergence of a 'medico–legal state'.[32]

Between roughly 1900 and 1930 scientific criminology and penology had its heyday in Latin America. Science and, quite prominently, medicine began to inform the design of prison regimes, the implementation of prison therapies and the evaluation of inmates' behaviour. Medical and criminological journals, university theses, international conferences and, especially, the implementation of research facilities inside prisons offered the spectacle of scientific, intellectual and social élites eager to study the 'social problem' of crime and put forward solutions that, because they were produced in the name of science, were expected to be embraced by society at large. Positivist criminology had a visible, but still uneven and ambiguous, impact on the prison systems in a number of countries in the

---

[30] For Mexico, see Buffington, *Criminal and Citizen*; for Cuba, Alejandra Bronfman, *Measures of Equality: Social science, citizenship, and race in Cuba, 1902–1940*, Chapel Hill, NC: University of North Carolina Press, 2004; for Peru, Carl Herbold, 'Developments of the Peruvian Administrative System, 1919–1939: Modern and traditional qualities of government under authoritarian regimes', Ph.D. dissertation, Yale University, 1973; for Argentina, Ricardo Salvatore, 'Positivist Criminology and State Formation in Modern Argentina (1890–1940)' in Peter Becker and Richard F. Wetzell (eds), *Criminals and Their Scientists: The history of criminology in international perspective*, New York: Cambridge University Press, 2006, pp. 253–80.

[31] Aguirre, *The Criminals of Lima*, pp. 53–60; Elisa Speckman Guerra, *Crimen y castigo: Legislación penal, interpretaciones de la criminalidad y administración de justicia (Ciudad de Mexico, 1872–1910)*, Mexico City: El Colegio de Mexico/UNAM, 2002, pp. 93–105; Buffington, *Criminal and Citizen*, pp. 120–3.

[32] Salvatore, 'Positivist Criminology', p. 254.

region. Two cases stand out as examples of these developments: the penitentiaries of Buenos Aires, Argentina and São Paulo, Brazil (later renamed as 'Institute of Regeneration'). The former, under the leadership of renowned criminologists Antonio Ballvé and José Ingenieros, was transformed into a massive research facility in which experts in medicine, public health, psychiatry, anthropology, psychology and criminology conducted research and produced a number of studies that would offer valuable insights into a number of social issues, not just criminality. Positivism guided these efforts. As Ricardo Salvatore has argued, 'positivism provided the ruling élite with the institutional spaces, the technologies of power, and the rhetoric needed to exercise power more effectively in the period of transition toward a more democratic republic.' Within that scheme, the penitentiary of Buenos Aires and, more precisely, its Institute of Criminology, came to play a crucial role.[33] In Brazil a similar role was played by the Institute of Regeneration of São Paulo, formed in 1914 after a complete renovation of the São Paulo penitentiary. A massive building resembling the architectural model of the panopticon, it contained a prestigious anthropometrical institute where research was conducted using inmates as subjects. For criminologists and penologists elsewhere in Latin America, the Institute of Regeneration was a source of both envy and pride.[34] Similar research facilities were created in various prisons throughout the region.[35]

These and other prisons thus became not only deposits of inmates and (allegedly) places for repentance and reform, but also sites for the production of knowledge about those inmates. They were constantly visited by physicians, doctors, psychiatrists and anthropologists in search of primary materials with which to offer interpretations about criminals and the social question. Pioneering criminological studies conducted by Julio Guerrero and Carlos Roumagnac in Mexico, Nina Rodrigues in Brazil, Fernando Ortiz and Israel Castellanos in Cuba and Abraham Rodríguez in Peru were all based on research conducted inside the prisons. Even if the outcome of their research was not always original, scientifically sound (even by the standards of that era) or particularly relevant, the production of knowledge based on prison research did have an impact on the ways in which the social and political élites viewed the 'social question' and tried to address the challenges that modernisation presented to their strategies of

---

[33] Ibid.
[34] Salvatore and Aguirre, 'The Birth of the Penitentiary', pp. 9–10.
[35] Nydia Cruz, 'Reclusión, control social, y ciencia penitenciaria en Puebla en el siglo XIX', *Siglo XIX: Revista de Historia*, 12 (1992); Aguirre, *The Criminals of Lima*, pp. 98–9.

governance. Although it is difficult to summarise the highly dissimilar production of these researchers, which in turn reflected the variety of social, political, cultural and racial settings in which their work was being conducted, there are a few common elements that surface from their work: 1) they posited, with different emphases, a combination of biological, cultural and social factors behind criminal behaviour; 2) they identified specific groups of individuals that were considered 'dangerous', when not inborn criminals, and who were usually members of the poor, uneducated and non-white social groups; 3) political doctrines such as anarchism and socialism were considered dangerous sources of unrest and violence, and thus also potential sources of criminal behaviour; 4) they offered solutions to crime and the social question that included more intrusive forms of state intervention such as compulsory education, urban reforms and various types of eugenicist proposals; and 5) many of them suggested that the assimilation of Indians and blacks and not their extermination (as previous evolutionary theories had suggested) was the desired path to build more inclusive but still hierarchically-ordered national communities. From elaborations on crime to ambitious proposals for social engineering and nation building, the work of positivist researchers was probably the most important contribution of this era of scientific penology in Latin America.

This era also brought about—and for the last time—a period of relative optimism in the implementation of prison reform packages; this time, however, the notion of the 'regeneration' of the criminal as the main goal was somehow overshadowed by the goal of transforming prisons into well-administered institutions. In other words, the 'reform of prisons' superseded, but did not completely suppress, the 'reform of prisoners' as the main objective of penal reformers. The optimism seems to have come mostly from the policy-makers' confidence in the ability of the state to effectively implement its mandates. The belief in the power of science to generate knowledge about, and solutions to, a wide array of social problems, including crime and criminal behaviour, infused the policies of both stronger and wealthier states. If anything, the era of scientific penology produced an increasing intrusion of the state into the daily lives of prisoners, as it did into the lives of subaltern groups more generally.

The implementation of research facilities inside prisons was in fact conceived as part of ambitious packages that included, among other reforms, building more and larger prisons, regulating and improving prison work, creating bureaus for the constant evaluation of prisoners, and centralising the administration of prisons under a single state agency. Techniques of identification and recording (the use of photographs, ID cards, biographical databases and dactyloscopic methods) were widely implemented from at least the 1880s.[36] The so-called Vucetich system epitomises the successes and hopes of this era of scientific and technological progress in crime control methods. Juan Vucetich, a Croatian immigrant in Argentina, was the first to develop an identification, classification and filing system based on fingerprints to replace the inadequate and 'annoying' Bertillon anthropometric method of identification and classification of criminals.[37] The Vucetich system—which allowed its creator to solve a case of infanticide in 1892, the first case allegedly to have been solved using fingerprints, and gave him, in a short time span, international celebrity—was quickly adopted in many other countries, even beyond the region, and was seen as an important step in the implementation of scientific forms of policing and crime control.[38] Closer and more efficient collaboration between prisons and police and judicial authorities were pursued and usually attained. Databases such as photographic records of criminals, biographical cards for criminals, workers and servants, health records for inmates, and many others were widely, albeit unevenly, implemented and used. As a result criminologists and penologists—again, probably for the last time—came to enjoy an unusual degree of social and political prestige and authority that reached well beyond the walls of prisons and institutes of criminology. As Salvatore has argued in the case of Argentina, the influence of positivist criminology could be identified in at least two interrelated areas: '(a) disciplinary institutions adopted ideas, concepts, and policies for the control, rehabilitation, and resocialisation of "deviant" populations suggested by positivist criminologists; and (b) the state's everyday practices came to reflect (in relation to the general population) concepts, categories, and procedures pioneered by criminologists.'[39]

What kinds of effects did the spread of scientific penology have on prisons? What were its implications for the treatment of prisoners and the vicissitudes of

[36] Aguirre, *The Criminals of Lima*, p. 73.

[37] On the Vucetich system see Julia Rodriguez, 'Encoding the Criminal: Criminology and the science of "Social Defense" in modernizing Argentina (1880–1921)', PhD dissertation, Columbia University, 1999, and 'South-Atlantic Crossings: Fingerprints, science, and the state in turn-of-the-century Argentina', *American Historical Review*, 109, 2 (2004). See also Kristin Ruggiero, 'Fingerprinting and the Argentine Plan for Universal Identification in the Late Nineteenth and Early Twentieth Centuries' in Jane Caplan and John Torpey (eds), *Documenting Individual Identity: The development of state practices in the modern world*, Princeton University Press, 2001, pp. 184–96.

[38] As Kristin Ruggiero points out, Vucetich's ambitious vision was to turn his system into something much larger than just a new criminological device. He envisioned a complete revolution in the means by which information about human beings was filed. The goal was to create 'a universal system of identification'. Ruggiero, 'Fingerprinting', p. 192.

[39] Salvatore, 'Positivist Criminology', p. 255.

daily life inside the institutions of confinement? Were state authorities able to reduce significantly previously existing hindrances such as overcrowding, corruption, abuse and inhumane conditions? Based on the available scholarship, the emerging picture is one of continuity with the past rather than change and improvement. With the possible exception of a few major detention centres, such as the penitentiary of Buenos Aires, that could be considered 'well-ordered prisons' (to borrow a phrase used by Randall McGowen),[40] most Latin American states failed to transform their prison systems. True, additional prisons were built, some existing ones were modernised, living conditions were improved for small numbers of inmates, and tighter security was added, but by the end of the 1930s in most countries of Latin America prison networks showed clear evidence of distress, inefficiency and corruption. Only in Argentina did the modernisation of the prison system under the aegis of positivism seem to have achieved at least some of its goals. As Lila Caimari wrote after summarising the changes effected between 1933 and 1940—which included the construction of eleven new 'model' prisons and the overhaul of a number of existing gaols—'the ideal of the ordered, modern and scientific prison confirmed its validity at the heart of the [Argentine] state.'[41] Almost everywhere else the picture offered by outside observers, prison administrators and inmates was one of corruption and inefficiency and, from the standpoint of the prisoners, of suffering and neglect. Science did not help redeem the prisoner.

DAILY LIFE AND PRISONERS' AGENCY

Although prison conditions were usually quite deficient for both men and women, the existing evidence suggests that the latter fared significantly better. Male prisons were usually described as true hells: overcrowding, violence, lack of hygiene, insufficient food, corporal punishment, terrible health conditions, sexual and other types of abuses and excessive work are just some of the features of life in prison that were constantly reported during most of the period under review. The Mexico City Belem gaol was described as 'a box that contains all the abjections and dejections of a society in formation'.[42] In Lima's Guadalupe gaol, according to a witness, 'a crowd of men were lying down, like incarnations of

[40] Randall McGowen, 'The Well-Ordered Prison: England, 1780–1865' in Norval Morris and David Rothman (eds), *The Oxford History of the Prison: The practice of punishment in Western society*, New York: Oxford University Press, 1995, pp. 71–99.

[41] Caimari, *Apenas un delincuente*, p. 123.

[42] Quoted in Padilla, *De Belem a Lecumberri*, p. 242.

brutal idleness! ... huge rooms, humid and poorly ventilated, serve as bedrooms; each bed is used by 40 or 50 prisoners ... Such a jail is unimaginable in this city, so proud of its lustre.'[43] Villa Devoto, an infamous gaol in Buenos Aires, was described in 1909 as 'a kingdom of arbitrariness, the absolute empire of dirtiness'.[44] Matters were significantly worse at some institutions, in certain locations and during certain periods, but overall, as in many other societies, daily life in prison was not particularly pleasant. However, one important caveat is worth mentioning: while more orderly and regimented prisons such as modern penitentiaries may seem to have offered better living conditions when compared to fetid gaols, the former were not necessarily perceived as such by some inmates who may have preferred a more untidy and poorly administered one, such as Guadalupe or Belem, where they would not feel the overwhelmingly intrusive presence of prison regulations and would have had much more leverage to negotiate their conditions of incarceration with 'weak' prison administrators.[45]

In the case of institutions of confinement for women, living conditions appear to have been more benign, although still lacking and at times quite poor. Although overcrowding was frequently reported, violence does not seem to have been as pervasive as in male prisons. Food and health were overall quite tolerable, but not for everybody. Scattered evidence suggests that mistreatment (including physical chastisement) was pervasive and that abusive behaviour on the part of the nuns was always an ingredient in the otherwise profoundly hierarchical relationship established within these prison-convents.[46] In both male and female prisons, though, conditions of living depended on specific configurations of power, prestige and status within the inmate population. There were always inmates that were able to secure relatively safe and benign conditions of incarceration, even inside overall rotten prisons.

The issue of race in the shaping of the world of the prison is more difficult to assess and summarise, especially because we lack studies on which to base any firm conclusions, and the countries we are surveying present quite dissimilar racial and ethnic configurations. The first and most obvious finding is that the majority of inmates generally belonged to the non-white racial groups. Prison populations overwhelmingly comprised poor Indians, blacks and *mestizos*, which

---

[43] Quoted in Aguirre, *The Criminals of Lima*, p. 103.

[44] Quoted in Caimari, *Apenas un delincuente*, p. 116.

[45] For prison conditions in different countries of the region see Aguirre, *The Criminals of Lima*, passim; León León, *Encierro y corrección*, vol. II, chapter 7; Fernández Labbé, *Prisión común*, pp. 107–19; Padilla, *De Belem a Lecumberri*, pp. 203–49; Piccato, *City of Suspects*, pp. 189–209.

[46] Aguirre, 'Mujeres delincuentes', pp. 223–4; Ruggiero, '"Houses of Deposit"', pp. 126–8.

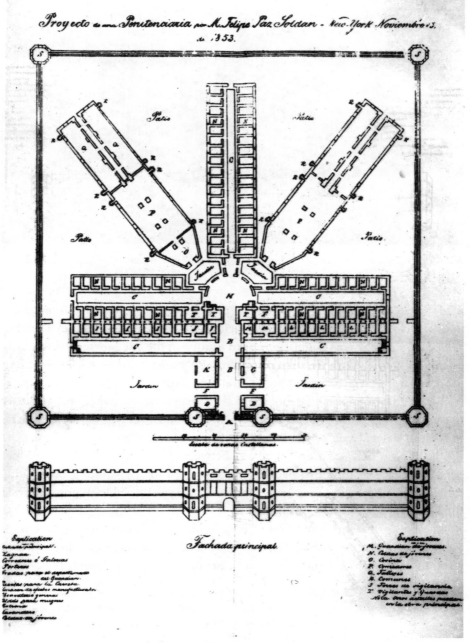

1. Original plan of the Lima penitentiary, by Mariano Felipe Paz Soldán. [Mariano Felipe Paz Soldán, *Examen de las penitenciarías de los Estados Unidos*, New York: S. W. Benedict, 1853]

2. Postcard showing the façade of the Lima penitentiary, *c.* 1900. [From the collection of Carlos Aguirre]

made incarceration as a social and legal practice one that greatly reinforced the overall socio-racial structures of these societies. In cases such as Argentina that received large immigrant populations from Europe in the late nineteenth and early twentieth centuries, those foreign groups also came to represent a significant proportion of the incarcerated population (and a subject of constant preoccupation for authorities and criminologists).[47] In Brazil the overwhelming majority of prisoners were Afro-Brazilians. Between 1860 and 1922, for example, inmates of African descent comprised 74 per cent of the incarcerated population at the Recife House of Detention.[48] In Peru between 1870 and 1927 about 85 per cent of inmates at the Lima penitentiary belonged to non-white groups, and a similar percentage (82.6 per cent) was found among the inmate population at the Guadalupe gaol.[49]

In terms of the administration of prisons, the classification and separation of inmates according to race was never legally sanctioned, but racial divisions and tensions clearly shaped the forms and distribution of punishment, the alloca-

---

[47] See especially Ricardo D. Salvatore, 'Criminology, Prison Reform, and the Buenos Aires Working Class', *Journal of Interdisciplinary History*, 23, 2 (autumn 1992), pp. 279–99, and Eugenia Scarzanella, *Ni indios ni gringos: Inmigración, criminalidad, y racismo en la Argentina, 1890–1940*, Buenos Aires: Universidad Nacional de Quilmes, 2002.

[48] Huggins, *From Slavery to Vagrancy*, pp. 88–9.

[49] Aguirre, *The Criminals of Lima*, p. 228.

tion of prison space and privileges, and the distribution of resources within the prison.[50] Racial biases informed the way inmates were treated by authorities, guards and fellow prisoners, with indigenous and black prisoners usually receiving poorer treatment than whites and *mestizos*. Authorities and guards, but also fellow inmates, would generally share pervasive notions of social 'worthiness' when dealing with individuals from different ethnic backgrounds. Based on what we know about the functioning of prisons, it seems fair to suggest that daily life inside prisons reproduced the forms of interaction, hierarchies and conflict among different ethnic groups that existed in the outside world. In many cases departments or special accommodations were created for 'distinguished' inmates, usually members of the upper and white/*mestizo* classes.[51] Thus, even if prisons were not conceived of as racially-segregated institutions, as in other areas of the world, they usually reproduced, in their daily functioning, the racial structures of Latin American societies. What is worth emphasising is that racial divisions were not always forcefully imposed by prison authorities but were in fact sometimes promoted by inmates themselves, who put in practice ideas and notions about racial hierarchies learned in the outside world.

Another important issue is that 'race' was frequently codified in the use of descriptive socio-cultural labels that designated 'lowly' individuals and helped demarcate boundaries of acceptable behaviour, citizenship rights and social worthiness, both outside and inside the prisons. Terms such as *lépero, ratero, roto, jíbaro, malandro, atorrante* and the like, though not necessarily 'racial' idioms, contributed to stigmatise large segments of the non-white population that were viewed as 'unworthy' and undeserving. Cultural constructions of race were intricately connected to discussions about criminality and marginality. The result was the usual collapsing, in the imagination of state authorities, criminologists, journalists and ordinary people, of socio-legal and racial categories, which contributed to the intensification of discriminatory practices against non-white, lower class populations, and their mistreatment by the criminal justice systems. When a police officer apprehended a suspect and filed him with the label of, say, 'recalcitrant *ratero*', he was doing much more than simply putting an individual through the intricate labyrinth of the judicial system: he was triggering off a series of actions and reactions that, in most cases, would disadvantage such an individual.[52]

---

[50]   Ibid., pp. 176–9.

[51]   Piccato, *City of Suspects*, p. 201.

[52]   Pablo Piccato, 'Cuidado con los Rateros: The making of criminals in modern Mexico City' in Salvatore, Aguirre and Joseph (eds), *Crime and Punishment*, pp. 233–72; Aguirre, *The Criminals of Lima*, pp. 120–3.

As in other societies, inmate communities created their own 'prison sub-cultures' that strongly resonated both inside and outside the prison. Specific forms of jargon, the use of tattoos, the various practices associated with homosexual relations, certain forms of masculinity connected to various forms of criminal behaviour, and the pervasive recourse to violence to settle differences were all cultural devices that developed and were nurtured inside prisons, even if they sometimes originated in the outside world. These manifestations of prison sub-culture contributed to create bonds of cooperation and horizontal reciprocity among inmates, but also nurtured (and were nurtured by) acute forms of competition and conflict. Prison communities, after all, were never homogeneous human conglomerates but rather quite heterogeneous and fragmented collectives. On the other hand, inmates were usually proactive in seeking forms of socialisation, entertainment and recreation that would allow them, whenever possible, to alleviate the torments of prison life. The practice of football and other sports, especially after the turn of the twentieth century, was popular among inmates and was usually encouraged by prison authorities who saw in them important means to promote healthy and safe distractions for inmates. Prisoners also engaged in activities such as drinking and gambling that, although prohibited by prison bylaws, were frequently allowed by authorities when it was convenient to their interests. As a result of these social practices, prison life could be at once colourful and dreadful, fun and horrific, violent and placid.

Prisoners' responses to incarceration should not be framed in terms of a dichotomy between resistance and accommodation. More productive is to see their behaviour (both individual and collective) as encompassing a series of complex, ambiguous and shifting mechanisms of coping with their conditions of incarceration. Again it is difficult to make crude generalisations, but certain patterns emerge from the available literature, patterns that, in fact, seem to be quite similar to those found in other societies. Prisoners' attitudes varied widely depending on the institution they were secluded in, their individual conditions (age, sex, place of origin, race/ethnicity, social status, criminal background and so forth), the legal condition and length of their confinement and the particular relationship established between inmates, guards and prison authorities. The first conclusion is that prisoners were always active seekers of greater degrees of autonomy and leverage in the negotiation of prison rules, both among themselves and with prison guards. This involved a number of different strategies including violence (or the threat of violence) and the forging of patronage ties with authorities and other members of the prison community. Also important to underline is the fact that prison communities were highly differentiated social groups within which clearly-established and often quite brutal hierarchies (based on the combination of criminal experience, control of existing resources and illegal trades, and the use of violence) existed. Thus inmates, besides having to cope with the oppressiveness of prison structures, also had to recognise that they now belonged to a community in which they would negotiate their way by confronting structures of power that sometimes they did not quite understand. Horizontal relations of solidarity—based on racial, regional, sexual or even political affinities—were common, albeit also fragile. Entering into relations of patronage and complicity with prison administrators and guards was fairly common, but also doubled-edged and even dangerous. Resorting to desperate attempts at ending the oppression of prison life through escapes, suicide and riots was certainly an option (often quite risky), although less commonly pursued than the other strategies. There were other forms in which prisoners demonstrated their willingness to fight back and, in doing so, they definitely shaped the world of the prison and the nature of the prison regimes being imposed upon them: writing letters to newspapers, authorities and other outsiders, for instance, to denounce their living conditions and to call attention to their suffering, or manipulating the kinds of information they gave to prison experts and criminologists during interviews or evaluations.[53] Collective forms of resistance and organisation surfaced from time to time, and it seems that they became more common when inmates began to interact with radical political prisoners, especially in the early twentieth century.[54]

POLITICAL PRISONERS

In most countries of Latin America, political imprisonment was widely used throughout the nineteenth century against members of opposing factions, outgoing administrations and conspirators, typically, albeit not solely, belonging to the upper classes of society. Authoritarian administrations such as the Rosas regime in Argentina (1829–52) used imprisonment as a central ingredient of their overall strategy of government and repression against political opponents; in fact, it set a precedent that would reverberate throughout Latin America during the various periods of successive military dictatorships. Other administrations made less systematic use of political imprisonment, although it was always a resource they had at hand, especially given the highly volatile political climate that

[53] Caimari, *Apenas un delincuente*, pp. 137–61; Aguirre, *The Criminals of Lima*, pp. 203–9.
[54] For detailed portraits of prison life in various countries see León León, *Encierro y corrección*; Padilla, *De Belem a Lecumberri;* Caimari, *Apenas un delincuente*; Picó, *El día menos pensado*; Aguirre, *The Criminals of Lima*; Fernández Labbé, *Prisión común*.

characterised most Latin American countries during this period of protracted and uneven state formation.

Political prisoners were usually secluded in separate sections of gaols, police stations, prisons and military barracks since tradition, legislation and the political inmates' own determination almost always guaranteed that they would not be mixed with common criminals. The category of political prisoner included various types of offender: members of the armed forces involved in attempted coups; officers of outgoing administrations deemed politically dangerous; conspirators and plotters against the ruling party; individuals involved in disturbances against voting procedures; and opponents of colonialism in the case of Cuba and Puerto Rico. Political imprisonment in the nineteenth century was, from time to time, the subject of public denunciations, but only rarely did it reach wide audiences or have an impact—as a subject of discussion—on broader political or legal debates. An important exception is the pamphlet written by Cuban patriot José Martí, *Political Imprisonment in Cuba* (1871), a damning indictment of Spanish colonialism in Cuba and a powerful call for patriotic action against it.[55]

The use of political imprisonment would become much more widespread and sustained towards the late nineteenth and early twentieth century, when radical social, political and labour movements influenced by anarchist, socialist, communist and nationalist ideologies challenged the oligarchic state and were confronted with massive repression, including the political imprisonment of hundreds, if not thousands, of individuals belonging, for the most part, to the middle and working classes of society. The administrations of Leguía in Peru (1919–30), Machado in Cuba (1925–33), Juan Vicente Gómez in Venezuela (1908–35), Porfirio Díaz in Mexico (1876–1911) and various regimes in Argentina (1900–30) made systematic use of political imprisonment. Infamous prisons such as the Islas Marías penal island, the San Juan de Ulúa fortress and the Mexico City penitentiary (also known as the 'Lecumberri Palace') in Mexico, the Ushuaia penal island and the Villa Devoto gaol in Argentina, the Juan Fernández archipelago in Chile, the Lima penitentiary or 'panóptico' and the El Frontón penal island in Peru, or the Presidio Modelo in Cuba hosted scores of political prisoners and became synonymous with oppression and torture.

One of the most interesting (and potentially disrupting) issues regarding political imprisonment was the relationship between political inmates and common criminals. The presence of large numbers of political prisoners among the criminal population created tensions between those two groups, but also the potential

---

[55] José Martí, *El presidio politico en Cuba*, Madrid, 1871.

for further destabilisation of the prison system. The cohabitation with common criminals was a source of constant debate and protest on the part of political prisoners; while in most cases they were housed in separate cells, pavilions or buildings, there were instances in which, as a means to make their punishment even harsher, political prisoners were forced to share the same space with common criminals.[56] Generally political prisoners detested the population of common criminals on the basis of their supposed lack of political consciousness, their alleged moral degeneration, the recruitment of criminals as informants working for the political police and, quite frequently, the racial and class prejudices held by political prisoners. They always tried to convey a sense of moral superiority vis-à-vis common criminals and, in front of prison guards and authorities, they wanted to appear more 'worthy' than the vulgar thief or the dreadful assassin. They adamantly demanded respect for their rights and expected to receive appropriate treatment from the authorities, which typically meant not to be treated 'like criminals' or physically mixed with them. At the same time, though, the presence of political prisoners belonging to radical movements was bound to generate tensions that jeopardised the internal order of prisons, not least because of their potential impact on the community of common criminals. In fact there were occasions in which both groups joined forces to confront authorities and demand certain rights or the fulfilment of obligations. In addition political prisoners saw in common criminals potential collaborators and on occasions made proselytising efforts among them. As Lila Caimari suggests, the experience of the prison allowed leftist militants to accumulate information on the realities of prisons and made them more sensitive to the needs of the criminal population.[57] For common criminals, on the other hand, the presence of political prisoners was an opportunity to seek an alliance with individuals who, due to their social connections, knowledge of the legal intricacies of the justice system and levels of organisation both inside and outside the prison, represented important resources in their efforts to improve their conditions of incarceration and possibly to attain freedom or parole. Caimari recounts the case of a lieutenant imprisoned in 1932 for leading a failed conspiracy. Common inmates kept telling him they were innocent and were unjustly serving prison time, but once they discovered that he did not have any connections to authorities that could help them with their situation, they did not hesitate to confess their crimes to him.[58]

[56] Caimari, *Apenas un delincuente*, pp. 124–35; Aguirre, *The Criminals of Lima*, pp. 132–9.
[57] Caimari, *Apenas un delincuente*, p. 126.
[58] Ibid.

Political prisoners wrote memoirs and testimonies, smuggled letters, organised party cells inside prisons, and engaged in myriad other ways of confrontation with state power. By doing so they created a powerful imaginary about the prison that resonated widely throughout society—more widely, certainly, than common prisoners' voices. Testimonies such as *La Tiranía del Frac ... (Crónica de un preso)* by the Argentine anarchist militant Alberto Ghiraldo; the series of articles and the book about the Cuban 'Presidio Modelo' written by the Puerto Rican Pablo de la Torriente Brau; or *Hombres y Rejas*, a novel by the Peruvian Aprista author Juan Seoane about his imprisonment in the Lima penitentiary, among others, contributed to amplify the debates about prison conditions.[59]

BEYOND PRISON WALLS

The increased role of prisons as both sites of research about the 'social question' and destinations for political prisoners—and thus objects of political denunciation—was compounded by a series of social developments that amplified the significance of the prison in the imagination of large sectors of the population. Public attention to the conditions of prisons and prisoners, for example, multiplied with the emergence of mass print media. Newspaper reporters visited prisons with a voyeuristic eye, ready to reveal the 'mysteries' of prisons to the outside reader.[60] Sensational stories about famous criminals were endlessly told, usually after interviewing the perpetrators inside their cells. Front-page drama—depicting in great detail episodes of theft, murder, suicide and prison escapes—became a common feature for newspaper readers in most Latin American urban spaces.[61] In Mexico, broadsheets, including those featuring engravings by renowned artist José Guadalupe Posada, chronicled and denounced the horrors of imprisonment

---

[59] Alberto Ghiraldo, *La tiranía del frac ... (Crónica de un preso)*, Buenos Aires: Biblioteca Popular de Martín Fierro, 1908; Pablo de la Torriente Brau, *Presidio Modelo*, Havana: Instituto del Libro, 1969; Juan Seoane, *Hombres y rejas*, Santiago de Chile: Ediciones Ercilla, 1937.

[60] Bretas, 'What the Eyes Can't See'.

[61] See for instance Alberto del Castillo, 'Entre la moralización y el sensacionalismo: Prensa, poder y criminalidad a finales del siglo XIX en la ciudad de México' in Ricardo Pérez Montfort *et al.*, *Hábitos, normas y escándalo: Prensa, criminalidad y drogas durante el porfiriato tardío*, Mexico City: CIESAS/Plaza y Valdez, 1997, pp. 15–73; Lila Caimari, 'Pasiones punitivas y denuncias justicieras: La prensa y el castigo del delito en Buenos Aires, 1890–1910' in Paula Alonso (comp.), *Construcciones impresas: Diarios, panfletos y revistas en el origen de las naciones latinoamericanas*, Buenos Aires: Fondo de Cultura Económica, 2004, pp. 297–320; Sylvia Saitta, 'Pasiones privadas, violencias públicas: Representaciones del delito en la prensa popular de los años veinte' in Sandra Gayol and Gabriel Kessler (eds), *Violencias, delitos y justicias en la Argentina*, Buenos Aires: Manantial/Universidad Nacional de General Sarmiento, 2002, pp. 65–85.

(but also of criminal behaviour).[62] Popular songs and ballads told stories about criminal and prison life to the usually illiterate masses of recently-arrived immigrants in various urban areas around the region. The increasing popularity of the photographic genre, as a technique of identification as well as a feature accompanying sensational stories in newspapers, greatly helped make the criminal underworld 'known' to the population at large.[63] As a result the outside population developed a relationship with the prison that was at once more intimate and increasingly distant. On the one hand the population in general came to 'know' much more about prisons than ever before. They could 'see', 'smell' and 'feel' what prison life was like, including its most sordid aspects. On the other hand the way prisons were generally portrayed in media accounts, as places of suffering but also as 'schools' of vice and crime whose populations engaged in repugnant forms of behaviour, made the public perceive them with horror and repulsion. This latter point is particularly important, since the notion that criminals, and not only prisons, belonged to a world of degradation and dreadfulness was instrumental in the shaping of a public opinion not very sympathetic to initiatives aimed at improving the lives of inmates. Although much more research is needed to assess the impact of these views about criminals on the absence of meaningful initiatives towards the amelioration of prison conditions, the exposure of the intimacies of prison life to the outside population did not necessarily generate sympathies towards inmates, mainly because of the way in which 'criminals' were depicted, as unfortunate and suffering individuals, but also as belonging to a class of degenerate and immoral subjects. This may help explain why public campaigns for the reform of prisons initiated by philanthropic societies (called 'Patronato de Presos' in some countries), religious individuals and groups, and a few humanitarian personalities, that strove to move public opinion and state officials towards a compassionate attitude towards prisoners, were generally isolated, weak and short-lived. They stumbled against authoritarian views that deemed criminals as deserving the suffering they were enduring in gaols and prisons.

CONCLUSION

As in other parts of the world, prisons in Latin America during the period under study were far from model institutions performing the functions expected of

---

[62] Frank, *Posada's Broadsheets*, chapters 1 and 2.

[63] The role of criminal photography in shaping both efforts at crime control and attitudes towards criminals is analysed in Fernández Labbé, *Prisión común*, pp. 197–234.

them. The summary of the history of prisons in Latin America between 1800 and 1940 outlined above offers a mostly negative assessment of their role in their respective societies: states and reformers failed, for the most part, to transform prisons into sites for the regeneration of criminals, and prisons did not offer inmates humane conditions. Prisons, the evidence also suggests, did not occupy a central place in the strategies of domination and control implemented by the élites and the state.

Several explanations could be offered in trying to understand why this was the case. Financial limitations and political instability account for the lack of enthusiasm in the formulation and implementation of ambitious plans for the reform of prisons. Weak state structures and corrupt mechanisms of recruitment and control over the different levels of state bureaucracy also created problems in the management of prisons and the enforcing of the bylaws. Beyond these administrative and managerial impediments, however, the nature of the larger socio-political structures of these nations must account for the fate of prisons in the region. Post-independence Latin American societies were, to varying degrees, highly exclusionary, hierarchical, racist and authoritarian structures that, behind the legal façade of liberal democracies, maintained oppressive social and labour forms of domination that included slavery, peonage and servitude. Citizenship rights were denied to major sectors of the population. Profound social, regional, class and ethnic fractures divided the populations, resulting in socio-political regimes in which small élites (landowners, financiers, export-oriented entrepreneurs, military bosses) exercised domination over the urban and rural indigenous and black masses. This implied a flagrant contradiction to the republican ideals of citizenship and inclusion upon which these nation-states were supposedly founded. Within these structures, punishment was rarely viewed as an opportunity for the repentance and reform of the criminal or for the display of humanitarianism on the part of the state; instead punishment was generally seen as the privilege and duty of the ruling groups in their efforts to control unruly, degenerate and socially and racially inferior peoples incapable of civilization and unworthy of legal and civic rights. Instead of republics of citizens, as their constitutions usually proclaimed, Latin American societies were, during most of the nineteenth century, neo-colonial structures in which the state operated mostly as a tool in the hands of oligarchic groups.

Around the turn of the twentieth century the growth of export-oriented economies, the combined effects of migration and urbanisation, the emergence of radical and middle-class social and political movements, the implementation of reforms aimed at enlarging the participation of the population in electoral politics, and the consolidation of relatively modern state structures, brought about significant changes in the nature of the relations between state and society. Slightly more inclusive social and political projects were formulated and implemented, challenging the rule of oligarchies whose power had been sustained by dictatorial political structures and export-oriented economic models. The single most important outcome of all these changes was the growth and modernisation of the state and the greater capacity it now had to intervene in the regulation of society. Within this context a renewed effort was made to transform prisons into loci for the regulation of lower-class behaviour, as well as for the production of knowledge about crime, criminals and the 'social question'. Prisons and prisoners witnessed the increasing presence of the state in the form of techniques of identification and recording, research facilities, centralised administrative bureaus, closer integration between the different levels of the criminal justice system and the like. Generally guided by positivism, these efforts allowed the state greater institutional ability to claim control and authority not only over prison populations but over society as a whole. Although for prisoners themselves these changes meant very little—they continued to suffer from poor living conditions, abuse and neglect—some of these developments (the increasing presence of political prisoners or the greater visibility of the prison in the wider society) did resonate among them, opening up new spaces for contestation and struggle.

BIBLIOGRAPHICAL NOTE

The literature on the history of prisons in Latin America is still relatively undeveloped and quite uneven in its coverage. A few countries, especially Argentina and Mexico, have received much greater attention than others, and certain periods, for instance the decades between 1870 and 1930, have been studied far more than others. Nevertheless, the literature produced in the last ten or fifteen years has substantially advanced our knowledge about prisons and punishment in the region, as this short essay attempts to show.

Scholarly interest in the study of crime and punishment in Latin American history can be traced back to the early 1970s. A series of pioneering monographs on urban and rural crime, banditry, policing and punishment were written in the 1970s and early 1980s. These works, that were variously informed by Marxist, *dependentista* and social history theories, include Colin MacLachlan, *Criminal Justice in Eighteenth-Century Mexico: A study of the tribunal of the Acordada*, Berkeley, CA: University of California Press, 1974; Patricia Aufderheide, 'Order and Violence:

Social deviance and social control in Brazil, 1780–1840', PhD dissertation, University of Minnesota, 1976; Linda Lewin, 'The Oligarchical Limitations of Social Banditry in Brazil', *Past and Present*, 82 (1979); William Taylor, *Drinking, Homicide, and Rebellion in Mexican Colonial Villages*, Stanford University Press, 1979; Richard Slatta, 'Rural Criminality and Social Control in Nineteenth-Century Buenos Aires Province', *Hispanic American Historical Review*, 60, 3 (1980); Gabriel Haslip-Viera, 'Crime and the Administration of Justice in Colonial Mexico City, 1690–1810', PhD dissertation, Columbia University, 1980, which was subsequently published as *Crime and Punishment in Late Colonial Mexico, 1692–1810*, Albuquerque, NM: University of New Mexico Press, 1999; Blanca Silvestrini, *Violencia y criminalidad en Puerto Rico, 1898–1973: Apuntes para un estudio de historia social*, Río Piedras: Editorial Universitaria, 1980, on crime in twentieth-century Puerto Rico; Paul Vanderwood, *Disorder and Progress: Bandits, police, and Mexican development*, Lincoln, NE: University of Nebraska Press, 1981 (2nd ed., Wilmington, DE: Scholarly Resources, 1992); Julia Blackwelder and Lyman Johnson, 'Changing Criminal Patterns in Buenos Aires, 1890–1914', *Journal of Latin American Studies*, 14, 2 (1982), pp. 359–79; Laurence Rohlfes, 'Police and Penal Reform in Mexico City, 1876–1911: A study of order and progress in Porfirian Mexico', PhD dissertation, Tulane University, 1983; Michael Scardaville, 'Crime and the Urban Poor: Mexico City in the late colonial period', PhD dissertation, University of Florida, 1977; Alberto Flores Galindo, *Aristocracia y plebe: Lima, 1760–1830*, Lima: Mosca Azul Editores, 1984, on violence in late colonial Lima; Martha K. Huggins, *From Slavery to Vagrancy in Brazil: Crime and social control in the Third World*, New Brunswick, NJ: Rutgers University Press, 1985; David Trotman, *Crime in Trinidad: Conflict and control in a plantation society, 1838–1900*, Knoxville, TN: University of Tennessee Press, 1987; Richard W. Slatta (ed.), *Bandidos: The varieties of Latin American banditry*, New York: Greenwood Press, 1987; Louis Pérez, *Lords of the Mountain: Social banditry and peasant protest in Cuba, 1878–1918*, Pittsburgh, PA: University of Pittsburgh Press, 1989; and Rosalie Schwartz, *Lawless Liberators: Political banditry and Cuban independence*, Durham, NC: Duke University Press, 1989. Very few of these works, though, paid central attention to the prison system, although several of them did include changes in punishment methods in their coverage.

This situation would change in the 1990s. Historians of Latin America began to give much more attention to both institutional and informal forms of social control such as prisons, mental asylums, houses of correction, penal servitude and the death penalty. The influence of both Foucauldian and social history approaches were eclectically combined in a series of studies about prisons in connection to processes of state formation, formal and informal mechanisms of social control and, to a lesser extent, the experiences of subaltern groups. The 1990s initiated a period of intense research and debate about the history of the prison in Latin America. To be sure, it was part of a larger interest in the history of the law, justice, crime and punishment, which was reflected not only in the growing number of publications, but also of scholarly conferences, panels and associations. This trend has yielded a number of valuable monographs that illuminate various aspects of the history of punishment and prison in the region: the ideological and political foundations behind the adoption of 'modern' forms of incarceration; the connections between prisons and the implementation of various socio-political regimes; the impact of positivism and criminological theories on the management of crime and prisons; the porosity of carceral institutions and their relationship with the larger society; the racial and gendered dimensions of different forms of imprisonment and detention; and the prisoners' agency and the making of prison subcultures.

A great deal of the scholarship on prisons in Latin America has focused its attention on the period between 1870 and 1930. There are various reasons for that: it is the era of consolidation of the nation state and of the implementation of 'modern' prison regimes; it is also the period in which innovative doctrines and theories of crime and punishment (positivist criminology or the medicalisation of punishment, for instance) were adopted. Prison reform was part and parcel of the (always uneven) processes of modernisation that most Latin American countries went through during this period. Much less studied are the pre-Hispanic, colonial and early independent periods, as well as the post-1930 era. The exception to this is the proliferation of studies about political repression and incarceration during the authoritarian regimes of the 1970s and 1980s which, although they represent an important area of scholarly work, fall outside the chronological focus of this essay.

Argentina and Mexico are the countries most studied by historians of punishment and prisons in Latin America. For Argentina, Beatriz Ruibal, *Ideología del control social: Buenos Aires, 1880–1920*, Buenos Aires: Centro Editor de América Latina, 1993, offers an early and valuable synthesis of 'social control' discourses and debates in the period between 1880 and 1920; Ricardo D. Salvatore has studied criminology, prison reform and the spread of positivism in a series of illuminating articles: 'Criminology, Prison Reform, and the Buenos Aires Working Class', *Journal of Interdisciplinary History*, 23, 2 (1992), pp. 279–99, 'Penitentiaries, Visions of Class, and Export Economies; Brazil and Argentina compared' in Ricardo D. Salvatore and Carlos Aguirre (eds), *The Birth of the Penitentiary in*

Latin America: Essays on criminology, prison reform, and social control, 1830–1940, Austin, TX: University of Texas Press, 1996, and 'Positivist Criminology and State Formation in Modern Argentina (1890–1940)' in Peter Becker and Richard F. Wetzell (eds), *Criminals and Their Scientists: The history of criminology in international perspective*, New York: Cambridge University Press, 2006, pp. 253–80. The same author has looked at an earlier period and has studied coercion and conscription of rural subaltern subjects: 'Repertoires of Coercion and Market Culture in Nineteenth-Century Buenos Aires Province', *International Review of Social History*, 45, 3 (2000), and *Wandering Paysanos: State order and subaltern experience in Buenos Aires during the Rosas era*, Durham, NC: Duke University Press, 2003; and the connections between the death penalty and liberalism, 'Death and Liberalism: Capital punishment after the fall of Rosas' in Ricardo D. Salvatore, Carlos Aguirre and Gilbert M. Joseph (eds), *Crime and Punishment in Latin America: Law and society since colonial times*, Durham NC: Duke University Press, 2001. Lila Caimari has focused her attention on the cultural and political resonances of incarceration, 'Remembering Freedom: Life as seen from the prison cell (Buenos Aires province, 1930–1950)' in Salvatore, Aguirre and Joseph (eds), *Crime and Punishment*; 'Castigar civilizadamente: Rasgos de la modernización punitiva en la Argentina (1827–1930)' in Sandra Gayol and Gabriel Kessler (eds), *Violencias, delitos y justicias en la Argentina*, Buenos Aires: Manantial/Universidad Nacional de General Sarmiento, 2002, pp. 141–68; 'Psychiatrists, Criminals, and Bureaucrats: The production of scientific biographies in the Argentina penitentiary system' in Mariano Plotkin (ed.), *Argentina on the Couch*, Albuquerque, NM: University of New Mexico Press, 2003; *Apenas un delincuente. Crimen, castigo y cultura en la Argentina, 1880–1955*, Buenos Aires: Siglo XXI, 2004. Lila Caimari, 'Whose Prisoners are These? Church, state and patronatos and rehabilitation of female criminals (Buenos Aires, 1890–1970)', *The Americas*, 54, 2 (1997), pp. 185–208, Donna J. Guy, 'Girls in prison: The role of the Buenos Aires Casa Correccional de Mujeres as an institution for child rescue, 1890–1940' in Salvatore, Aguirre and Joseph (eds), *Crime and Punishment*, pp. 369–90, and Kristin Ruggiero, '"Houses of Deposit" and the Exclusion of Women in Turn-of-the-Century Argentina' in Carolyn Strange and Alison Bashford (eds), *Isolation: Places and practices of exclusion*, New York: Routledge, 2003, pp. 279–99, have paid close attention to the gendered dimensions of incarceration in a series of articles about houses of correction and reformatories for women and girls. Ernesto Bohoslavsky, 'La ystoria de migran padesimiento: Cárcel y literatura popular en Patagonia a principios del siglo XX' in Jorge A. Trujillo and Juan Quintar (eds), *Pobres, marginados y peligrosos*, Tepatitlán de Morelos, Jalisco: Universidad de Guadalajara and Patagonia, Argentina: Universidad Nacional del Comahue, 2003, and Bohoslavsky and Fernando Casullo, 'Apuntes para una historia de la cárcel de Neuquén (1904–1955)', unpublished manuscript, focused their efforts on the lesser-known cases of prisons in the Patagonia region. Kristin Ruggiero, 'Fingerprinting and the Argentine Plan for Universal Identification in the Late Nineteenth and Early Twentieth Centuries' in Jane Caplan and John Torpey (eds), *Documenting Individual Identity: The development of state practices in the modern world*, Princeton University Press, 2001, pp. 184–96, and Julia Rodriguez, 'Encoding the Criminal: Criminology and the science of "Social Defense" in modernizing Argentina (1880–1921)', PhD dissertation, Columbia University, 1999, and 'South-Atlantic Crossings: Fingerprints, science, and the state in turn-of-the-century Argentina', *American Historical Review*, 109, 2 (2004) pp. 387–416, have studied the implementation of techniques of observation of the criminal body.

For Mexico, the work of historians such as Pablo Piccato, Robert Buffington, Elisa Speckman Guerra, Nydia Cruz and Antonio Padilla Arroyo have illuminated various aspects of the development of the penal system, the functioning of prisons and the impact of criminological theories. Nydia Cruz, 'Los encierros de los ángeles: las prisiones poblanas en el siglo XIX' in Carlos Contreras (ed.), *Espacio y perfiles: Historia regional mexicana del siglo XIX*, Puebla: Centro de Investigaciones Históricas y Sociales de la Universidad Autónoma de Puebla, 1989, and 'Reclusión, control social y ciencia penitenciaria en Puebla en el siglo XIX', *Siglo XIX: Revista de Historia*, 12 (1992), studied the case of the Puebla penitentiary and the introduction of 'scientific' penology. Pablo Piccato, *City of Suspects: Crime in Mexico City, 1900–1931*, Durham, NC: Duke University Press, 2001, offers a multilayered account of crime, punishment and urban life in modernising Mexico City. Robert Buffington, *Criminal and Citizen in Modern Mexico*, Lincoln, NE: University of Nebraska Press, 2000, studied criminological theories in connection to discourses about race and nation in Porfirian and revolutionary Mexico. Elisa Speckman Guerra, *Crimen y castigo: Legislación penal, interpretaciones de la criminalidad y administración de justicia (Ciudad de Mexico, 1872–1910)*, Mexico City: El Colegio de Mexico/UNAM, 2002, surveyed the various scientific, juridical and public discourses on crime in Porfirian Mexico, while Antonio Padilla Arroyo, *De Belem a Lecumberri: Pensamiento social y penal en el México decimonónico*, Mexico City: Archivo General de la Nación, 2001, detailed the functioning of prisons in nineteenth-century Mexico.

The other countries of the region have received much less attention. For Chile, we have the encyclopedic, three-volume study of the formation of the prison system by Marco Antonio León León, *Encierro y corrección. La configuración de un sistema de prisiones en Chile (1800–1911)*, Santiago: Universidad Central de Chile, 3 vols, 2003, and the companion collection of documents compiled by the same author, *Sistema carcelario en Chile: visiones, realidades y proyectos (1816–1916)*, Santiago: Dirección de Bibliotecas, Archivos y Museos, 1997. Marcos Fernández Labbé, *Prisión común, imaginario social e identidad social, 1870–1920*, Santiago: Editorial Andrés Bello, 2003, covers the period 1870–1920, and focuses on the cultural resonances of incarceration. Women's prisons and houses of correction have been studied by María Soledad Zárate, 'Vicious Women, Virtuous Women: The female delinquent and the Santiago de Chile Correctional House, 1860–1900' in Salvatore and Aguirre (eds), *The Birth of the Penitentiary*, pp. 78–100, and María José Correa Gómez, 'Demandas penitenciarias: Discusión y reforma de las cárceles de mujeres en Chile (1930–1950)', *Historia* (Santiago de Chile), 38, 1 (2005), pp. 9–30, and 'Paradojas tras la reforma penitenciaria: Las casas correccionales en Chile (1864–1940)' in Ernesto Bohoslavsky and María Silvia Di Liscia (eds), *Instituciones y formas de control social en América Latina: 1840–1940. Una revision*, Buenos Aires: Prometeo Libros, 2006, pp. 25–48. Lastly, Eduardo Cavieres, 'Aislar el cuerpo y sanar el alma: El régimen penitenciario chileno, 1843–1928,' *Ibero-Amerikanisches Archiv* 21, 3–4 (1995), summarised the early development of penitentiary reform in that country.

For Brazil, we have solid accounts of policing in Rio de Janeiro: Thomas Holloway, *Policing Rio de Janeiro: Resistance and repression in a 19th-century city*, Stanford University Press, 1993, and Marcos Luiz Bretas, 'You Can't! The daily exercise of police authority in Rio de Janeiro, 1907–1930', PhD dissertation, Open University, Great Britain, 1994; the use of the army as a penal institution: Peter M. Beattie, *The Tribute of Blood: Army, honor, race, and nation in Brazil, 1864–1945*, Durham, NC: Duke University Press, 2001; the representations of the prison in literature, memoirs and the printed media: Marcos Luiz Bretas, 'What the Eyes Can't See: Stories from Rio de Janeiro's prisons' in Salvatore and Aguirre (eds), *The Birth of the Penitentiary*, pp. 101–22; and the connections between criminology, race and prison reform: Ricardo D. Salvatore, 'Penitentiaries, Visions of Class, and Export Economies: Brazil and Argentina compared' in Salvatore and Aguirre (eds), *The Birth of the Penitentiary*, pp. 194–223.

For Peru, Carlos Aguirre, *The Criminals of Lima and Their Worlds: The prison experience, 1850–1935*, Durham, NC: Duke University Press, 2005, focuses on prisoners' agency; the same author reviews informal mechanisms of incarceration for criminals and slaves, 'Violencia, castigo y control social: esclavos y panaderías en Lima, siglo XIX', *Pasado y Presente* (Lima), 1 (1988); female institutions of confinement in Lima, 'Mujeres delincuentes, prácticas penales, y servidumbre doméstica en Lima, 1862–1930' in Scarlett O'Phelan et al. (comp.), *Familia y vida cotidiana en América Latina, Siglos XVIII–XX*, Lima: IFEA/Instituto Riva Agüero/ Pontificia Universidad Católica, 2003, pp. 203–26; the connections between race and criminology, 'Crime, Race, and Morals: The development of criminology in Peru (1890–1930), *Crime, History, Societies*, 2, 2 (1998), pp. 73–90; and the use of clientelistic tactics by male inmates in Lima's prisons, 'Los usos del fútbol en las prisiones de Lima (1900–1940)' in Aldo Panfichi (ed.), *El Perú a través del fútbol*, Lima: Fondo Editorial de la Universidad Católica del Perú, 2007.

For Puerto Rico, Fernando Picó, *El día menos pensado: Historia de los presidiarios en Puerto Rico (1793–1993)*, Río Piedras: Editorial Huracán, 1994, summarises the prisoners' experience with incarceration from the late eighteenth through to the late twentieth centuries, and Kelvin Santiago-Valles, '"Forcing Them to Work and Punishing Whoever Resisted": Servile labor and penal servitude under colonialism in nineteenth-century Puerto Rico' in Salvatore and Aguirre (eds), *The Birth of the Penitentiary*, pp. 123–68, offers a synthesis of penal servitude and colonialism in the late nineteenth century.

The literature about criminological and racial discourses in Cuba, especially Alejandra Bronfman, *Measures of Equality: Social science, citizenship, and race in Cuba, 1902–1940*, Chapel Hill, NC: University of North Carolina Press, 2004, helps us understand the context for prison reform in that country, even if we lack specific studies about the prison.

In Ecuador, the work of Ana María Goetschel, 'El discurso sobre la delincuencia y la constitución del estado ecuatoriano en el siglo XIX (períodos Garciano y liberal)', Master's thesis, Flacso (Quito), 1992, illuminates the relationship between liberalism and penal reform in the nineteenth century.

For Colombia, a valuable study of nineteenth-century prisons in Antioquia is found in Rodrigo Campuzano Cuartas, 'El sistema carcelario en Antioquia durante el siglo XIX', *Historia y Sociedad* (Medellin), 7 (December 2000), pp. 87–122; while for Venezuela, Ermila Troconis de Veracoechea, *Historia de las cárceles en Venezuela, 1600–1890*, Caracas: Academia Nacional de la Historia, 1983, has reconstructed the history of prisons from colonial times to the late nineteenth century.

Finally, a series of collective, usually multi-national volumes has greatly contributed to our knowledge of crime, banditry, policing and punishment in the region: Carlos Aguirre and Charles Walker (eds), *Bandoleros, abigeos y montoneros: Criminalidad y violencia en el Perú, siglos XVIII–XX*, Lima: Instituto de Apoyo Agrario, 1990; Lyman L. Johnson (ed.), *The Problem of Order in Changing Societies: Essays on crime and policing in Argentina and Uruguay, 1750–1940*, Albuquerque,

NM: University of New Mexico Press, 1990; Ricardo D. Salvatore and Carlos Aguirre (eds), *The Birth of the Penitentiary in Latin America: Essays on criminology, prison reform, and social control, 1830–1940,* Austin, TX: University of Texas Press, 1996; Carlos Aguirre and Robert Buffington (eds), *Reconstructing Criminality in Latin America,* Wilmington, DE: Scholarly Resources, 2000; Ricardo D. Salvatore, Carlos Aguirre and Gilbert M. Joseph (eds), *Crime and Punishment in Latin America: Law and society since colonial times,* Durham, NC: Duke University Press, 2001; Sandra Gayol and Gabriel Kessler (comps), *Violencias, delitos y justicias en la Argentina,* Buenos Aires: Manantial/Universidad Nacional de General Sarmiento, 2002; Jorge A. Trujillo and Juan Quintar (eds), *Pobres, marginados y peligrosos,* Tepatitlán de Morelos, Jalisco: Universidad de Guadalajara y Patagonia, Argentina: Universidad Nacional del Comahue, 2003; and Ernesto Bohoslavsky and María Silvia Di Liscia (eds), *Instituciones y formas de control social en América Latina: 1840–1940. Una revision,* Buenos Aires: Prometeo Libros, 2006.

THE SHADOW OF RULE: COLONIAL POWER AND MODERN PUNISHMENT IN AFRICA

Florence Bernault

At the end of the nineteenth century, European colonisers in Africa imposed prison systems on a massive scale as soon as they secured control over people and territories. Yet the project did not emerge as part or sequence of a global 'carceral archipelago' in Foucault's sense. While a great number of devices of confinement were tested in African colonies (asylums, hospital wards, industrial work camps, corrective facilities for children etc.), they always proved limited in medical scope and disciplinary ambition. Racial segregation and social distance between Europeans and Africans served as an enduring, though tacit, basis for the architectural, moral and bureaucratic management of the colonial penitentiary. The principle of repentance, one of the major sources of prison reform in the West, thus experienced considerable alteration in the colonies. While the Western penitentiary reframed free individuals as equal citizens and legal *subjects*, the colonial prison primarily constructed Africans as *objects* of power.[1] In doing so, the history of the colonial prison speaks to a host of long-debated questions on the parallels between modern governance and the decline of state-inflicted destruction.[2]

To a large extent the advent of the custodial prison in African colonies can be described as a never-ending enterprise of territorial and human conquest. Custodial prisons were foreign to nineteenth-century African penal systems.

---

[1] This parallels, but does not overlap entirely David Arnold and Megan Vaughan's arguments on the ways in which the British prison in India, and colonial biomedicine in Africa, constructed the colonised as objects of knowledge. David Arnold, 'The Colonial Prison: Power, knowledge and penology in nineteenth century India' in David Arnold and David Hardiman (eds), *Subaltern Studies VII: Essays in honour of Ranajit Guha*, Oxford University Press, 1994; Megan Vaughan, *Curing Their Ills: Colonial power and African illness*, Stanford University Press, 1991.

[2] For a recent discussion, see Achille Mbembe, 'Necropolitics', *Public Culture*, 15, 1 (2003), pp. 11–40.

Colonizers imposed them as tools of social disorder rather than civil discipline, consolidating social divides and rulers' political control. But their centrality to the colonial project, their success at rounding up black workers, codifying criminality and, ultimately, at surviving the demise of the colonial state, points to the prison's overwhelming efficiency and resilience in colonial and postcolonial Africa.

CUSTODIAL CAPTIVITY, 1880s–1910s

The birth of the prison in Africa can be traced to three main sources: first, the gaols set up in coastal forts and garrisons established by Europeans from the sixteenth century onward; second, the devices of bodily constraint and physical confinement used during the slave trade; and finally, starting in the 1880s, the military lock-ups deployed during the imperial conquest. Only after the 1910s did colonisers start to build a methodical network of custodial facilities in the colonies. Yet the new prisons did not entirely break from earlier models. By origin and by function, colonial prisons emerged as places of captivity rather than of custody, reviving, far from Europe, a specific breed of penal archaism.

Custodial sentences did not exist in nineteenth-century sub-Saharan Africa, and penal procedures seldom utilised spatial confinement as a way to measure and deter criminal activities. Rather than the lack of bureaucratic institutions, this can be explained by the particular configuration of the relationships between men and space that structured public authority across the diverse polities south of the Sahara. Although social groups were located in socially defined territories, power was generally exercised over people rather than space.[3] In this context judicial techniques did not privilege spatial confinement as a punitive method. For minor offences, procedures tended to rely on compensation and fines. For the most serious crimes, punishment consisted in the death sentence and other forms of radical exile from the community. Sale into slavery, in particular, subjected criminals not only to exclusion, but also to destructive geographical and social displacement.[4] Only rarely did extreme sentences retain the accused within the community, sometimes placing them in ostracised grounds associated with spiritual pollution, a form of social, rather than spatial, isolation comparable to death.[5]

---

[3] Christopher Gray, *Colonial Rule and Crisis in Equatorial Africa: Southern Gabon ca. 1850–1940*, University of Rochester Press, 2002.

[4] For slave narratives of spatial and social wanderings, see Marcia Wright, *Strategies of Slaves and Women in East Africa: Life stories from East/Central Africa*, New York: L. Barber Press, 1993.

[5] For a case-study of Bandjoun ostracism in Cameroon, see Thierno Bah, 'Captivity and Incar-

In this context, physical reclusion occurred as a transitory moment that underscored the exercise of sovereignty, aiming less to correct than to seize the criminal's body in order to inflict punishment and allow legal reparation. While small scale and decentralised societies usually chained or restrained the accused in the open, some centralised states in West Africa possessed permanent places for holding convicted criminals or suspects before trial, a form of physical constraint comparable to gaoling convicts in *ancien régime* Europe. Instruments of aristocratic power, these locales did not seek to rehabilitate criminals, or to enforce standardised sentences. Few specialised buildings have been documented. Royal courts and buildings sometimes provided quarters to restrain criminals, such as the compounds in the royal palace at Abomey, the capital of the kingdom of Dahomey.[6] In most cases judicial confinement and captivity seem to have been temporary and preventive, holding the accused before trial and sentence, or keeping war captives before they could be exchanged among victorious parties, then killed, enslaved or integrated into a household as a dependent.

One should not deduct from this brief overview that the later archaisms associated with the colonial prison derived from African practices in the nineteenth century.[7] Local systems had not developed in isolation, and European influence had proved a significant factor in shaping African penal systems since the sixteenth century.

At the end of the fifteenth century, following the reconnaissance of the African coast by Portuguese navigators, Europeans had started to sign treaties with local rulers and establish trading forts and military garrisons along the shoreline. White authorities had little or no judicial control outside European settlements, with the possible exception of the Portuguese *prazos* of Moçambique and, in the nineteenth century, of a few settlement colonies such as the British colony of Freetown (Sierra Leone), where a prison opened in 1816; or the French trading and military stations of St-Louis and Gorée (Senegal), where, in July 1867, a *senatus-consulte* allowed the construction of prisons to control the African itinerant

---

ceration in Nineteenth-Century West Africa' in Florence Bernault (ed.), *A History of Prison and Confinement in Africa*, Portsmouth, NJ: Heinemann, 2003, p. 75. See also how the great warrior Samori imprisoned his own son who was accused of treason, and made him die of hunger, a form of destructive captivity and extreme bodily torture. Ibid., p. 73.

6   Ibid., pp. 71–2.

7   The best critique of evolutionary and functionalist views of pre-colonial law in Africa is to be found in Martin Chanock, *Law, Custom and Social Order: The colonial experience in Malawi and Zambia*, Portsmouth, NJ: Heineman, reissued 1998, pp. 19 and 25–31. See also his critique of anthropological myths on dispute settlement in Africa, ibid., pp. 5 and 219–20.

population and petty urban criminals.[8] In most cases these gaols incarcerated military personnel or delinquent traders and, occasionally, a marginal fraction of the racially mixed inhabitants of the colony. Moreover, they had remained largely unaffected by the reform movement taking place in Europe, and continued to work as *ancien régime* gaols, that is, as places where convicts could be held before trial. As such they bore considerable similarity to contemporary African systems of restraint and captivity, and never worked as nodes of modernising influence.[9]

Indeed, while prison reform was sweeping America, Europe and other parts of the world, the intensification of the slave trade in the eighteenth and nineteenth century, and the violence it entailed at the time of abolition (1809–65), meant that unprecedented numbers of Africans faced capture and enslavement, and that Europeans' pre-colonial influence over African penal systems came mostly from the diffusion of antiquated devices of bodily restraint and torture. In nineteenth-century Angola, for instance, traders (*pombeiros*) used iron shackles, neck-rings and chains to restrain slaves, and during the abolition period grouped them in enclosed compounds, *quintals* and *barracons* (from the Portuguese *barracão*, a large cabin or hangar) in order to escape the surveillance of the abolitionist naval patrols.[10] During the same period missionaries and abolitionist associations organised semi-enclosed communities to house and supervise slaves recaptured by French or British patrols along the coast of Africa, called, inappropriately, 'villages of liberty'.[11]

The development of the slaving economy caused the value of the free person to decline. In the eighteenth century it was easier for rulers and powerful men to accumulate dependents through the slave trade than through the nurturing of natural reproduction and the protection of families and kin groups. Very low dependency status appeared, and in certain polities large settlements of slave-workers were attached to free families.[12] The whole fabric of those societies

[8]   A.W. Lawrence, *Trade Castles and Forts in West Africa*, London: Jonathan Cape, 1963. Slaves usually stayed in open quarters outside the fort.

[9]   A situation quite different from nineteenth-century China, as demonstrated by Frank Dikötter, *Crime, Punishment and the Prison in Modern China*, London: Hurst, 2002.

[10]   Jan Vansina, 'Confinement in Angola's Past' in Bernault (ed.), *A History of Prisons*, pp. 62–4. See also Paul du Chaillu's visit to the Sangatanga barracoons in 1856, as quoted by K. David Patterson, *The Northern Gabon Coast to 1875*, Oxford: Clarendon Press, 1975, pp. 83–6: 'Men were chained in collars in groups of six, but women and children were allowed to wander at will within the well-guarded compound. The slaves subsisted on rice and beans while awaiting shipment.'

[11]   Denise Bouche, *Les villages de liberté en Afrique noire française, 1887–1910*, Paris, La Haye: Mouton, 1968.

[12]   This pattern is well described along the Congo River by Robert Harms, *River of Wealth, River*

exposed to slavery suffered from this process. Local judicial systems tended to inflict sentences of enslavement for an increasing range of offences, thus fuelling the production of slaves for the benefit of a few. The cosmopolitan élites living on the coast, often Western-educated and well-travelled across the Atlantic, seldom served as intermediaries between global reform ideas and rulers in the hinterland. Those who did, generally lacked political influence.[13]

By the second half of the nineteenth century, therefore, far from benefiting from reform, penal economies in Africa had experienced a dramatic inflation of sentences, enforcing social death (slavery) as a more frequent punishment, and encouraging a deflation in the value of the person. This in turn caused devices of physical restraint to be more closely associated with the threat of captivity and enslavement.

At the turn of the twentieth century colonial confinement worked as a catalyst to make these experiences overlap. The prisons set up by European conquerors directed African convicts into new geographical/social displacements, ending up, this time, within the tight walls of central buildings. Their failure to short-circuit the negative connotations inherited from earlier forms of physical confinement, captivity and enslavement proved surprisingly enduring, underlining the lasting coercive nature of colonial imprisonment. During the early colonial penetration (*c.*1880s–1910s) the gaols set up by European authorities seldom resembled reform prisons, but answered immediate military and political needs to tame political resistance. Hastily erected in military garrisons and European posts, they aimed at imprisoning local leaders until they submitted to foreign occupation. Those who resisted were executed or exiled in faraway locations, a strategy similar to nineteenth-century military campaigns and slave raiding.[14] Under the name of 'administrative internments' these sentences sustained the war against political opponents of colonisation. The frequent suicide of prisoners who were

---

of Sorrow: The central Zaire basin in the era of the slave and ivory trade, 1500–1891, New Haven, CT: Yale University Press, 1981. For slave clusters in West Africa, see Martin Klein, *Slavery and Colonial Rule in French West Africa*, New York: Cambridge University Press, 1998.

[13] African and Afro-American missionaries in West Africa did lead anti-slavery campaigns in West Africa, but had little impact on penal procedures. James Fairhead (ed.), *African-American Exploration in West Africa: Four nineteenth-century diaries*, Bloomington, IN: University of Indiana Press, 2003.

[14] Samori Touré, the leader of the Juula revolution and a fierce opponent of the French conquest of Western Sudan, was exiled to Gabon in 1895; many other leaders were deported, for example Queen Ranavalona III of Madagascar or the Asantehene (king) after the conquest of the Asante empire by the British.

leaders and nobles demonstrates how incarceration resonated with local ideas about slavery and the loss of freedom and personal dignity.[15]

During the first two decades of the twentieth century major transformations occurred. Up to the 1910s the European military and administrative presence had remained superficial, concentrated only in a few strategic points that kept fluctuating under the pressure of local resistance. By the 1920s colonial rulers had created a tighter network of permanent administrative posts endowed, for the most important ones, with a prison. By enforcing taxes, censuses, portage and forced labour, Europeans and their auxiliaries were now able to control population movements and local economies. The prison played a central role in this transition.

ROUNDING UP THE NATIVES, 1910s–1950s

Because colonial power answered specific needs and purposes, the nature and length of custodial sentences in African colonies differed significantly from metropolitan ones. From the 1910s to the 1950s the prison touched African lives mostly through short and arbitrary detentions falling upon a wide spectrum of the adult male population. Perhaps best captured by the term 'pervasive' rather than 'massive', this form of incarceration imposed high levels of short, widely distributed custodial sentences that proved remarkably enduring throughout the colonial period. The dissemination of prison sentences at the grass-roots resulted from the criminalisation of native life and the building of permanent facilities, almost never from penal debates.[16] Prison ideologies thus need to be read directly from judicial ordinances and regulations, architectural devices and diagrams, and prison practitioners' scattered comments.

Legal apparatuses

By the 1900s seven European nations had carved more than thirty colonial enclaves across sub-Saharan Africa, each equipped with a particular governmental, judicial and penal apparatus. The latter were multifaceted in ways unknown to metropolitan regimes. Yet prison custody was adopted as the primary and referential sentence in all sub-Saharan colonies. More than the fate of convicts,

---

[15] Ibrahima Thioub, 'Sénégal: La prison à l'époque coloniale' in Florence Bernault (ed.), *Enfermement, prison et châtiments en Afrique du 19ème siècle à nos jours*, Paris: Karthala, 1999, pp. 287 and 292–3.

[16] On the ideological limits of colonial penology, see Florence Bernault, 'The Politics of Enclosure in Colonial and Post-Colonial Africa' in Bernault (ed.), *A History of Prison*, pp. 23–6.

however, colonial rulers were concerned primarily with bureaucratic efficiency, anticipated economic benefits and the need to enforce native submission.[17]

In the colonies under direct administration (French, Belgian, Spanish and Portuguese) and in those under indirect rule (British and German) the enforcing of different levels of civil rights, criminality and sentences generated particularly complex legal situations. The same law did not apply to white settlers and black 'natives', resulting in different penal codes and racially segregated tribunals. In the French colonies, for instance, 'native tribunals' (*tribunaux indigènes*) presided over by a white judge (usually the local French administrator) arbitrated offences and conflicts committed by Africans by taking account of local 'customs'. Meanwhile French and European settlers could be tried only by 'second-degree courts' (*tribunaux de second degré*) run by French judges and juries that followed the judicial codes in use in metropolitan France.[18] The system of indirect rule in a few British colonies, such as the Protectorate of Northern Nigeria, respected the judicial sovereignty of native authorities (in the emirates, the Muslim *qadis*, and in non-Muslim areas, local chiefs) and, in theory, left them in charge of managing local police forces, penal laws, native courts and native prisons.[19] Yet in the same colonies, Africans living in regions under direct British administration would be tried by native tribunals controlled by the colonial authorities.

Negotiated between African and European rulers, customary laws, far from preserving pre-colonial juridical regimes, encouraged the diffusion of prison sentences. British rulers proscribed native courts from applying sentences such as mutilation, enslavement and torture, deemed, in the words of Lord Frederick Lugard, the founder of indirect rule, 'repugnant to natural justice and

[17] Native is a colonial term that, *lato sensu*, opposed Africans to white colonists. The French equivalent is *indigène*. I use it here to illuminate the racial divides at work in the colonial situation.

[18] For instance, in French Equatorial Africa, 'Décret du 12 mai 1910 portant réorganisation de la justice en AEF', *Journal officiel de l'Afrique équatoriale française* [hereinafter *JOAEF*], 15 October 1910, pp. 527–52; 'Circulaire du 17 novembre 1910 sur le fonctionnement de la justice indigène', *JOAEF*, 15 December 1910, pp. 675–81. These decrees were modified several times until 1927, when three different levels of court were organised; conciliatory tribunals (*tribunaux de conciliation*, former *tribunaux indigènes*), first degree tribunals and second degree tribunals, the last two being presided over by French administrators and judges.

[19] On Native Authorities and Native Courts ordinances, see David Killingray, 'Punishment to Fit the Crime? Penal policy and practice in British colonial Africa' in Bernault (ed.), *A History of Prison*, pp. 97–118. There is a considerable literature in African history on the fallacy of the British endeavour to preserve existing ('customary') polities and authorities in the African colonies. The academic consensus is that British rule reinvented or fossilised what the British saw as 'traditional' authorities, while transforming the nature of their public legitimacy.

humanity'.[20] Moreover, native courts could not pronounce the death sentence (with the exception of northern Nigeria and Buganda), thus encouraging recourse to prison sentences. In the French colonies the organising of native justice (*justice indigène*) and native tribunals from 1910 onward explicitly forbade the use of criminal sanctions 'contrary to the principles of French civilisation'.[21] Fines, imprisonment and death were the sole punishments *tribunaux indigènes* and second degree courts could inflict. Local tribunals should submit sentences longer than two years (including the death penalty) to a higher court that confirmed or overturned the decision.[22] This encouraged tribunals to pronounce shorter prison terms, thus avoiding long confirmation delays and loss of control over local conflict resolution.

In French colonies the penal provisions known as the *régime de l'indigénat* proved particularly efficient in disseminating short-term imprisonment at the grass-roots level.[23] First promulgated in Algeria in 1881, extended to the colony of Senegal in 1887, in French West Africa in 1904, and in French Equatorial Africa in 1910, and abrogated only in 1946, the *indigénat* allowed white local administrators, without trial, to punish a large range of offences with a maximum of fifteen days in prison.[24] Belgian authorities in the Congo and in Ruanda–Urundi relied on a similar system of 'disciplinary sentences'.[25] In the first decades of the twentieth century, and sometimes as late as the aftermath of the Second World War, tax demands, subsistence crises and the slow increase in monetary circulation made fines unrealistic sentences. In 1914, for instance, an administrator in southern Gabon (French Equatorial Africa) explained the rising number of im-

---

[20] Lord Lugard, *Political Memoranda: Revision of instructions to political officers on subjects chiefly political and administrative, 1913–18*, 1st ed. 1906; 2nd ed. 1919, reprinted London: Cass, 1970, part III, para. 30, pp. 97–8; quoted by Killingray, 'Punishment to Fit the Crime?', p. 99.

[21] 'Décret du 12 mai 1910 portant réorganisation de la justice en AEF, article 47', *JOAEF*, 15 October 1910, p. 532.

[22] Ibid., article 49 and 54, *JOAEF*, 15 October 1910, p. 532.

[23] For a recent reappraisal of the *Régime de l'indigénat*, see Isabelle Merle, 'Retour sur le régime de l'indigénat: Genèse et contradictions des principes répressifs dans l'empire français', *French Politics, Culture & Society*, 20, 2 (summer 2002), pp. 77–97.

[24] 'Décret du 31 mai 1910 portant le règlement sur l'indigénat en AEF', *JOAEF*, 1 August 1910, pp. 377–8. In 1910 misdemeanours punished by the *indigénat* ranged from refusal to pay taxes to vagrancy, public disorder, smuggling, desertion of porters, illegal burials and the cultivating of Indian hemp. 'Arrêté déterminant les infractions spéciales à l'indigénat', *JOAEF*, 15 September 1910, p. 485.

[25] In 1956 27,209 sentences for crimes and common offences and 21,192 disciplinary sentences were pronounced in the Belgian Congo. A. Rubbens, 'Congo Democratic Republic' in Alan Milner (ed.), *African Penal Systems*, London: Routledge and Kegan Paul, 1969, p. 27.

prisoned convicts in his area, saying: 'I would have preferred, of course, to inflict fines, but how would I have been paid? Ultimately, I would have had to imprison reluctant payers. I decided therefore to confine them right away.'[26]

Administrative and short-term sentences thus provided tremendous leverage for taking hold of the colonised and, as we shall see, for controlling local economies and native labour. The building of local facilities in the 1910s and 1920s, the petty criminalisation of native life (accusations of vagrancy, failure to pay colonial taxes, resistance to new constraints) and the systematic use of prison sentences at the grass-roots level resulted in considerable ratios of imprisonment.

Pervasive imprisonments

Colonial imprisonment ratios remained on average three to six times higher than in the West. From the 1930s to the 1950s they ranged approximately between one in 300 and one in 600 persons.[27] By comparison, ratios for the same period in Britain (England and Wales) and France ranged from one in 1,100 to one in 2,700.[28]

---

[26] 'Rapport trimestriel du chef de la circonscription de l'Ogooué-Ngounié, signed Gaignon, 1914'. Archives nationales du Gabon, Fonds Présidentiel [hereinafter ANG/FP] 522.

[27] Estimates from available data in the Belgian Congo, Gabon, Burkina-Faso, Senegal, Kenya, Tanzania, Nigeria. Note that colonial sentences of short-term imprisonment were not usually counted in penal statistics outside the colony. The League of Nations, for instance, listed only the number of criminal detainees in Africa. 'The Prisoner Population of the World', *Howard League for Penal Reform* (1936), pp. 1–10.

[28] For the UK, official ratios amounted to 1 in 1,371 (1910), 1 in 2,784 (1930) and 1 in 2,142 (1950); for France they ranged from 1 in 1,812 (1910–11), to 1 in 2,062 (1930) and 1 in 1,138 (1950). Slightly higher numbers are found in the United States after the 1940s, with a maximum of 1 in 846 in 1950. Lionel W. Fox, *The English Prison and Borstal Systems: An account of the prison and Borstal systems in England and Wales after the Criminal Justice Act 1948, with a historical introduction and an examination of the principles of imprisonment as a legal punishment*, London: Routledge and Kegan Paul, 1952, pp. 118 and 218–19. For France, Georg Rusche and Otto Kirchheimer, *Punishment and Social Structure*, New York: Columbia University Press, 1939, p. 146, and Pierre Pedron, *La Prison sous Vichy*, Paris: Les Editions de l'Atelier, 1993, pp. 48 and 199. For the United States, Frank Hobbs and Nicole Stoops, 'Demographic Trends in the 20th Century', *Census 2000 Special Reports*, Washington, DC: US Government Printing Office, 2002, p. 11. For population statistics, England: The Registrar General, *Statistical Review of England and Wales for the Year 1941*, London: His Majesty's Stationery Office, 1946, p. 2; France: République Française, Ministère des Finances et des Affaires Économiques, Institut National de la Statistique et des études Économiques, *Statistique du mouvement de la population années 1950 et 1951*, Nouvelle Série, vol. XXV, Paris: Imprimerie Nationale, 1956, p. 19; the United States: Margaret Werner Cahalan, *Historical Corrections Statistics in the United States, 1850–1984*, Rockville, MD: Westat, 1986, p. 29. I thank Lisa Cline for helping me to compile this data.

However, average ratios tend to sanitise the impact of colonial incarcerations at the grass-roots. The following examples shed light on a grimmer situation and provide a more realistic assessment of Africans' prison experience. In the Belgian Congo in the late 1930s annual detainees represented 10 per cent of the male population. In the mid-1950s almost 7 per cent of the adult males in the province of Kivu were spending some time in prison at any given time of the year.[29] In French Equatorial Africa, where detailed archival data is available, similar patterns can be documented. In 1915, for instance, in a district of southern coastal Gabon, as much as 21.4 per cent of the male population spent at least one day of the year in prison.[30] Thirty years later, in 1944, records of *indigénat* sentences for the colony show that the number of days in prison had reached forty-two per 100 adult males.[31] Higher rates were not uncommon: in 1943 in the district of Tchibanga (southern Gabon) 12,358 days of imprisonment were enforced over a local population of 5,700 males, i.e. a ratio of 216 days of prison for 100 men.[32]

Statistics on the daily number of detainees help refine the picture.[33] Colonial Kenya is a particularly well-documented case, although judicial authorities here incarcerated a far greater proportion of the native population than in other East

[29] Figures in Marie-Bénédicte Dembour, 'La chicote comme symbole du colonialisme belge?' *Canadian Journal of African Studies*, 26, 2 (1992), pp. 207–28.

[30] Imprisonment topped the payment of fines as the major sentence. In the Oroungou area adult men were likely to pay 0.30 French francs on average per year in fines, a relatively low sum compared to the financial burden imposed by head taxes (about 3 French francs per person [*impôt de capitation*], or 6 French francs per household [*impôt de case*]). Catherine Coquery-Vidrovitch, *Le Congo au temps des grandes compagnies concessionaires, 1898–1930*, Paris, The Hague: Mouton, 1972, p. 119. 'Relevé des peines disciplinaires en 1915, chef de la circonscription des Oroungous', n.s. ANG/FP 633.

[31] 'Tableaux récapitulatifs des sanctions de police administrative au cours du 3ème et du 4ème trimestre 1944, Libreville, February 17 and May 11, 1945, signed Mercoy'. ANG/FP 910. Note that the Second World War led to increasing economic and social demands and discipline in French Equatorial Africa, as the natives were asked to supply war resources. Florence Bernault, *Démocraties ambigües en Afrique centrale, Gabon, Congo-Brazzaville, 1940–1965*, Paris: Karthala, 1996.

[32] Unfortunately the archives remain silent on the number of sentences corresponding to the number of days in prison. The only example I could find is for the year 1943 in the district of Fougamou in southern Gabon (total population of 17, 378). A total of 179 *indigénat* sentences resulted in 2,057 days in prison, or an average sentence of over eleven days of prison. 'Rapport politique de la Ngounié, 1943, n.s'. ANG/FP 418.

[33] See also complaints and reports pointing to the chronic overcrowding of facilities. For instance, the prison at Kindia (Guinea), consisting of two rooms of five metres by six metres, contained twenty-nine prisoners in December 1907. Mamadou Dan Diallo, *Répression et enfermement en Guinée: Le pénitencier de Fotoba et la prison centrale de Conakry de 1900 à 1958*, Paris: L'Harmattan, 2005.

African British colonies.[34] From 1911 to 1938 the daily average of people incarcerated in the thirty prisons of Kenya (twenty-three of which were district
prisons) tripled, increasing from 1,541 to 4,700. In 1931 penal facilities were
holding approximately 28,000 detainees (1/146 Africans). For comparison, imprisonment ratios in Great Britain during the same period hardly reached thirty
prisoners per 100,000 people, or a ratio of one in 3,333, twenty-two times less
than in Kenya. In the colony and in absolute numbers the convict population
rose to 36,000 in 1941 (1/136), 55,000 in 1951 (1/109) and 86,000 in 1955. By
1946 the convict population averaged 7,215 daily; in 1951, prior to the Mau
Mau rebellion, it reached 11,630.[35] According to Daniel Branch, in the 1930s
the increase resulted from the economic depression, tax defaults and a shortage
of cash for fines; and from the better organisation of colonial courts. The Second
World War boosted the lingering agrarian crisis in the native reserves, and aggravated economic demands. By the late 1940s and early 1950s Kenya's high ratio of
imprisonment derived from the pervasive use of convict labour, combined with
heightened economic issues and social tensions.[36]

This data suggests that colonial prisons did not serve to detain a marginal population of criminals, but instead participated in taming political, economic and
cultural resistance to white domination. In this system delinquency was defined
as a racial trait, encompassing the entire spectrum of the African population.[37]
Colonial prisons' undermining of the disciplinary and reformative functions of
the modern penitentiary thus derive little from failing penal policies, or the
prisons' incomplete success as bureaucratic institutions.[38] To the contrary, the

---

[34] Daniel Branch, 'Escaping the Carceral Archipelago: Imprisonment and colonialism in Kenya,
c.1930–52', *International Journal of Historical African Studies* (forthcoming).

[35] Leonard C. Kercher, *The Kenya Penal System: Past, present and prospect,* Washington, DC: University Press of America, 1981, p. 138. The African population of Kenya was estimated, for these
three years, at about 4.1 million (1931), 4.8 million (1941) and 5.9 million (1951). John D. Fage
and Roland Oliver (eds), *The Cambridge History of Africa*, vol. 3, Cambridge University Press,
1975, p. 576; and for 1951 to 1955, Branch, 'Escaping the Carceral'.

[36] On dire economic conditions in Gikuyuland, see Carolyn Elkins, *Imperial Reckoning: The untold
story of the end of empire in Kenya*, New York: Henry Holt, 2004. On pastoral economies, Richard
Waller, 'Rough and Ready Injustice? Stock theft legislation in colonial Kenya', paper presented
at the African Studies Association Conference, 14 November 2004.

[37] In a different context, for a discussion of delinquency as a political tool of social discrimination,
see Michel Foucault, *Discipline and Punish: The birth of the prison*, New York: Pantheon Books,
1977, part 4, chapter 2.

[38] Peter Zinoman, *The Colonial Bastille: A history of imprisonment in Vietnam, 1862–1940*, Berkeley,
CA: University of California Press, 2001, makes the opposite argument, and sees the colonial

low-disciplinary nature of the colonial penitentiary answered, in efficient and cost-effective ways, the task of routinised economic and political coercion.

Monumental disseminations

By the early 1920s, with the securing of colonial state budgets and bureaucracies, the transitory period of make-shift gaols and cells hastily set up in the first administrative or military garrisons was over. Newly built facilities emerged, along with the church and the administrator's residence, among the early, prominent architectural markers of the European presence. In today's Africa many remain among the most visible legacies of colonial rule.

In British territories, early colonial governments issued a comprehensive series of prison ordinances in the 1900s and, in regions under indirect rule, allowed paramount chiefs to open their own facilities. By the late 1920s a regular and hierarchical network of local and central prisons existed in most African colonies. However, increasing contradictions in the prisons' penal function prompted considerable adjustment in their geographical locations. Early on, security incentives had encouraged the building of remote facilities for criminals and opponents to colonial rule (penitentiaries built on islands or in the Sahara desert): at the same time, prisons were established in the centre of large white settlements in order to counter urban delinquency and petty criminality (Dakar, Freetown). In the 1930s and 1940s fear of epidemics combined with expanding urban development, new concerns with the beautification of white districts, and efforts to segregate African neighbourhoods triggered the relocation of prison facilities at the margins of colonial towns.[39] Meanwhile the need for convict labour encouraged the building of temporary labour camps adjacent to construction projects (Senegal, Kenya). Prison networks thus experienced important geographical fluctuations according to the contradictory imperatives of economic profitability and racial segregation.[40]

---

prison as an antiquated and failing institution where prisoners could resist confinement and undermine the colonial project.

[39] Odile Goerg, 'Colonial Urbanism and Prisons in Africa: Reflections on Conakry and Freetown, 1903–1960' in Bernault (ed.), *A History of Prison*, pp. 119–34; Dior Konaté, 'A History of the Penal State in Senegal: Repressive architectures and the life of prison detainees from the 19th century to the present', PhD dissertation, University of Wisconsin-Madison, chapter 2.

[40] For a case-study of colonial rehabilitation projects for urban minor delinquents and their relocation to rural penitentiaries, see Ibrahima Thioub, 'Juvenile Marginality and Incarceration during the Colonial Period: The first penitentiary schools in Senegal, 1888–1927' in Bernault (ed.), *A History of Prison*, pp. 79–96.

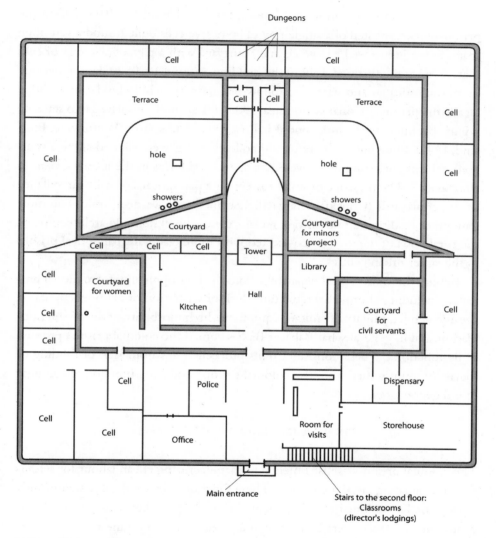

Dungeons

Cell   Cell

Terrace   Cell   Cell   Terrace   Cell

Cell   hole   hole   Cell

showers   showers

Courtyard   Courtyard for minors (project)

Cell   Cell   Cell   Tower   Library

Cell   Courtyard for women   Hall

Cell   Kitchen   Courtyard for civil servants   Cell

Cell

Cell   Cell   Dispensary

Cell   Police   Room for visits   Storehouse

Cell   Cell   Office

Main entrance

Stairs to the second floor:
Classrooms
(director's lodgings)

1. Central Prison of Brazzaville, Congo, 1995 (original design from 1949)

By contrast the principles that shaped the prisons' inner designs proved remarkably enduring. Colonial Africa's penal architecture adhered to strict racial discrimination, the de-individualisation of the African convict population and a pervasive neglect of the latter's conservation. From outside, and even in the inner lay-out of convicts' quarters, colonial penitentiaries did not seem to differ dramatically from reformed Western prisons. Designs were standardised, symmetrical and even panoptical. Among the oldest models (1910s–1920s) the prison-block consisted of a single row of collective cells built around a vast open space. Some juxtaposed a large central courtyard with a rectangular ring of cells that served as the fortified walls of the building. Around 1920–30 designs became more sophisticated and started to follow panoptic models. Behind a monolithic façade the prison at Conakry (Guinea, 1903), for example, displayed two separate wings spanning out from a central hall (schema dating from Pentonville, England, 1842). Elsewhere courtyards and collective cells were aligned along a symmetrical axis consisting of a covered or open corridor, as in the *maison centrale* in Brazzaville.[41] The presence of watchtowers for a panoptical, constant surveillance of the courtyards (Conakry, Brazzaville) seemed to have been quite common. Panoptical facilities did not always replace prison-blocks: simple architectures in the rural posts of the interior co-existed with more elaborate, panoptical prisons in the larger urban centres.

Behind the walls critical departures from the metropolitan reform model prevailed, including chronic overcrowding, lack of separation of prisoners by status, age and gender, paucity of sanitary equipment, high morbidity of the prison population, and in general what Babacar Bâ has coined the colonial prison's promise of dysfunction.[42] These consistent traits proceeded less from lack of funding or social constraints, than from the colonial prison's enduring function: the taming of indigenous societies.[43]

PRODUCING LABOUR AND RACE

The colonial prison was instrumental in manufacturing cheap labour for settlers and consolidating racial inequalities. These functions did not decline significantly during the late colonial era. Instead, prisons endured as key sites for preserving economic and racial hierarchies, remaining remarkably immune to reforms implemented in the late colonial period.

[41] On Pentonville, see Robin Evans, *The Fabrication of Virtue: English prison architecture, 1750–1840*, New York: Cambridge University Press, 1982; and on panoptical design, Foucault, *Discipline and Punish*. I drew the plan of the central prison of Brazzaville during a visit to the facility in the summer of 1995.

[42] Babacar Bâ, 'L'enfermement carcéral pénal au Sénégal: 1790–1960. Histoire de la punition pénitentiaire coloniale', doctoral dissertation, University of Cheikh Anta Diop, 2004.

[43] Bernault, 'Politics of Enclosure in Colonial and Post-Colonial Africa', pp. 14–16 and 38. Achille Mbembe, *On the Postcolony*, Berkeley, CA: University of California Press, 2001.

Labour

Most African convicts, including women, had to work.[44] No geographical exceptions existed: both urban and rural prisons made systematic use of penal labour. No noteworthy reform curbed the iron law of generalised penal labour, even during the later phase of colonial rule. Penitentiaries imprisoned Africans who resisted forced labour and colonial extractions and, in turn, African detainees were considered a significant source of reliable and cheap labour. The prison thus participated in the artificial economic system of the colonies, where surplus value derived from wages maintained at a low level.[45]

The case of Senegal offers an exemplary case-study of convict labour regulations. Here penal labour originated before the colonial conquest in the gaols of the coastal trading stations, and developed in direct connection with the slaving economy. First legalised in the nineteenth century for slave prisoners in St Louis, labour was rapidly imposed on all convicts (1927), including prisoners for debt (1932), a considerable innovation in French law.[46] Forced labour was made available to private entrepreneurs (1892) and later channelled to temporary penal camps next to road sites, mines and salt marshes.[47] Inspired by the model of the Louga facility (1931), seven penal camps opened along main routes in the colony, uprooting several hundred male convicts who were forced to work long and hard for months and sometimes years.[48] These camps remained in use till independence. Permanent prisons thus became reservoirs for frontier projects that blurred private and public need for a docile and cheap native workforce. Similar developments

---

[44] Only the infirm and the sick were exempt. I could not find reliable data, however, on convict labour in the native prisons in territories under indirect rule. Also note that in practice some facilities lacked the means to put convicts to work. Konaté, *A History of the Penal State in Senegal*.

[45] See a similar view in D. Williams, 'The Role of Prisons in Tanzania: A historical perspective', *Crime and Social Justice* (1980), pp. 27–38.

[46] In metropolitan France, the penitentiary regime applied to debtors was equivalent to that for an accused, thus significantly lighter than that for regular convicts.

[47] 'Arrêté de 1841, article 10, and Arrêté de 1892. Circulaire du gouverneur général, 3 mars 1927, and Arrêté du 22 janvier 1927'. Archives nationales du Sénégal, 3F86. Arrêté général du 28 octobre 1932 modifiant l'arrêté de 1927. Archives nationales du Sénégal, 3F1. All quoted in Bâ, 'L'enfermement carcéral pénal'.

[48] 'Mission et Rapport Monguillot sur le travail pénal'. Bâ, 'L'enfermement carcéral pénal'. The Louga camp served the colony's longest road project between St Louis and Dakar. Five other camps opened in the 1930s, one along the Thiès-Mekhé road, one along the Fatick-Bambey road, two in the Casamance region, and one for building a military camp near Thiès in 1944. That same year the Louga camp was transferred with 300 prisoners to serve a private company (Société des Salins du Siné-Saloum) that exploited salt fields near Koutal. In 1945 a seventh camp opened at Hann for prisoners from the Dakar prison to labour in stone quarries and road works.

can be traced in French Equatorial Africa, where in 1955, work in labour camps was mandated for all convicts sentenced to more than one year in prison.[49]

In most African colonies penal labour endured as a hidden form of forced labour, even after the liberalisation of labour laws in the 1930s and 1940s[50], supplementing, and sometimes competing with, free labour for unskilled tasks such as work on quarries, roads, construction sites (wharves, bridges), rubbish disposal, ship loading or warehousing in colonial towns. In a confusion typical of the colonial situation, the recourse to penal labour obliterated the barriers between the private and public sectors. The tight administrative control over labour markets sustained a constant flux between workers being sent to prison and convicts being used in various workplaces outside the prison. While inmates provided a cheap and malleable work force, the prison population was reproduced by induced native resistance to labour laws and economic regulations (forced labour and cultivation, pass laws, vagrancy, taxes). An early example of such practices is preserved in the archives of Niger (French West Africa). In the mid-1920s, in the jurisdiction of Maradi, men resisted forced labour and military conscription by fleeing to neighbouring British Nigeria, thus undermining the availability of native labour. In 1926 the local *commandant* ordered local chiefs to send sixty young males to register at the district headquarters and to provide ten days of mandatory labour on the prison construction site. Fifteen of the workers were drafted for military service on the spot. The remainder were sentenced to forty-seven days in the prison they had just built before being transferred to the military recruiting commission as conscripts.[51]

In British colonies, where forced labour was never legalised, convict labour inside and outside prisons proved nonetheless significant. In Kenya, for instance, the courts could rely on *corvée* tax labour and the petty criminalisation of natives,

[49]   For 60 hours a week (including travel time). The prison administration received a fee calculated according to the minimum wage practiced in the territories, and the prisoner received only a portion of this money (*pécule*)—fixed by the order of the territorial chiefs. Article 6, arrêté du 18 août 1955, *JOAEF*, 15 September 1955, p. 1189.

[50]   By way of comparison, the transfer of prison labour gangs to private entrepreneurs had been forbidden in metropolitan France at the end of the nineteenth century. Jacques-Guy Petit, *Ces peines obscures: La prison pénale en France, 1780–1875*, Paris: Fayard, 1990. Forced labour was abolished for free citizens in the French colonies in 1946.

[51]   'Enquête et plaintes concernant le maintien des recrues à Maradi, 1927'. Archives nationales du Niger, 3N 35. Later examples abound. In Tanzania, in the 1940s and 1950s, the state punished peasants resisting terracing schemes by imprisoning them on a large scale. Williams, 'The Role of Prisons in Tanzania', p. 28; and Steve Feierman, *Peasant Intellectuals: Anthropology and history in Tanzania*, Madison, WI: University of Wisconsin Press, 1990.

2. Convict labour in Mombassa gaol, *c.* 1900. [*Commonwealth in Focus: 130 years of photographic history*, Sidney: International Cultural Corporation, 1982]

generating imprisonment ratios comparable to those in French and Belgian colonies. In the mid-1920s administrative recourse to convict labour assisted the opening of new facilities. Kenya's Prison Board classified penitentiaries according to the duration of the detainees' sentences: two prisons held long-term prisoners (sentenced to more than three-years detention), five accommodated medium-term sentences (six months to three years), and twenty-three, labelled 'district prisons', received short-term prisoners. Starting in 1925 convicts were relocated according to productive tasks: in 1927 twenty-two 'detention camps' supervised hard labour in the territory. By 1933 the government had begun building 'prison camps' entirely devoted to agricultural and public works.[52] In the mid-1950s the Mau Mau crisis triggered unprecedented levels of penal detention in Kenya, leading to the incarceration of large segments of the Kikuyu population. The extreme violence used both in the fifty 'emergency camps', in which entire villages were forced to resettle, and in the dreadful 'rehabilitation camps', where

[52] Statistics from Kercher, *The Kenya Penal System*, pp. 14–15. In less than twenty years the number of penal institutions doubled, from 85 to 177 facilities.

thousands of suspects were screened and tortured under the pretence of political cleansing, indicates the highly punitive, even destructive agenda of this detention policy.[53] But if the goals differed, coercive techniques did not: in the emergency villages and in the rehabilitation camps, warders imposed forced labour to tame the prisoners' resistance.[54]

Colonisers kept complaining about labour shortages in the colonies and justified the recourse to convict labour as compensation for weak labour markets. In fact labour shortage in Africa was largely produced by inadequate wages. Therefore, by keeping wages and labour rights at an artificially low level, forced labour and convict labour contributed to solidifying the system, rather than compensating for it. If the respective weight of convict, forced and free labour in colonial economies is difficult to establish, the key fact in African colonies is precisely the lack of clear differences between these categories. The pervasive use of penal labour was hardly the exception to the rule in a developing labour market or a temporary response to contextual labour needs. Instead, it contributed to larger colonial efforts to produce a cheap, steady and disciplined native workforce. Convict labour was one of the many forms of mandatory labour in the colonial economy, itself a surviving and transitional form of slave labour in post-emancipation Africa.[55] The indiscriminate use of convict labourers on public works and in private establishments blurred the lines between the realm of the public and the private, while the circulation of free and penal workers across the walls of the colonial prison induced a structural confusion between the labour market and the space of unfree labour.[56] Last but not least, the system masked the divide between the space of punishment (the prison) and the space of sovereignty (outside the prison).

[53] Elkins, *Imperial Reckoning*, and Branch, 'Escaping the Carceral Archipelago'. For further statistics and analysis of British confining policies during the Mau Mau crisis, see David Anderson, *Histories of the Hanged: The dirty war in Kenya and the end of empire*, New York and London: W.W. Norton, 2005, pp. 311–16.

[54] Most of the Kikuyu prisoners were not tried, but treated as prisoners of war. On Kikuyu reserves and emergency villages, and on punitive work in hard core camps, both for male and female suspects, see Elkins, *Imperial Reckoning*, pp. 117, 141–2, 196, 224 and 242.

[55] Klein, *Slavery and Colonial Rule*, and Frederick Cooper *et al.*, *Beyond Slavery: Explorations of race, labor, and citizenship in post-emancipation societies*, Chapel Hill, NC: University of North Carolina Press, 2000, pp. 107–49.

[56] For the relationship between forced labour (*shibalo*) and prison labour in Mozambique, see Jeanne Penvenne, *African Workers and Colonial Racism: Mozambican strategies and struggles in Lourenço Marques, 1877–1962*, Portsmouth, NJ: Heinemann, 1995.

Race

In late-eighteenth-century Europe prison reform had emerged at the heart of a social consensus, in response to a series of convulsive transformations: an increasing sensitivity to pain and bodily torture, the passage of Western economies to industrial capitalism, the resulting threat of social disruption, and innovative ideas of social control. Instead of celebrating the king's ruling and punitive power, new modes of governance relied on the bureaucratic management of the political body and on individual reformation through discreet forms of standardised and democratic punishment.

In Africa, by contrast, the endurance of white rule depended on asserting social and political divides between colonisers and Africans, rather than on crafting integrative ruling strategies. While the reformed penitentiary in Europe promoted the virtue of punishment and the rationality of social control, colonial prisons encouraged the preservation of social antagonisms vital to white hegemony and contributed actively to the task of ascribing race as the major marker of difference between rulers and ruled.

If this policy is hardly surprising, the practical details are worth scrutinising. Prison regulations and architectural design worked to achieve three basic goals: the separation of black and white convicts, the de-individualisation of black prisoners, and the maintenance of very low standards of living for African convicts. White prisoners lived in separate quarters and enjoyed preferential treatment.[57] They were provided with better food, sanitation and clothing, and remained exempt from forced labour.[58] Colonial visions of Africans as an undifferentiated mass of gregarious people, defined by collective bonds rather than individual autonomy and responsibility, militated against isolating black convicts in individual cells. Most African prisons, therefore, accommodated native prisoners in collective chambers.[59] Material conditions remained dire and resisted reform. In black quarters, chronic overcrowding reigned, as well as a lack of structural separation of native convicts according to gender, age and the nature of the crime. The

[57] In early facilities that did not allow for separation, Europeans were incarcerated in police stations, or in administrative buildings. Most were rapidly transferred to Europe for trial. For a spectacular example of sentence evasion, see Michael Crowder, *The Flogging of Phineas McIntosh: A tale of colonial folly and injustice, Bechuanaland 1933*, New Haven, CT: Yale University Press, 1988.

[58] See a case-study of Burkina Faso in Laurent Fourchard, 'Between Conservatism and Transgression: Everyday life in the prisons of Upper-Volta' in Bernault (ed.), *A History of Prison*, pp. 135–54.

[59] Colonial prison design sometimes provided special gaols for African guards and warders. See for instance the Magaria prison in Niger, 1929 in Bernault, 'Politics of Enclosure', p. 20.

separation of male and female prisoners was generally ignored. Lack of funds and political concern everywhere prevented the building of separate quarters for minors.[60] Last but not least, penal policies worked as a social conservatory. As several studies have shown, no significant reform of the colonial penitentiaries came to fruition in Africa, even during the 1940s and 1950s when forced labour was abolished, racial segregation challenged in the electoral and judicial systems, and labour rights achieved by trade-unions. Late in the colonial period black prisoners experienced little if any improvement in their detention conditions and labour tasks.[61]

Yet penal policies did not rely entirely on pre-determined notions about racial difference. While judicial inequality remained the norm throughout the colonial period, the rule of penal difference did not remain inert or follow simple racial lines.[62] Instead, imprisonment contributed to the invention of racial divides. In some places, ideas of individual reform, for instance, cut across race and applied to white and black minor prisoners. Punishment through the loss of freedom seemed to some colonialists too weak a deterrent for African convicts. Some custodial practices employed legal, cultural and historical differences to justify the separation of black convicts from white prisoners and the nature of the punishment that should fall upon them.

Changing overlaps between race and class, in particular, played a crucial role in the emergence of the colonial penitentiary in South Africa, where penal segregation succeeded in the nineteenth century only after an initial attempt to establish non-racial reform prisons. At the end of the Dutch occupation in the Cape, which had started as a small merchant colony in the seventeenth century, a policy of deportation and public punishment applied to all offenders. With no distinction according to race, this penal system closely resembled the *ancien régime* punishment that then existed in Europe and in North America. In 1808 pass laws started to target Blacks and to swell the black convict population.[63] In 1843 the

---

[60] Women were commonly forced to suffer sexual abuse from both prisoners and guards. Their mandatory labour as cooks and maids in the maintenance of prison buildings was not recognised by law, and was thus not remunerated. Dior Konaté, 'Ultimate Exclusion: Imprisoned women in Senegal' in Bernault (ed.), *A History of Prison*, pp. 155–64.

[61] Bâ, 'L'enfermement carcéral pénal'; Konaté, 'A History of the Penal State in Senegal'; Fourchard, 'Between Conservatism and Transgression'.

[62] On similar views in the realm of citizenship, see Frederick Cooper, 'Deracializing Imperialism? Citizenship and conflict in French Africa after World War II', unpublished article, 2004.

[63] After the abolition of slavery in the Cape Colony (1809), settler communities developed pass laws to control the movement of the black population and reduce the cost of labour. A large population of Khoi Khoi and Bushmen offenders ended up in local gaols ('lockups'), whereas

new Colonial Secretary of the Cape, John Montagu, inspired by reformers' ideals in Europe and the United States, emphasised the reform role of the prison and the importance of penal labour.[64] The reform prompted the construction of large, portable wooden convict stations that could be transported to the sites of public works, where prisoners laboured in chain gangs. Montagu's project still ignored racial distinction and promoted a reformative classification based on each prisoner's behaviour.

By the late 1880s, following the discovery of diamonds and gold in the Boer provinces and the rapid transformation of the regional economy, an increasing number of white offenders ended up in prison for diamond smuggling. These were refined, intelligent and rich convicts who started to encourage discriminatory views about good and bad criminals and the need for separate punishment. In 1884 a Cape Town magazine complained how '[in prison] the coarser criminal, the black, the brute, has a more comfortable life than probably he had before his "punishment" commenced, while ... the white man has every decent susceptibility [to be] everlasting shocked and outraged.'[65] By the early 1890s John Montagu's rehabilitation ideals were replaced by a racialised, differential treatment, imposing hard labour for black convicts and reformative treatment for white ones. In 1892 the penal administration introduced racial separation of inmates inside all penal facilities in Cape Town, segregated diets (1898) and physical punishment for black prisoners.[66]

In later African colonies, racial segregation, if radically observed with white inmates, was further broken down among black offenders through a complex

---

criminals sentenced to long terms were detained in newly created 'convict stations'. By the 1900s pass laws generated the largest number of black convicts. Between 1916 and 1986 over 17 million blacks were imprisoned for breaking the pass laws. In addition to Cape Town's facilities the prison at Robben Island served for deported convicts, both white and black, from South Africa, and from the British East Indies. Harriett Deacon (ed.), *The Island: A history of Robben Island, 1488–1990*, Cape Town: Mayibuye Books, 1996, pp. 1–32. See also Dirk Van Zyl Smit, 'Public Policy and the Punishment of Crime in a Divided Society: A historical perspective on the South African penal system', *Crime and Social Justice*, (1984), pp. 148–9.

[64] Harriett Deacon, 'Racial Segregation and Medical Discourse in Nineteenth Century Cape Town', *Journal of Southern African Studies*, 22, 2 (1996), p. 305.

[65] Ibid.

[66] White detainees could choose to attend skills and industrial training in special prison workshops. By 1901 the Breakwater Prison in Cape Town was exclusively reserved for white prisoners. The first segregated prison to open outside the Cape Colony was in Kimberley, the capital of diamond mining. Vivian Bickford-Smith, *Ethnic Pride and Racial Prejudice in Victorian Cape Town*, New York: Cambridge University Press, 1995, p. 139, and Deacon, 'Racial Segregation and Medical Discourse', pp. 306–7.

web of differential legal status. In the French colonies, for instance, African 'administrative detainees' sentenced through the *code de l'indigénat* could be detained in separate quarters from black offenders tried by native tribunals.[67] Such distinction overran differences in age and gender, with the exception of a few attempts to send young delinquents to penitentiaries' schools or farms. Similar developments could be seen for *évolués* in the Belgian colonies and *assimilados* in the Portuguese, a status that granted a few civil and legal privileges to a handful of Western-educated Africans, yet did not endow them with full citizenship. In British colonies a number of scandals involving 'non-native' Africans condemned by native courts confirmed how colonial punitive practice enforced powerful divides among Africans—and within the larger category of race—according to their standing vis-à-vis colonial jurisdictions.[68]

Last but not least, penal raciology built upon considerable concern over convicts' imagined mental ability and cultural assets. In South Africa notions of race, education and inner feelings towards punishment did not merge before the 1890s. In colonies conquered after the mid-1880s the fusion was immediate. Most of the time, of course, colonisers paid attention to black convicts' minds only to deny their ability to understand confinement, an opinion well illustrated by the commissioner in charge of the supervision of prisons in Guinea in 1909: '[the elimination of meat and fish from the prisoners' diet] has produced an excellent effect: the condemned will no doubt eventually understand that imprisonment is a punishment, not a compensation for their misdeeds.'[69] Yet in the violent context of colonial rule, the idea that punishment should be measured against convicts' needs and inner psyche underlines how racial stereotypes could not entirely undo the premises of the reform model.

THE FABRICATION OF VIOLENCE

The uneasy filiation colonial penology in Africa entertained with the reform model can be further investigated through one of its most perplexing features: the revival and institutionalising of corporal punishment. The significance of this fact goes beyond a simple confirmation of imperial brutality, racism or archaism. Carefully fabricated and disseminated across various segments of the colonial

[67] See design of Magaria prison, in Bernault 'Politics of Enclosure', pp. 19–20. However, colonisers did not seem to have organised significant ethnic differences among convicts.

[68] Steven Pierce, 'Punishment and the Political Body: Flogging and colonialism in northern Nigeria', *Interventions*, 3, 2 (2001), pp. 206–21.

[69] Rapport de 1909, quoted by Diallo, *Répression et enfermement en Guinée*, p. 206.

3. 'Colonie belge' (whipping in Belgian Congo Prison), painting by Tsibumba Makundu.

society, corporal sanctions were part of colonial attempts to open hegemonic dialogues among white rulers and with local élites: at the ideological level by securing acceptance of legitimate forms of violence; and at the practical level by sharing the task of enforcing it across various segments of the colonial society. The penal ideology that supported these efforts proved highly original: corporal punishment, not imprisonment, emerged as the device that colonisers saw fit to discipline the natives, and the one they chose to promote hybrid forms of reformation.

Bodily punishment and penal archaism

In territories under indirect rule, African 'native' courts and 'customary' legislation supervised by Europeans legally enforced whipping, caning and beating. In British colonies (with the exception of Ghana) whipping sentences endured until the 1930s, only to be replaced by cane beating after local legislative councils rejected the Colonial Office recommendation that physical punishment should be entirely abolished in African colonies.[70] Beyond native courts most colonial legislations allowed physical punishment against black prisoners. The *chicote*—a whip made out of a bull or hippo's nerve—was the major punitive device used by the police and warders in Belgian Congo prisons up to independence. Under increasing criticism from Belgian opinion and from the international community, the law limited the number of blows to fifty in 1906, a dozen in 1923, eight in 1933 and four in 1951.[71] Outside the prison the unregulated use of the *chicote* by police guards of the Force Publique was so widespread that it later became an icon of colonial rule in the Congo.[72] Last but not least, when the law did not allow corporal sentences, officers and warders seldom refrained from using it against African convicts. In French colonies such breaches were common. In 1906 in Cotonou and Porto Novo (Benin) guards violently beat detainees' hands twenty or thirty times with a flat wooden cane (*correction palmatoire*) to force them to comply with the prison's internal regulations.[73] In Equatorial Africa chaining prisoners was still common in the late 1940s.[74]

Meanwhile classic histories of the penal reform in the West have made a strong case in presenting the birth of the modern penitentiary as paralleling the decline of physical torture. Representative of this school of thought, Michel Foucault and Robin Evans have argued how custodial sentences for criminals, breaking from the regime of public torture in the *ancien régime*, derived from a core belief in the possibility of altering the individual's willpower through rational architecture and regulated physical exercise (treadmill). The adoption of standardised imprisonment in rationally designed, curative and hygienic buildings has been usually explained by increasing sensitivity in the West to torture as unacceptable, by the loss of faith in the reformative power of pain, and by the rise

[70] Alan Milner, *The Nigerian Penal System*, London: Sweet and Maxwell, 1972, 297ff; Milner (ed.), *African Penal Systems*; and Kercher, *The Kenya Penal System*, pp. 72–5. For an interpretative essay, see David Killingray, 'The "Rod of Empire": The debate over corporal punishment in the British African colonial forces, 1888–1946', *Journal of African History*, 35 (1994), pp. 201–16, and idem, 'Punishment to Fit the Crime?'.

[71] See Dembour, 'La chicote', pp. 207–8. The sentence was finally abolished in 1959.

[72] See the series of paintings of *Colonie belge* by artist Tshibumba, analysed in Johannes Fabian, *Remembering the Present: Painting and popular history in Zaire*, Berkeley, CA: University of California Press, 1996. In German East Africa before the First World War, colonial agents used the *kiboko* whip.

[73] 'Rapport du governeur du Dahomey au gouverneur général de l'AOF, no. 378, March 31, 1906', Archives nationales du Sénégal.

[74] 'Lettre du gouverneur général de l'AEF sur l'enchaînement des prisonniers, no. 941/AP2, July 23, 1947'. ANG/Ndjolé-6. In the French colonies the *code de l'indigénat* did not allow corporal punishment, yet the archives show how beating and chaining prisoners remained common practice until after the Second World War. See Bâ, 'L'enfermement carcéral pénal'.

of bureaucratic modes of governing preoccupied with cheap yet efficient ways of preserving social order.[75] As a result the emergence of the reformed prison in the West is contextualised as part of a new regime of disciplining tactics aimed at touching the individual's soul and behaviour through an influence rendered as little physical as possible.[76]

The restoration of corporal punishment in African colonies belies this historical trajectory and as such questions both dominant narratives of Western punishment and important tenets in colonial history. Using African bodies to bear the physical mark of colonial rule does not differ essentially from the punitive tactics of the old Sovereign, and seems hardly to correspond to a modern disciplining agenda, in the Foucaldian sense of the term.[77] The process also interrogates the argument that sees European empires as global 'laboratories of modernity'.[78] The fabrication of colonial *supplice* thus relocates colonial power within two discreet yet suggestive genealogies: the brutality of current African regimes and Western teleological paradigms of social progress.[79] Did colonial prisons shelter a marginal revival of archaic violence confined to empires? Or did they arise as discreet 'frontier institutions', revealing the failure of the Western penal reform at large?[80]

[75] Historians disagree on the major causes in this dynamic, yet usually consent to its sequential logic. Foucault, *Discipline and Punish*; Evans, *The Fabrication of Virtue*; Pieter Spierenburg, *The Spectacle of Suffering: Executions and the evolution of repression: From a pre-industrial metropolis to the European experience*, Cambridge University Press, 1984; Karl Shoemaker, 'The Problem of Pain in Punishment: Historical Perspectives' in Austin Sarat (ed.), *Pain, Death and the Law*, Ann Arbor, MI: University of Michigan Press, 2003, pp. 15–41.

[76] According to Foucault: 'La prison ... a toujours ménagé une certaine mesure de souffrance corporelle ... Que serait un châtiment incorporel? Demeure donc un fond suppliciant dans les mécanismes modernes de la justice criminelle—un fond qui n'est pas tout à fait maîtrisé, mais qui est enveloppé, de plus en plus largement, par une pénalité de l'incorporel'. *Surveiller et punir. Naissance de la prison*, Paris: Gallimard, 1975, p. 21.

[77] Foucault, *Discipline and Punish*, section 3, chapters 1 and 2. It is important to note how Foucault's conceptualisation of the verb in English (to discipline) and in French (*discipliner*), emphasised its alternate meaning as training, educating, controlling and normalising, thus breaking away from the common sense of punishing. The colonial situation, as we will see, provided the term with original semantics.

[78] Paul Rabinow, *French Modern: Norms and forms of the social environment*, Cambridge, MA: MIT Press, 1989.

[79] Mbembe, 'Necropolitics'. For critiques of the modernity of colonial rule, see Zinoman, *Colonial Bastille*.

[80] Extreme schemes of repression/confinement in Europe have been analysed as a rupture with normal forms of retribution and imprisonment (Hannah Arendt) and limited aberrations to the penitentiary model (Patricia O'Brien and Michelle Perrot). Fewer studies have identitifed 'archaic' or pre-modern forms of punishment as structural parts of modern punitive devices. For comparison between the British Mau Mau camps in Kenya and the Soviet Gulag, see Marshall

Sharing violence and manufacturing consent

The larger economy of violence in which corporal sentences were embedded reveals significant archaic features in the deployment of colonial rule. Almost everywhere assaulting Africans was a practice accepted beyond the confines of prisons, native tribunals and police malpractice. Private European settlers enjoyed impunity when physically mistreating and beating Africans. White missionaries and African catechists participated in these abuses.[81] The ubiquitous use of physical power across dominant classes, and colonial authorities' reliance on private actors betrays significant lapses in the colonial state's monopoly of legitimate force. To a large extent, the tactic ran parallel to the colonial authorities' lack of concern towards (indeed encouragement of) the generalised use of penal labour by private companies. Both strategies provided considerable support in the production of economic dominance and political authority.

Beyond the diffusion of private violence, however, colonial authorities' enforcement of corporal punishment helped to promote hegemonic conversations with native élites.[82] Indeed historical evidence shows that a number of judicial articulations did take place around the legalising of physical punitive practices.[83] Historians have interpreted colonial flogging in Nigeria and in Uganda, for instance, as a way of manufacturing consent between white rulers and local élite males: the flogging of undisciplined women by native courts helped to assert a double patriarchal control over female labour, and in Uganda to secure cotton cultivation for the benefit of local entrepreneurs.[84] Regulated corporal sanctions hence helped punitive alliances crystallise across colonial divides.

Clough, *Mau Mau Memoirs: History, memory, and politics*, Boulder, CO: Lynne Rienner, 1998, p. 205; Anderson, *Histories of the Hanged*, pp. 311–16; and Elkins, *Imperial Reckoning*.

[81] ANG/FP 809. 'Procès verbal de plainte contre le catéchiste Zouma, no 1032', signed by G. Thomas, district chief of Mekambo. ANG/FP 629. 'Procès-verbal de plainte contre le Père Le Clanche, tribunal de Mékambo, August 2, 1943'. ANG/FP 8-308.

[82] On the weakness of colonial rule in Africa and its ability to be built from the bottom up, see Bruce Berman and John Lonsdale, *Unhappy Valley: Conflict in Kenya and Africa*, vol. 1, London: James Currey, 1992.

[83] This contradicts the paradigm of colonialism as a form of 'dominance without hegemony'. See Ranajit Guha, 'Colonialism in South Asia: A dominance without hegemony and its historiography' in *Dominance without Hegemony: History and power in colonial India*, Cambridge, MA: Harvard University Press, 1997. For a critique of this idea, see Berman and Lonsdale, *Unhappy Valley*, and Jean and John Comaroff, *Of Revelation and Revolution: Christianity, colonialism and consciousness in South Africa*, University of Chicago Press, 1991.

[84] Carol Summers, 'Whips and Women: Forcing change in eastern Uganda during the 1920s', unpublished article; and Pierce, 'Punishment and the Political Body'.

Yet physical punishment also served to secure racial hierarchies. Colonial representations[85] set it firmly in the realm of indigenous practices, while legal practice confined the performing of corporal sentence to native authorities, black warders and African delinquents.[86] In European views, Africans complied with judicial beating either because they did not take issue with the virtue of bodily pain, were not sensitive to it, or accepted it as a 'traditional' sentence.[87] This doctrine naturalised, traditionalised and, to a large extent, patronised physical violence as a marker of racial difference, thus constructing significant biological and cultural divides (the ability to feel pain or preferring one's customs) in the realm of penal practice. The enforcement of physical torture was also predicated on moral grounds. Since Europeans made considerable use of corporal brutality, they tended to put forward subtle contrasts between action and intention, suggesting how their strategic acceptance of 'native ways' was achieved at a high moral cost, only by overcoming personal disgust ('repugnant') and ethical norms ('disquieting').[88] Colonial representations, in short, drew a forceful contrast between a determined African compliance with force, cast as cultural or biological, and a rationalised European acquiescence, envisioned as a matter of moral choice and self-inflicted political necessity.[89]

Disciplining violence

In this ideological context physical punishments were imagined and imposed as hybrid sentences borrowing from African and Western punitive regimes in which measure, regulation and predictability would function as the imprint of white penal civilisation on local physical hubris. Whipping, for instance, was consciously justified as a modern and standardised form of bodily retribution deemed to replace traditional mutilation, stoning or death.[90] Colonial law

---

[85] For lack of evidence, I need to limit my discussion to white representations of physical sentences.

[86] For a rare exception, see Crowder, *The Flogging of Phineas McIntosh*.

[87] For the classic critique of the colonial concept of tradition, see Eric Hobsbawm and Terence Ranger (eds), *The Invention of Tradition*, New York: Cambridge University Press, 1983; and for a recent reappraisal, Thomas Spear, 'Neo-Traditionalism and the Limits of Invention', *Journal of African History*, 44 (2003), pp. 3–27.

[88] Pierce, 'Punishment and the Political Body'; Killingray, 'The "Rod of Empire"'.

[89] In French, self-inflicted decisions are tellingly rendered by the expression *se faire violence*. For a study of colonialism as work on the self, see Emmanuelle Saada, 'The Empire of Law: Dignity, prestige and domination in the "Colonial Situation"', *French Politics, Culture and Society*, 20, 2 (summer 2002), pp. 98–120.

[90] On British colonies, see Killingray, 'The "Rod of Empire"'; and 'Punishment to Fit the Crime?'. On Belgian colonies, Dembour, 'La chicote'.

carefully ordered the details of public performances, tuning the exact number of cat, whip or cane lashes to be exacted, how blows should strike the victim, and which parts of the body could be exposed.[91] The length, diameter and weight of the caning stick was prescribed by law and varied from one colonial territory to another.[92] The new whipping or caning procedure was supposed to comfort African spectators as a familiar, legible form of sentence, at the same time the careful calibration of lashes was to display the educative virtue of Western reform. Around colonial scaffolds, where a large public was summoned, bodily chastisements were performed therefore as a *reformed spectacle*, differing both from native punitive practices and the legacy of ancient Western *supplices*.

Colonial authorities invested considerable scrutiny on native courts' performances and occasional mishaps. As Steven Pierce shows for Northern Nigeria, incidents were blamed on procedural problems, not ideological flaws: 'flogging administered when they should not have been, meted out to inappropriate people, too many lashes delivered, lashes applied improperly.'[93] On these unfortunate occasions, technical 'lapses' prompted didactic spectacles to degenerate into scandals, ruining the performative virtue of regulated punishment.

Colonial concerns about the irregular, indecent or cruel ways in which native courts might inflict flogging and caning demonstrate, moreover, that the object of colonial disciplining was, to a large extent, the treatment itself. In colonisers' minds, monitored beating seemed to have held greater reformative potential than imprisonment, as custodial confinement was frequently seen as a non-indigenous treatment incompatible with the gregarious, family-bonded and undisciplined African, too desperate to survive incarceration or too lazy to understand it as punishment.[94]

It is therefore no coincidence that colonisers talked about beating recalcitrant prisoners or rebellious women in the vocabulary of discipline (in French, *discipliner*), a repertoire seldom used in commenting on the colonial penitentiary. From the colonial rulers' viewpoint, if bodily retribution was better accepted by Africans than custodial incarceration, if it conformed to old customs, if it encouraged the maintaining of African authority and answered the lack of bodily sensitivity particular to the natives, a mutual dialogue could occur between colo-

---

[91] Pierce, 'Punishment and the Political Body'; and Summers, 'Whips and Women'.

[92] Killingray, 'Punishment to fit the crime?', p. 107.

[93] Pierce, 'Punishment and the Political Body', p. 209. See also Steven Pierce and Anupama Rao, 'Discipline and the Other Body: Correction, corporeality and colonial rule', *Interventions*, 3–2 (2001), pp. 159–68.

[94] Pierce, 'Punishment and the Political Body', pp. 213–14.

nisers, local élites and African commoners. Then physical punishment, not incarceration, could serve for judicial conversations, disciplinary experiments and the possibility of reform. A new compromise between the violence of native repression and the kindness of colonial retribution, construing bodily pain as blending 'traditional customs' and the calibrating force of modern colonial power, stood as the Europeans' main reformative ambition. In British Central Africa, crimes punished by flogging reflected colonial efforts to instil in Africans new notions of social order and individual discipline: wasting time instead of buying food was punished by four lashes, sitting around the fire instead of working by five to ten lashes.[95] As a result a particular disciplinary project emerged in the colonial context, drawing back together what Western penal ideologues had sought to separate since the eighteenth century: the confluence of physical pain, punishment and individual reform.

Hence colonial punishments and disciplinary tactics mobilised a double level of sentence and purpose in symmetrical opposition to the European reform model: well-ordered prison architectures served primarily to organise violent coercion (forced labour and racial segregation), while physical punishment was promoted to effect discipline and reformation. The tropical prison, enduring as an operational contradiction in terms, thus survived as a project as 'impossible' as its Western counterpart.[96] Failing to serve the reformation of African subjects, colonial confinement and discipline both disengaged from the reform paradigm. Yet it cannot be reduced to mere revivals of penal archaism. Indeed, beyond the great divide described by Foucault, colonial penal violence did not celebrate the new ruler's absolute power on the native body, as much as it aimed at preserving, controlling and re-inscribing onto this very body the defeated laws of the old Sovereign.

APPROPRIATION AND ESCAPE

The meaning of the modern prison in Africa cannot be found only at the heart of imperial projects, even if the colonial prison left little room for African initiatives. Indeed the penal system could be diverted from the reproduction and consolidation of colonial inequalities only with great difficulty. Prisons emerged

---

[95] Chanock, *Law, Custom, and Social Order*, p. 108, quoted in Killingray, 'Punishment to Fit the Crime?', p. 108.

[96] Michelle Perrot (ed.), *L'impossible prison: Recherches sur le système pénitentiaire au XIXe siècle*, Paris: Seuil, 1980.

as central instruments of state power while they achieved little legitimacy as a form of punishment in the African public. The legacy of this contradiction can still be seen today.

Serving political repression and economic extraction, colonial prisons engendered considerable resistance among ordinary Africans. By all accounts this rejection appears not only to have been ubiquitous, but also to have persisted well beyond the first years of the century.[97] Early on, the frequency of suicide and morbid forms of prostration among African prisoners suggest how detainees, especially free men, experienced imprisonment as an extreme situation.[98] Even if the historical experience of captivity and slaving played a determining role in this repulsion, colonial imprisonment seems to have exacerbated the association of capture with personal degradation.[99] Those who crossed the prison threshold expected to be stripped of their social and physical integrity and their spiritual protection. In colonial Guinea informants compared the prison to a grave, a vision fuelled by detainees' testimonies about the obscurity of the stockades, the darkness of the gaols and chambers. Many believed in the otherworldly nature of the prison, describing how those who had the misfortune to be imprisoned for more than three months would progressively lose their vision, becoming totally blind after a year inside.[100] Images of physical and spiritual decay resonated with

[97] For a reconstituted narrative of prison experience, see Charles Van Onselen, 'Crime and Total Institutions in the Making of Modern South Africa: The life of Nongoloza Mathebula, 1867–1948', *History Workshop Journal*, 19 (1985), pp. 62–81. Bandits and rebels generated an extensive literature in the 1980s. See David Crummey (ed.), *Banditry, Rebellion and Social Protest in Africa*, London: Heinemann, 1985; and S. Cohen, 'Bandits, Rebels or Criminals: African history and Western criminology (Review Article)', *Africa*, 56, 4 (1986), pp. 468–83.

[98] Prisoners' life stories are difficult to document, not only for moral and social reasons but because the prison was often experienced as a space of annihilation and silence. One has to rely on former prisoners' autobiographies, political denunciation and works of fiction, although such narratives cannot entirely express what lies behind the silent experience of those who did not testify. Among many outstanding works, see J.M. Kariuki, *Mau Mau Detainee* (1963), George Simeon Mwase, *Strike a Blow and Die: A narrative of race relations in colonial Africa* (1967), Wole Soyinka, *The Man Died: Prison notes* (1972), Ngugi Wa Thiong'o, *Detainee: A writer's prison diary* (1981), Ken Saro Wiwa, *A Month and a Day: A detention diary* (1995), the novel by Ibrahima Ly, *Toiles d'araignées* (1982), and the recent collection edited by Jack Mapanje, *Gathering Seaweed: African prison writing*, Portsmouth, NH: Heinemann, 2002.

[99] Thioub, 'Sénégal: la prison à l'époque coloniale. Significations, évitement et évasions' in Bernault (ed.), *Enfermement*, p. 292, explains how free men (*gor*) and nobles (*garmi*) experienced the prison as an unbearable social degradation. Several followed the example of the ruler (*damel*) of Kayor, Samba Yaya Fall, who committed suicide after he was confined to the Island of Gorée in 1891.

[100] Diallo, *Histoire de la répression pénitentiaire en Guinée*, p. 125.

the ancient fear of the vampirisation of souls and black bodies by Europeans and their henchmen.[101]

Escapes proved the major form of revolt against the prison, and remained high throughout the colonial period. Escapees benefited from many forms of complicity: the help of African guards, protection from relatives and public refusal of the prison as a tool of foreign oppression. Spiritual initiatives emerged as well. In Senegal charms such as the '*ndémène* horn' (*lokki ndémène*) or the *koular* charm, could protect one from becoming involved with the administration and could render the individual invisible. Other charms could help restore the detainee's spiritual protection after incarceration.[102]

The intrusive presence of the custodial prison in the legal sphere introduced new repertoires of grass-roots judicial practice. First, the prison transformed collective sentences into standardised, individual punishments applied to all. This radically challenged older practices of proportional compensation based on the social status of the conflicting parties. The prison also individualised punishments by truncating social responsibilities, severing the criminal from collective protection, and preventing the victim from mobilising powerful patrons for reparation and vengeance. Second, imprisonment circumvented public vengeance on delinquents, leaving the victim in the shadows—a crucial shift from past judicial procedures. In a few instances the influence of the prison model could derive from its very proximity with local understanding. For example, forced penal labour could be understood in terms of compensatory reparation or as a form of pawning to the benefit of the new (white) masters. But in this case again the overarching meaning of punishment changed radically. Forced labour as 'compensation' no longer contributed to the resolution of local conflicts and the production of local hierarchies, but served the foreign, arbitrary power of Europeans.

Colonial prisons contaminated local taxonomies and popular imaginations. European missionaries and African catechists served as zealous intermediaries in this rhetorical diffusion: in 1936, for example, a ten-year-old girl claimed a certain Zouma, a village catechist in southern Gabon, had accused her of singing badly during the night prayers, ordered her 'to stay in prison' in his own house,

---

[101] On idioms of extraction during the time of the slave trade, see Joseph C. Miller, *Way of Death: Merchant capitalism and the Angolan slave trade, 1730–1830*, Madison, WI: University of Wisconsin Press, 1988, pp. 157–8. And on their endurance throughout the colonial and postcolonial periods, see Luise White, *Speaking with Vampires: Rumor and history in colonial Africa*, Berkeley, CA: University of California Press, 2000.

[102] Thioub, 'Sénégal', p. 294.

and raped her.[103] In 1943 a conflict involved a white Catholic missionary, Father Le Clanche, and several African Protestant converts. The father had threatened the plaintiffs that he would ask the commandant to put them in prison.[104]

Chérif Diallo finds that in Guinea-Conakry, popular consent to the prison can be detected by the 1930s.[105] A significant number of Africans had entered the prison as indigenous guards and warders—although little is known about their origins and motivations. For the ruling class and for some ambitious individuals the new penal system presented obvious opportunities. Aside from the few paramount chiefs who ran their own prisons, some did not hesitate to take advantage of the possibility of incarcerating undesirable people. We know how an administrative agent of the jurisdiction of Dori (Niger) managed to devise a whole series of clandestine operations around the local prison. Denouncing criminals and petty offenders to the French administrator in residence, he ransomed families under the pretence of being able to help the prisoners survive or escape. In 1915 the district authorities arrested the zealous agent after three individuals protested against the confiscation of twenty of their cattle.[106] This episode speaks to the ambiguity of the punitive compromise between the colonial state and indigenous élites. Apart from native courts and the few paramount chiefs who were allowed to manage their own gaols, ordinary Africans could also find ways to make use of the colonial prison. But most had to do so through illegal enterprises, not as recognised partners of the colonial authorities.[107]

Appropriations of the prison thus further cast Africans as subaltern agents of the colonial system. Although open riots organised by prisoners have been documented, it seems that pervasive and low-key resistance, consisting of systematic incidents with warders and the authorities, the organising of mutual aid among prisoners, political education, faking disease, and escaping, provided favourite means of opposing colonial imprisonment.[108]

---

[103] 'Procès verbal de plainte 1032, to G. Thomas, chef de poste à Mékambo, April 1, 1936'. ANG/FP 629.

[104] 'Procès verbaux d'enregistrement de plainte, Tribunal indigène du 1er degré de l'Ogooué-Ivindo, August 1, 1943'. ANG/FP 8-308.

[105] Diallo, *Histoire de la répression pénitentiaire en Guinée*, p. 122.

[106] 'Minutes du tribunal de subdivision de Djibo, cercle de Dori. Audience du 18 mai 1915'. Archives nationales du Niger, 7-8-2.

[107] Some could ally with African civil servants against the threat of the prison. In early colonial Sierra Leone, for example, the courts realised that a number of suspects had evaded the law by bribing the court messengers on their way to arrest them. C. Magbaily Fyle, *History and Socio-Economic Development in Sierra Leone*, Freetown, 1988, pp. 91–2.

[108] For case-studies of political resistance, see Anderson, *Histories of the Hanged*, pp. 324–7. On the

Most colonial penitentiaries thus survived until decolonisation in a context of undisturbed inequality, their walls delimiting a space of domination that, while surely not infallible or total, resisted any significant sharing of power between colonisers and colonised. This coercive agenda has been largely carried on by postcolonial regimes.

WORKING LEGACIES, 1960s–2000s

The three decades from the 1960s to the late 1980s saw the exacerbation of the colonial model, paralleling in many countries a steady loss of state authority. During this period, national debates on the role of retribution and punishment proved exceedingly rare. Most African penitentiaries remained shaped by colonial legacies, localised power relations and the uneven deployment of public and private violence on the ground. In the early 1990s new initiatives surfaced among the public, voicing concerns about criminality, prisoners' rights and the need to reform penal practices.

Ambivalent penitentiary regimes

In the 1970s and 1980s the extreme violence exerted in a few infamous African prisons was exacerbated under postcolonial dictatorships. Sékou Touré's Camp Boiro in Conakry (Guinea), Jean-Bedel Bokassa's prison at Ngaragba (Central African Republic) and Idi Amin Dada's gaols in Kampala (Uganda) evoked the sinister images of Nazi camps or Soviet gulags. However, as Didier Bigo argues in his provocative study of Ngaragba, the comparison obscures, rather than illuminates, the logic of these prisons. Bokassa's prison did not operate according to the panoptical laws of the modern and bureaucratic penitentiary; instead it responded to the imperatives of a local political culture shaped by arbitrariness, physical torture and the personalisation of violence.[109] Unlike Nazi concentration camps, driven by industrial and impersonal technique, Ngaragba functioned as an open-air theatre, where torturers and prisoners enacted tragic scenes of power and submission that celebrated Bokassa's personal will and grandeur. An excrescence of arbitrary

---

formation of gangs and hidden associations in colonial prisons, see Fourchard, 'Between Conservatism and Transgression' in Bernault (ed.), *A History of Prisons*, pp. 142–7; and Van Onselen, 'Crime and Total Institutions'. Konaté, 'A History of the Penal State in Senegal,' pp. 227–65, shows in detail the multiple channels through which convicts defeated or undermined prison regulations, but also intrigued to accommodate the system.

[109] Didier Bigo, 'Ngaragba, "L'impossible prison"', *Revue française de science politique*, 39, 6 (1989), pp. 867–85.

power, the prison and its involuntary actors theatralised the cruel confrontation between the weak and the strong, in an institution where inconstancy, contingency and unpredictability—not bureaucratic routine—provided the organising principle. In contrast with the model of the Weberian or the Foucauldian state, based on bureaucratic techniques of power, general surveillance and the citizens' internalising of omnipresent discipline, these extreme cases of detention and torture speak both to the colonial prison's prevalent use of coercion over protection and to newer, extravagant forms of personalised power.[110]

During the same period the diffusion of clandestine lock-ups set up by paramilitary gangs and militias has shown how African states engulfed in wars and civil conflicts were no longer able to exercise a monopoly of (il)legitimate violence. These transient, localised tactics of incarceration continue to this day to reinforce local networks of power and to expose the existence of many social and geographical zones where the state is unable to penetrate. Across the African continent the multiplication of refugee camps has further revealed the state's increasing loss of control over confinement policies and national boundaries.

Starting in the 1960s a few regimes tried to restructure the legal systems inherited from the colonial past. The creation of special courts in Nigeria, the adoption of customary laws in Zimbabwe along with the creation of village and community courts, and the sweeping replacement of Portuguese courts by people's tribunals in Mozambique marked this period of renovation.[111] Yet most initiatives failed to lessen the coercive agenda of the colonial prison and to renew the penal link between the state and civil society. A majority of penal regimes, for instance, continued to enforce corporal punishment.[112] Up to the 1990s man-

---

[110]   Achille Mbembe, 'Traditions de l'autoritarisme et problèmes de gouvernement en Afrique sub-saharienne', *Africa Development*, 17, 1 (1992), pp. 37–64. Roland Marchal, 'Surveillance et répression en postcolonie', *Politique africaine*, 42 (1991), pp. 41–50.

[111]   In Ghana the government made efforts to transform penal labour from a productive to a reformatory technique. In 1961 the establishment of revolutionary tribunals in Ghana reflected Nkrumah's long-standing suspicion that the existing legal system had served 'an imperialist and colonial purpose'. See an excellent overview by R. Gocking, 'Ghana's Public Tribunals: An experiment in revolutionary justice', *African Affairs*, (1996), pp. 197–223. Also Williams, 'The Role of Prisons in Tanzania', pp. 32 and 36–7.

[112]   This is the case for the criminal codes of Nigeria, Kenya (1973) and Uganda. See Milner (ed.), *African Penal Systems*, p. 111, and *The Nigerian Penal System*, p. 305. See also Kercher, *The Kenya Penal System*, p. 250. In Tanzania the government introduced a 'Minimum Sentences Act' in 1963, that required caning for scheduled offences such as robbery, cattle theft and theft by public servants and state officials. The Law provoked vigorous criticism in Tanzania until a new law cancelled all physical punishment in 1972. See discussion of the 1963 Act in J.S. Read, 'Minimum Sentences in Tanzania', *Journal of African Law*, 9, 1 (1965), pp. 20–39. For a good analysis of

datory convict labour remained widespread, while penal labour contributed significantly to national production, especially in the agricultural and public works
sectors.[113] Although the material degradation of African penitentiaries can be
traced to colonial times, the building of new facilities and the maintenance of
prisons inherited from the colonial period have often remained relegated to the
margins of national budgets. Recent efforts to modernise the prison system have
met with mixed results. The maximum security ('C-Max') facility opened in
1997 in the prison at Pretoria (South Africa) is renowned for its dreadful living
conditions.[114] In Ghana and Ivory Coast, public rumour describes the recently
built, ultra-modern and maximum security prisons as horrific and impersonal
places where wardens can exert unchecked, sometimes lethal, violence on detainees.

New public engagement

Despite a lack of reliable studies and statistics, highly divergent visions of the
prison system seem to endure in post-independence public views. On the one
hand civil opinion, at least in the cities where urban crime is high, accepts and
encourages the incarceration of criminals and delinquents. On the other hand
numerous signs of the rejection of carceral institutions remain palpable con-
tinent-wide. Escapes, for example, increased drastically in postcolonial prisons,
suggesting enduring support for escapees as well as a remarkably negligent attitude on the part of the penal administration. In the 1960s and 1970s official
figures for successful escapes from prisons in Congo-Kinshasa were three times
those at the end of the colonial period.[115]

---

the 1972 Act, and discussion of earlier debates, see D. Williams, 'The Minimum Sentences Act,
1972, of Tanzania', *Journal of African Law*, 18, 1 (1974), pp. 79–91. In Ghana the British colonial
government never legalised corporal punishment. R.B. Seidman, 'The Ghana Prison System: A
historical perspective' in Milner (ed.), *African Penal Systems*, pp. 68 and 85.

[113] See the construction of the airport at Embakasi in Nairobi. James S. Read, 'Kenya, Tanzania,
and Uganda' in Milner (ed.), *African Penal Systems*, p. 137.

[114] Detainees spent 23 hours a day in complete isolation, and could exercise only in a caged courtyard. Amanda Dissel and Stephen Ellis, 'Ambitions réformatrices et inertie du social dans les
prisons sud-africaines', *Critique internationale*, 16 (2002), pp. 137–52.

[115] In 1956 1,425 escapes for 22,680 (6.3 per cent) prisoners; in 1963, 4,743 escapes for 12,285
detainees (38.6 per cent); in 1973, 3,126 for 15,322 (20.4 per cent). Administration pénitentiaire, Imprimerie de Ndolo, Archives nationales du Congo. Gaining access to even imperfect
figures on this point is extremely difficult. Milner (ed.), *African Penal Systems* and *The Nigerian
Penal System*; and Kercher, *The Kenya Penal System*, are silent on escapes. In addition, available
data are hardly reliable as figures can be manipulated to put pressure on governments to increase budgets for maintenance and security.

Juridical practices have reflected this ambivalence, at least till the 1990s. In some countries only specific categories of people lacking strong social connections and protection, such as labour migrants and foreigners, ended up in prison and lived out their sentences.[116] Large-scale financial fraud or crimes perpetrated by high-placed persons could escape judicial sanctions entirely. At the other extreme of the social ladder, compensation for petty crimes was often managed within families and neighbourhoods or negotiated at the level of local police precincts.[117] In a more dramatic context, spontaneous sentences initiated by angry crowds—stoning, beating, murder by fire—remained frequent. In Cameroon in the mid-1990s, plagued by road squads (*coupeurs de route*), popular views justified violent retaliation against petty thieves to prevent the development of underworld bosses (*katchika*).[118] The endurance of this 'second legal economy' points to the perpetuation of rich layers of informal, hidden judicial tactics initiated during the colonial period, when European law touched upon only a superficial stratum of crimes and conflict resolution.

State negligence in maintaining facilities has resulted in initiatives to improve detainees' living conditions. In the mid-1990s, in two countries as different as Niger and Congo-Brazzaville, the general neglect that reigned both inside and outside the prison was striking. Dating from the colonial period, the buildings were no longer maintained. Financial resources were nonexistent or unpredictable, a situation that forced prison directors to rely on charitable organisations and the detainees' families to ensure the prisoners' subsistence (food, clothing, bedding, health care). Such outside support was facilitated by the considerable permeability of the prison buildings. Families and donors entered the prison yard on a daily basis, while prisoners could leave the buildings for work, visits, walks, errands or casual conversation with visitors.[119] As a result many older facilities ended up preserving social connections between prisoners and their relatives,

---

[116] In Brazzaville in 1995 detainees were reputed to be mostly of foreign origin, in particular from Congo-Kinshasa. Social vulnerability can result from the nature of the crime itself. In the case of witchcraft, a crime legally recognised in several countries, incarceration is an effective means of protecting the alleged criminal from popular vengeance. See Cyprien Fisiy and Michael Rowlands, 'Sorcery and Law in Modern Cameroon', *Culture and History* (Copenhagen), 6 (1990), pp. 63–84; and Cyprien Fisiy and Peter Geschiere, 'Judges and Witches: Or how is the state to deal with witchcraft? Examples from southeastern Cameroon', *Cahiers d'études africaines*, 118 (1990), pp. 135–56.

[117] Serge Nédélec, 'Etat et délinquance juvénile' in Bernault (ed.), *Enfermement*, pp. 411–35.

[118] Sabou Issa, 'La répression du grand banditisme au Cameroun', unpublished article.

[119] Author's visits to the prisons at Tillabéry, Niamey, Daikana and Kollo (Niger, 1992); and to the central prison of Brazzaville (Congo, 1995).

thus offering milder experiences of incarceration than in modern Western prisons. The existence of these 'open prisons' does not result only from the depletion
of colonial facilities but also from creative strategies promoting the prisoners'
physical conservation and continuing socialisation.

The most promising penal initiatives in the last years of the twentieth century
were carried out by the African public and by prisoners themselves. Recent research on refugee camps in Algeria, Mali and Libya by Pierre Boilley, and in Tanzania by Liisa Malkki, suggests how sites of massive confinement can promote
social renewal.[120] Press campaigns, emerging academic research and pressure from
NGOs and human rights activists have increased public awareness about the fate
of prisoners and the need to reform the penal system. This sometimes goes hand
in hand with public pressure for more repressive confinement policies, for instance in post-apartheid South Africa, where the dismantling of racialised facilities and efforts to reform prisons did not curb rising criminality and mounting
public concern.[121] Yet the notion of prisoners' rights plays a new role in the South
African debate, and has now taken root in a majority of African countries.

Civil society's involvement in the execution of penal sentences and the
search for non-custodial alternatives appear as central pillars in current efforts
for penal reform.[122] To counter the enduring overcrowding of facilities and to
answer emerging public concerns about prisoners' rights, English-speaking African countries (Nigeria, South Africa, Zimbabwe, Namibia and Cameroon) have
adopted the use of supervised deferred sentences and probation orders. In cases
of minor offences a court can adjourn the sentencing process for a period during
which the convict is placed under the supervision of probation officers. In Cameroon the court can delegate the probation officer's function to a social worker,
a relative or a friend of the offender, who agrees to help him reintegrate into
society. In 1993, Senegal introduced a range of non-custodial orders to punish
petty crimes or contractual offences, and appointed 'post sentencing' or review
judges to monitor penalties according to individual circumstances. The review

[120] Pierre Boilley, 'Administrative Confinements and Confinements of Exile: The reclusion of
nomads in the Sahara' in Bernault (ed.), *A History of Prison*, pp. 221–37; Liisa Malkki, *Purity
and Exile: Violence, memory and cosmology among Hutu refugees in Tanzania*, University of Chicago
Press, 1995.

[121] Dissel and Ellis, 'Ambitions réformatrices'. See also Dirk van Zyl Smith, 'South Africa' in Dirk
van Zyl Smith and Frieder Dünkel (eds), *Imprisonment Today and Tomorrow: International perspectives on prisoners' rights and prison conditions*, Kluwer Law International, 2001.

[122] Odette-Luce Bouvier, 'The Senegalese Reform Project on Alternatives to Imprisonment',
Seminar on Community Service, Bangui, Central African Republic, 2–5 November 1998.
Article available at <http://www.penalreform.org>.

judge does not work alone but is assisted by a consultative committee made up of prison administrators, social workers and civil volunteers.

A crucial feature of these penal initiatives is the way in which official projects parallel, and frequently stem from, civil activism. In several countries considerable mobilisation has emerged among human rights activists, churches, NGOs and lawyers, leading to proposals and actions to improve prisoners' detention, education, training and social reinsertion.[123] Multiple pressures for reforming the prisons have led to the organising of two major conferences, in 1996 (Kampala, Uganda) and in 2002 (Ouagadougou, Burkina-Faso). The Kampala Declaration on Prison Conditions in Africa, adopted at the closure of the 1996 conference, has since served as a benchmark for prison and penal reform in Africa.[124] While it is too early to assess their achievements, these initiatives clearly derive from considerable changes in the public's awareness of and engagement with the role of prisons, the fate of prisoners, and the meaning of punishment in modern Africa.

BIBLIOGRAPHICAL NOTE

The history of prisons in the thirty or more countries south of the Sahara has been unevenly treated, even if the field is now attracting considerable attention from historians. Arnold W. Lawrence, *Trade Castles and Forts in West Africa*, London: Cape, 1963, provides an elaborate study of the gaols present in the trading castles and stations built on the coast of Africa between the fifteenth and the nineteenth centuries, accompanied by superb illustrations. Unfortunately, no equivalent work exists for African systems of punishment and captivity during this period. For the colonial and post-independence era, the rich collection edited by Alan Milner, *African Penal Systems*, London: Routledge & Kegan Paul, 1969, offers extensive information on a selection of countries. A few monographs have focused on national penal systems or some famous facilities, such as D. Williams, 'The Role of Prisons in Tanzania: A historical perspective', *Crime and Social Justice*, 1980, pp. 27–38; Taslim Olawale Elias (ed.), *The Prison System in*

---

[123]　For instance, the association *Prisonniers sans frontières*, organised among Catholic activists in the Ivory Coast in the mid-1980s, was 500 members strong in 2005 and sponsored several dozen groups of local volunteers, present in the penal facilities of Benin, Burkina-Faso, Cameroon, Congo-Brazzaville, Mali, Niger, Senegal and Togo.

[124]　Pan African Conference on Prison Conditions, co-organised by the NGO Penal Reform International (PRI) and the African Penitentiary Association (APA). Information available at <http://www.penalreform.org>.

Nigeria, Lagos, 1965; Alan Milner, *The Nigerian Penal System*, London: Sweet and Maxwell, 1972; and Didier Bigo, 'Ngaragba: L'impossible prison', *Revue française de sciences politiques*, 1989, on Jean-Bedel Bokassa's dictatorial regime in the Central African Republic. The recent collection edited by Florence Bernault, *Enfermement, prison et châtiments en Afrique du 19ème siècle à nos jours* Paris: Karthala, 1999, followed by a revised version in English (*A History of Prison and Confinement in Africa*, Portsmouth, NJ: Heinemann, 2003), proposes an interpretative overview of the custodial prison in sub-Saharan Africa from the nineteenth to the late twentieth century, followed by historical case-studies on Rwanda, Senegal, Angola, Burkina-Faso, Guinea-Conakry and Liberia. In the same collection, David Killingray's chapter covers the history of prisons in British colonies. Based on doctoral research at the University of Cheikh Anta Diop in Dakar and the University of Wisconsin-Madison, Dr Ibrahima Thioub, Babacar Bâ and Dior Konaté are currently writing on prisons in Senegal. Representative of this new school of research in West Africa is Mamadou Dan Diallo, *Répression et enfermement en Guinée: Le pénitencier de Fotoba et la prison centrale de Conakry de 1900 à 1958*, Paris: L'Harmattan, 2005. In Anglophone Africa, South Africa and Kenya have drawn the most sustained attention from historians. After Leonard C. Kercher, *The Kenya Penal System: Past, present and prospect*, Washington, DC: University Press of America, 1981, new research has investigated the coercive system developed during the Mau Mau crisis with attention to prisons, most notably Carolyn Elkins, *Imperial Reckoning: The untold story of the end of empire in Kenya*, New York: Henry Holt, 2004, and David Anderson, *Histories of the Hanged: The dirty war in Kenya and the end of empire*, New York and London: W.W. Norton, 2005. On convicts' testimonies, see Marshall Clough, *Mau Mau Memoirs: History, memory and politics*, Boulder, CO: Lynne Rienner, 1998. South Africa offers the largest and most comprehensive body of work on prisons and prisoners, starting with Charles Van Onselen's pioneer study on 'Crime and Total Institutions in the Making of Modern South Africa: The life of Nongoloza Mathebula, 1867–1948', *History Workshop Journal*, 19 (1985), pp. 62–81. On prisons during the apartheid era, see Dirk Van Zyl Smit, 'Public Policy and the Punishment of Crime in a Divided Society: A historical perspective on the South African penal system', *Crime and Social Justice*, 1984, pp. 148–89. On the birth of the segregated prison in South Africa see Linda Chisholm, 'The Pedagogy of Porter: The origin of the reformatory in the Cape Colony, 1882–1910', *Journal of African History*, 27 (1986); 'Crime, Class and Nationalism: The criminology of Jacob de Villiers Roos, 1869–1913', *Social Dynamics*, 13 (1987); and 'Education, Punishment and the Contradictions of Penal Reform: Alan Patton and the Diepkloof reformatory,

1934–1948', *Journal of Southern African Studies*, 17, 1 (1991). On the most infamous prison in South Africa, see the detailed study by Harriett Deacon (ed.), *The Island: A history of Robben Island, 1488–1990*, Cape Town: Mayibuye Books, 1996. Amanda Dissel and Stephen Ellis, 'Ambitions réformatrices et inertie du social dans les prisons sud-africaines', *Critique internationale*, 16 (2002), pp. 137–52, and Dirk van Zyl Smit and Frieder Dünkel (eds), *Imprisonment Today and Tomorrow: International perspectives on prisoners' rights and prison conditions*, The Hague: Kluwer Law International, 2001, address the recent challenges faced by the penitentiary system in post-apartheid South Africa. To approach prisoners' experiences, see C. Driver, 'The View from Makana Island: Some recent prison books from South Africa', *Journal of Southern African Studies*, 2, 1 (1975) and the recent Paul Gready, *Writing as Resistance: Life stories of imprisonment, exile, and homecoming from apartheid South Africa*, Lanham, MD: Lexington Books, 2003. In the rest of the African continent, prisoner memoirs and novels provide a rich entry into convicts' experiences and the political function of the prison. Although the following selection represents but a fraction of this literature, see Josiah Mwangi Kariuki, *Mau Mau Detainee*, Nairobi: East African Publishing House, 1963; Ngugi Wa Thiong'o, *Detained: A writer's prison diary*, London and Exeter, NH: Heinemann, 1981; George Simeon Mwase, *Strike a Blow and Die: A narrative of race relations in colonial Africa*, Cambridge, MA: Harvard University Press, 1967; Wole Soyinka, *The Man Died: Prison notes*, New York: Harper & Row, 1972; Ken Saro Wiwa, *A Month and a Day: A detention diary*, 1995; Ibrahima Ly, *Toiles d'araignées*, Paris: L'Harmattan, 1982, and the recent collection edited by Jack Mapanje, *Gathering Seaweed: African prison writing*, Portsmouth, NH: Heinemann, 2002.

REGULATION, REFORM AND RESISTANCE IN THE MIDDLE EASTERN PRISON

Anthony Gorman

The modern prison emerged in the Middle East from the second third of the nineteenth century onwards as it progressively replaced traditional corporal, capital and financial punishments. Marginal in indigenous penal traditions, prison was restyled as a progressive institution consistent with the claims of a modern state and civilised society. Its adoption was not sudden, uniform or complete but occurred over time as local practices and political structures accommodated European ideas and influence. In Algeria from the 1830s, prisons were transformed under the impact of direct French colonial rule. More common was the piece-meal adaptation of existing prison structures and administration. In the Ottoman Empire the beginnings of change, in word if not in practice, began under the impetus of the modernising reforms of the Tanzimat. In Egypt the prison was already a significant feature of the modernising programme of Muhammad Ali and much more so after the British occupation in 1882. Elsewhere the modern prison was consolidated under French and British mandatory administrations after the First World War. States not directly colonised, such as Turkey and Iran—both radical modernising regimes—recast their justice and prison systems by drawing heavily on European models during the 1920s and 1930s. The increasingly global dialogue on prison practice, penal law and criminology served as a forum for the dissemination of new ideas. In this evolution, native traditions of punishment, local political requirements, economic and social factors all came to play a part in the creation of state institutions of confinement that included hard labour prisons, agricultural colonies and reformatories. Thus, pervasive as a global idea and appropriated as a modern institution, the Middle Eastern prison also embodied the local traditions and customary order, reflecting in its practice the political, social and economic tensions between indigenous élites and masses.

BEFORE THE MODERN PRISON

While imprisonment was far from unknown in the early Islamic period—the Prophet himself is said to have sent someone to prison—in the Arabian tradition it was looked upon as 'a rather doubtful procedure'.[1] Little discussed in *fiqh* literature, prison was an unusual and supplementary rather than primary punishment, favoured as a pre-trial or administrative measure to ensure attendance, elicit information or produce repentance.[2] Debtors were imprisoned less as a penalty than as a means to extract money from a defaulter or to establish the inability to pay. When employed, imprisonment was not applied uniformly across all social classes but was more likely to be prescribed for offenders from the élite than from a lower social order, who would be flogged for the same transgression. The absence of imprisonment as a prescribed penalty in Islamic law (*shari'a*) meant that its application, as a punishment and a disciplinary practice, was associated with offences against political authority, to punish those who broke man-made law (*qanun*) such as disturbers of public order, disobedient officials and those who failed to pay their taxes.[3] In Ottoman law it was also employed to punish or constrain individual enemies and persons awaiting the sultan's judgement.

The close association of the prison with the will of the temporal ruler was evident in its location. Usually set within or near the official residence of the governor, the citadel, seraglio or Kasbah, prisons were not usually purpose-built structures but buildings and rooms adapted for the purpose, such as the Bagnio (literally 'bathhouse') in Istanbul. As a space linked to the authority of the ruler, the prison could be a target for political opposition. During serious civil disturbances, mobs often stormed prisons, seeing them as symbols of political repression and seeking to liberate those held inside to express their discontent. Conversely, release from prison could serve as an expression of the magnanimity

I wish to thank my fellow contributors and Wayne Dooling for their comments on earlier drafts.

[1] Franz Rosenthal, *The Muslim Concept of Freedom, prior to the Nineteenth Century*, Leiden: EJ Brill, 1960, pp. 38–42. See also *Encyclopedia of Islam*, s.v. *sidjn*. The normal Arabic word for prison, *sijn* (pl. *sujun*), may be of Greek origin but it is worth noting that some important convict prisons used another term, such as the Liman in Egypt, from the Turkish and Greek word for 'port' (so named because of its location in the harbour of Alexandria), and the *Zindan/a* or *Zindala* in Istanbul and Tunis, which are derived from the Persian word for prison.

[2] Irene Schneider, 'Imprisonment in Pre-Classical and Classical Islamic Law', *Islamic Law and Society*, 2, 2 (1995), pp. 157–73.

[3] Rosenthal, *Muslim Concept of Freedom*, p. 54.

1. A visit to a Turkish Prison: Prisoners in the 'salon' or main hall, amusing themselves. One of the favourite amusements of the prisoners was to race cockroaches or waterbugs. Each one guides and encourages his insect with a bit of straw. The man with the champion cockroach wins a day's ration of bread. [Men and Insects (W. T. Maud/H. Lanos), Wellcome Library]

and mercy of a ruler.[4] The physical conditions of imprisonment varied widely from comfortable confinement to disgusting dungeons, depending on the clientele and the proprietor of the prison. In Istanbul, Yedi Kuleh, built by Mehmet II in the fifteenth century, was used to imprison ambassadors.[5] Other, less salubrious prisons accommodated debtors, thieves (*sijn al-lusus*) or slaves.

THE OTTOMAN PRISON

By the middle of the nineteenth century prisons were a regular feature of Ottoman urban administration.[6] Found in provincial centres, which usually had two,

[4] Ibid., p. 65. Some jurists discussed the rights of prisoners to pray and have sexual relations, Rosenthal, *Muslim Concept of Freedom*, pp. 53–4. On the duties of the ruler to the imprisoned, see Abu Yusuf Ya'qub al-Kufi (731–98), *Kitab al-Kharaj*, Lahore: Islamic Book Centre, 1979, p. 233.

[5] A. Griffiths, *Oriental Prisons*, London: Grolier Society, [c.1918/19], p. 270.

[6] Unless otherwise indicated, the following is based on a survey of Ottoman prisons carried out by British consular officials in 1851, Foreign Office papers, British National Archives [hereinafter FO] 195/364, Letters relating to Prisons in Turkey.

although Istanbul had six, they varied in size from the Bagnio, which held up to five hundred prisoners, to the prison at Ghadames in the Sahara, which had an average of two or three inmates. Conditions were generally appalling. The prison at Mosul in Iraq was typical:

... wretched, and filthy beyond conception, vermin of every description abounds, the flooring is of mud, quite bare and uncommonly damp, there is a sad want of ventilation and the atmosphere is tainted with all manner of disgusting and disagreeable odours ... The more indigent class are obliged to huddle together at night for warmth ... Many of the prisoners are almost in a state of nudity and the few rags they have hanging about them are perfectly loathsome.

The sick were given little consideration and disease and death were frequent. In Alexandretta it was popularly remarked 'if a prisoner was not liberated in 110 days death would liberate him', and of the Bagnio, 'It is a place that would kill an Englishman in a week.'[7]

These dreadful physical conditions were matched by a lack of order and organisation. Prison terms were not usually fixed and many were imprisoned for long periods before trial, prompting one observer in the 1840s to note, 'The greatest danger is to be forgotten.'[8] Instructions issued periodically from the capital were either not received or seldom enforced by local authorities who were rarely held to account. In theory prisoners could petition officials but this required literacy in Turkish, access to official paper, and risked the ill will of the gaoler. In some places, like Smyrna, representatives of the local council could directly intervene in a case but redress was mostly in the hands of the governors, whose diligence in enforcing rules varied greatly. In Baghdad during the 1840s the bastinado, frequently threatened and sometimes used to extract a confession or payment of a debt under one governor, was forbidden under another. The lack of uniform practice notwithstanding, prisoners were generally imprisoned in three separate groups: serious offenders, petty criminals and debtors. Treatment depended little on ethnic or religious identity and more on social status and the ability to pay bribes to secure more favourable conditions. In Istanbul higher social ranks were confined to the apartments of the Minister of Police, while in Damascus those able to pay were given a separate room.

[7]   Nassau W. Senior, *A Journal Kept in Turkey and Greece in the Autumn of 1857 and the Beginning of 1858*, London: Longman, Brown, Green, Longmans, and Roberts, 1859, p. 70 (quoting Major Gordon).

[8]   J.A. Blanqui, 'Rapport à Monsieur le Comte Duchatel, ministre secrétaire d'état de l'interieur sur le régime des prisons de la Turquie' in France, Ministre de l'Intérieur, *Rapports sur les prisons de la Prusse sur le régime de quelques prisons de l'Espagne, de l'Angleterre et de l'Allemagne et sur le régime des prisons de la Turquie*, Paris 1843, p. 80.

Prison practice suggested little beyond punishment and incarceration. While repentance was not an alien concept in Ottoman law—*fatwas* sentencing convicts to galley service stipulated punishment until 'his repentance and moral improvement have become manifest' (*tövbe ve salahi zahir olınca*)—it was unclear how such improvement might occur.[9] Some prisons included places of worship, but there was scant encouragement to religious observance and less to education. Apart from galley service, prison inmates were not required to work. Far from being an institution of correction, many outside observers saw the mid-nineteenth-century prison as an instrument of personal vengeance and source of enrichment where innocent people were held from whom money was extorted.

However, in the course of the nineteenth century, as European ideas of punishment were disseminated, some changes were taking place in Ottoman prisons, particularly in the greater responsibility taken by officials and the decline in the use of torture, but the changes were often more in principle than practice. In early 1858, Edmund Hornby and Major Edward Gordon were sent by the British government to inspect the prisons in Istanbul and assist the Turkish authorities in building new ones 'in accordance with the principles acknowledged and acted upon in Europe'.[10] The following year the two officers reported that 'we have wholly failed to produce any good results ... [since] the local authorities regard the subject from so utterly a different point of view from what we do.' In the treatment of suspects, Gordon complained that the Turkish authorities confined them in solitary cells as a way of forcing them to confess, while the convicted were imprisoned in large cells where they mixed freely with one another. The Turks regarded space dedicated to exercise as wasted, prison clothing 'a useless expense', and 'any attempt to enforce a strict system of discipline as likely to occasion disturbances on the part of the prisoners and render necessary a large and costly guard'. Gordon's experience was not uncommon. British officials, such as Lord Cromer, regularly complained of the cosmetic adoption of laws by Eastern governments: 'Oriental rulers have ... discovered ... they can satisfy European reformers without incurring all the consequences which would result from the execution of a reforming policy. Broadly speaking, this plan consists in passing a law, and then acting as if the law had never been passed.'[11]

[9]   U. Heyd, *Studies in Old Ottoman Criminal Law*, Oxford: Clarendon, 1973, p. 302.
[10] FO 97/417, Hornby to Earl of Malmesbury, no. 13 enclosure of 6 December 1858, and FO 97/418, Turkey, State of Prisons, 1857–59.
[11] Earl of Cromer, *Modern Egypt*, London: Macmillan, 1908, vol. II, p. 491. Cromer's view, as ever, should be taken with some caution. Ottoman law was not so undiscriminating. The Ottoman

2. Cairo Central Prison c. 1909. One of the new prisons built at the end of the 19th century under the newly-organised Prison Department, Cairo prison housed both male prisoners (left wing) and female prisoners (right wing). [Arnold Wright, *Twentieth Century Impressions of Egypt: Its history, people, commerce, industries and resources*, London: Lloyd's Greater Britain Publishing Co., 1909]

Despite its reluctance to initiate substantive prison reform, the Ottoman government kept abreast of developments in international prison practice. Turkish representatives attended the first International Penal Congress in London in July 1872 and other congresses thereafter. Some of the new ideas found their way into Ottoman legislation in the 1870s, which enjoined district officials to maintain prison registers and submit written reports.[12] Governors were authorised to appoint prison directors, guards and committees of preliminary enquiry, made up of Muslim and non–Muslim members, empowered to obtain information from the police and secure the release of those detained unjustly. Subsequent legislation underlined the separation of gaols and prisons, laying down measures against illegal detentions and setting out conditions for the rehabilitation of the prisoner after release.[13] It seems likely that these laws were not strictly enforced, and when the Committee of Union and Progress came to power in 1908 prison reform was once again on the agenda.[14]

penal code of 1858, largely based on the 1810 French code, excluded important sections regarding citizens' rights, Fouad Ammoun, *La Syrie criminelle*, Paris: Marcel Giard, 1929, pp. 122–30.

[12] George Young, *Corps de droit ottoman*, 7 vols, Oxford: Clarendon, 1905, 'Instructions sur l'administration des vilayets', 21 February 1876, vol. I, pp. 88–91; 'Code of procédure pénale', 26 June 1879, vol. VII, pp. 226–8, 295–300.

[13] Young, *Corps de droit ottoman*, 'Réformes pour l'Anatolie', 20 October 1895, vol. I, pp. 97, 103.

[14] For some recent ongoing work on this period, see Kent Schull, 'Counting the Incarcerated:

EGYPT

In Egypt during the rule of Muhammad Ali (1805–49) the basis for a modern state was being laid, with the establishment of a conscript army, significant educational reforms, the reorganisation of civil administration, and a new economic regime. Designed to produce a disciplined society, this new order (*nizam jadid*) sought to maximise the country's economic and military potential.[15] Integral to the project was an Egyptian penal code, first issued in 1829, which abandoned the numerous traditional punishments of Ottoman law for a more limited repertoire of flogging, capital punishment and imprisonment with forced labour.[16] The last was a means of 'correction' (*al-tarbiyya*) and 'discipline' (*ta'dib*) with a specified length—also a departure from Ottoman practice—which could be reduced if there was evidence of repentance and potential economic benefit.[17] The code still upheld the traditional notion of differential punishment according to social class, laying down a graduated scale of punishments for state employees guilty of extortion: senior officials were imprisoned at Abu Qir, junior officials at the Liman (Arsenal Prison), village shaykhs were flogged. These distinctions had ethnic overtones since higher officials were drawn from the Turko-Circassian élite, while lesser officials were of Egyptian origin. The code also reproduced some religious discrimination, with Coptic officials being more harshly punished than their Muslim counterparts.[18]

The elimination of corporal punishment from the penal code in 1861 marked a milestone in the shift from the deterrence of 'cruel' and 'exemplary' punishment

---

YoungTurk attempts to systematically collect prison statistics and their effects on prison reform, 1909–1919', conference paper, Boğaziçi University, 3–4 December 2005.

[15] Timothy Mitchell, *Colonising Egypt*, Cambridge University Press, 1988, pp. 34–43.

[16] Rudolph Peters, '"For His Correction and as a Deterrent Example for Others": Mehmed 'Ali's first criminal legislation (1829–1830)', *Islamic Law and Society*, 6, 2 (1999), pp. 165–92. For other relevant discussions on nineteenth-century Egyptian penal law, see Gabriel Baer, 'Tanzimat in Egypt' in *Studies in the Social History of Modern Egypt*, University of Chicago Press, 1969, pp. 109–32; Rudolph Peters, 'The Codification of Criminal Law in 19th Century Egypt' in J.M. Abun-Nasr (ed.), *Law, Society and National Identity in Africa*, Hamburg: Buske, 1990, pp. 211–25.

[17] 'if it is known that those criminals will be useful for the prosperity of the region and the well-being of the state and that they are repentant and penitent' [article 4]. Quoted in Peters, '"For His Correction ..."', p. 185.

[18] Peters' suggestion that the practice was due to 'perceived social distance' between Turkish speakers and the rest of Egyptian society may be sound, but it also reflects traditional penal practice, see, '"For His Correction ..."', p. 179.

to a policy of measured discipline.[19] Facilitated by the growing efficiency of the police force and law courts, it also had the political utility of promoting the ruler as a patron of justice and not an arbitrary despot.[20] As the prison regime was being assembled, other institutions of social control were being dismantled or wound down. The Egyptian army, a formidable military force and an instrument of collective discipline under Muhammad Ali, was substantially reduced under the terms of the London Convention in 1840, and again after the unsuccessful 'Urabi revolt in 1882. Slavery, officially abolished in 1854, though persisting for some time, was in terminal decline. The prison, as a provider and conduit of forced labour, offered economic benefits to the state, providing a workforce for industrial enterprises and public works, but also serving as an institution of restraint and regulation. In addition, it emerged as an important locus of public health awareness.[21] While the prison system itself remained an unconsolidated disciplinary apparatus controlled by a plurality of jurisdictions—it was not united under the Ministry of Interior until 1878—it functioned as a central site for political, economic, social and medical practice.[22]

THE BRITISH PREOCCUPATION WITH PRISONS

The British occupation in 1882 brought Egypt into direct contact with imperial rule and began a period of great political and administrative reorganisation. Critical of Eastern penal practice for decades, British authorities quickly carried out a series of prison inspections in Lower Egypt which produced a grim picture, little different from their survey of Ottoman prisons thirty years earlier.[23] Many pris-

---

[19] Rudolph Peters, 'Administrators and Magistrates: The development of a secular judiciary in Egypt, 1842–1871', *Die Welt des Islams*, 39, 3 (1999), p. 385.

[20] Khaled Fahmy, 'The Police and the People in Nineteenth-Century Egypt', *Die Welt des Islams*, 39, 3 (1999), pp. 340–77; Peters, '"For His Correction ..."', pp. 172–9.

[21] Khalid Fahmy, 'Medical Conditions in Egyptian Prisons in the Nineteenth Century' in R. Ostle (ed.), *Marginal Voices in Literature and Society*, Strasbourg: European Science Foundation, 2000, pp. 135–55; Rudolph Peters, 'Controlled Suffering: Mortality and living conditions in 19th century Egyptian prisons', *International Journal of Middle East Studies* [hereinafter *IJMES*], 36 (2004), pp. 387–407.

[22] Among those that operated prisons were the *qadi* (head of the religious court), the Police, the Navy Department, the Department of Industry, the Governorates (*mudiriyyat*), the Prefect, the Courts of Justice, the Mixed Courts, the War Office and a number of foreign consulates, FO 881/5369, 'Commission of inquiry into the facts connected with the recent epidemic at Tourah Prison', August 1886, p. 18.

[23] See Stewart's Report on Tanta Prisons, 30 October 1882, Wilson on Cairo, 12 and 20 November

ons were overcrowded, woefully furnished and inadequately provisioned. One inspector noted, 'no report can convey the feeblest impression of the hopeless misery of the mass of prisoners who live for months like wild beasts without change of clothing.' The failure to classify prisoners was singled out for special censure, 'The greatest blot on the Oriental system is the herding together of all categories of prisoners. In the East practically every man is treated as if guilty of the offence of which he is accused, until he has established his innocence.' Another report deemed 'corrective discipline impracticable' because of the time and money required to remedy the system, and suggested that recourse to other punishments, such as flogging, would be more feasible.[24]

A new prison administration (*Maslaha al-sujun*), set up in 1883 and headed by a surgeon, Henry Crookshank (later Pasha), was charged with remedying the situation. Prison regulations issued in 1885, more a statement of intent than actual practice, introduced a system of registration and classification, prescribed appropriate accommodation arrangements, and stipulated that clothing, bedding and food would be provided by the department.[25] The health of the prison population was to be monitored, and personal hygiene, including daily washing and a weekly haircut and shave, stressed.[26] Smoking and gaming were forbidden, and special punishment was limited to solitary confinement.

The reorganisation was informed by British metropolitan practice as well as prison administration elsewhere in the empire. In this dialogue of imperial experience, India was especially important, not least because many officials in Egypt had previously served there.[27] Indian influence could be found both in the abstract and the concrete. The 1901 prison law, the framework for the service for the next fifty years, incorporated elements from the Indian Prison Regulations.[28] The ambitious building programme that began in the late 1890s adapted

---

1882, and Chermside's report to Dufferin, 6 December 1882, 'Further Correspondence respecting the Affairs of Egypt', *Parliamentary Papers (House of Commons)*[hereinafter PP], LXXXIII (1883).

[24] See Justice West, *The Times*, 29 May 1885.

[25] FO 141/205, Crookshank, 'Cairo Prison, changes introduced and present administration', 29 February 1884.

[26] The inquiry into the outbreak of an epidemic at Tura in 1885, in which almost 300 prisoners died, strongly criticised Crookshank and revealed bureaucratic rivalry between the Prisons Department and the Sanitary Administration, FO 881/5369, 'Commission of inquiry into the facts connected with the recent epidemic at Tourah Prison', August 1886.

[27] Among these were the long-serving Consul-General, Lord Cromer, as well as the first two Directors General of the Prisons Department, Henry Crookshank Pasha and Charles Coles Pasha.

[28] 'Reports by Her Majesty's Agent and Consul-General on the Finances, Administration and Condition of Egypt and the Soudan in 1900', *PP*, XCI (1901), p. 37.

architectural designs from Indian and English models that owed little to Bentham's Panopticon. Rectangular, usually four storeys high, with individual cells on the first two floors and communal accommodation on the upper two, the prison block had a gridiron roof which allowed ample ventilation. The offices, kitchen, bathroom and store facilities were located in smaller buildings nearby.[29]

The new system was built not only on imperial practice but also rested on indigenous foundations. The 1901 prison law retained much previous legislation, itself a mixture of the French and local penal codes. As Nathan Brown has argued, the development of the legal system in Egypt under European occupation was not a matter of wholesale imposition but the result of an accommodation between Western and indigenous traditions and a compromise between the imperial and local élites.[30] Believing the faithful reproduction of European judicial systems was unsuitable for colonial situations, British policy was willing 'to tolerate a certain amount of inefficiency, and to be content with relatively slow progress, rather than to adopt [the] extreme process of eliminating native agency from the administration.'[31] This approach guaranteed the persistence of established practices and customary attitudes in the operation of the justice and penal system. One such element was the misconduct and abuse by public officials, particularly mudirs, who pursued personal vendettas by imprisoning enemies on the basis of false accusations, sometimes for years.[32] This practice continued, and may even have expanded after 1882. Individuals and powerful groups accommodated and appropriated the new structures, securing appointments as judges and manipulating the judicial system to their advantage.[33] Use of the court system was not confined to the élites. Egyptians from relatively humble backgrounds showed a readiness to seek judicial redress for a perceived wrong or to pursue an enmity.[34] After 1882, recourse to the courts, far from diminishing, actually

[29] These prisons came to be known as Coles' Hotels (*Lukandaat Koles*) after the Director of Prisons, Charles Coles Pasha, *Recollections and Reflections*, London: St Catherine Press, 1918, pp. 99–100.

[30] Nathan Brown, *The Rule of Law in the Arab World*, Cambridge University Press, 1997, pp. 1–22.

[31] Reports by Her Majesty's Agent and Consul-General on the Finances, Administration and Condition of Egypt and the Soudan in 1902, PP, LXXXVII (1903), p. 39. See also Cromer, *Modern Egypt*, p. 517 quoting M. de Lavigne Sainte-Suzanne.

[32] Examples are numerous. See Borg's report on the case of Emin Bey Shamsy and Sir Charles Wilson on the prisoners at Cairo, 'Further Correspondence respecting the Affairs of Egypt', PP, LXXXIII (1883); also the letters of John Ninet (*The Times*, 31 October 1882) and Charles Cook (*The Times*, 19 April 1884) and Cromer's remarks, *Modern Egypt*, vol. 2, p. 485.

[33] Cromer, *Modern Egypt*, p. 519.

[34] Fahmy, 'The Police and the People in Nineteenth-Century Egypt', p. 342.

increased.[35] The manufacture of false charges, 'one of the curses of this country', saw personal interest turn the judicial and consequently the prison system to its own purpose.[36]

Despite British attempts to make it a closed institution, the prison was constantly penetrated by outside social forces, a process exacerbated by restricted financial resources and limited institutional capacity. Until the late 1890s the majority of prisoners relied on family and friends for food. Some prisoners were even forced to beg in the street. Authorities believed that these practices undermined the disciplinary regime and reduced the sense of punishment. As Cromer pointed out, 'The mere confinement in the society of their fellow-prisoners, with frequent opportunities of seeing and conversing with their relations when bringing their supply of food is hardly felt as a punishment.'[37] To limit this interaction, the administration undertook the feeding of all prisoners by 1901, but the change was made possible only through the revenue generated from prison labour, much of it outside the walls, which itself undercut the disciplinary regime. These ambitions were further undermined by 'constant and excessive' overcrowding.[38] Convict and central prisons were regularly required to accommodate numbers well above, sometimes as much as three times, their official capacity. The obstacles to constructing a closed prison environment seemed insuperable. Financial resources were limited and the reliance on communal accommodation meant that cellular imprisonment was available to only a minority of inmates. There were almost no individual cells in local prisons and only limited capacity in other prisons, further eroded by overcrowding.[39] Limited space also hindered the introduction of labour into many prisons and, save for the segregation of the sexes, there was often little categorisation and separation of different classes of inmates.[40] To ease the situation, labour in lieu of imprisonment and conditional

---

[35] 'Reports by Her Majesty's Agent and Consul-General on the Finances, Administration and Condition of Egypt and the Soudan in 1900', *PP*, XCI (1901), p. 36.

[36] Frederic M. Goadby, *Commentary on Egyptian Criminal Law and the Related Law of Palestine, Cyprus and Iraq*, Cairo: Government Press, 1924, p. 319. See also Raoul Darmon, *La Tunisie criminelle*, Tunis, 1942, pp. 41–2. For a comparable example of how a local population embraced the colonial rule of law to its own advantage, see Thomas W. Gallant, *Experiencing Dominion: Culture, identity, and power in the British Mediterranean*, University of Notre Dame Press, 2002.

[37] 'Reports on the Finances, Administration and Condition of Egypt and the Progress of Reforms in 1897', *PP*, CVII (1898), pp. 25–6.

[38] Prisons Department, *Report for the Year 1904*, p. 25.

[39] In 1904, for example, only 10 per cent of prisoners in convict prisons and 17 per cent in central prisons were in individual cells, Prisons Department, *Report for the Year 1904*, Table II.

[40] See Crookshank, *The Times*, 21 May 1884.

release was introduced, and temporary camps set up in the Delta and Upper Egypt, but this further weakened the controlled, corrective character of a prison term.[41]

WOMEN BEHIND BARS

The confinement of women has a long tradition in the Middle East, evident not only in the harem, so central to the Western orientalist imagination.[42] Institutions that restrained a woman's liberty in a variety of circumstances, such as the *Dar al-thiqa* ('House of Trust'), *Dar sukna bi husna* and the *Dar jawad*, are attested in sixteenth-century Tunisia.[43] Separate women's prisons, like the *Dar 'adil* ('House of Justice'), were operating by the eighteenth century and by the mid-nineteenth century were not uncommon.[44] In Algeria an old hospital building, the Lazaret, served as the prison for a whole range of female prisoners, old and young, native and European.[45] Even the damning British survey of Ottoman prisons in 1851 had saved some praise for the conditions of women, noting that 'Eastern delicacy has already adopted the principle of separation with respect to the sexes.'[46] The more usual practice throughout the Ottoman Empire at this time was that convicted women be confined in the house of religious leaders or of married public officials where they would perform domestic work. In Egypt in the early 1830s women served their imprisonment at the *Bayt al-wali* (literally, 'the house of the governor'), though other women's prisons in Cairo and Alexandria were also operating about this time.[47] Conditions varied greatly. At Damanhur in the Delta, women were held in a well-ordered separate section, while at Mansura they were

[41] Coles, *Recollections*, p. 103.

[42] Anthony Gorman, 'In Her Aunt's House: Women in prison in the Middle East', *International Institute for Asian Studies Newsletter*, 39 (December 2005).

[43] See Abdelhamid and Dalenda Larguèche, *Marginales in terre d'Islam*, Tunis: Cérès, 1992, pp. 85–111. The first two were places where married couples were confined to deal with marital difficulties. The last, which provided for the confinement of disobedient or rebellious women, had less positive connotations and represented an unmistakeable assertion of patriarchal authority. See also Abdelhamid Larguèche, *Les Ombres de la Ville: Pauvres, marginaux et minoritaires à Tunis (XVIIIème et XIXème siècles)*, 1999, pp. 239–42.

[44] The continued use of the word *dar* ('house') makes clear the domestic lineage of the institution.

[45] Emile Larcher and Jean Olier, *Les institutions pénitentiaires de l'Algérie*, Paris and Alger, 1899, pp. 198–200.

[46] FO 195/364, Letters relating to Prisons in Turkey.

[47] Rudolph Peters, 'Egypt and the Age of the Triumphant Prison: Legal punishment in nineteenth century Egypt', *Annales islamogiques*, 36 (2002), pp. 270–1.

3. The female ward at Cairo Prison at the beginning of the twentieth century. Note the female staff in attendance. [Arnold Wright, *Twentieth Century Impressions of Egypt: Its history, people, commerce, industries and resources*, London: Lloyd's Greater Britain Publishing Co., 1909]

crowded into a 'squalid den' without their own facilities, a humiliating punishment, whether specifically intended or not, in a sexually segregated society.[48]

After 1882 women came to occupy a small but more defined position in the Egyptian prison system. New prison regulations laid down special conditions, requiring that women be searched only by female prison staff, and granting rights to pregnant inmates and those with small children.[49] A new women's prison at Bulaq built in 1891 brought together two hundred inmates, about half of the national female prison population at the time. Separate women's prisons at Shibin al-Kum and Asyut soon followed.[50] By the turn of the century, women represented about ten per cent of the Egyptian prison population, but the figure quickly dropped to five per cent by 1906, and did not rise significantly above this by 1952. In religious identity and education women prisoners reflected the composition of female society at large, being more than 90 per cent Muslim and almost entirely illiterate.

A NEW SYSTEM IN PLACE

By the end of the nineteenth century, imprisonment progressively dominated the penal code. Corporal punishment had been long abandoned and the private use of the whip (*kurbash*) by landowners banned in the 1880s.[51] The decline of capital punishment, already evident in the time of Muhammad Ali, continued.[52] Though executions were still carried out, by 1905 they had been removed from the public gaze to a specially designated room inside the prison.[53] By contrast, prisoner numbers steadily increased. Utilising an expanding body of legislation, Egyptian judges proved willing, even zealous, in sentencing offenders to impris-

---

[48] See Chermside's report to Dufferin, 6 December 1882, Further Correspondence respecting the Affairs of Egypt, PP, LXXXIII (1883); Judith Tucker, *Women in Nineteenth-Century Egypt*, Cambridge University Press, 1985, pp. 160–2, but cf. Peters, 'Egypt and the Age of the Triumphant Prison', p. 270 n. 107.

[49] FO 141/205, General Rules for Prisons [1884].

[50] Report on the Finances, Administration, and Condition of Egypt, and the Progress of Reforms, PP, XCVI (1892), p. 28; Report on the Finances, Administration, and Condition of Egypt, and the Progress of Reforms, PP, CXI (1893–4), p. 23.

[51] Cromer, *Modern Egypt*, vol. II, pp. 397–405.

[52] Sir John Bowring, *Report on Egypt*, 1823–38, p. 324.

[53] Prisons Department, *Report for the Year 1905*, p. 5. Even after 1905 there were occasions when public executions were held, infamously in June 1906 when four fellahin were hanged at Dinshawai for an attack on British officers, Afaf Lutfi al-Sayyid, *Egypt and Cromer, A Study in Anglo-Egyptian relations*, London: John Murray, 1968, pp. 171–5.

onment. By 1904 the average number of inmates in all Egyptian prisons at any one time numbered almost 12,000, and through the course of the year, just over 106,000 persons. Almost three quarters of these (73 per cent) received sentences of a month or less, and those serving more than a year behind bars made up less than four per cent.[54] Prisoners were overwhelmingly male, illiterate (94 per cent) and between the ages of fifteen and forty (83 per cent). Almost certainly poor, over half were agricultural workers, and a large number of offences involved theft or various types of assault.[55] By 1930 the prison population had risen to just over 30,000, an increase reflected in the expanding prison budget and staff.[56]

The prison system was organised in a three-tiered structure. The most punitive arm, the convict prisons or *bagnes* (Arab. *liman* pl. *limangt*), held those under sixty years of age sentenced to penal servitude and forced labour for offences such as murder, robbery and rape, and made up roughly a quarter of the total prison population. The original convict prison, the Liman, had closed in May 1885 and been replaced by Tura, just south of Cairo, which initially accommodated 500 inmates but in time would hold more than four thousand.[57] Two other convict prisons operated at Abu Za'bal to the north of Cairo and at Qanatir (Barrage) in the Delta. The second tier comprised the central prisons (*sujun 'umumiyya*), found in regional centres, which held the majority, perhaps two thirds of all prisoners, who had been condemned to more than three months' imprisonment, to detention, and all women and men over sixty years of age sentenced to forced labour. The third tier, the local prisons (*sujun markaziyya*), located throughout the country, held those awaiting trial or sentenced to three months or less.[58] Accommodating much smaller numbers, these were far less 'total' institutions than the convict and central prisons, for example, allowing inmates to arrange for their own food.

SPECIALISED INSTITUTIONS

While this triad served as the primary institutions of confinement, specialised institutions were established to deal with more specific transgressions of the law.

---

[54] Prisons Department, *Report for the Year 1904*, p. 5.

[55] In Algeria in 1903 the situation was comparable with an even greater percentage coming from an agricultural background and about two-thirds of those being convicted of theft.

[56] Between 1884 and 1944 the budget increased from LE 20,371 to LE 778,135 and from 1885 to 1936, the personnel grew from 55 to 2,587.

[57] 'Report by Dr Crookshank on the present condition of Egyptian prisons', Reports on the State of Egypt and the Progress of Administrative Reforms, *PP*, LXXXIX (1884–5).

[58] Ministry of the Interior, Egypt, *Police Regulations, 1914*, Cairo, 1914, pp. 186–9.

Perhaps the most innovative of these was the reformatory, an institution for re-peat offenders.[59] Since at least the 1880s the Egyptian penal code had recognised this criminal category and had provided for stronger prison sentences. Inside prison, various measures were employed to segregate recidivists from others: they were given a distinctive black dress—hence their name 'the Black Gang'—and their conditions of imprisonment—cell confinement, harder labour and fewer visitors—were more onerous.[60] The lack of success of these measures became evident with the improvement in methods of record-keeping and the use of new scientific techniques of identification, such as fingerprinting, photography and measurement.[61] In 1907 a new approach was adopted, informed by the school of positivist criminology that stressed criminal types above the crimes themselves, and saw the establishment of an Adult Reformatory (*islahiyya*) at the Barrage. Sentenced to indeterminate periods of up to six years, recidivists or 'habituals' served their first nine to twelve months in solitary confinement, allowing prison officials to study their character and aptitude, and prepare a full dossier includ-ing medical reports.[62] During this time each inmate received daily instruction, schooling and an hour of exercise working the pumps. A weekly wage was paid, half used as a credit in the canteen, with the other half banked for eventual re-lease. Stars and stripes were awarded to prisoners to indicate conduct, proficiency in a craft and the length of time inside. Clothes of black, blue and white were designated for different classes. A prisoner was released when his conduct and proficiency at a learned handicraft was satisfactory. Those sentenced to the re-formatory a second time were detained, and expected to earn their subsistence through the handicraft already learned but no further attempt was made to re-form them.[63]

---

[59] The idea was not entirely new. In the 1850s a 'reform unit' (*al-firqa al-islahiyya*) had been estab-lished for vagrants and those serving sentences of less than three years, where they were trained in a skill that could support them after release, Rudolph Peters, 'Egypt and the Age of the Tri-umphant Prison', p. 273.

[60] On the following see Coles, *Recollections*, pp. 106–12.

[61] Reports by His Majesty's Agent and Consul-General on the Finances, Administration and Condi-tion of Egypt and the Soudan in 1903, *PP*, CXXX (1902), pp. 30–1; and in 1904, *PP*, CIII (1905), pp. 50–1. Anthropometric Bureaus were also set up in Tunisia and Algeria, L. Paoli, 'L'anthropométrie en Algérie', *Bulletin de La Société Générale des Prisons* [hereinafter *BSGP*], 22 (1898), pp. 1251–7; L. Paoli, 'Les questions pénitentiaires en Algérie en 1899', *BSGP*, 24 (1900), pp. 479–80.

[62] A 'habitual' was defined as someone who had served two sentences of more than one year, or three of less than one year for certain offences.

[63] *Révue pénitentiaire et de droit pénal*, 44 (1920) pp. 223–36.

Regarded as an advanced penological approach by some legal commentators, the reformatory attracted criticism even from within the Egyptian government. It was expensive—about twice the cost of the upkeep of an ordinary prisoner—and some, notably the British Consul General, Lord Kitchener, believed it deprived the authorities of free labour for public works. The task of teaching suitable skills to physically and mentally feeble inmates, particularly drug addicts, a significant proportion of the confined, was proving difficult, and in 1911 a mutiny and the discovery of a counterfeiting ring inside further undermined public confidence in the institution.[64] Admitting these teething problems, the director nevertheless remained convinced that inmates could be taught a livelihood, although he conceded that at worst it was successful in 'ridding the community of these pests'.[65] These reservations notwithstanding, the reformatory system remained in place and testified at least to an ongoing rhetorical commitment to the reform of hardened criminals. The Barrage reformatory continued to operate with numbers increasing to over 1,500 inmates by the mid-1940s. However, no equivalent institution was ever established for women who, when sentenced to special internment, served a year in Cairo before being transferred to the central prison at Asyut.[66]

CONFINING YOUTH

Ottoman prisons in the mid-nineteenth century had provided for some separation, though no different treatment, for young inmates, but it was not unusual for juveniles to be detained in ordinary prisons even at the end of the century. In Egypt in 1904 almost 2,400 convicted prisoners, about three per cent of the total, were under fifteen years of age.[67] The specific causes of the growth of juvenile delinquency in these years, the nature of the pressures on the traditional family unit, and the dislocation wrought by economic changes, require more study. But the institutional response was no doubt motivated by some awareness of the distinctive problems of juvenile delinquency and a belief in the greater reformability of youth.

[64] In 1911 thirty-six of fifty-six prisoners in the Reformatory were addicted to drugs, *Report for the Year 1911*, pp. 17–18.
[65] Coles, *Recollections*, p. 111.
[66] Albert Chéron and Aly Badawi, *Nouveau code pénal égyptien annoté: Doctrine, jurisprudence, droit comparé*, Cairo, 1939, p. 265.
[67] Prisons Department, *Report for the Year 1904*, Table VII.

The opening of a reformatory for young offenders in Alexandria in 1896 marked the first significant measure to address juvenile crime in Egypt.[68] Initially set up as a philanthropic institution, the reliance on private funds proved impractical and in 1897 it moved to Bulaq, now under the supervision of the Prisons Department, and ultimately Giza.[69] Modelled on the County Council School for Waifs and Strays near London and the reformatory at Ypres, the new reformatory provided accommodation for 300 boys in a barrack system of huts radiating from a central courtyard, with a garden of seven acres. Aged between eight and fifteen, the inmates came from all parts of the country, though principally Cairo, Alexandria and the Delta. Few had any education, most had been sentenced for theft and a quarter had previous convictions.[70]

Discipline, surveillance and control were the central principles of the reformatory. School and vocational training were provided each day. Reading, writing and arithmetic were taught, as well as religion and study of the Quran, according to the tradition of an Islamic school (*kuttab*). Skills taught included printing, bookbinding, carpentry, shoemaking, tailoring, smithing and gardening. Health was closely monitored, with an hour each day dedicated to exercise and time allowed for cleaning and recreation. Half doors in toilets meant boys were potentially never out of the sight of guardians. The strict disciplinary code was derived from police regulations, with the addition, which the director noted with some satisfaction, that this was the only school in Egypt with corporal punishment.[71] This approach—education, vocational training and corporal punishment—reflected the view that minors were more malleable and capable of rehabilitation than adult criminals. No longer used on adult offenders, whipping (*jald*) was widely prescribed for boys and administered under supervision at central and local prisons. In 1905 more youths were whipped than were sent to prison, and the method continued to be employed certainly into the mid-1930s, although it was dropped by the early 1950s.[72]

Despite the considerable investment in tackling juvenile delinquency, the reformatory was hampered by organisational problems.[73] Slow to introduce trade

---

[68] For the following, see Hassan Nachat, *Les jeunes délinquants*, Paris, 1913, pp. 375–85.

[69] Coles, *Recollections*, pp. 113–20.

[70] Prisons Department, *Report for the Year 1905*, pp. 38–52.

[71] '... for some reason or other the educational authorities have pandered to the absurd prejudice in vogue in the country against this description of punishment', Coles, *Recollections*, p. 116.

[72] Prisons Department, *Report for the Year 1905*, p. 47; Hassan Nachat Pasha, 'Égypte, Aperçu du système pénitentiaire', *Recueil de documents en matière pénale et pénitentiaire*, VI (September 1937), p. 29.

[73] For the following, see Ahmed Sami, 'Juvenile Vagrants and Delinquents', *L'Égypte contemporaine*, 14 (1923), pp. 250–72.

instruction, its limited capacity meant that many youths still had to wait in prison before a place became available. More serious, the practice of putting young criminals together with juvenile vagrants failed to discriminate between two quite different social problems. Indeed, one commentator believed that the reformatory operated much like a prison. In July 1921 a permanent commission was constituted to examine the causes of crime among children and propose new measures to deal with them. The move recognised the need for special methods in dealing with young offenders and highlighted the importance of supervising procedures in youth institutions. It is unclear how effective this body was, but in the following years, two more youth reformatories were opened, one for girls at Giza, using a similar educational programme as the boys but instead teaching cooking, laundry, dairy work and dressmaking, and the al-Marg Reformatory for rural youths that was taken over from the Ministry of Public Instruction. By the end of the 1930s these three institutions held over 1,700 inmates.

By the early 1950s convicted juveniles in Egypt could be confined in a number of institutions depending on their age and the offence committed: the Model Farm, where they received an education, industrial or agricultural vocational training; the reformatory; or a range of private institutions. Youths convicted of serious offences were still sent to prison but neither penal servitude nor the death penalty could be administered to those under seventeen. Across the Middle East, practices varied, with only very few countries—among them Lebanon and Algeria—with private institutions, and a somewhat greater number with reformatories. Thus, while there was a broad recognition of the special needs of young criminals, prison still remained the main option in most countries.[74]

SOCIAL STATUS AND FOREIGN NATIONALITY

Specialised institutions, such as the adult and youth reformatories, the shelters for the poor (see below) and the asylum, held only a minority of the confined. The majority of inmates were accommodated in the general prison system, but even here conditions could differ considerably. One significant factor was the social status of a prisoner. Although differential punishment according to social rank had been formally abandoned in law in 1837, the application of uniform sentences in a society as diverse as Egypt troubled some prison administrators.

[74] United Nations, Dept of Social Affairs, Division of Social Welfare, *Comparative Survey on Juvenile Delinquency*, Part V, *Middle East*, New York, 1953, pp. 41–5, 51.

In Egypt one law for the rich and the poor works out very unfairly as the modes of life vary so that what is little short of torture to one may be comparative luxury to another, yet it cannot be well left to a prison official or even to a judge to discriminate. It is some satisfaction to feel that if in the case of the well-to-do the punishment is relatively severe, he is as a rule less deserving of sympathy and has not the same motive for committing crime as one from the lower classes.[75]

The 1901 law reintroduced some flexibility on the basis of social background, by granting those sentenced to simple imprisonment and 'having regard to their accustomed lifestyle' exemption from work in return for a daily fee. Differential treatment was formally revived in the 1949 legislation that set up the categories of class A (broadly Europeans, middle and upper class Egyptians) and class B prisoners (all other Egyptians) to operate in local and central prisons. The former, 'because of their customary way of life, the nature and circumstances of the crime committed, or because of their social situation', were accorded preferential treatment in accommodation, exercise privileges and reading material.[76] The system continued to operate after 1952, though by the mid–1950s, there was discussion of extending class A rights to all prisoners.[77]

The principle of differential prison treatment was most apparent in the case of foreign nationals. Since before the time of Muhammad Ali, Egypt had hosted a considerable foreign resident population of Greeks, Italians, Levantines and others. Under the Capitulations that dated back to the early modern period, European states enjoyed extraterritorial powers that granted nationals the right to be judged according to their own national laws by the local consular court. Under its provisions, in the nineteenth century those sentenced to short terms were held in small consular prisons. By the early twentieth century few of these prisons were still operating, and most foreigners were instead held in Egyptian prisons, though in separate cells and supplied with food by their consul.[78] Numbers, while small, were not negligible—over a thousand foreign nationals, almost 1.5 per cent of the prison population, were imprisoned in 1904.[79]

---

[75] Prisons Department, *Report for the Year 1904*, pp. 10–11.
[76] Article 9: 'en raison de leur genre habituel de vie, de la nature ou des circonstances du crime dont il sont coupables, ou bien en raison de leur condition sociale'.
[77] Prisons Administration, *Cairo Prison, Correctional Institution*, Cairo, 1955, pp. 6–7.
[78] The Mixed Courts, a jurisdiction for disputes between those of different nationality, established in 1876, also had its own prison until 1912, Jasper Yeates Brinton, *The Mixed Courts of Egypt*, New Haven, CT: Yale University Press, 1930, p. 211.
[79] Prisons Department, *Report for the Year 1904*, Table VI. By 1912–13 the number had dropped to 283 foreigners, Arrest of Alexander Adamovitch, *PP*, LXXXI (1913), pp. 3–4.

During the interwar period European inmates were brought together and imprisoned at Hadra prison in Alexandria or, prior to conviction, at the foreigners' gaol in Cairo, at some remove from their Egyptian counterparts. At this time British concern with Egyptian prisons centred on the presence and condition of foreign prisoners rather than the state of the prisons themselves, a view captured in the comment of one British official:

European prisoners are a nuisance in Egyptian prisons, particularly the Alexandria type of low European. Owing to their general undesirability from the point of view of cleanliness and behaviour, and the desirability of limiting their contact with Egyptian prisoners, they are put in the most easily accessible part of the prison.[80]

Egyptian demands in the 1920s for the annulment of the extraterritorial powers were part of a widespread international call for the recognition of national sovereign rights.[81] The Capitulations, abolished at Montreux in 1937 following British agreement to support the Egyptian request, came about as a direct result of the Anglo-Egyptian defence treaty agreed the previous year, itself precipitated by the growing threat of war in Europe. While the issue of prison reform was not central to discussions at this time, it was taken up in subsequent negotiations between the British and Egyptian governments as 'a deferred fragment of the Montreux Conference'.[82] Here the British strongly argued the case for preferential conditions for European inmates on the basis of their physical constitution.

Conditions of imprisonment in Egypt which might be supportable for a short period, might become for climatic reasons impossible for a long period, so that care must be taken not to treat a gently nurtured person in a manner which from pure reasons of the effect of the climate upon his health might become inhuman.[83]

Negotiations dragged on with the existing preferential treatment for foreign prisoners being maintained in the interim. The issue was not resolved for another twelve years, until the 1949 prison law was passed, which established the class A category as the basis under which foreign inmates could be guaranteed a certain standard of treatment.

[80] Keown–Boyd, European Dept to First Secretary, Residency, 23 December 1928, FO 141/470, Imprisonment of British subjects in Egypt, Imprisonment of Foreigners in Egypt. These included ethnic Arabs and Egyptians who held foreign nationality.
[81] Frank Dikötter, *Crime, Punishment and the Prison in Modern China*, London: Hurst, 2002, pp. 42–3.
[82] CO 323/1610/20, Egyptian Affairs, Abolition of Capitulations.
[83] FO 371/ 20873, Keown–Boyd to 'Abd al-Hamid Badawi Pasha, 16 April 1937.

ALGERIA

The French invasion of Algiers in 1830 and the subsequent extension of control inland laid the foundation for a prison regime in Algeria that was more explicitly based on a division between native and foreigner. The presence of a large European settler population in the country—never the case in Egypt—that numbered over half a million by the end of the century was reflected in the administration of justice and the operation of the prison system.

Built just outside Batna in 1852 to hold French political prisoners, Lambese was probably the first prison in the Middle East constructed according to the latest contemporary European ideas. An extensive complex enclosing a large rectangular area, according to Lespinasse, the inspector of civil prisons in Algeria, it was 'one of the most beautiful penal establishments in Europe', though to another observer it was simply a 'large ugly-looking stone building three stories high'.[84] Organised according to the Auburn system of individual cells with communal eating and working, Lambese embodied the practice of 'total care', providing two meals a day and meat twice a week for all prisoners. Although viewed by the authorities as an opportunity for 'a uniform penitentiary regime, strong and repressive enough to intimidate them and to force them to better behaviour', this was to be a limited uniformity. Lespinasse had himself made clear that one of the advantages of Lambese was its great size—it had more than 500 cells with an overall capacity of over 1,500. This made it possible to avoid the 'genuine monstrosity' of mixing natives and European prisoners. Planned, promoted and initially used as a modern, standardised prison, Lambese soon became an expression of colonial rule and racial hierarchy.

The incorporation of Algeria into the metropolitan French administration in the 1850s had threatened to undermine the legal basis of separation between natives on the one hand and French nationals and other European prisoners on the other. Two legal devices, one spatial and the other relating to personal status, were introduced to shore up the difference in judicial status between these groups. The first was the division of the country into three jurisdictions based putatively on the different levels of local civic development and the size of the native population.[85] The second was the *Code de l'Indigénat*, the native penal code, passed in

---

[84] Lespinasse, Inspector of civil prisons in Algeria to Préfet, 7 July 1860, Archives d'Outre-Mer, Algeria/GGA (French National Archives) [hereinafter AOM], 10 G/17 Locaux et Comptabilité; Rev. Joseph Williams Blakesley, *Four Months in Algeria*, Cambridge: Macmillan, 1859, pp. 306–7.

[85] These were the *communes de plein exercice*, the *communes mixtes* and the *territoire de commandement*.

1881 and in force continuously until 1914, which gave the administration 'the power to fine or imprison natives, individually and collectively, without trial for various offences supposedly subversive of law and order'.[86] Unlike resident Europeans or even Algerian Jews, who were collectively given French nationality, the great majority of Muslims, while French subjects, were not French citizens. As *indigène* they alone were subject to the *Indigénat*. The direction of Algerian prisons, though legally operating according to the same laws and regulations that obtained in France, was qualified by administrative orders based on special jurisdiction and national status that underpinned a dual system. Even advocates of the *Indigénat* agreed this was contrary to the principles of 1789 but defended the anomaly on the grounds that civilised criminal codes were meant for civilised people. Since Muslim society was not 'an advanced civilisation', and Arabs only understood 'severe and terrible' justice, laws were required 'to make up for the insufficiency in an Arab country of the French legislation and justice'.[87]

This supposed civilisational difference between European and native Algerian inmates was manifest in the policy taken towards 'reform' of the prisoner. At Lambese, for example, Europeans who knew a trade or were capable of being taught one were encouraged to practice their trade or train in one. By contrast, Arab inmates were regarded as 'maladroit' and thus unsuited to anything other than striking the forge. Further, collective punishment, meted out to native families and 'bandit' tribes, contradicted the concept of individual rehabilitation. Put bluntly, 'The difficult problem of rehabilitation is impossible to resolve for the native: there is only one way to avoid recidivism, it is the method of elimination, and it is necessary to apply it without gentleness.' Even as he censured the lack of access to religious guidance, educational opportunities and visitors for European prisoners for hindering their rehabilitation, Larcher saw the reform of the native as a task beyond human capability.[88]

In fact practical difficulties of prison management often undermined the principle of separation between native and European prisoners. At Berrouaghia and Harrach, prisoners were mixed, and in smaller prisons, segregation was probably

---

Each was held to influence the behaviour of the native Arab: 'In military territory the Arab who meets the European greets him; in the commune mixte, he passes without saying a word, in the commune de plein exercice, he spits to mark his aversion towards the roumi [Christian]', Emile Larcher and Jean Olier, *Les institutions pénitentiaires de l'Algérie*, p. 13.

[86] Charles-Robert Ageron, *Modern Algeria*, London: Hurst, 1991, p. 53.

[87] Larcher and Olier, *Les institutions pénitentiaires*, pp. 11, 72, 79. Emile Larcher was Professor of Law at the University of Algiers and the great authority on Algerian law and penal institutions.

[88] Larcher and Olier, *Les institutions pénitentiaires*, pp. 207 n. 2, 194–6.

less rigorously maintained. In women's prisons such as the Lazaret there was little separation between Europeans and natives.[89] Nevertheless, the principle of separation was one favoured by the French and other colonial regimes. In Libya foreigners were kept separate from natives, with Italians sentenced to longer terms being removed to Syracuse or elsewhere in Italy, whereas Libyans were imprisoned locally.[90]

The justification for this policy of segregation was sometimes couched in practical terms. Some suggested, for example, that Algerian natives readily learnt the vices of Europeans, and so needed to be insulated from them, or that those of mixed race were predisposed to greater criminal behaviour.[91] While such assertions are evidence for the racial nature of much of this literature, the principle of official hierarchies within prison regimes reflected a broader and more profound conception. The colonial order was based on a series of hierarchies from which flowed understandings of power, social structure and cultural superiority. The principle of separation at many levels guaranteed and reinforced the maintenance of this order. As an important arm of the administration required to uphold these values, the prison system reproduced the hierarchy of coloniser and colonised. In a non-colonial or 'soft' colonial situation the political and social order was no less important to preserve, and underlay the separation of prisoners on the basis of class, gender and political status.

PENAL LABOUR

Although regarded by commentators on Islamic law as contrary to religious values, being corruptive of both polity and economy, penal or forced labour (*sukhri* or *tashkir*) is attested from the early Islamic period.[92] In the sixteenth century it was employed especially by the Ottomans when the need for oarsmen saw service in the galleys (*kürek*) commonly prescribed as a punishment.[93] By the nineteenth century convict labour had moved to agriculture and small-scale industry where it provided a reliable workforce and, particularly in the colonial context, manpower for public works projects. In the Egyptian penal code of 1829, forced

---

[89] Larcher and Olier, *Les institutions pénitentiaires*, p. 199.

[90] Ravizza, 'Il lavoro dei condannati e la colonia penitenziaria agricola <Volpi> in Tripolitania', *Rivista penale di dottrina, legislazione e giurisprudenze*, vol. C (*c*.1924), p. 385.

[91] Larcher and Olier, *Les institutions pénitentiaires*, p. 7. See also Larcher's explanation for the different crime rates between resident Europeans and native Algerians, pp. 54–8.

[92] Rosenthal, *The Muslim Concept of Freedom*, pp. 77–80.

[93] U. Heyd, *Studies in Old Ottoman Criminal Law*, Oxford: Clarendon, 1973, pp. 304–7.

labour (*al-istikhdam fi al-ashgal al-sufliyya*) was regarded as the most serious punishment apart from the death penalty. Defined as employment with feet chained, the specific work was determined according to the capabilities of the prisoner. The healthy were employed at the Liman, the Bulaq iron foundry or at government building sites. Those with small children were sent to the tailors, arms factories and other industrial establishments.[94] Young men were conscripted into the army. In this period, penal labour appears not to have been particularly punitive since prisoners worked alongside free workers, but it nevertheless played a significant role in Muhammad Ali's programme of economic development and industrialisation.[95]

Under the British occupation a more systematic approach to penal labour was adopted. Hitherto in a state of enforced idleness, all male prisoners over sixteen at Cairo Prison were now required to contribute to an ambitious programme of prison industries that included cleaning, whitewashing, water carrying, stonemasonry, carpentry and mat-making.[96] Only slowly extended through the prison system because of practical difficulties (principally overcrowding) sweeping and cleaning of the cells and other domestic tasks inside the prison were prescribed in the 1901 legislation for those sentenced to simple imprisonment.[97] The work designated for women sat squarely within a traditional framework. Since 1856 those sentenced to hard labour worked in the textile workshop (*iplikhane*) in Bulaq, the industrial centre of Cairo, and effectively became the seamstresses of the prison system, making clothes for inmates and guards.[98]

Despite the repeated claim that labour was a means of disciplining individuals by training them in the virtues of sustained effort, the primary purpose of penal labour was its economic value to the prison service, both in providing cheap labour and in securing earnings. Employed at Tura in 1884–5, prison labour was used to build many new prisons thereafter. During the 1890s it was extended

[94] Bowring, *Report on Egypt*, p. 121 on Bulaq; Peters, 'Egypt and the Age of the Triumphant Prison', pp. 266–8.

[95] Rudolph Peters, 'Prisons and Marginalisation in Nineteenth-Century Egypt' in E. Rogan (ed.), *Outside In*, London and New York: IB Tauris, 2002, pp. 42–3.

[96] FO 141/205, Crookshank, 'Cairo Prison, changes introduced and present administration', 29 February 1884.

[97] 'Report by Dr Crookshank on the present condition of Egyptian prisons', Reports on the State of Egypt and the Progress of Administrative Reforms, *PP*, LXXXIX (1884–5). Eight years later the administration still regarded 'the introduction of labour is out of the question', Administration, Finances and Condition of Egypt, *PP*, XCVI (1892), p. 29.

[98] Rudolph Peters, 'Controlled Suffering: Mortality and living conditions in 19th century Egyptian Prisons', *IJMES*, 36 (2004), p. 389.

beyond prison walls when, drawing on the inspiration of standing prison camps in India, labour camps were established in each province to carry out canal work, road construction and other public works.[99] The expansion was well timed, and almost certainly not coincidental with, the abolition of the *corvée* in the early 1890s. Extramural labour produced raw materials, such as stone, bricks and gypsum, which were sold to the Public Works Department for the maintenance of Cairo's roads and pavements.[100] Sometimes convict labour was employed further afield. Since the 1840s convicts had been sent to work in the Sudan at Jabal Fazughli and later on military works at Suakin and Trinkitat. During the summer of 1896 many were employed on the Dongola expedition, where they unloaded war matériel from boats and railway wagons and worked on railway construction at Aswan and Wadi Halfa.[101] Again, at the end of 1913, convicts sentenced to long terms were sent to work in the Sudan.[102]

Within the prison, work regimes produced a wide range of articles manufactured for the use of the prisons department, or to be sold to other government departments and the public. At Tura, lime, bread, biscuits, doors and windows, buckets, iron, panelling and sleepers for carriages and tramways were turned out by prisoners working eight hours a day. Other prisons took on more specialised tasks. Cotton spun by hand at Beni Suef, Minya, Asyut, Suhag and Banha was woven to produce cloth at Giza prison, where shoes and slippers were also made. Mats for inmates were produced at Fayum.[103] Overseen by a Directorate of Prison Industries, the range of products continued to expand. By 1911 saddles, brushes, doormats, *libdat* (felt skullcaps), *maqatif* (baskets), brooms, lime, *humra* (brick dust), leather, wood, in addition to laundry, farming and gardening, featured on the prison inventory and produced steadily increasing profits.

Penal labour was not without a rehabilitative dimension. The 1910 Egyptian prison report stressed that the 'useful and practical tuition' given to prisoners using tools available in the village would serve as 'a means to ... redemption from crime and a direct path to a straighter and better life', even if it admitted that the 'uneducated adult fellah' was not proving receptive to such opportunities.[104]

[99] Coles, *Recollections*, p. 101.
[100] Administration and Condition of Egypt and the Progress of the Reforms, *PP*, XCVII (1890–1), p. 25.
[101] 'Prisons égyptiennes', *BSGP*, 21 (1897), pp. 967–70; Administration and Condition of Egypt and the Progress of the Reforms, *PP*, XCVII (1896), p. 18.
[102] 'Convicts for the Sudan', *Egyptian Gazette*, 29 December 1913.
[103] 'Les prisons égyptiennes', *BSGP*, 18 (1894), p. 722.
[104] See statements of Delanoy in Prisons Department reports for the years 1909 and 1910.

Nevertheless, the use of penal labour was primarily justified by economic profitability and public benefit, and further prompted by the inability of the prison system to cope with the sheer weight of numbers. Inspired by the practice of *corvée*, labour in lieu of imprisonment allowed those sentenced for minor offences to reduce their sentence at a set rate per day, by working for a government department or municipality, sweeping and cleaning streets, working on public roads, breaking stones, loading and unloading matériel, filling in marshy ground, and destroying cotton worms. During 1898, its first year of operation, over forty thousand prisoners took up this option, and the prisons for petty offences in Cairo and Alexandria were closed down.[105]

In Algeria the practice of penal labour was tied even closer to economic interests and to the colonial project. Following French practice, most Algerian prisons were run according to the enterprise system, whereby the state engaged private contractors to provide prisoners' food, clothing and fuel at a fixed rate per person per day.[106] Opportunities for profit extended to running the prison canteen, operating prison workshops and hiring prison labour to private employers outside. Formally subject to state scrutiny, prison entrepreneurs were from time to time accused of excessive profit-making, sometimes in complicity with state officials. The type of work varied from prison to prison. At the Lazaret women were employed in sewing, dressmaking and making matchboxes. At Lambese and Harrach, prisoners made *crin végétal*, matchboxes and straw baskets or worked in the garden or *sparterie*.[107] The network of *chantiers* (worksites) most clearly expressed the role of convict labour in colonial development. Used for the construction of roads, railways, irrigation works, dams and the clearing of land (*défrichements*), these labour gangs, at the direction of state authorities, individual businesses and settlers, assisted substantially in the creation of the infrastructure of the country.[108]

Agricultural penitentiaries in Algeria and Libya offered a variation on this theme and perhaps more plausibly established a work regime based on the maxim,

[105] Report by Her Majesty's Agent and Consul-General on the Finances, Administration and Condition of Egypt and the Soudan in 1898, *PP*, CXII (1899), p. 28.

[106] Patricia O'Brien, *The Promise of Punishment: Prisons in nineteenth-century France*, Princeton University Press, 1982, pp. 155–63. The exceptions were Berrouaghia and Birkadem, the youth reformatory.

[107] A *sparterie* was where *esparto* or needle grass, used in paper manufacture, was prepared.

[108] AR, 'Chantiers extérieurs en Algérie', *BSGP*, 22 (1898), pp. 761, 1333–4; A. Rivière, 'Main-d'oeuvre pénale en Algérie', *BSGP*, 19 (1895), pp. 430–6; J. Astor, 'La main-d'oeuvre pénale en Algérie', *BSGP*, 21 (1897), pp. 928–34; 'La main-d'oeuvre pénitentiaire en Algérie', *BSGP*, 24 (1900), pp. 285–96.

'Improve the land with the man and the man with the land.'[109] At Berrouaghia, a site of 880 hectares established in 1879, more than a thousand long term inmates were employed in the growing of cereals and rearing livestock, as well as in a number of workshops. Its most profitable activity was wine production where it contributed significantly to an emerging industry.[110] At the agricultural penitentiary of Sghedeida in Tripolitania, Italian authorities put convicts to work growing vegetables, experimenting with tobacco cultivation, and improving land subsequently sold off as private farms.[111] Although some critics complained that life there was not sufficiently punitive, the advocates of Berrouaghia stressed the rehabilitative value of learning farming skills and the beneficial aspects of working outside.[112] Nor were the economic benefits of penal labour policy uncontested in Algeria. At the end of the nineteenth century the use of convict manpower became a controversial issue, where some argued that it hindered economic development, was expensive, and competed unfairly with free labour, especially in areas where work was scarce. Others insisted on its penological value—simple imprisonment was an insufficient deterrent for Arabs. A compromise was struck by deciding to maintain penal labour on projects that were prohibitively expensive when privately funded.[113]

The predominantly agricultural economies of Egypt and Algeria required not a disciplined and skilled urban proletariat but cheap, unskilled labour. British economic policy in Egypt aimed to develop the country as a source of raw materials, principally cotton, for British textile mills. Penal labour was occupied in the construction and maintenance of the infrastructure for this economy and not for industrialisation which, even by the late 1940s, was still relatively underdeveloped. Similarly in Algeria, the penal labour regime embodied the economic priorities of French colonial rule. Work inside prison was manual in character and of limited value, with opportunities for learning a trade confined to European inmates. Berrouaghia, the most positive example in providing inmates with vocational skills, contrasted with the native penitentiaries (see below) reserved for Algerian Muslims, which were little more than slave labour camps. *Chantiers*, whether publicly or privately managed, promoted the development of a colonial economy, even if it may have had a negative impact on the settler working

---

[109] Ravizza, 'Il lavoro dei condannati...', p. 390.

[110] 'Il Penitenziario agricolo di Berrouaghia in Algeria', *Rivista penale*, 29 (1889), pp. 408–9.

[111] Claudio G. Segrè, *Fourth Shore: The Italian colonization of Libya*, University of Chicago Press, 1974, p. 79.

[112] Larcher and Olier, *Les institutions pénitentiaires*, pp. 189–90.

[113] 'La main-d'oeuvre pénitentiaire en Algérie', *BSGP*, 24 (1900), pp. 285–96.

class. The failure to develop a significant industrial base in Algeria ensured the continuation of these work practices. In 1948 outside work was performed by almost 15 per cent of prisoners, mostly in agriculture and notably vineyards. A larger number worked in industrial workshops turning out the same small-scale products they had for decades, and it was not until the early 1950s that inmates were provided with any real vocational training.[114]

NATIONAL PRISON SYSTEMS AND INTERNATIONAL PRACTICE

The creation of new states in the Middle East after the First World War, amidst local emergent nationalism, heightened widespread expectations of political and social change. In the former Arab territories of the Ottoman Empire, French and British mandate administrations were entrusted with the task of nurturing a system of modern governance and state institutions, including a reformed prison system. Elsewhere other states were eager to present themselves as new, respectable members of the international community, informed by modern penal ideas and practice. With the abolition of the Capitulations in 1928, the Persian government committed itself to the construction of new, hygienic prisons run according to prison regulations based on a European model.[115] The most well-known of these was at the Qajar Palace which opened the following year. Designed by a Russian architect, it was inspired by Western design but incorporated ancient Persian architectural motifs.[116] In the resolutely secular and nationalist Turkish Republic of Kemal Ataturk, a new system introduced in the mid-1930s aimed to deal with the 'uncontrolled primitive instincts' of prisoners and turn them into 'respectable members of society'.[117] A series of model prisons and penal settlements were built, such as on the island of Imrali where a community of 400 convicts was housed in the open air, taught how to read and write, and instructed in various trades. Illiteracy, which afflicted more than 90 per cent of the Turkish population, had been targeted since 1927 with the establishment of an education programme where, according to *The Times* correspondent, 'If the Board of Education has its way, no prisoner will be discharged, no matter what the sentence, unless he knows his alphabet.'[118]

[114] See Gouvernement Général de l'Algérie, *Exposé de la situation générale de l'Algérie en 1948*, pp. 748–50 and *Exposé de la situation générale de l'Algérie en 1952*, p. 909.
[115] For the text of the new regulations, dated *c.*1929, see PRO FO 370/486/L1883.
[116] FO 371/13800/E6780; Ervand Abrahamian, *Tortured Confessions*, Berkeley, CA: University of California Press, 1999, p. 27.
[117] 'New Prison System, Lessons from Other Lands', *The Times*, 9 August 1938.
[118] *The Times*, 15 June 1927.

In Egypt, following the new constitutional arrangements of 1922, the prison administration came under the direction of an Egyptian for the first time in June 1924. The next year Egypt attended the International Penal Congress in London where it presented a short history and a film on its prison system.[119] It was not the first time that Egypt had been represented at the congress, but the prevailing spirit of national optimism provoked a great deal of discussion in the Egyptian press and emphasised the government's wish to conform to international prison norms.[120] One pressing issue of international policing and enforcement in this decade was drug trafficking. Egypt, due to its proximity to drug-producing areas (Greece, Syria, Turkey), its lenient drug laws—until 1925 the maximum penalty for drug trafficking was a one pound fine and seven days in prison[121]—and the additional protection that the Capitulations afforded foreign nationals, was regarded as having an increasing drug problem.[122] The Egyptian government responded by increasing penalties to six years' imprisonment for some drug offences, and establishing a Narcotics Bureau in 1928 to provide surveillance and enforcement of the law. There was considerable debate about the appropriate punishment for offenders. The Prisons Department called for a special sanatorium and a law that allowed for indeterminate sentences. Russell Pasha, the British head of the Narcotics Bureau, proposed that drug traffickers be sentenced to the lash, arguing that while not an appropriate penalty for addicts, since hardy Egyptian peasants could tolerate such punishment, it would be effective for the trafficker who 'is a very different type ... an Armenian, a local Greek or a local Jew, generally of miserable physique and an arrant coward and the mere sight of the lash will be enough for him. ... physical pain to this type means something very real whereas mere imprisonment under modern conditions means very little ...'[123] Imprisonment was preferred, and Egyptian prisons quickly filled with drug offenders, numbering over 7,000, or about 30 per cent of all inmates, by the end of 1929. Although drug offenders were held in many prisons, Tura Farm, a large agricultural site next to the convict prison, came to be the favoured place

---

[119]   Unfortunately no copy of the film appears to have survived.

[120]   See the three part series 'In the World of Prisons' by lawyer Husni 'Abduh al-Shintanawi in *al-Ahram*, August 1925, and the historical survey of prisons by 'Ali Hilmi Bey, one of the Egyptian representatives at the conference *Misr wa al-nazm al-ta'dibiyya*, Cairo [1925].

[121]   'The Magnetic Page', *al-Ahram Weekly*, 19–25 July 2001.

[122]   See James H. Mills, *Cannabis Britannica: Empire, trade and prohibition, 1800–1928*, Oxford University Press, 2003, pp. 152–87.

[123]   Central Narcotics Intelligence Bureau, *Annual Report for the Year 1929*, pp. 68–70, 89–90.

for their confinement.[124] By the end of the 1930s Russell Pasha was trium-
phantly claiming a victory over heroin use throughout the country.[125]

CUSTOMARY PRACTICES

The emerging internationalisation of penal norms did not preclude the maintenance of local traditions. Rather the prison was articulated with customary practice to reinforce them. Before the modern period, indigents had been interned in
the Mahall al-Fuqara', part of the medieval Maristan Qalawun. From the middle
of the nineteenth century an increasingly intrusive and centralising state com-
mandeered such traditional institutions to deal with the issue of public mendi-
cancy.[126] From the 1840s beggars and vagrants were confined in state-run shelters
(*takiyya* pl. *takaya*) in Cairo and Alexandria, administered by the new Ministry
of Religious Endowments (Waqfs).[127] Never comprehensively prosecuted, confinement was nevertheless applied at times with great rigour, overwhelming the
limited capacity of the shelters. In 1897 a new law on vagabondage prescribed
prison sentences of up to a week for those begging in prohibited public places.
This approach was further extended, most significantly in relation to child vagabondage, in 1908, and again in 1923, to provide for the imprisonment of those
without means or fixed address, gamblers, procurers of prostitutes, gypsies (*ghajar*)
and suspicious persons.[128] With the declining economic circumstances of the
late 1920s and the fragmentation of social support networks, there were calls for
'moral purification' as a way of addressing the social ills of gambling, drug use and
alcohol abuse.[129] By the early 1930s, a series of hospices (*malja'* pl. *malaji*) was set
up throughout the country for the use of beggars, with those who did not use
them liable to a term of imprisonment.[130]

---

[124] Nachat, 'Égypte, Aperçu du système pénitentiaire', p. 36. Tura Farm was for occasional rather
than hardened criminals.

[125] *Egyptian Gazette*, 13 July 1938.

[126] Mine Ener, 'Getting into the Shelter of Takiyat Tulun' in E. Rogan (ed.), *Outside In*, pp. 53–76;
Mine Ener, *Managing Egypt's Poor and the Politics of Benevolence*, Princeton University Press, 2003.

[127] Among these were the Takiyyat Tulun, which had a capacity of 500, and the smaller establishments Takiyyat Tura and Takiyyat 'Abdin (the latter for women) in Cairo, and the Takiyyat
Qabbari in Alexandria, Ener, *Managing Egypt's Poor*, pp. 94–5.

[128] See Law 2 (1908) and Law 24 (1923).

[129] 'Moral Cleansing', *Al-Ahram Weekly*, 6 June 2002.

[130] See Law no. 49 against begging (22 June 1933) and the decree organising a network of *malaji*
(7 January 1934). The *dépôts de mendicité* established in Algeria in the late 1870s may be comparable institutions, J. Astor, 'Les dépôts de mendicité de l'Algérie', *BSGP*, 19 (1895), pp. 596–9.

The prison was also appropriated to customary political practices. In Egypt the tradition of freeing prisoners and of general amnesties had been employed by rulers since at least Mamluk times to demonstrate their clemency or as an act of thanksgiving for recovery from illness.[131] The custom was still being practised in the nineteenth century when prisoner amnesties were issued to mark special occasions, such as the capture of Acre in June 1832, the circumcision of the Khedive's son in March 1861, and the visit of the Austro-Hungarian Emperor to Egypt in December 1869.[132] By the end of the century a more regular pattern of releasing prisoners for good conduct who had served three quarters of their sentence was established, now tied to four specific religious and royal occasions each year: the two Muslim feasts of Bairam, the birthday of the ruler and the anniversary of the ruler's accession to the throne.[133] By the 1940s such releases were extended not only to other religious feasts but to commemorate recent and celebrated political events, such as Independence Day and National Struggle Day.[134] From an instrument of the ruler's will in the pre-modern period, the prison, now as a state institution, accommodated the new political discourse of the twentieth century, punctuating its administration according to the rhythms of religion, nation and royalty. Prisoner releases not only affirmed an existing regime but promoted the legitimacy of a new one. Following the coming to power of the Committee of Union and Progress in Turkey and the restoration of constitutional rule in 1908, political prisoners were released in the capital and elsewhere in the Ottoman empire.[135] Common criminals liberated at Prevessa were 'asked to take an oath that they would live in harmony with all their fellow citizens without distinction of creed'.[136] In Egypt in 1924 the first popularly-elected Wafdist government quickly took up the issue of Egyptians imprisoned by British military courts. Their speedy release prompted enthusiastic demonstrations in Cairo and Alexandria.[137]

[131] Adam Sabra, *Poverty and Charity in Medieval Islam, Mamluk Egypt 1250–1517*, Cambridge University Press, 2000, pp. 63–6.

[132] Rudolph Peters, 'Egypt and the Age of the Triumphant Prison', p. 282.

[133] Report by Her Majesty's Agent and Consul-General on the Finances, Administration and Condition of Egypt and the Soudan in 1898, *PP*, CXII (1899), p. 28.

[134] *Al-Ahram*, 17 January 1943. Other days included New Year's Day, the Prophet's Mawlid, Sham al-Nassim, first of Ramadan, Constitution Day, and the birthday of Faruq's mother, Queen Nazli.

[135] *The Times*, 29, 31 July, 1, 7, 12, 31 August 1908. In fact all prisoners were liberated, leading a delegation to complain to the Grand Vizier that ordinary criminals had been released to discredit the new government. Bandits and robbers were subsequently rearrested. For Damascus, see FO 618/3, Damascus General Reports 1909.

[136] *The Times*, 12 August 1908.

[137] See the series of articles in *Egyptian Gazette*, 8–15 February 1924.

PRISON REFORM

Far from a mere slogan, prison reform (*islah al-sujun*) became a mantra in the Egyptian press in the 1930s, and the specific remit of a number of government committees set up during that decade and the next.[138] Concern for the rehabilitation of prisoners who had served their sentences was taken up in public discussion and new legislation which set up a mechanism for the restitution of an individual's judicial rights.[139] Education was targeted. In 1936 the Ministry of the Interior proposed the introduction of a system of compulsory education for prisoners, teaching basic literacy, numeracy, moral education and some science.[140] A later measure, part of the campaign against public illiteracy, made specific provision for prisoners serving more than nine months to receive instruction.[141] A special education programme proposed the teaching of housekeeping and embroidery for women prisoners.[142] This change in emphasis in prison administration, from an aspect of domestic security to a complex social issue, was given official recognition with the transfer of the Prisons Department from the Ministry of the Interior to the Ministry of Social Affairs in 1939.[143]

The impetus for these changes came from more than one source. An international dialogue on prison practice, penal law, drugs and criminology conducted at a series of conferences underlined the global concern with prison reform.[144] The Egyptian prison law of 1949 was prepared, according to the government, on the basis of international standards of prison practice laid down over the previous decade and a half.[145] In the months after the Free Officers took power in

---

[138] These were launched in 1939, 1943 and 1949.

[139] Law 41 (1931); *al-Ahram*, 23 May 1935; 'al-Ijram am al-islah wa sa'il islah al-masjunin ba'd al-ifraj anahum (1 and 2)', *al-Muqtataf*, 96 (1940).

[140] *Al-Ahram*, 19 September 1936.

[141] See August 1944 Law no. 110 [relative à la lutte contre l'analphabétisme] article 11, and *al-Ahram*, 9 January 1947.

[142] *Al-Ahram*, 2 July 1945.

[143] The Prisons Department was subsequently transferred to the Ministry of National Defence (later the War Ministry) in the late 1940s, and returned, full circle, to the Ministry of the Interior in the 1950s.

[144] In addition to the quinquennial meetings of the International Prison Congress, these included the Second International Opium Conference (Geneva, 1925), the International Congress of Penal Law (Brussels, 1926) and the first International Conference of Criminology (Rome, 1938).

[145] Among these were the 'Rules for the Treatment of Prisoners' endorsed by the League of Nations in 1935, the resolutions of the Prisons and Punishment Conference at Berlin (1935), the Criminal Code Conference (Paris, 1937) and the International Commission for Prisons

July 1952, prison reform was embraced to highlight the progressive programme of the new order and to stress the shortcomings of the old. In December 1953 Egypt hosted the Middle East seminar on crime in Cairo and attended the first United Nations Congress on the Prevention of Crime and Treatment of Offenders in Geneva in August 1955. In the same year Egyptian prison officers and government officials visited prisons in the United States.[146] Explaining the motives behind the reforms of these years, such as the introduction of recreation in 1953 and the banning of irons in 1955, the administration stated that 'Infliction of pain and torment had to be replaced by correction and redress.' Such statements should be taken with a grain of salt. The prison record of this decade and the next, certainly in respect of political prisoners, was far from impressive. Yet at another level they indicate a rhetorical commitment to international norms by which the government was keen to establish its credentials.

Academic and scientific opinion both influenced and participated in this trend. European work on criminality in the Middle East had first appeared late in the nineteenth century when French scholars studied indigenous criminal behaviour in Algeria.[147] Anthropometric bureaus set up in Algeria and in Egypt in the 1890s reflected the influence of positivist criminology, while the work of Cesare Lombroso was discussed in Arabic language journals.[148] In Egypt modernist learned societies such as the Institut d'Égypte (est. 1859) and the Royal Society of Political Economy, Statistics and Legislation in Egypt (est. 1909), served as forums for discussion and commentary on penal reform and criminality.[149] In time local scholars like Hassan Nachat in Egypt, Fouad Ammoun in Syria and Sa'di Bisisu in Iraq employed their Western academic training to analyse the justice and penal systems of their own countries.[150] In Turkey, Institutes of Criminology

---

(August 1946), Ministry of War, Republic of Egypt, *The Egyptian Prisons under the New Regime* [1955], pp. 1–2.

[146]   *Egyptian Prisons under the New Regime*, pp. 7, 15, 37.

[147]   For example, A. Kocher, *De la criminalité chez les Arabes au point de vue de la pratique médico-judiciaire*, Paris, 1884.

[148]   See *al-Muqtataf*, 32 (February 1907), pp. 112–16, and Lombroso's obituary, 'al-Ustadh lumbruzu', *al-Muqtataf*, 35 (November 1909), pp. 1099–100.

[149]   One of the earliest recorded discussions of prison reform in Egypt was by Colucci Bey at a meeting of the Institut d'Égypte in August 1862, *Bulletin de l'Institut d'Égypte*, 1, 8 (1864), pp. 35–6. The journal of the Royal Society, *L'Égypte contemporaine*, regularly published articles on issues of penal law, see J.E. Marshall, 'Prison Reform', *L'Égypte contemporaine*, 12 (1921), pp. 476–86 and 'The Egyptian Penal Code', *L'Égypte contemporaine*, 13 (1922), pp. 324–31 which argued for the use of the lash, especially with the fellahin, because prison was not an adequate deterrent.

[150]   Hassan Nachat, *Les jeunes délinquants*, Paris, 1913; Fouad Ammoun, *La Syrie criminelle*, Paris:

set up in Istanbul (1944) and Ankara (by 1950), and in Cairo (by 1953) testified to an increasing concern with criminal behaviour. More research needs to be done to determine how influential these bodies were on government policy but they at least indicate a local engagement with wider international debates.

Less significant a force in prison reform was an activist public. As early as the middle of the nineteenth century there is evidence that local communities could act as a curb on the abuses of officials.[151] By the 1890s the Howard Association in England maintained a modest network of local correspondents in Morocco, Lebanon and Egypt who reported on aspects of prison administration.[152] Nevertheless, locally based private associations were slow to take an interest in prison affairs. In his survey of the Syrian prison system in the 1920s, Ammoun explicitly criticised the indifference of public opinion to prison conditions and the treatment of prisoners.[153] When civil society did take up these causes, women's organisations were notably at the forefront in articulating such concern. In Beirut, the Society to Stop Crime and Improve Prisons was founded in 1928, and the Iranian Women's Party secured permission from the Ministry of Justice to investigate the condition of women in prisons in 1947.[154] In Egypt it was not until 1952, when the Popular Committee for Prison Reform was established by Jamal al-Banna, that a specific association took up the cause of the welfare of prisoners.[155] In juvenile affairs, private agents and organisations played a greater role through their management of non-state institutions, and may have exercised some influence on government policy.[156] These efforts notwithstanding, non-governmental actors were of relatively little account in determining prison

---

Marcel Giard, 1929; Sa'di Bisisu, *Mahakim al-ahdath wa al-madaris al-islahiyya*, 1949.

[151] In 1851 the British Vice-Consul at Alexandretta had written that 'public opinion acts as a restraint upon the authorities and the jailor.' FO 195/364.

[152] The Howard Association, established in 1866, took its name from John Howard, the great penal reformer of the eighteenth century. In the Middle East it took a particular interest in Morocco.

[153] Ammoun, *La Syrie criminelle*, pp. 425–6. See also Ahmed Sami's comments, 'Juvenile Vagrants and Delinquents', p. 272.

[154] Elizabeth Thompson, *Colonial Citizens*, New York: Columbia University Press, 2000, p. 97; Parvin Paidar, *Women and the Political Process in Twentieth-Century Iran*, Cambridge University Press, 1995, p. 127.

[155] Jamal al-Banna, *Takwin wa 'amal al-jam'iyya al-misriyya li-ri'ayya al-masjunin wa usrihum*, Cairo, n.d.

[156] Sami, 'Juvenile Vagrants and Delinquents', p. 269, citing the examples of the Liberty Asylum and Brotherhood Waifs and Strays Home in Shubra. For similar institutions in Algeria, such as Bon Pasteur and others, see Gouvernement Général de l'Algérie, *Exposé de la situation générale de l'Algérie en 1948*, pp. 760–1. See also Hassan Nachat, 'Le patronage des jeunes libérés', *L'Égypte contemporaine*, 5 (1914), pp. 209–22.

practice, and such changes as occurred were driven more by modernist reformers and policymakers amongst state élites. If the emergence of the Howard Association in England was testimony to the strength of civil society in an emerging liberal democracy, so its weakness in the Middle East spoke of a political culture of muted social engagement.

ENEMIES OF THE STATE:
THE PRACTICE OF POLITICAL IMPRISONMENT

The detention of political rivals or of hostages to guarantee the good behaviour of a tribe had a long tradition in the Middle East. But the rise of mass political participation in the twentieth century saw the practice of political imprisonment evolve on a more systematic basis. Particularly under repressive colonial administrations, mass internment was employed to suppress nationalist opposition but even in the post-independence era, authorities readily appropriated the use of torture and arbitrary detention to the new political configuration. Formerly a personal enemy of the ruler, the political prisoner was now recast as an enemy of the state and the social order.

From the early 1850s in Algeria political prisoners were part of a two-way traffic across the Mediterranean. While metropolitan radicals were shipped south to serve their sentence, unruly tribal chiefs were dispatched to Ile Sainte-Marguerite, just off the Algerian coast, or to agricultural penitentiaries (*pénitenciers agricoles*) in Corsica.[157] Others were transported to more remote locations, such as New Caledonia, particularly after the crushing of the Kabyle revolt of 1871. Yet in time exile was discarded for domestic reclusion to an area remote from tribal territory or local internment in a native penitentiary (*pénitencier indigène*). Described as 'undoubtedly the most original and Algerian institution' of the penal system, the native penitentiary interned those accused of offences not provable in court.[158] They held an exclusively native, that is, Muslim population, sentenced by disciplinary commissions or by administrative order for a range of offences that included making a pilgrimage to Mecca and preaching holy war and hatred of the *roumis* (i.e. Christians). Internment could also be applied to the relatives and friends of a wanted criminal or to relocate bandits and their families far from their tribal lands. Punishment was usually for six or twelve months but it could be for shorter or even indeterminate periods. Critics, who pointed out that a

---

[157]   AOM 10G/39, Sec of State for War to Gov Gen, Paris, 14 August 1854. See also A. Rivière, 'Les établissements pénitentiaires et le patronage en Corse', *BSGP*, 15 (1891), pp. 1206–14.

[158]   Larcher and Olier, *Les institutions pénitentiaires*, p. 259.

simple theft could involve an indefinite penalty and condemnation of an entire family were dismissed as 'ignorant' of Algerian affairs.[159] In the 1860s native
penitentiaries held over 900 detainees, but by the end of the century mounting
opposition to inhumane aspects of the system and high maintenance costs saw it
slowly dismantled. As a legal punishment internment was abolished in July 1914
and the last native penitentiary, Tadmit, closed in 1919.[160]

The native penitentiary suggested nothing that was rehabilitative and much
that was repressive. On his arrival the prisoner was shaved all over, a procedure
repeated each week. Labour, for which internees received rations but no remu-
neration, was mandatory and could be in agriculture, animal husbandry, rock
breaking or on public works. Hours were long, usually from sunrise to sunset,
with a break in the middle of the day, although a special schedule applied during
Ramadan. Prisoners 'sous garde' were expected to march in order and silence to
their work. Work was dangerous and unhealthy, especially in the extreme south.
Even advocates of native penitentiaries admitted, 'We are sceptical of the moral
effect of these ... but we do not call for their repression; they serve a political necessity. The native only respects force. It is necessary to make those who would
contest our authority feel it.'[161]

In Egypt, Bedouin hostages had been held as guarantees for the loyalty of
tribes from the 1850s and probably much earlier.[162] Following the suppression of
the 'Urabi revolt in 1882 the British, like the French, preferred to exile prominent political opponents to distant parts of the Empire—'Urabi himself was
sent to Ceylon and some of his supporters were banished to the Sudan.[163] The
practice continued but, with opposition to British rule growing, some nationalists were interned in Tura during the First World War. In the interwar period
Egyptian nationalists of various shades enjoyed an ambiguous status as legitimate
political opposition while more radical groups, particularly communists and the
Muslim Brotherhood, came to be regarded as a more serious challenge to the
political order.[164] A series of crackdowns conducted after the Second World War
saw many party cadres detained. When their imprisonment in ordinary prisons

[159]   Ibid., p. 262.
[160]   AOM 9H/111; 10G/40.
[161]   Larcher and Olier, *Les institutions pénitentiaires*, p. 262.
[162]   Rudolph Peters, 'Prisons and Marginalisation in Nineteenth-Century Egypt' in E. Rogan (ed.),
        Outside In, p. 40.
[163]   Richard Hill, *Egypt in the Sudan, 1820–1881*, Oxford University Press, 1959, p. 163.
[164]   The Press Law (no. 20) of 1936, which aimed to curb press criticism of the government and
        provided for those convicted to be held in special prisons, was part of this repressive strategy.

situated within the city granted them visibility, albeit muted, and the opportunity for sympathy among the local population, they were moved to concentration camps (*mu 'taqalat*) in remote locations, such as at al-Tor in the Sinai and at Wahat oasis in the Western Desert of Egypt. In general political prisoners enjoyed better conditions than ordinary criminals from whom they were kept separate, but their treatment depended much more on the vagaries of the political climate.

In Iran the short-term detention of communists, begun in the late 1920s, developed into long prison terms after the passing of the 'Black Law' in 1931 which prescribed solitary confinement for membership of organisations with 'collectivist ideology'.[165] Held at Qasr Palace prison, where they received better treatment than ordinary prisoners, politicals made up about 10 per cent of the total of two thousand inmates held there in 1940. In Iraq the imprisonment of communists began in earnest in the late 1940s, particularly at Nuqrat al-Salman, a desert prison near the Saudi Arabian border. Here the physical conditions were more gruelling, the administration less scrutinised and the difficulties for visiting families and friends much greater.[166] When the communal nature of the housing, usually tents or large dormitories, was found to nurture an atmosphere of self-organisation and solidarity, authorities responded by returning inmates to the bricks and mortar of small prison cells, where dissent could be more easily and often brutally controlled, as happened during the 1950s at al-Mahariq and Abu Za'bal in Egypt, and at the new prison at Baquba in Iraq.

RESISTANCE AND PRISON SUBCULTURE

Despite the attempts of the state to confine, constrain and control the prison population, its authority was by no means uncontested. The agency of the prisoners themselves significantly determined prison practice by directly resisting the dictates and officers of the regime, and by constructing a subculture through which the prisoners associated and organised themselves. Available sources provide only a limited idea of the actions, much less the thoughts, of inmates, but even from official reports it is clear that rules and regulations were far from unchallenged and that a persistent tension existed between inmates and authorities, ranging from uneasy calm to overt conflict. The catalogue of official prison punishments alone—solitary confinement, flogging, irons and transfer—document a

---

[165]   Ervand Abrahamian, *Tortured Confessions*, Berkeley, CA: University of California Press, 1999, pp. 27–9.

[166]   Interview with Hisqail Kojaman (former inmate of Nuqrat al-Salman, Kut and Baquba prisons).

record of low level attrition. In Egyptian prisons in 1904 almost seven thousand such offences were listed, although it was reported with some satisfaction that the 'acts of violence and murderous assaults' on prison guards at Tura had declined.[167] Resistance provoked direct retaliatory reaction from authorities but it could also play a part in shaping prison practice. At Harrach in Algeria, in order to provoke an uprising, prisoners were allowed to mix day and night, a practice normally avoided.[168]

Riots and mass protests were the most dramatic confrontations between prisoners and authorities. At Tura from the early 1890s regular uprisings testified to a persistent antagonism between inmates and guards, even if particular episodes were usually ignited by specific grievances. In January 1911 authorities were faced with simultaneous mass protests at the Barrage Reformatory and Tura prison.[169] At the former the inmates, all sentenced to indeterminate terms, demanded to know the exact length of their sentence. Refusing to re-enter their cells, they used tools to defend themselves until the authorities regained control by force in the ensuing struggle. At Tura prisoners were protesting the change from a wheat to a maize bread diet. After failed negotiations, mutineers armed themselves with water cans, but after the ringleader was shot dead, order was restored and the change of diet maintained. Three years later, again at Tura, a more substantial mutiny occurred when prisoners started pelting warders with missiles and debris during roll call. After firing a round of blanks, the armed guards followed with real shot, killing a number of convicts and injuring many others, including a prison officer. Press reports suggested that the reasons for the incident may have been long-running ill treatment by unqualified warders, anxiety caused by the recent dispatch of convicts to the Sudan, or a replay of a recent bread and water riot.[170] Events outside the prison could also provoke unrest. In 1909 the increase in prison offences was explained 'as due to a certain extent to the wave of unrest and want of respect for constituted authority which was making itself manifest throughout Egypt'.[171] When Ibrahim al-Wardani, the assassin of Prime Minister Butrus Ghali, was imprisoned prior to his execution in 1910, rumours of a prison mutiny circulated, though this did not take place.[172] In April 1919 a

---

[167] Prisons Department, *Report for the Year 1904*, p. 9.
[168] Larcher and Olier, *Les institutions pénitentiaires*, p. 209.
[169] For Coles' account of these events, see *Recollections*, pp. 131–3.
[170] *Egyptian Gazette*, 5 January 1914.
[171] Prisons Department, *Report for the Year 1910*, p. 7.
[172] Coles, *Recollections*, p. 137.

mass breakout at Tura was part of the general disorder occurring throughout the country, protesting against the continued British occupation.[173]

Prison authorities were constantly concerned with escape, despite periodic claims that prison life was too comfortable or that Arabs were apathetic about imprisonment. Some prisoners exhibited special talents. Andrus, a repeat offender, developed a reputation as an escape artist before ending up in Tura. Shihata Ibrahim, a former police guard, escaped twice from custody before being shot dead during a robbery.[174] Mass escapes, often made while working outside, could be desperate affairs. In 1881, as the gate of the prison at La Goulette in Tunis opened at sunset, a group of about fifty convicts burst out, armed and free of their chains, sending a wave of panic through the town.[175] In 1893 a gang returning to Tura prison from work in the quarries attempted a mass getaway. Fired upon by troops, thirty-nine were killed but the remainder escaped.[176] Successful breakouts were not always the result of prisoners outwitting or overpowering prison officers but could involve their complicity, or even assistance. Speaking of the Bagnio in Istanbul, one visitor commented that 'permitted escape' was an incentive offered by gaolers to deserving prisoners.[177] In September 1919 the escape of a large number of prisoners, accompanied by three warders from the Central Prison in Istanbul, was said to have been arranged by an outside political organisation and corrupt elements in the prison administration.[178]

Hunger strikes were a more specific form of protest, made viable in Egypt after the state took over responsibility for feeding prisoners at the end of the nineteenth century. Although there had been earlier protests regarding the quality of food at Tura, one of the first hunger strikes occurred in early 1922 when Muhammad Kamil Husayn, a trade unionist, was reported to have refused food.[179] Members of the Egyptian Communist Party arrested in 1925 adopted the same tactic.[180] Thereafter hunger strikes, empowered by a strong sense of prisoners' rights, were regularly used to press certain demands. At Huckstepp camp outside Cairo, political prisoners went on strike for better conditions in 1949. Later a strike at Cairo Prison won an improvement in the status of some political pris-

---

[173] *The Times*, 17 April 1919; *Egyptian Gazette*, 15 April 1919.

[174] Coles, *Recollections*, pp. 137–8; Prisons Department, *Report for the Year 1905*, p. 11.

[175] *The Times*, 16 August 1881.

[176] *Annual Register*, 1893, p. 36.

[177] 'Turkish Prisons – The Bagnio', *The Times*, 20 December 1855.

[178] *The Times*, 8 September 1919. The correspondent commented pithily, 'The usual inquiry is being made and will probably be followed by the usual results.'

[179] *The Times*, 26 January 1922.

[180] AS 'Dans les prisons anglo–égyptiennes', *La correspondance internationale*, 94 (21 August 1926).

oners.[181] In Iraq a string of hunger strikes by political prisoners during the 1950s secured improvements in food, the right to wear their own clothing and even the temporary closure of Nuqrat al-Salman.[182] Resistance to prison authority could take less collective, more internalised forms. Suicides, though not numerous, occurred regularly.[183] Self-mutilation expressed psychological turmoil or the wish to avoid work, though a more common strategy for the latter was to feign illness and be confined to the hospital.[184]

The culture of prison life was framed not only by the hostility between the prison authorities and inmates but by the informal organisation of the prisoners themselves. Nineteenth-century prison regimes were little concerned with what happened behind locked doors. Detainees were usually left to feed, maintain and organise themselves according to their own resources. Describing an Istanbul prison in 1843, Blanqui commented:

Prisoners have established their own order and hierarchy among themselves: the debtors are in one part of the cell, the children in another, the murderers in a third, each with consent of all, the false vendors alone are excepted from this methodical and free classification, as a prey to the aggression of their comrades of misfortune, in token of the deep contempt that the crime for which they have been rendered guilty inspires ... the guards do not often go inside the internal courtyards without great caution for their health and safety because of the contagious state.[185]

Unwilling or incapable of maintaining surveillance over inmates, authorities were content that 'The strong and the healthy bully and tyrannise over the weak and the sick', as one observer reported of the Bagnio.[186] Yet even after ostensibly more disciplinary regimes were instituted, the daily prison routine continued to be moderated through the complex relations among inmates. Differences in social status and economic resources between prisoners could reproduce themselves inside. One prisoner at Tura, Muhammad al-Minshawi, sentenced to twenty years

[181] Workers imprisoned for political reasons were granted class A status: interview with Yusuf Darwish (a former inmate of Cairo Prison, Wahat and Abu Za'bal).

[182] Interview with Hisqail Kojaman.

[183] See, for example, *al-Ahram*, 5 April 1948. In the first years of the twentieth century, between one and three prisoners were listed as committing suicide each year in Egypt.

[184] At the native penitentiary at Tadmit in the south of Algeria, one inmate reportedly reacted to the harsh climate and heavy agricultural work by deliberately inflicting cuts and wounds on himself with a razor blade, *Dépêche algérienne*, 11 October 1907. On malingering, see John Warnock, 'Twenty-eight Years' Lunacy Experience', *Journal of Mental Science*, 70 (1924) p. 584.

[185] Blanqui, 'Rapport à Monsieur le Comte Duchatel', p. 82.

[186] Senior, *Journal*, p. 70.

for brigandage, exercised great authority within the prison. The son of a pasha, he inherited a fortune on his father's death which he used to influence prisoners and obtain favours from prison staff, ultimately marrying a daughter of the deputy governor of the prison.[187]

Self-organisation was strongest among political prisoners, particularly in concentration camps, which allowed the establishment of organised networks that were effectively autonomous. In Cairo Prison in 1950 communist inmates formed an organisation to manage the distribution of extra food among members and to represent them in discussions with prison authorities, a model that came to be adopted by Marxist groups throughout Egyptian prisons.[188] A similar system in Iraq, first organised by the communist leader Fahd while in Kut prison, allowed party members to live in a self-managed community where each member was allotted particular duties such as cooking, cleaning and laundry. After a hunger strike the authorities agreed to recognise a prisoners' representative who acted as their spokesman in any negotiations.[189] The official policy of quarantining political cadres from ordinary criminals, while limiting the opportunity for dissemination of propaganda, allowed the flourishing of a prison culture in which internees studied language, literature and performed theatre. Indeed it is ironic that the communist movement in Egypt, working underground and notoriously fragmented during the 1940s and 1950s, was arguably at its most united in prison. Imprisoned Islamists, members of the Muslim Brotherhood in Egypt and the Hizb al-Istiqlal in Iraq, also organised themselves, although on different, more hierarchical lines.

Other non-political activities also inscribed social life in prison. Chess, played with pieces shaped from bread, cards, and gambling on insect races provided a medium of interaction and means of distraction. Illegal drugs and alcohol, such as *hubhub*, a spirit made by inmates at Abu Za'bal fermented from a bread mixture, were used to lubricate the tedium.[190] The demand for contraband within the prison offered opportunities for smuggling networks and the potential for cooperation and conflict between different groups and criminal gangs. Although rarely explicitly attested in the sources, oblique references to 'unnatural practices' suggest that homosexuality was practised.[191]

---

[187]   Coles, *Recollections*, pp. 134–5.
[188]   Interview with Yusuf Darwish.
[189]   Interview with Hisqail Kojaman.
[190]   Interview with Yusuf Darwish.
[191]   For a study of women's relationships in an Egyptian prison in the 1960s, see Christianne Gear-

4. Tattoos of Egyptian prisoners, *c.* 1920. Among the examples shown here are designs worn by Muslim inmates. [From M. Caloyanni, 'Étude des tatouages sur les criminels d'Égypte', *Bulletin de l'Institut d'Égypte*, V (1923), pl. VII]

Prison subculture was mediated not only through the pattern of relations between inmates but in the self-identification of prisoners themselves. One such medium was the use of tattoos as a counter to the 'depersonalising life of the institution'.[192] A pioneering study of the tattoos of Egyptian prisoners in the early 1920s categorised them as professional, decorative, sentimental and cura- tive in character.[193] Although senior criminals were rarely tattooed, men, women and youths tattooed with figures or animals were usually from the criminal class, with such symbols as the fish, snake, lion, warrior or a woman with swords denoting particular grades of thief or circles of association. Some tattoos ex- pressed religious affiliation. Copts marked themselves with crosses, Muslims with mosques or prayer mats. By contrast, Bedouins were rarely tattooed, regarding it as shameful. Other designs, such as the name of a wife or a husband, expressed an emotional tie. The most common type of tattoo was curative in purpose, often consisting of simple points and circles to deal with illnesses such as eye prob- lems, migraines, rheumatism, local inflammation and tumours. Obscene tattoos,

geoura, 'Women's Prisons: Cohesion and social structure, a study of Qanater's women's prison', MA thesis, American University in Cairo, 1969.

[192] Patricia O'Brien, *The Promise of Punishment*, p. 87. On tattooing as practised in French prisons, see pp. 77–80.

[193] M[egalo] Caloyanni, 'Étude des tatouages sur les criminels d'Égypte', *Bulletin de l'Institut d'Égypte*, V (1923), pp. 115–28. In seeing tattoos as an expression of the external life of an indi- vidual, Caloyanni was closer to the views of Lacassagne than of Lombroso who believed they testified to a criminal or immoral nature. For earlier studies of tattoo practice among Arabs, see Alexandre Lacassagne, *Les tatouages, étude anthropologique et medico-légale*, Paris, 1881, pp. 13–16, and Kocher, *Criminalité*, pp. 64–72.

common in European prisons, were unknown. These inscriptions of the body denoting professional status, religious allegiance, emotional ties or medical therapies functioned as an affirmation of individuality or a self-assigned collective identity. They also served as a symbolic subversion of the branding practice employed by some prison authorities, such as the Liman, where inmates were marked with the letter 'L' (*lam*).[194]

THE GUARDED AND THE GUARDS

The relationship between prison staff and prisoners was central in determining the character of prison culture and the effectiveness of the disciplinary regime. For most of the nineteenth century, when few prisons received regular state funds and the gaoler often no salary, the prevailing picture was of predictable corruption and graft where money was extorted routinely from prisoners. Officially abolished during the Tanzimat, the charging of prison release fees to supplement a gaoler's income nevertheless persisted in some places. In Egypt, prison guards, usually ex-soldiers, received a regular if modest salary but the dominant image there and elsewhere, found in both official and press reports, is of unqualified and incompetent staff. The turnover of personnel was high, and increasingly stronger measures were authorised to deal with disciplinary problems amongst guards.

Religious and ethnic divisions could reinforce the natural hostility between inmates and guards. At Beirut prison in the mid-nineteenth century, where all gaolers were Muslims, religious difference may have been the reason for the alleged harsher treatment meted out to Christian prisoners.[195] In Egypt, at least till the 1880s, the Turko-Circassian élite monopolised prison governorships and, in some Egyptian prisons, made up most or all of the prison guards. The 'Urabi uprising, which saw a group of native Egyptian officers challenging Turko-Circassion dominance, had obvious implications in such a context. As one British official reported, 'The present crisis is a reign of terror on a small scale ... and a considerable proportion [of prison governors], as is natural, seem animated by vindictive feelings.'[196] Specialised troops from a different ethnic background might be used to maintain security outside the prison or camp. At Tura, Sudanese troops watched over work gangs, and the *Hajjana*, Sudanese or Bedouin camel corps patrolled the area around the desert camps in Egypt and Iraq. Yet

---

[194] Khaled Fahmy, *All the Pasha's Men: Mehmed Ali, his army and the making of modern Egypt*, Cambridge University Press, 1997, p. 106.
[195] FO 195/364, Letters relating to Prisons in Turkey.
[196] FO 141/170, Major Herbert Chermside to Dufferin, 6 December 1882.

successful prison management also depended on a degree of consent between prison officers and prisoners. In Algeria discipline on the labour gangs and in the dormitories was supervised by *prévots*, prisoners entrusted with various responsibilities, who worked in conjunction with the guards.[197]

While an instinctive antagonism might exist between guards and guarded, relations within the ranks of prison officers and warders were not necessarily harmonious. The composition of prison staff reflected the local political hierarchy. In Algeria senior posts were held routinely by French officers, while Algerians occupied the more junior positions. After 1882 the appointment of British prison officers over Egyptian warders characterised the new political order. In April 1924, not long before the handover of the prisons department to an Egyptian officer, warders of Cairo Prison gave voice to a long standing resentment by presenting a petition which complained of their working conditions, and asked for an improvement in working hours, a limitation on the powers of the governor to inflict fines, free travel on trains and free lodging. The British officer, Inspector Moberley Bey, responded by arresting the chief warder and assistant, who protested that 'the days of tyranny were over and they were now in the days of justice and independence'.[198] As well as shedding light on contemporary expectations of the post–1919 political arrangements, the episode highlights significant cleavages within the prison staff that must have chronically impaired the institutional efficiency of the prison.

SOCIAL DETERRENCE AND POPULAR PERCEPTIONS

Part of the purpose of the prison was to deter wrongdoers by its sheer physical hardship. Prison administrators in the Middle East were constantly troubled that an improvement in prison conditions, particularly in the provision of food and clothing, undermined its deterrent value. In 1892 Crookshank had warned, 'I am of the opinion that simple imprisonment as it exists can never act as a deterrent to, or a commensurate punishment for, crime, unless the Government provides prisons where separate confinement and labour can be enforced, and where all interviews with relatives and friends are done away with.'[199] Forty years later, press reports that certain individuals dealt openly in small amounts of drugs in order that they be arrested and sent to prison, where they would be fed and

---

[197] See, for example, the regulations of the agricultural penitentiary of Ain el-Bey, AOM 10G/40.
[198] 'Incidents at a Prison', *Egyptian Gazette*, 9 April 1924.
[199] Report on the Finances, Administration, and Condition of Egypt, and the Progress of Reforms, *PP*, XCVI (1892), p. 29.

housed at government expense, reinforced such perceptions.[200] The reality was certainly mixed. In some circumstances prison may have been preferable to avoid military service or fend off hunger. But the record of escapes and the large numbers of people who opted for labour in lieu of imprisonment in Egypt suggest that prison life was less than comfortable, an assessment that accords with the traditional Arabic saying, 'Prison is for real men' (*al-sijn lil-jad'an*).

While prison authorities had some control over the prisoners' material comfort, they were much less able to shape social attitudes towards prison. In his study of prison in nineteenth-century Egypt, Peters argues that there was probably little stigmatisation or social exclusion in such punishment, given that confinement did not completely isolate the individual, many crimes were not regarded in moral terms, and the inconsistencies of the legal system undermined its ethical force.[201] Certainly many Europeans and British officials commented on the prison's general lack of deterrence.[202] Cromer bewailed its failure to inspire fear: '[it] is not a place sufficiently dreaded', and the 'disgrace of being put in prison ... is scarcely felt by the mass of the population here'.[203] The absence of social stigma, found particularly among the illiterate Egyptian peasantry, the largest element among the general prison population, continually frustrated legal authorities.[204] However, it is not surprising that a social group that viewed the state as a traditional source of oppression, and probably saw the prison as representative of that order, regarded confinement as little to do with justice. Amongst the professional criminal classes prison served as a rite of passage. In calling for a return to corporal and capital punishment, even exile, for drug offenders in the 1930s, Shaykh al-Taftazani asserted that for such criminals, 'Prison is still something to brag about [and] iron fetters are ornaments to vaunt.'[205]

In the colonial context, imprisonment, far from being a disgrace, could take on noble associations of the national struggle against an oppressive foreign, Christian

[200] *Al-Ahram*, 13 December 1932.

[201] Peters, 'Prisons and Marginalisation in Nineteenth-Century Egypt', pp. 31–52.

[202] On the views of Clot Bey and others, see Peters, 'Prisons and Marginalisation in Nineteenth-Century Egypt', pp. 45–6.

[203] Report on the Finances, Administration, and Condition of Egypt, and the Progress of Reforms, *PP*, CXI (1893–4), p. 22; and Report on the Finances, Administration, and Condition of Egypt, and the Progress of Reforms, *PP*, CVII (1898), pp. 25–6. For similar statements, see Report on the Finances, Administration, and Condition of Egypt, and the Progress of Reforms, *PP*, XCVI (1894), pp. 16, 28, and Warnock, 'Twenty-eight Years' Lunacy Experience', p. 384.

[204] See Goadby, *Commentary on Egyptian Criminal Law*, p. 237n, quoting the Judicial Adviser's Report (1913).

[205] 'Fast Talk', *Al-Ahram Weekly*, 31 October–6 November 2002.

power. For this reason some argued that simple imprisonment was an ineffective punishment for Arabs since it offered them not only better living conditions but the status of martyr among their coreligionists. Colonial authorities were perplexed at the lack of social opprobrium directed towards those sentenced to internment or transportation for commonplace crimes. As a journalist in Algeria reported:

Liberated prisoners or convicts are received with open arms, feted as honest travellers who have come from afar and have been long absent. At Constantine in 1896 a former *qadi* [judge] returned from Cayenne after having served seven years of forced labour for forgery and fraud; knowing that he was going to arrive by train, a number of natives went to wait at the station and gave him a real ovation.[206]

Indeed the arbitrary fashion in which regimes clamped down on political opposition meant that rather than stigmatising prisoners, a term of imprisonment could be perceived as evidence of virtue.[207]

The full social meaning and significance of prison was clearly determined neither by political authority nor prisoners themselves but by a more complex and multi-layered social matrix. One significant element has been the literary imagination found in the well-established tradition of Arabic prison literature (*adab al-sujun*), first in verse and later taken up by prose writers in the twentieth century.[208] The richness of this tradition has been due not simply to the fact that many of the authors have themselves been imprisoned, usually for political reasons, but because, as an institution of control, repression and brutality, the prison has lent itself as a metaphor for a society dominated by an authoritarian state.[209] The prison has also been used by filmmakers to highlight social issues and political struggles.[210] On a linguistic level the range of terms used to describe the

---

[206] Edmond Norès [avocat général à la cour d'appel d'Alger], *L'oeuvre de la France en Algérie*, Paris: Félix Alcan, 1931, pp. 350–1, quoting Hugolin, *Le banditisme en Algérie*, 1896, p. 10.

[207] Abdelwahab Bouhdiba, *Criminalité et changements sociaux en Tunisie*, Tunis, 1965, p. 67.

[208] On poets, see Rosenthal, *Muslim Concept of Freedom*, pp. 66–77. Among prose writers are Egyptians Yahya Haqqi (*Qissa al-sijn*, 1939), Fathi Ghanem (*Hikayat Tu*, 1987) and Sunallah Ibrahim (*Sharaf*, 1997), Saudi Abd al-Rahman al-Munif (*Cities of Salt*) and Syrian Nabil Sulayman (*al-Sijn*, 1972).

[209] Sabry Hafez, 'Torture, Imprisonment, and Political Assassination in the Arab Novel', *al-Jadid* (winter 2002), pp. 16–17. See also Isabella Camera d'Afflitto, 'Prison Narratives: Autobiography and fiction' in Robin Ostle *et al.* (eds), *Writing the Self*, London: Saqi, 1998, pp. 148–56.

[210] Among many are *Ja'launi mujriman* ('They Made Me a Criminal'), directed by Atif Salim in 1953, with a screenplay by Nagib Mahfuz, which addresses the social conditions that can lead to crime, and *Fi baytina rajul* ('There's a Man in Our House') 1960, directed by Hinri Barakat, based on the novel by Ihsan 'Abd al-Quddus set in the 1940s, which tells the story of a nationalist escaped from prison and discusses, among other things, the practice of torture.

prison, from the official to the colloquial, and the humorous to the ironic, reflects its complex and contradictory senses. *Dar khaltu* ('the house of his aunt'), *karraka* ('the incubator'), *bou daffa* ('the great vagina'), *fi qalbu* ('in his heart') and *sabbat al-dhalam* ('archway of darkness') straddle a broad canvas of meanings from the familiar to the terrifying.[211]

CONCLUSION

The widespread adoption of imprisonment and the corresponding decline of traditional modes of punishment across the Middle East from the nineteenth century was an acknowledgement that local customary practice had become outdated. The prison in the Middle East and elsewhere now became a yardstick by which the 'civilised' nature of society was measured. The change was substantially driven by European influence but it fitted well with the aspirations of Middle Eastern states to become members of the international community. As the resources of the state expanded, specialised approaches were devised to deal with different categories of offenders, either by adapting traditional institutions such as the *Dar jawad* and the *takaya* to a modified purpose, or by defining new categories of imprisonment, like the reformatories for recidivists and for youth. There was a gradual improvement in prison standards from the nineteenth century and more so from the 1920s, stimulated by a desire to develop the prison as an effective institution of reform. Educational and vocational programmes designed to deal with illiteracy and the lack of employment skills, and the attempts to assist in rehabilitation of prisoners after release testify to a commitment to social betterment.

Yet while the universal rhetoric of the prison may have been embraced by local modernist élites, actual practice was permeated by indigenous political structures, social hierarchies and cultural context. In the colonial situation the prison reflected the political priorities and economic demands of empire. Overwhelmingly poor and illiterate, prison populations were harnessed to provide the manpower for public works projects, land improvement and small-scale manufacture, as well as the perpetuation of the prison system itself. Extraterritorial powers protected the privileged position, even criminality, of foreign nationals. Political imprisonment, both in the colonial and postcolonial period, was embraced by élites as a tool of exclusion, to constrict and control the arena of legitimate political activism. Moreover, the impetus for reform was driven largely from the top

---

[211] Bouhdiba, *Criminalité*, p. 65.

and was not the result of popular agitation. While public sensibilities may have been affronted by certain penal practices, civil associations concerned with the welfare of prisoners were few and without much influence. Prison administrations thus reflected the interests of the state and the social perspective of its élite, and any genuine reform was circumscribed by and subjugated to those priorities. Whenever necessary, humanist convictions and prisoners' interests were overridden by political contingencies, social perceptions and budgetary considerations in a manner that perpetuated rather than reduced criminal categories.

However, prison practice was not solely determined by state authorities. Prison regimes were riddled with systemic flaws, such as chronically corrupt and unqualified staff, limited resources and residual archaic practices. More than this, the agency of prisoners themselves who resisted, negotiated with or submitted to the authorities was a significant factor in shaping the dynamics of prison life. The widespread use of the communal mode of imprisonment, amplified by overcrowding, facilitated an ethic of resistance and cultivated a vibrant subculture. Political prisoners in particular were able to challenge and modify the system through collective action from within. Far from isolating inmates from their community, prison walls were constantly permeated by political and social forces from without. This was the paradox of the prison in the Middle East and the basis of its failure. Promoted as a civilising institution, the modern prison in the Middle East was appropriated as an instrument to reinforce rather than reform the existing social order. Associated with the discourse of discipline and social improvement, the prison was a site of multivalent and contradictory transactions that nurtured social difference, institutionalised criminality, and sustained a restrictive political culture.

BIBLIOGRAPHICAL NOTE

National archives offer a rich and largely untapped source of information on Middle Eastern prisons. In the Middle East, the Ottoman archives, particularly the records of the Directorate of Prisons, and those of the Prisons Department in the Egyptian National Archives (*Dar al-Watha'iq*), contain important documentation on prison administration and related matters, such as court records. From European state collections, the British National Archives (Kew) holds valuable material relating to the Ottoman Empire, Egypt after 1882, and records on mandate Palestine and Iraq. The French national archives at Aix-en-Provence

(*Archives d'outre-mer*) contain much relevant material on the Algerian prison system.

Official prison publications remain an essential source particularly for statistical information. From 1882 until 1914 the annual reports on Egypt and the Sudan to the House of Commons feature a section on prisons, and the reports of the Egyptian Prisons Department itself offer a greater wealth of data from the late nineteenth century. Similarly valuable material can be found for the mandatory administrations in Iraq and in Palestine (*Blue Books*). The equivalent publication for the French mandates of Lebanon and Syria is the multi-volume *Rapport sur la situation de la Syrie et du Liban*, Geneva: League of Nations, 1923–39. By the 1940s, some prison data was published in annual statistical reports by most Middle Eastern states. More specific monographs, such as those issued by the Egyptian Ministry of War, *Cairo Prison, Correctional Facility*, and *The Egyptian Prisons under the New Regime*, both published in 1955, should be consulted even if they provide an over sanguine picture, a routine feature of government literature. For an international context the published proceedings of the International Penal Congresses from the late nineteenth century onwards, usually under the title of *Actes du congrès pénitentiaire internationale*, contain some material on Middle Eastern developments. *Egypt and the Penal System* (*Misr wa al-nazm al-ta'dibiyya*) [c.1925] by Ali Hilmi Bey, an Egyptian delegate at the 1925 London congress, sets the Egyptian system in a comparative historical and international framework.

Secondary literature on the history of Middle Eastern prisons is surprisingly scanty. For the pre-modern period, the *Encyclopedia of Islam*, s.v. *sidjn* provides a useful summary of the scholarship. Franz Rosenthal, *The Muslim Concept of Freedom, prior to the Nineteenth Century*, Leiden: EJ Brill, 1960, and Irene Schneider, 'Imprisonment in Pre-Classical and Classical Islamic Law', *Islamic Law and Society*, 2, 2 (1995), pp. 157–73, discuss imprisonment in Islamic thought and law respectively. For the modern period, the literature on nineteenth–century Egypt is the most developed. Over the last decade, Rudolph Peters has produced an illuminating stream of articles on the prisons and Egyptian penal law, the most relevant being '"For His Correction and as a Deterrent Example for Others": Mehmed 'Ali's first criminal legislation (1829–1830)', *Islamic Law and Society*, 6, 2 (1999), pp. 165–92; 'Prisons and Marginalisation in Nineteenth-Century Egypt' in Eugene Rogan (ed.), *Outside In*, London and New York: IB Tauris, 2002; 'Egypt and the Age of the Triumphant Prison: Legal punishment in nineteenth century Egypt', *Annales islamologiques*, 36 (2002), pp. 253–85; and most recently 'Controlled Suffering: Mortality and living conditions in 19th century Egyptian prisons', *International Journal of Middle East Studies*, 36 (2004), pp. 387–407. Khaled Fahmy has also made a substantial contribution to our understanding of prisons in his monograph, *All the Pasha's Men: Mehmed Ali, his army and the making of modern Egypt*, Cambridge University Press, 1997, and more particularly in his article, 'Medical Conditions in Egyptian Prisons in the Nineteenth Century' in R. Ostle (ed.), *Marginal Voices in Literature and Society*, Strasbourg: European Science Foundation, 2000, pp. 135–55. An early work by Ahmad Hilmi, *al-Sujun al-misriyya fi 'ahd al-ihtilal al-inglizi* [Egyptian prisons in the period of the English occupation], 1911, takes the narrative into the period of the British occupation.

For Iran, Ervand Abrahamian, *Tortured Confessions*, Berkeley, CA: University of California Press, 1999, and Darius M. Rejali, *Torture and Modernity: Self, society and state in modern Iran*, Boulder, CO: Westview Press, 1994 provide the most accessible English language literature, placing the development of prisons in the context of the practice of torture. Abdelhamid Larguèche, with Dalenda Larguèche, in *Marginales in terre d'Islam*, Tunis: Cérès, 1992, and alone in *Les ombres de la ville: Pauvres, marginaux et minoritaires à Tunis (XVIIIème et XIXème siècles)*, 1999, offers pioneering research on Tunisian prisons from the eighteenth and nineteenth centuries, based on close use of archives. The work of the Professor of Law at the University of Algiers, Emile Larcher, with Jean Olier, *Les institutions pénitentiaires de l'Algérie*, Paris and Alger, 1899, is indispensable for an understanding of the Algerian situation, even if it clearly reflects the interest of the French colonist. Fouad Ammoun provides a detailed coverage of Syrian penal law and institutions in *La Syrie criminelle*, Paris: Marcel Giard, 1929 that stresses continuities with earlier practice. A more extensive legal literature that places imprisonment in the fuller context of Middle Eastern law can be consulted with profit. Among the more important works are Uriel Heyd, *Studies in Old Ottoman Criminal Law*, Oxford: Clarendon, 1973, Frederic M. Goadby, *Commentary on Egyptian Criminal Law and the Related Law of Palestine, Cyprus and Iraq*, Cairo: Government Press, 1924, and Emile Larcher, *Trois années d'études algériennes*, 1902. On youth delinquency, the works of Hassan Nachat, *Les jeunes délinquants*, Paris, 1913, and Sa'di Bisisu, *Mahakim al-ahdath wa al-madaris al-islahiyya* [Youth courts and reformatory schools], 1949, set local Middle Eastern practice within a comparative framework.

Contemporary periodicals, such as the annual reports of the Howard Association and the *Bulletin de Société Générale des Prisons* published in France deal with a range of issues on Middle Eastern prisons from the late nineteenth century onwards, particularly on Morocco, Algeria and Egypt. Discussions on aspects of penological law and prison administration can also be found in Egyptian periodicals such as *L'Égypte contemporaine* and the Arabic language *al-Muqtataf.* Where exact dates are known, local press coverage of specific events, such as prison riots, mass releases, escapes, hunger strikes and topical prison issues, can provide invaluable supplementary material and social perspective.

A number of Middle Eastern prison officials and administrators have published their memoirs. Probably the most well-known is *Recollections and Reflections*, London: St Catherine Press, 1918 by Charles Coles Pasha, the Director General of Prisons in Egypt from 1897–1913. Another director of Egyptian prisons, Muhammad Shahin Kifah, wrote *al-Jarima* (Crime), 1936, while the memoir *With the Communists in their Prisons* by 'Abd al-Jabbar 'Ayyub, a director of Baghdad Prison, later executed for his conduct in office, appeared in the 1950s (the last two unseen by the author).

The memoirs of former prisoners offer a necessary contrasting perspective. For the most part written by those imprisoned for political reasons, this literary genre has burgeoned in recent years and includes the work of some prominent literary figures such as Nawal al-Sa'dawi (*Memoirs from the Women's Prison*, London: Women's Press, 1986). For the period discussed here, Mahmud 'Abbas al-'Aqqad's, *'Alam al-sudud wa al-quyud* [The world of bars and shackles], Cairo, 1937, offers important insights. For a wider consideration of prison literature, the article by Sabry Hafez, 'Torture, Imprisonment, and Political Assassination in the Arab Novel', *al-Jadid* (winter 2002), pp. 16–17, provides a good starting point. Prisoner interviews are an obvious source for the more contemporary period. Some have been published, such as a collection of interviews of former female internees in Egypt, as *Misriyyat fi al-sujun wa al-mu'taqalat* [Egyptian women in prison and concentration camps], Markaz al-buhuth al-'arabiyya, 2003.

Finally, those interested in prisons in the broader context of the poor and socially marginal classes might explore recent works on these themes: Robin Ostle (ed.), *Marginal Voices in Literature and Society*, Strasbourg: European Science Foundation, 2000; Eugene Rogan (ed.), *Outside In*, London and New York: IB Tauris, 2002; Mine Ener, *Managing Egypt's Poor and the Politics of Benevolence*, Princeton University Press, 2003; and Michael Bonner, Mine Ener and Amy Singer (eds), *Poverty and Charity in Middle Eastern Contexts*, Albany, NY: State University of New York Press, 2003.

INDIA: THE CONTESTED PRISON

David Arnold

The prison has a long history in South Asia. Places of confinement existed as early as the reign of the Buddhist emperor Ashoka in the third century BC, as well as under subsequent Hindu and Muslim regimes. Their use, however, was seldom as an aid to ordinary punishment but as a way of detaining rebels and rivals for the throne, often in the dungeon of a secure fort.[1] Until the late eighteenth century imprisonment was less common than other forms of punishment, such as execution, fines and mutilation. Where lock-ups (*hajats*) existed, it was generally as places of temporary or pre-trial detention. Pre-colonial regimes arguably lacked the means to create a fully-fledged prison system, for as Sumit Guha has observed, 'Only a government with considerable administrative and fiscal resources could afford to lock up any large number of persons in (however unluxurious) a state of idleness.'[2]

The prison in India was not therefore an entirely colonial invention, but it underwent a revolution in form and function with the establishment of British rule. The history of the Indian prison can thus be understood as the story of a largely alien institution, its evolution reflecting shifts in metropolitan fashion as well as changes in the nature and requirements of the colonial regime. This 150-year history can be divided into three phases of roughly equal duration. During the foundation period between 1790 and the 1850s, use of the prison became widespread, complementing and underpinning other aspects of the colonial

---

[1] A.L. Basham, *The Wonder That was India*, New Delhi: Rupa, 1985, p. 118; Peter Jackson, *The Delhi Sultanate: A political and military history*, Cambridge University Press, 1999, pp. 157, 176, 200; François Bernier, *Travels in the Mogul Empire*, Westminster: Archibald Constable, 1891, pp. 106–7.

[2] Sumit Guha, 'An Indian Penal Regime: Maharashtra in the eighteenth century', *Past and Present*, 147 (1995), p. 119.

administration. British penal practices, including transportation, were introduced or adapted to local circumstances, but in general India's prisons remained poorly managed and subject to frequent disturbances and escapes. A second phase of more systematic prison discipline and gaol construction followed, lasting from the 1850s into the 1890s and beyond. Greater emphasis was given in this period to prison management and convict employment: transportation was phased out, central gaols were created and intramural industries established. During these first two phases, however, the death-rate in prisons remained high, and this was one reason (apart from the absence of any specialised prison agency) why the responsibility for prison administration was assigned to colonial medical officers. At its height in the late nineteenth century this medicalisation of the prison was indicative of the extent to which the gaol served not only as a place of confinement but also as a site of colonial knowledge, a means of acquiring insight into the material conditions of the population at large.

The final phase of India's colonial prison, from the 1890s through to the end of the Second World War, was marked by contrasting trends. One was growing pessimism about the prison's ability to reform India's 'criminal tribes'. Identified as an increasingly large percentage of the prison population, recourse was also had to non-carceral means in order to curb their activities. This growing preoccupation with the 'criminal tribes' accompanied the rise of colonial criminology in India, and greater responsibility was accordingly assigned to the police in issues relating to crime control and prison policy. A second feature of the period was the growth of organised anti-colonial movements, spearheaded by Indian nationalism. The colonial authorities sought to contain political opposition through extensive use of the prison (among other coercive measures), but, especially under Gandhi's leadership, nationalists responded by making 'gaol-going' a fundamental feature of their campaigns. The prison became a highly contested site between the colonial state and its political adversaries, helping to set the stage for the British departure in August 1947.

The contestation surrounding the prison thus occurred at several different, if interrelated, levels. The nature and purpose of the prison was a subject of sustained debate within the colonial regime itself. It was generally accepted that prisons were necessary and preferable to the 'barbaric' penal practices identified with pre-colonial regimes, but there was extensive discussion as to who should run the prisons, how much money and administrative effort should be invested in them, how far Indian 'prejudices' should be accommodated within the prison, and ultimately what the function of the colonial prison should be. Among the Indian population at large, the prison was loathed and feared: it was seen to be a site not only of colonial oppression but also of systematic attempts to break caste and impose Christianity. Resistance within the prison was matched by extramural protest, making the prison part of a wider network of Indian alienation and resistance. From the 1890s the rise of Indian nationalism and other opposition movements added a new layer of contestation. Political prisoners struggled to assert their identity and rights within the prison system, contested the privileges given to European prisoners while simultaneously distancing themselves from 'common criminals'. The contested nature of the colonial prison reflected its practical and symbolic importance in the evolving struggle between Indian subjects and British rulers, but also conflicts within the prison itself, between convicts and warders, between high- and low-caste prisoners, between an educated élite of political prisoners and the bulk of ordinary convicts.

THE BIRTH OF THE COLONIAL PRISON

It was perhaps inevitable that, in extending their control over India in the late eighteenth and early nineteenth centuries, the British should import penal institutions familiar to them at home and held to be progressive and civilised. But the history of the colonial prison is not simply one of unidirectional institutional transfer. As the instrument of British administration, the East India Company (until its abolition in 1858) sought to retain indigenous institutions and practices as far as seemed compatible with its political ambitions and economic interests. A policy of non-intervention appeared the most economical and effective way of deploying its resources and securing Indian acquiescence. Thus in Bengal from the 1760s the British sought to utilise the existing courts and Islamic system of punishments. However, in the closing years of the century they began to amend or reject judicial and penal practices they found unacceptably 'barbaric' or excessively lenient towards Brahmins and other high-status groups. Despite the severity of Britain's own penal system at the time, which included greater use of the death penalty than in India, the British recoiled from such practices as mutilation and impaling, 'the very mention of which', observed Sir John Shore in 1782, 'makes me shudder'.[3] With the arrival of Lord Cornwallis as Governor-General of India in 1786, Islamic law and its customary punishments were steadily replaced by measures the British considered more consistent with 'reason and

---

[3] Jörg Fisch, *Cheap Lives and Dear Limbs: The British transformation of the Bengal criminal law, 1769–1817*, Wiesbaden: Franz Steiner Verlag, 1983, p. 37.

humanity'.[4] This 'humanitarian' approach ultimately resulted, too, in the criminalisation and suppression of such Hindu practices as *sati* and female infanticide.

In setting the new prison system on firmer foundations, from 1790 British magistrates in Bengal were vested with powers of management and control over the gaols in their districts. Company officials sought a more extensive and systematic use of imprisonment, and, in addition to utilising various existing buildings, began to construct purpose-built prisons. Imprisonment, however, was never the sole mode of punishment and deterrence. The British made greater use than their Indian predecessors of capital punishment, especially for *dacoity* (gang robbery), seen as one of the greatest threats to colonial authority and to stability and revenue-collection in the countryside. A further innovation was the transportation of perpetrators of serious crimes: begun in 1787, when the first convicts were shipped to Benkulen in Sumatra, this was soon extended to other parts of the Indian Ocean region.[5]

From the 1790s colonial prison discourse and practice revolved around three main sets of concerns that reflected the limitations as much as the perceived capabilities of British authority in India. There was, firstly, the question of how far India presented physical and cultural constraints (or, alternatively, penal opportunities) different from those in the West. This occasioned a debate within the colonial administration about racial difference and cultural accommodation. The British sought to remove the privileged penal status of Brahmins (who had rarely been executed or imprisoned under previous regimes),[6] while believing that an essential distinction had to be maintained between European and Indian prisoners. As the framers of India's draft Penal Code put it in 1837: 'The physical difference which exists between the European and the native of India renders it impossible to subject them to the same system of prison discipline ... It would be cruel to subject an European for a long period to a severe prison discipline, in a country in which existence is almost constant misery to an European who has not many indulgences at his command.' It would, they argued, be undesirable to allow Indians to see 'Englishmen of the worst description, placed in the most

---

[4] Ibid., pp. 43–85. See also Radhika Singha, *A Despotism of Law: Crime and justice in early colonial India*, Delhi: Oxford University Press, 1998.

[5] Tapas Kumar Banerjee, *Background to Indian Criminal Law*, Bombay: Orient Longman, 1963, chapter 6.

[6] Visiting Cuddapah gaol in the Madras Presidency in 1809, one surgeon remarked on the leniency given to Brahmin prisoners, but added that they particularly hated being hanged by a Chuckler, the lowest of outcastes: Benjamin Heyne, *Tracts, Historical and Statistical, on India*, London: Robert Baldwin, 1814, p. 322.

degrading situations, stigmatised by the courts of justice, and engaged in the ig-nominious labour of a gaol.'[7]

Conversely, it was held that imprisonment alone was an insufficient means of punishment and deterrence for most Indians, unless supported by such ad-ditional means as branding convicts with the mark of their crime (*godena*),[8] or by transportation overseas, which Hindus were thought particularly to dread as violating the taboo against crossing the 'black water' (*kala pani*) and consequently entailing loss of caste. But the heterogeneity of India's prison population posed as great a problem as its collective alterity. With such a diversity of castes, races and religions, it was difficult to pursue, with respect to such matters as diet, dress and labour, a uniform prison policy. Indeed one strand in Company thinking was that significant local differences must be respected. In the 1790s it was proposed that Hindu and Muslim, as well as male and female, prisoners should be kept apart; subsequently it was recommended that Hindus and Muslims be allowed to ob-serve their religious festivals and be exempted from labour on holy days.[9]

Secondly, a complex spatial geography informed colonial penal practice. In part this related to India's 'tropical' location. While prison might be deemed a suitable mode of punishment in Europe, in India, especially during the hot sea-son, it was intolerable (not least for European prisoners), 'worse than the worst dungeon in our western world'.[10] But the vastness of the Indian Empire and the Indian Ocean territories associated with it—from Aden and Mauritius to the Andamans and Singapore—meant that there were perceived advantages in mov-ing refractory or long-term prisoners away from their home localities, where they might remain in close contact with relatives and friends, to far-off locations where, especially among illiterate convicts, such ties would be severed. While the prison in India remained remarkably permeable to local influences, geographical space could be manipulated to provide the kind of punitive isolation that Euro-pean and American reformers sought to create institutionally within the confines of a well-ordered prison. But the mobility forced upon many nineteenth-century prisoners was no less a consequence of their labour value. Just as from the 1830s Indian indentured labourers were recruited for service in India and overseas, so

[7] 'On the chapter of punishments', *The Indian Penal Code as Originally Framed in 1837*, Madras: Higginbotham, 1888, pp. 95–6.
[8] Clare Anderson, *Legible Bodies: Race, criminality and colonialism in South Asia*, Oxford: Berg, 2004.
[9] Banerjee, *Background*, pp. 329, 345.
[10] Jones to William Pitt, 5 February 1785, in Garland Cannon (ed.), *The Letters of Sir William Jones*, vol. 2, Oxford: Clarendon Press, 1970, p. 661.

prisoners were mobilised to provide much-needed labour on the roads and on public works across the subcontinent or in penal settlements abroad.

Thirdly, the colonial prison was a site of conflicting economic ambitions. On the one hand the labour of prisoners was highly valued, whether in repairing roads or in the proliferating gaol industries of the late nineteenth century. By their toil, prisoners could contribute to the cost of their upkeep and satisfy the colonial desire to run the prison system as inexpensively as possible. But on the other hand the Indian prison had to grapple with the problem of acute rural poverty. The majority of Indian prisoners came from the poorest agrarian classes, driven to commit crime by stark necessity. These were men and women for whom prison, in times of dearth and famine, represented an escape from utter destitution and starvation. It was much debated whether prisons should in such circumstances recognise an obligation to provide food and shelter or should, conversely, become even more harshly punitive, shedding their reputation as places of relative comfort,[11] in order to chastise and discourage those who, for whatever reason, took to crime.

THE PRISON DISCIPLINE COMMITTEE, 1836–8

The emergence of a local critique of India's existing prison system broadly corresponded in time and intent to the penal reform movement in Britain and North America,[12] but its effects were far more restricted. The first significant expression of the need for systematic reform was the Committee on Prison Discipline, appointed in 1836 and reporting two years later in 1838.[13] This Calcutta-based committee was charged with investigating the physical and moral condition of India's prisoners and recommending improvements. Significantly, the enquiry was not prompted by a humanitarian outcry over prison welfare or by a principled concern to promote the reform and rehabilitation of prisoners. Instead it was impelled by the need to support a reformed Indian penal code

---

[11] Prisoners were sometimes said to refer to prison as 'my father-in-law's house'. In 1809 Heyne reported that the Company's *donkalus* (thieves) were said to 'look like bridegrooms' in prison, fat and well looked after: Heyne, *Tracts*, p. 322.

[12] See Randall McGowen, 'The Well-ordered Prison, England, 1780–1865' in Norval Morris and David J. Rothman (eds), *The Oxford History of the Prison: The practice of punishment in Western society*, New York: Oxford University Press, 1995, pp. 71–99, and David J. Rothman, 'Perfecting the Prison: United States, 1789–1865' in *The Oxford History of the Prison*, pp. 100–16.

[13] 'Prison discipline' might sound Foucauldian but the term reflected contemporary usage and the existence since 1816 of the Society for the Improvement of Prison Discipline in Britain; cf. Michel Foucault, *Discipline and Punish: The birth of the prison*, Harmondsworth: Penguin, 1977.

with an effective prison system, and by the perceived threat from unruly prisoners in Calcutta, the colonial metropolis. The immediate cause was a disturbance in April 1834 at Alipur gaol on the outskirts of the city, during which the district magistrate was killed.[14] Built in 1810, this gaol was one of the largest in India, accommodating more than a thousand prisoners, and it was here that many convicts from northern and eastern India were held awaiting transportation. Ways were accordingly sought to control more securely 'the immense concourse of desperate and turbulent criminals who are, ... when assembled ... in one body, an object of terror to their keepers'.[15]

The committee sought information from district officials throughout Bengal and the northwest, and these enquiries provide the first detailed picture of prisons and imprisonment in India. In 1836 there were reported to be 118 prisons across British India (more than half of them containing civil as well as criminal prisoners). These held 56,632 prisoners, with the largest numbers in Bengal (23,622) and the North-Western Provinces (18,355). The ratio of prisoners to population varied widely, averaging 69 per 100,000 in Bengal but as high as 96 in Bombay: across India the average was 62. The data indicate that in India at the time there was no 'great confinement'. A daily tally of little more than 56,000 prisoners in a country estimated at the time to possess more than 90 million people was not a particularly large number.[16] Although as many as 10 per cent of prisoners were registered as re-offenders, most prisoners served sentences of under a year and generally no more than a month or two. Given this rapid turnover, in any given year many more than 56,000 individuals experienced prison life. The smallness of the prison population may partly reflect the sentencing of serious offenders (such as murderers and dacoits) to transportation overseas, removing them from the Indian statistics.[17] The low figure is also indicative of the extent to which punishments

---

[14] In India, 'prison' and 'jail' (or 'gaol') were used synonymously, without distinction between lockups for under-trial prisoners and places of long-term confinement. The terms 'house of correction' and 'penitentiary' were less common: *Report of the Indian Jail Conference*, Calcutta: Home Secretariat Press, 1877, pp. 11–14.

[15] Resolution, Legislative Department, 8 October 1838, *Report of the Committee on Prison Discipline*, Calcutta: Baptist Mission Press, 1838, p. 13.

[16] Ibid., p. 9. Relatively low rates of incarceration have historically been the norm in South Asia: in the 1990s India had only 23 prisoners per 100,000 of the population compared to Northern Ireland (126), South Africa (368), the United States (519) and Russia (558): Graeme Harper, 'Criminal Minds and Felonious Nations: Colonial and postcolonial incarceration' in Harper (ed.), *Colonial and Postcolonial Incarceration*, London: Continuum, 2001, p. 8.

[17] Until abandoned in 1825 Benkulen accommodated up to 900 Madras and Bengal convicts: J.F.A. McNair and W.D. Bayliss, *Prisoners Their Own Warders*, Westminster: Constable, 1899, p.

(such as fining and flogging) were still widely used without recourse to prison,[18] and suggests that a large proportion of crimes escaped detection by the unre-formed police or were dealt with locally by village headmen and caste *panchayats* (councils).

Already in 1838 the view was well established that India's prison population presented features not encountered in the West. In north India a substantial sec-tion of prisoners came from high castes, such as Rajputs, sentenced for 'honour' or revenge killings, affrays and other 'heinous crimes'; but many of those con-victed, especially for robbery and theft, belonged to low castes, including mem-bers of 'criminal tribes and castes'. These castes were alleged to have inherited their criminal proclivities from their ancestors and belonged to communities that had committed crime 'time out of mind'. Trying to reform individuals so 'addicted' to crime was deemed virtually impossible.[19] The steady rise in colo-nial perception and prison statistics of the 'criminal tribes' constitutes one of the principal subplots in India's prison history. Another aspect of prison life much remarked upon (and which, in this Orientalising discourse, further differentiated India from Europe) was the impact of caste, on prisoners and the prison admin-istration alike. Life inside the prison tended to replicate that outside: high-caste prisoners continued to enjoy superior status and even to retain, in their style of dress and the manner of wearing their hair, some of the physical emblems of their caste. Conversely, untouchable or low-caste prisoners from 'sweeper' castes were expected to clean the gaols, reproducing within prison the same degrading role they performed outside.[20]

In Bengal and the North-Western Provinces (NWP), prisoners were given a cash allowance to buy food from visiting traders and were allocated space within the prison yard to cook and eat their meals separately. While some officials saw this as a necessary accommodation of caste (violation of which would constitute additional and unauthorised punishment), others informed the Prison Discipline Committee that this amounted to an unwarranted indulgence, giving prisoners too much freedom. It resembled paying them a wage and, in allowing them the

---

7. See Clare Anderson, *Convicts in the Indian Ocean: Transportation from South Asia to Mauritius, 1815–53*, Basingstoke: Macmillan, 2000; Anand A.Yang, 'Indian Convict Workers in Southeast Asia in the Late Eighteenth and Early Nineteenth Centuries', *Journal of World History*, 14, 2 (2003), pp. 179–208.

[18] In 1855 158 convicts were sentenced to flogging in Madras Presidency, 53 to death and 55 to transportation: *Report of the Inspector of Prisons, Fort St George, 1856*.

[19] *Report ... on Prison Discipline*, pp. 69–70, 97.

[20] Ibid., p. 16.

'pleasures' of trading for, and cooking, their own food, undermined prison discipline.[21] Conversely, some respondents felt that caste gave the colonial authorities exceptional leverage: having to mix with low-caste prisoners was one of the most repugnant aspects of prison life for the higher castes, just as the loss of caste caused by labouring on roads or through transportation made imprisonment, if not a deterrent, then at least a source of considerable 'disgrace'.[22]

Information supplied to the committee revealed other practices that militated against effective control or appeared repugnant to enlightened penology. Most striking was the large number of prisoners who worked on the roads: in Bengal alone they numbered 13,000 (roughly three-quarters of the total prison strength). While recognising the value of prison labour to the state, the committee and its informants saw many disadvantages to this practice. Those who had the means to bribe their overseers were virtually exempt from hard labour, the burden falling on poor convicts instead. Road-gangs were poorly supervised: prisoners chatted to family members and friends, receiving from them food, opium, tobacco or a share of their criminal spoils. Such contact violated the belief that 'privation of intercourse with the world' was one of the 'legitimate aggravations' the state imposed on prisoners, without which 'all attempts to reform the character are futile'.[23] The laxity of extramural labour was one of the commonest reasons why prisoners were able to escape, usually by bribing their guards.[24] Work on the roads had other disadvantages too that made it 'incompatible with any improvement of prison-discipline'. Convicts were sent far away from their prisons, out of reach not only of effective supervision but also suitable food, shelter and medical attention. It was unhealthy work, especially during the monsoons, with many more prisoners dying on the roads than in prison.

Although the Prison Discipline Committee included no medical expert, high levels of sickness and death were deemed a legitimate cause for state concern and added momentum to the case for urgent reform. It was widely accepted that mortality in gaols greatly exceeded that outside. Since 1817 cholera epidemics had raged across India and the poor sanitation in prisons made them particularly susceptible. In the early 1830s as many as a fifth of gaol deaths were attributed to this.[25] But other diseases—including 'gaol fever' and dysentery—were also rife.

[21] Ibid., pp. 30–5.
[22] Ibid., pp. 69–70, 215–29.
[23] Ibid., pp. 38, 61.
[24] Ibid., pp. 11–17. NWP Criminal Judicial Procs. (CJP), no. 268, 24 April 1845, Oriental and India Office Collections (OIOC), British Library, London.
[25] In Bengal and NWP in 1833 there were 2,613 deaths, of which 585 were from cholera; in

In a single season prisons might lose a third or more of their inmates through disease: at Mangalore in 1838 151 prisoners (57 per cent) died, at least half of them from cholera.[26] Heavy mortality was thus a further factor in keeping India's prison populations relatively small. Overcrowded and poorly ventilated, full of filth and foul odours, prisons were seen in the medical topography of the time as paradigmatic sites for the generation of 'miasmatic' diseases. Few contemporary medical texts failed to mention them or see them as less than a pestilential threat to the towns and districts in which they were located.[27]

The Prison Discipline Committee called for a radical overhaul of Indian prisons: the substitution of work tasks within the prison for extramural labour; the replacement of food allowances by common messing; a more systematic division of prisoners into classes; increased use of solitary confinement and transportation, and less resort to fetters and chains; urgent improvement in prison health and sanitation; the recruitment of more dependable prison guards; and the construction of central prisons (or penitentiaries) where troublesome prisoners could be kept under close surveillance. However, the committee's recommendations left the Government of India unenthusiastic. Excessive cost was the main objection, especially as Lord Auckland's government had recently embarked on an expensive war in Afghanistan. But there were other considerations too that emphasised the inherent differences between prisons in India and Britain. Auckland remarked unfavourably on the 'extraordinary expense' of prison reform, but added that in no country was it

likely that greater difficulty will be experienced than in this. For the mere locality of the prison—that which is healthy in one season, may become a pest-house by a blast of fever or of cholera in another. For its form—the close yard which is adapted for classification and is not unwholesome in England, would be a sink of malaria in India. For food, for labour, and for consort—there are habits and an inveteracy of prejudice and of feeling bearing upon health, and almost upon life, opposing difficulties to the just management of prisons, such as are not elsewhere to be encountered, and, superadded to all this, is the absence of fitting instruments for control and management [upon which] ... the success of every scheme of discipline has been found to depend.[28]

1834, 472 deaths were from cholera and 2,236 from other causes: *Report ... on Prison Discipline*, appendix 19, pp. 1–3.

[26] *Report of the Inspector of Prisons, Fort St George, 1856*.

[27] For example, James Ranken, *Report on the Malignant Fever Called the Pali Plague*, Calcutta: G.H. Huttmann, 1838, pp. 198–206.

[28] Auckland, 8 October 1838, *Report ... on Prison Discipline*, p. 3. For further discussion of this report, see Singha, *Despotism of Law*, chapter 6.

The objections raised by Lord Auckland were to haunt prison policy and practice in India for decades to come. In the short term, most of the recommendations of the Prison Discipline Committee were ignored or postponed indefinitely and even those that were attempted soon encountered considerable difficulties.

REFORM AND RESISTANCE

However ineffective, the Prison Discipline Committee nonetheless marked the start of a series of all-India prison committees and conferences (1864, 1877, 1889, 1892, 1919–20), and from the 1840s a number of changes did begin to influence the ways in which India's prisons were run. One of the most evident changes was the construction of new prisons. Particular attention was given to building central gaols, and by 1877 there were twenty-six of these across British India.[29] It was in the central gaols in particular, confining those convicted of the most serious crimes, that attempts were made to incorporate the characteristic features of British and American penitentiaries, including high perimeter walls, separate accommodation for different classes of prisoner, cells for solitary confinement, yards for prison exercise, workshops for prison labour and an internal layout with a central tower and radiating wings that emulated London's Pentonville prison (completed in 1842).

The most influential proponent of the new prison regime was William Woodcock. A member of the Bengal Civil Service, Woodcock was appointed Inspector of Prisons for the North-Western Provinces in 1844 in order to recommend improvements and economies in the province's gaol administration. In practice Woodcock, subsequently elevated to the grander title of Inspector-General,[30] called for far-reaching reforms. That this reforming zeal came from NWP, rather than Bengal, might simply reflect the strength of Woodcock's personality and convictions. But it might also be indicative of the colonial belief that north India held a far more 'turbulent' population than Bengal (or Madras), and that this called for sterner discipline and more effective surveillance. Hailed as the 'pioneer of all jail improvements in India', and even as the 'Howard of India',

---

[29] *Indian Jail Conference* (1877), p. 14. For new central and district gaols in Madras, see W.J. Wilson, *Memorandum on the Progress of the Jail Department in the Madras Presidency from 1865 to 1874* (OIOC).

[30] The Government of India approved a permanent post of Inspector-General of Prisons for NWP in 1850: other provinces followed suit. A.P. Howell, *Note on Jails and Jail Discipline in India, 1867–68*, Calcutta: Superintendent of Government Printing, 1868, p. 4.

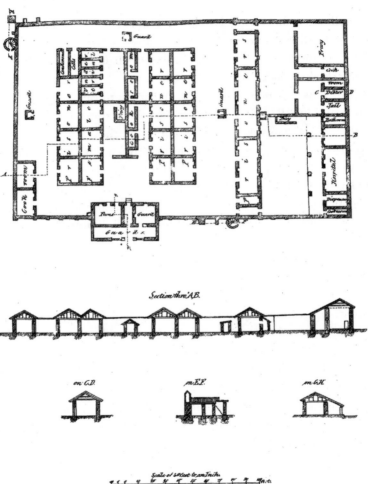

1. Plan and section of Coimbatore district gaol, 1856. [Library of the School of Oriental and African Studies].

Woodcock first drafted plans for a reformed prison in 1846.[31] Inspired less by the Prison Discipline Committee's report than by recent developments in Europe and America, Woodcock urged the NWP government to build central gaols that would allow separate confinement for different classes of prisoner (he believed there should be at least eight categories, including women, juveniles and lifers) and especially for total night-time segregation (along the lines of the 'separate system'). He praised the example of Allahabad gaol, completed in 1840, which had forty separate cells, used for short-term prisoners, hardened criminals and those in breach of gaol rules. He believed that this system produced in prisoners a 'quiet and subdued demeanour': it served to 'subdue the most refractory characters and to enforce the discipline of the prison'.[32] Construction of a new gaol to his own specifications began at Agra in 1849, incorporating both barracks on the 'associated' principle as well as cells for separate confinement, 'similar to those at Pentonville'. Agra gaol had a central tower 'from which radiate to the circumference 25 subdivisions, separated from each other by a blank wall high enough to prevent communication from one to the other. On top of the tower stands the sentry who commands all the radii ...'[33]

Similar plans for the 'economical' construction of prisons on the 'cellular system' were drafted in the 1850s, and the twenty-year period from the late 1840s marks the principal phase of 'modern' prison construction in India.[34] Considerable attention to technical detail went into the making of these prisons—it was extensively debated, for instance, whether, in India's hot and humid conditions, 500 cubic feet per prisoner provided sufficient air and ventilation.[35] It should be noted, though, that prison design and practice did not entirely follow metropolitan precedents. Most prisoners continued to be confined at night in barracks or wards. Separate or solitary cells were generally considered too costly for India, and even when such cells were built, or central observation towers erected, they rapidly fell into disuse, as was the case with Salem gaol in the Madras Presidency. It contained a central tower but, being accessible to so many prisoners, it was considered a potential source of danger, and abandoned.[36] In 1868 the Government

[31] Stewart Clark, *Practical Observations on the Hygiene of the Army in India*, London: Smith, Elder, 1864, p. 151.

[32] Woodcock, Report on NWP Jails, 29 January 1846, NWP CJP, no. 19, 4 March 1846 (OIOC).

[33] C.G. Wiehe, *Journal of a Tour of Inspection of the Principal Jails in India*, Bombay: Education Society's Press, 1865, p. 38.

[34] NWP CJP, no. 106, 9 May 1854 (OIOC).

[35] J. Rohde, *Report of the Inspector of Prisons, Fort St George, 1856*.

[36] Wiehe, *Journal*, p. 8.

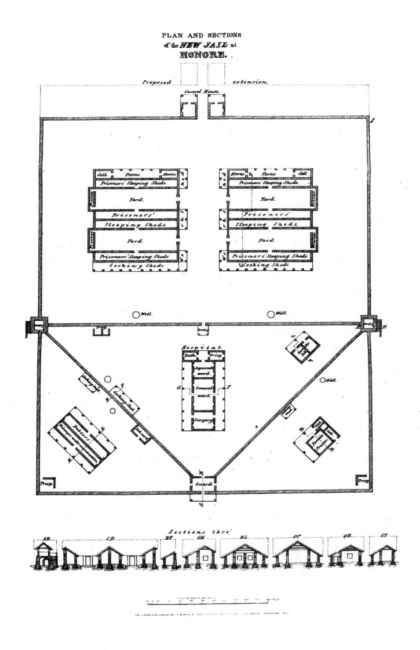

2. Plan and sections of the new district gaol, Honoré, 1856. [Library of the School of Oriental and African Studies]

of India formally abandoned the idea of single cells for Indian prisoners—partly for financial reasons, and on the grounds that in the Indian climate, small cells were difficult to ventilate, but also because, it claimed, India had fewer 'habitual' criminals than Britain. Moreover, Indians, being 'by nature gregarious', were unable to withstand the strain of solitary confinement. By the same token, however, as one viceroy noted, separation was the 'only punishment that a Native dreads'.[37]

By contrast with the central gaols, most district gaols remained modest affairs. Without surveillance towers and radiating wings, and with few facilities for solitary confinement, they often—as Figures 1 and 2 of the gaols at Coimbatore and Honoré (Honavar) in North Kanara in the mid-1850s show—consisted of single-storey buildings, surrounded by a perimeter wall, and equipped with a few guardhouses and sentry posts. Instead of an austere Benthamite panopticon, district gaols in South India followed a more relaxed principle of spatial separation, with ordinary convicts confined in 'sleeping sheds' or barracks, divided by internal walls from under-trial and female prisoners, 'lunatics' and debtors. Separate workrooms, cooking sheds and hospital wards were also provided and, as the cross-section of Honoré gaol shows, the buildings were constructed in a local style, with tiled roofs and *pials* or raised platforms, where prisoners, like their domestic counterparts, might sit to perform their daily tasks or relax and sleep.

Despite the recommendations of the Prison Discipline Committee, extramural work on the roads was only slowly phased out: many provincial administrations continued to believe it a cheap and efficient way of mobilising the labour needed for public works.[38] In 1844 in Madras more convicts worked on the roads than were kept in gaols, and in 1855, three-quarters of the 6,000 convicts still worked on the roads and related tasks. In 1877 the Indian Jail Conference affirmed the value of properly supervised labour on projects such as canal construction.[39] It was not until 1920 that the Indian Jails Committee directed that extramural labour finally be wound up in the few places where it still continued—Assam and the Andamans.[40] The continuing need for labour, especially in an era of state-funded public works, made governments reluctant to relinquish

[37] Howell, *Note on Jails*, pp. 18–19; Home Judicial (HJ), 14–15, 19 June 1869, National Archives of India, New Delhi (NAI); *Indian Jail Conference* (1877), p. 95.

[38] Appendix B to East India: Lords' Third Report, *Parliamentary Papers, Reports from Committees*, vol. 23, 1852–3, pp. 114–17.

[39] Ibid., p. 118; 'General statement of convicts', *Report of the Inspector of Prisons, Fort St George, 1856; Indian Jail Conference* (1877), pp. 109–12.

[40] *Report of the Indian Jails Committee, 1919–20*, vol. 1, Simla: Government Press, 1920, pp. 129–31.

this readily available source, and the contribution it made to projects essential to the development of India's economic infrastructure.

But increasingly prisoners were obliged to labour inside the gaols. The incentives for this shift were largely financial, though the change was justified as being more conducive to prison discipline and reform, as the prisoner's 'life of ease' was replaced by one of improving toil.[41] In the second half of the nineteenth century prisons became major manufactories, producing gunny bags, blankets, carpets, boots and other industrial goods; some made paper and ran quality printing presses. In addition to meeting the prison's internal needs, gaol industries also supplied other government departments, including the police and army. Workshops might (in theory) teach prisoners useful crafts, or (as with weaving and carpet-making) utilise skills already present among convicts, but they also generated a sizeable income, thereby saving the government a considerable part of prison costs. Alipur gaol became one of the most lucrative centres of prison industry: in 1861 its printing work earned Rs 210,000 and the manufacture of gunny bags a further Rs 59,952. Visitors were impressed—though often less by the penal effect of this labour than by 'the purely industrial nature of the institution'.[42] When Mary Carpenter, the only leading British penal reformer to visit nineteenth-century India, toured Alipur gaol in 1866 she found prisoners hard at work in the printing and lithography shops. They appeared to enjoy considerable freedom and to toil with apparent goodwill, without needing to be goaded by constant threats. She thought, however, that the system was too lax.[43]

By the early 1880s, as industry expanded elsewhere, the accusation was levied that these were in effect state-subsidised industries and so unfairly competitive with private enterprise. Manufacturers and chambers of commerce urged that their activities be restricted by being denied the use of steam-powered machinery. If only from financial self-interest, the government declined to comply.[44] Gaol industries were profitable and useful. And yet the relationship between the prison and the colonial economy was complex and often contradictory. Prisons could not simply be used to create or discipline a new labour force. The bulk of India's prisoners came from the rural population and, on their release from gaol, were

---

[41] 'Prison Discipline in India', p. 470.

[42] Wiehe, *Journal*, pp. 18, 23. 'In the Central Provinces the remunerative theory of labour has been pushed very far, so far in fact that, in reading the reports, it is often difficult to believe that prison labour and not factory labour is in question': Howell, *Note*, p. 42.

[43] Mary Carpenter, *Six Months in India*, London: Longman, Green, 1868, vol. 1, pp. 200–1.

[44] HJ, 121–52, October 1882; 328–51, June 1883; 14–23, September 1883 (NAI); *Indian Jails Committee* (1919–20), pp. 120–5.

unlikely to enter the urban, industrial sector. Although special laws were passed in the late nineteenth century to regulate labour in the tea-growing districts of Assam and the northeast, planters were reluctant to see absconding workers sent to gaol if they could be induced to return to work by other, less disruptive, means. Putting workers in gaol could do little to solve their desperate labour needs.[45]

Opportunities for escape diminished as new prisons were built and as gaol industries replaced extramural labour, but prisoners remained far from passive— or secure—in the hands of their warders. In a raid on Agra gaol in December 1846 fifty to sixty armed men scaled the prison walls, drove off the sentries, and freed 192 prisoners from their wards. Of the fifty-one inmates who fled the gaol, fifteen were killed and twelve wounded in the following pursuit.[46] Some prisoners objected to working the flourmills introduced at Agra and elsewhere in the 1840s and, in a prison version of 'everyday resistance', 'continued wilfully to injure the machinery, and to throw them out of gear, and themselves out of work for 4 or 5 days at a time'. Since the machines cost Rs 1,000 to 1,500 apiece, the Inspector of Prisons was hardly pleased.[47] Similarly, prison industries like shoemaking raised afresh issues about the recognition afforded to caste in prison and the differential treatment of prisoners. Since it was stated that prison labour should not cause the loss of caste, polluting leather working was confined to low-caste prisoners.[48]

On a second reforming front, efforts were made to replace the money doles given for prisoners to buy their own food with a more tightly disciplined system of common messing. Initial moves were made in 1841 but immediately encountered opposition. Rather than ignore caste altogether (as the Prison Discipline Committee had proposed), at Chapra gaol in Bihar in June 1842 the 620 prisoners were divided according to caste and religion into fifty-two messes, each with its own prisoner cook. The cooks, however, were first to rebel, and ten of them were whipped for disobedience. The prisoners then rose *en masse*, and though unable to break out of the gaol, some 3–4,000 townspeople (abetted by local *zamindars*

---

[45] *Special Report on the Working of Act I of 1882 in the Province of Assam, 1886–1889*, Calcutta: Superintendent, Government Printing, 1890, pp. 175–98.

[46] NWP CJP, no. 153, 26 January 1847 (OIOC).

[47] Woodcock, Report on NWP Jails (1846). On 'everyday resistance', see James C. Scott, *Weapons of the Weak: Everyday forms of peasant resistance*, New Haven, CT: Yale University Press, 1985.

[48] Madras Judicial Procs (MJP), no. 75, 19 April 1871; no. 98, 24 October 1871 (OIOC). 'In allotting labour to convicts reasonable allowance shall be made for caste prejudice, e.g., no Brahman or caste Hindu shall be employed in chucklers' [leather-workers'] work. Care shall, however, be taken that caste prejudice is not made an excuse for avoiding heavy forms of labour.' *The Madras Jail Manual*, Madras: Lawrence Asylum Steam Press, 1899, p. 121.

or landholders) gathered in their support. Peace was restored only when the magistrate, believing that force could not prevail against such strongly held 'prejudices', suspended common messing. Further disturbances followed across northern India, including at Patna gaol in September 1845, where again the military was called out, and eighteen prisoners died, and at Allahabad in May 1846 where four prisoners were killed and fifteen wounded. The ringleaders received thirty strokes of the rattan as punishment.[49]

By 1846 the new messing system had been introduced wholly or partly into twenty-five of the forty gaols in NWP, but many officials continued to believe it unenforceable. Even if Brahmin and Rajput prisoners were the principal antagonists, it was, said one judge, 'an universally acknowledged fact that the prisoners one and all are opposed to it'.[50] Woodcock, the provincial Inspector-General, believed that the loss of 'one of the luxuries of life, viz, of cooking their own food', and not caste, lay behind the disturbances, but the government was obliged to acknowledge that, whatever the underlying cause, the introduction of messing was making 'our prison system exceedingly unpopular with the country at large'.[51] F.J. Halliday, a former Secretary to the Government of Bengal, remarked with some scepticism that when the messing system was first introduced in Bihar, 'it was a matter of great surprise how many [caste] subdivisions arose, which nobody had heard of before, but which were admitted as such after full enquiry'. Some, he thought, were 'got up by the prisoners themselves in order to throw obstacles in the way of the scheme'.[52] The Bengal and NWP governments persisted with the system, supposedly without compulsion and without 'doing violence to the prejudices or the feelings of the people'.[53] Nonetheless, opposition rumbled on into the 1850s.[54]

This ongoing resistance demonstrated the practical limits to colonial authority, even within the seemingly assured environs of the gaol, but it also showed the extent to which the prison had become a battlefield over caste and what were

---

[49] 'Prison Discipline in India', *Calcutta Review*, 6, 12 (1846), pp. 492–4. Flogging remained common into the 1880s: 'Corporal punishment and mortality in Indian jails', *Parliamentary Papers*, 48, Cmd 3316, 1882, pp. 3–4.

[50] A. Lang to Woodcock, 20 May 1846, NWP CJP, no. 5, 1 July 1846 (OIOC).

[51] Woodcock to Sec., NWP, 30 May 1846; J. Thornton, Sec., NWP to Sec., Bengal, 1 July 1846, NWP CJP, no. 5, 1 July 1846 (OIOC).

[52] F.J. Halliday, evidence, 12 April 1853, East India: Lords' First Report, *Parliamentary Papers, Reports from Committees*, vol. 31, 1852–3, pp. 386.

[53] J. Thornton, 30 April 1847, NWP CJP, no. 103, 30 April 1847 (OIOC).

[54] NWP CJP, no. 296, 14 February 1854; nos 298–300, 368–70, 14 February 1854; no. 301, 16 March 1855 (OIOC).

seen to be the impositions of colonial rule. It was a particular concern to the British that the rebellious convicts enjoyed influential public support and that some of the leaders of gaol revolts came from the same castes—Brahmins and Rajputs—that were relied upon for recruitment into the Bengal Army. Indeed many of the issues affecting prisoners and the gaols (over dieting and dress, for instance, or transportation/service overseas), mirrored those that caused discontent in the army.[55] It was not surprising, then, that opposition within the gaols, and public support for it, carried over into the early stages of the sepoy mutiny and revolt of 1857. Mirat, where the uprising began, was one of several places where prisoners were liberated and gaol buildings destroyed.[56]

It was not only in the minds of colonial officials, or, from an opposing perspective, those of rebels and mutineers, that prisons constituted symbolic or exemplary sites. It was felt by some Europeans that the toleration of caste practices in prison, apart from undermining its deterrent effect, represented dire neglect of the government's Christian responsibilities. In 1858 the Scottish missionary Alexander Duff argued that the Mutiny showed the 'monumental evil of pandering or truckling to the prejudices and pretensions of caste'. He deplored the way in which caste had been 'basely and indecently succumbed to in our jails'. Prisoners had been 'allowed to purchase their own articles of diet, to cook and partake of their own food separately, to drink exclusively from their own *lotas* [water-pots] ... in short, to practise and preserve inviolate all the minutiae and mummeries of the caste system.' 'That caste usages should be ubiquitously yielded to in the case of otherwise well-behaved citizens is bad enough', he complained; 'but that these should be so unworthily submitted to in the case of *felons* or *condemned criminals* must surely be the very climax of sinful weakness.'[57]

Similar issues relating to caste and religion surrounded debates about education in Indian gaols. Duff was not alone in believing that prisoners should receive religious (i.e. Christian) instruction: Inspector J. Rohde, head of the Madras prisons, held a similar opinion in the 1850s. But, wary of antagonising prisoners and the public by seeming to favour proselytising, governments declined to sanction such proposals.[58] The general view was, anyway, that giving convicts an education

---

[55] In Awadh in 1862 nearly 30 per cent of prisoners came from the Brahmin and Rajput castes: *Report of the Inspector of Prisons in Oudh, 1862*, pp. 74–5. For grievances in the army, see Seema Alavi, *The Sepoys and the Company: Tradition and transition in northern India, 1770–1830*, Delhi: Oxford University Press, 1995, pp. 49–55, 75–9.

[56] Wiehe, *Journal*, p. 45; John Kaye, *History of the Indian Mutiny of 1857–8*, vol. 1, 2nd ed., London: W.H. Allen, 1891, pp. 141–5.

[57] Alexander Duff, *The Indian Rebellion: Its causes and results*, London: James Nisbet, 1858, pp. 354–5.

[58] MJP, no. 168, 7 February 1857 (OIOC). Cf. the more determined approach to prison education

was a waste of time and resources, or afforded them a privilege not enjoyed by others of their class.[59] Some secular instruction was given, but it was offered in 'a spirit of indifference', as much to aid gaol industries as to reform prisoners or benefit them on their release.[60]

Despite the absence of a medical expert on the Prison Discipline Committee of 1836–8, the gaols shifted from control of the magistracy into the professional and scientific care of the colonial medical service, so much so that by the close of the century it was authoritatively stated that 'medical administration is the most important of all matters affecting jail management'.[61] Concern at high rates of sickness and mortality was the main reason behind the appointment of a second prison committee in 1864, and led to the introduction of new measures to improve prison conditions (at the same time as fresh consideration was being given to army health and urban sanitation). Prison construction was accompanied by detailed attention to issues of ventilation, drainage and the proper disposal of human waste.[62] Most prisons possessed a hospital, however rudimentary, under an Indian doctor. The trend from the 1860s was for prison mortality to fall, and by 1919 prison officers could confidently claim that 'In no branch of Indian jail administration has progress been so marked and so satisfactory as in matters relating to the health of prisoners.'[63] The health, rather than the reform and rehabilitation, of prisoners became the standard by which the colonial prison administration judged its achievements, relative success in one sphere compensating for abject failure in the other. Short term, though, epidemics continued to wreak heavy mortality, as at Mirat in 1851 and 1856. Salem gaol had to be closed down and rebuilt in 1856 because mortality had been running at 18 per cent a year, half of

in Britain: William James Forsythe, *The Reform of Prisoners, 1830–1900*, London: Croom Helm, 1987, chapter 2.

[59] Martin Richard Gubbins, *An Account of the Mutinies in Oudh*, London: Richard Bentley, 1858, p. 77.

[60] NWP CJP, no. 112, 9 May 1854 (OIOC); *Report of the Committee Appointed on Jail Administration in India*, Calcutta: Superintendent of Government Printing, 1889, p. 80.

[61] *Rules for the Superintendence and Management of Jails in the Province of Assam*, vol. 1, Calcutta: Superintendent of Government Printing, 1899, p. 224. On the medicalisation of the prison, see David Arnold, *Colonizing the Body: State medicine and epidemic disease in nineteenth-century India*, Berkeley, CA: University of California Press, 1993, chapter 2, and 'The Colonial Prison: Power, knowledge and penology in nineteenth-century India' in David Arnold and David Hardiman (eds), *Subaltern Studies VIII*, Delhi: Oxford University Press, 1994, pp. 148–87.

[62] James Hutchinson, *Observations on the General and Medical Management of Indian Jails*, 2nd ed., Calcutta: G.H. Huttmann, 1845.

[63] J. Mulvaney, 2 September 1919, *Indian Jails Committee* (1919–20), vol. 2, p. 41.

it from cholera.[64] Over the quarter-century from 1843 to 1867, 40,550 prisoners died in the gaols of Bengal, more than a fifth of them from cholera.[65] Only gradually did prisons cease to be sinks of mortality.

In the absence of a dedicated prison service, from the 1860s members of the Indian Medical Service (whose principal duties were to provide medical aid to the Indian Army) supplied most of the inspectors–general of prisons and super-intendents of central gaols. The Indian Jail Conference of 1877 was essentially a medical affair, as, to a large degree, was its successor in 1889. Under the supervision of medical officers, gaols became convenient sites for the investigation and control of diseases affecting society at large. All prisoners were vaccinated against smallpox (unless already protected against the disease), and by the 1900s many prisoners were regularly dosed with quinine as a prophylactic against malaria.[66] Given the intensity of public opposition to post–mortems, prison was one of the few places where British doctors had access to Indian corpses for medical examination.[67] Pioneering research was conducted in the gaols into 'tropical' diseases like ankylostomiasis, beri-beri, cholera and *kala-azar*, which had important implications for the health and productivity of India's labouring classes.[68] Similarly, much of what came to be known about Indian diets and their physiological effects before the 1920s was drawn from prison observation.[69]

CHANGING PRISON POPULATIONS

The half-century following the report of the Prison Discipline Committee saw an overall increase in the size of India's prison population (British-held territory in India also expanded considerably during this period). In 1836 the average daily number of prisoners had been 56,632. For the ten years up to the end of 1862 the total number of prisoners passing through gaol annually (including

[64] John Murray, *Report on the Attack of Cholera in the Central Prison at Agra, in 1856*, Agra: Secundra Orphan Press, 1856; *Report of the Inspector of Prisons, Fort St George, 1856*.

[65] Howell, *Note*, p. 124.

[66] Home (Jails), nos 11–15, January 1910 (NAI).

[67] E.A. Parkes, *Remarks on the Dysentery and Hepatitis of India*, London: Longman, Brown, Green and Longman, 1846, p. x.

[68] For example, K.S. Mhaskar, 'Report on the Ankylostomiasis Inquiry in Madras', *Indian Medical Research Memoirs*, 1 (1924), pp. iii, 10–12.

[69] T.R. Lewis, 'A Memorandum on the Dietaries of Labouring Prisoners in Indian Jails', *Annual Report of the Sanitary Commissioner of the Government of India, 1880*, pp. 155–206; D. McCay, *Investigations into the Jail Dietaries of the United Provinces*, Calcutta: Superintendent Government Printing, 1912.

Burma and the princely states of Mysore and Hyderabad) was put at 589,981; for the subsequent ten years it was 883,990.[70] This still represented a small fraction of the total population. In 1875 that proportion varied from 190 prisoners for every 100,000 of the population in Punjab and NWP to 110 in Bombay, 90 in Bengal, and 80 in Madras. Nowhere in India proper did the figure approach the 460 per 100,000 of British Burma.[71]

There was much internal administrative debate about the factors underlying the apparent increase in crime, and hence in the number of those convicted. One cause was said to be 'the weakening of the collective responsibilities of villagers, the increased opportunities which improved methods of communication give to the criminal classes, and, more than all, the growth of individualism, and the gradual disintegration of the archaic ties by which Native society is held together'.[72] But the size of the prison population also reflected a number of short-term or cyclical factors. Among these was the impact of local uprisings, such as the Santhal Rebellion in 1855, and more especially the Indian Mutiny and Rebellion of 1857–8. Although large numbers of rebels were killed or summarily executed in the suppression of this revolt, thousands more were sentenced to long-term imprisonment. Many were sent to Port Blair in the Andamans, where the penal settlement came to hold not just mutineers but also those convicted of murder and other serious offences. By 1866 over 6,000 convicts were located there.[73] In 1857 transportation had been abolished in Britain, and in India in 1868 it was restricted to life convicts (though some exceptions were made for Port Blair). Only by the 1880s had transportation finally become discredited as a deterrent. 'The returned convicts from Port Blair, who give glowing accounts of the life of a self-supporting settler, have entirely dissipated that idea.'[74]

The establishment of provincial police forces in the late 1850s and early 1860s may have contributed to the growing number of prisoners, as detection rates rose; so too may the declining use of capital punishment and whipping.[75] But

[70] *Indian Jail Conference* (1877), p. 125. The average *daily* number of prisoners in Bengal between 1863 and 1892 was 17,329.

[71] Ibid., p. 22. See Ian Brown's essay in this volume for the possible factors behind high rates of incarceration in Burma.

[72] *Indian Jail Conference* (1877), pp. 18–19.

[73] Howell, *Note*, pp. 62–3.

[74] *Committee … [on] Jail Administration in India*, p. 137.

[75] In 1868 it was claimed that imprisonment was used in 99 per cent of all sentences: Howell, *Note*, p. 1. However, as late as the 1940s the rate of executions remained high—in Punjab alone around 200 a year. F.A. Barker, *The Modern Prison System of India*, London: Macmillan, 1944, p. xiii.

the fluctuating size of prison populations also reflected recurrent food shortages and the famines that repeatedly struck India in the second half of the century. In the Madras Presidency, for instance, the average number of individuals passing through the gaols for each of the three years 1863–6 was 24,737, but in the famine year 1866–7 it reached 31,692, before falling back to 29,060 in 1867–8. In Bengal, prison numbers rose from 77,091 in 1863–4 to 81,970 in 1864–5, and 90,333 in 1865–6, but, reflecting the impact of dearth and famine in Orissa and neighbouring areas, jumped to 114,870 in 1866–7, before declining to 89,120 the following year. Most of those convicted in connection with 'famine crime' were given short sentences, occasioning a debate as to whether those sentenced had actively sought prison as a means of ensuring their survival, and so did not form part of the 'criminal classes' as such, and whether prison life should be made even harsher so as to deter people whose existence outside the gaol was already as bad as, if not worse than, inside it.[76] In practice the medicalisation of the prison militated against more punitive arguments. Close attention was paid to giving prisoners sufficient food to maintain health and a capacity for labour. It was sometimes felt that this was done at the expense of effective discipline, but that there was little choice. If prisoners were not adequately fed, or if they were subjected to stern discipline, they tended to 'die off'. 'The constitution of the Native prisoners apparently will not bear it', Halliday claimed in 1853. Few suicides were reported, but prisoners became 'depressed' and were inclined to 'sink under what we should think but a moderate amount of discipline within a gaol'.[77]

Roughly a third of prison sentences before 1914 were for less than one month—hence the disparity between the relatively small average daily tally of prisoners and the far larger number who passed through gaol each year.[78] From the few detailed breakdowns that exist of prisoners' backgrounds it is clear that they were drawn from a wide cross-section of the population—mostly rural, but ranging from high-caste Hindus and high-status Muslims to low-caste groups and untouchables. In Awadh in the early 1860s more than half the prisoners were cultivators, but substantial numbers also came from 'service castes', the labouring classes and trading communities, with smaller numbers of *zamindars*, shopkeepers,

---

[76] *Indian Jail Conference* (1877), pp. 20–1. During the famines recourse was also had to other state institutions, including dispensaries and even lock hospitals intended for the confinement and treatment of prostitutes: Sarah Hodges, '"Looting" the Lock Hospital in Colonial Madras during the Famine Years of the 1870s', *Social History of Medicine*, 18, 3 (2005), pp. 379–98.

[77] East India: First Lords' Report, *Reports from Committees*, 1852–3, p. 385.

[78] *Indian Jails Committee* (1919–20), p. 227. This was not very different from the situation in England and Wales: cf. Forsythe, *Reform of Prisoners*, p. 94.

weavers, goldsmiths and 'beggars'. Fewer than 5 per cent of the 4,458 prisoners in Awadh's gaols were literate.[79]

On the other hand, accumulating statistical evidence was taken to indicate that the number of reconvicted prisoners—put in the early 1870s at 10 to 20 per cent—was increasing. Behind this, it was believed, lay the pernicious presence of India's 'criminal tribes and castes', whose reform could not be achieved by imprisonment alone.[80] From 1871 a series of Criminal Tribes Acts restricted the movements of repeat offenders, subjecting them to close surveillance by the police and magistracy, and imposing virtual detention without trial and confinement to specially designated settlements (which lay outside the control of the prison authorities and beyond the purview of gaol statistics).[81] This trend reflected a growing colonial engagement with the ideas of criminology emanating from Europe, associated from the late 1870s with Cesare Lombroso's work on 'criminal types', and supported by a close alliance between anthropology and colonial control.[82] However, in India this new criminal sociology was directed not, as in Europe, at a new underclass of migrant workers and urban poor but at long-established caste groups and marginalised rural populations. One of its consequences was to diminish the authority medical officers had hitherto held over prison discipline and the treatment of prisoners, and to increase the role of police officers and civil servants, groups that were far more strongly represented in the prison conferences and committees of 1892 and 1919–20 than in those of previous years.

PRISON LIFE

We can use the period of the mature prison system, between the 1840s and 1890s, to consider more closely prisoners' experience of gaol life and how prisons actually functioned. While the higher echelons of the prison administration were staffed by European civil servants and medical officers, the lower ranks were largely tenanted by Indians. As seen in Figs 1 and 2, most of the subordinate

---

[79] *Report of the Inspector of Prisons in Oudh, 1862*, pp. 52–77.

[80] *Indian Jail Conference* (1877), pp. 22, 33–8.

[81] There is an extensive literature on the Criminal Tribes legislation, including Anand A. Yang, 'Dangerous Castes and Tribes: The Criminal Tribes Act and the Magahiya Doms of northeast India' in Anand A. Yang (ed.), *Crime and Criminality in British India*, Tucson, AZ: University of Arizona Press, 1985, pp. 108–27; David Arnold, *Police Power and Colonial Rule: Madras, 1859–1947*, Delhi: Oxford University Press, 1986, pp. 138–47.

[82] Nicholas B. Dirks, *Castes of Mind: Colonialism and the making of modern India*, Princeton University Press, 2001, pp. 181–8; Anderson, *Legible Bodies*, chapter 6.

prison staff lived inside or on the perimeters of the gaol, in close proximity to the prisoners. The gaol establishment consisted of a head gaoler, aided by warders (*peons*), a 'native' doctor or dresser, and several clerks, sometimes augmented by an executioner. A recurrent colonial complaint was that India could never possess as effective a prison system as Britain or the United States because it lacked reliable warders. 'We have not an unlimited command of European agency', lamented A.P. Howell in 1868, 'and it is difficult to find good agents for such a purpose among our Native subjects.'[83] European gaolers were mostly limited to central gaols, like the Madras Penitentiary, or wherever significant numbers of white prisoners were held.[84]

It was at the interface between prisoner and warder that many of the evils of the prison system arose. Warders abused their powers by extorting money, goods and services from prisoners, beating or confining them without authorisation.[85] As late as the 1850s a significant proportion of warders were themselves punished each year for neglecting their duties. Some ended up behind bars for smuggling in tobacco and betel or aiding prisoners to escape; others were fined, lost wages or were dismissed.[86] Warders were usually local men, who, like the majority of prisoners in district gaols, were bound by shared 'ties and sympathies' to the extramural population.[87] Prison work was generally unpopular as well as poorly remunerated: in the early twentieth century the annual turnover of prison warders in the Bombay Presidency was as high as 25 per cent. Moreover, as the 1919–20 Indian Jails Committee remarked, the warder was 'but little less of a prisoner than the inmates whom it is his duty to guard'.[88]

In a further blurring of the distinction between convicts and warders, Indian gaols made extensive use of prisoners as warders, a practice that began among Indian convicts in Malaya, then spread back to India.[89] By the late nineteenth century as many as 10 per cent of prisoners were employed as 'convict officers'. The argument for their use was primarily one of economy, though it was also claimed that giving deserving convicts responsibility for other prisoners aided their reform.

[83] Howell, *Note*, p. 1.
[84] 'Permanent establishment of the several jails', *Report of the Inspector of Prisons, Fort St George, 1856*.
[85] HJ, nos 1–7, 1 July 1864 (NAI).
[86] *Report of the Inspector General of Prisons, Madras, 1857–58*, pp. 57–69.
[87] Fred J. Mouat, *Report on Jails Visited and Inspected in Bengal, Behar, and Arracan*, Calcutta: Military Orphan Press, 1856, p. 109.
[88] *Indian Jails Committee* (1919–20), p. 56.
[89] *Indian Jail Conference* (1877), pp. 70–3. In Bengal in 1867 1,647 prisoners served as warders, guards and overseers, roughly 8 per cent of the total: Howell, *Note*, p. 87.

They were entrusted with keeping order over fellow inmates, in return for which they were given minor (but valued) concessions, such as being allowed to smoke or excused from wearing the standard prison uniform. They were permitted to eat and sleep apart from other prisoners, and in NWP were paid Rs 3 or 4 a month and authorized 'to wear their hair and beards as in ordinary life'.[90]

Since some convict warders came from the lower castes, even from 'criminal tribes', their position could represent a significant inversion of the normal caste hierarchy, a reversal many high-caste prisoners strongly deprecated. Critics of the system also argued that convict warders were responsible for much of the criminality and vice in prison (especially at night when they had charge of locked sleeping sheds)—smuggling drugs and other prohibited items into the prison, extracting bribes and sexual favours from both male and female inmates, directing the assaults and murders that kept other prisoners under their sway. It was they, many critics alleged, who turned Indian prisons into 'schools of vice'.[91] In her account of Ahmedabad gaol in 1866, Mary Carpenter complained that the 'salutary' effect on prisoners of a day's labour was 'completely neutralised, or even worse, by the corrupting influences of the night'. She may have had sexual practices in mind (what others referred to as 'the evils of night association' or 'unnatural crimes'),[92] but it was the transmission of criminal, rather than carnal, knowledge that she emphasised. 'No man', she declared, 'convicted of a first offence only can enter this place, which ought to be one of punishment and attempted reformation, without the greatest probability of contamination, and in gaining experience in evil from the adepts of crime who are confined with him; no young boy can enter without his fate being sealed for life!'[93]

Inmates often evaded regulations or turned them to their own advantage. They smuggled in goods they were not officially permitted to possess but which might help to preserve their individuality or sanity, or which entered the commerce of the gaol—books, writing materials, musical instruments, playing cards, betel, tobacco, opium, bhang, knives and the occasional file. As elsewhere, Indian prisoners found opportunities to communicate among themselves (even when

---

[90] William Walker, *Rules for the Management and Discipline of Prisoners in the North-Western Provinces and Oudh*, Allahabad: North-Western Provinces and Oudh Government Press, 1882, pp. 42, 115–16.

[91] Mary Carpenter, 'On Reformatory and Industrial Schools for India', *Journal of the National Indian Association*, 47 (1874) p. 277.

[92] Wiehe, *Journal*, pp. 33, 48.

[93] Carpenter, *Six Months*, vol. 1, p. 49; cf. V.O. Chidambaram Pillai's evidence to *Indian Jails Committee* (1919–20), vol. 2, pp. 268–9.

confined in 'separate' cells),[94] and with relatives and friends outside the prison. They also feigned infirmity or insanity to avoid hard labour or in the hope that being sent to the prison hospital would facilitate their escape. Apart from aiding medical knowledge, one function of the post-mortems carried out in gaols was said to be to deter prisoners from trying to escape by pretending to be dead.[95]

By the 1870s prison manuals had been compiled for every province of British India. Part of the wider move in the second half of the nineteenth century to systematise colonial knowledge, the manuals sought to lay down regulations for virtually every aspect of gaol life, dividing prisoners into different classes (according to the nature of their crimes and by age, sex and race) and specifying appropriate forms of punishment, labour and dietary regime. Inmates were usually dressed in prison uniform, though even here concessions might be made according to caste and religion. They were required to wear a wooden ticket, coloured clothing or some other device to indicate the nature of their crime and length of sentence. Disobedience was met in a variety of ways—by solitary confinement, whipping, a reduced diet or loss of privileges. The use of the rattan to maintain internal discipline long remained in force: officially it was applied to the bare buttocks and not the back of the prisoner and, in Bengal at least, restricted to no more than thirty strokes. In 1875 there were 13,301 cases of corporal punishment in Indian gaols, but by 1914–18 this had dropped to 293 a year.[96] One of the duties of prison doctors was to sanction physical punishments on those deemed healthy enough to withstand them or, conversely, to grant exemptions. This unpopular duty brought them into the frontline of gaol discipline.

Prison food was intended to be as basic as that of the poorest labouring classes outside: it generally consisted of rice, wheat or millet (according to the local staple), supplemented with a few vegetables and condiments. Some even received ghee; a luxury men of their class would never know at home, declared Inspector F.J. Mouat of Bengal in 1856, ordering its withdrawal.[97] But in matters of diet, as in many other regards, differences were observed with respect to race and religion. In particular, European prisoners (of whom there were a substantial number)[98] received larger portions of food and were given a diet (including

---

[94] Wiehe, *Journal*, p. 53.

[95] Walker, *Rules*, p. 57. For further discussion of prison 'sub-culture', see Arnold, 'Colonial Prison'.

[96] George Alexander Hodge, *The Bengal Jail Manual*, Calcutta: Thomas S. Smith, 1867, p. 100; Barker, *Modern Prison*, p. 34.

[97] Mouat, *Report*, p. 105.

[98] In 1878 there were 1,230 male and fourteen female European prisoners: the figure included some Eurasians and military convicts sentenced by courts martial. *Indian Jail Conference* (1877), pp. 176–7.

beef and potatoes) that accorded with their presumed customs and constitutional needs. Chinese and Malay prisoners also received special dietary treatment.[99] Such was the concern not to diminish the status of whites by close confinement with Indians that separate wings, even entire prisons, were built exclusively for Europeans. Such gaols were usually situated in the cooler climate of a hill-station like Ootacamund.[100] White prisoners were almost invariably placed under European gaolers (commonly ex-soldiers), and their labour might be no more arduous than tailoring or digging in the prison vegetable garden. In the Madras Penitentiary in the 1860s Europeans were allowed books, but, unlike Indians, were obliged to attend divine service once a week. They also had a separate hospital.[101]

The treatment of women prisoners is more difficult to determine, partly because they were far fewer in number than men. At Agra gaol in 1844 there were forty-six female to 937 male convicts (5 per cent): here women tended trees in the yard while men toiled on the roads.[102] By the 1860s Bengal had its own women's prison at Russa near Alipur, which housed around 170 women and where the warders' duties were performed by female convicts.[103] In 1881 there were 402,823 male prisoners in British India but only 23,718 females (5.9 per cent): in 1891 the figures were 526,804 to 24,933 (4.7 per cent). In Britain the proportion of women prisoners was roughly twice as high, around 9 per cent.[104] While it was claimed that women committed crime from 'passion and impulse' rather than from material want,[105] by the late nineteenth century, as the targeting of 'criminal tribes and castes' increased, many low-caste women were gaoled for belonging to 'thieving and begging castes'. Women also came under increased judicial scrutiny following the Infanticide Act of 1870, which made them liable to imprisonment for killing their babies (often the unwelcome result of cross-caste liaisons or prohibitions on widow remarriage). They were imprisoned too

---

[99] For example, J. Cruikshank, *A Manual of Jail Rules for the Superintendence and Management of Jails in the Bombay Presidency*, Bombay: Government Central Press, 1876, pp. 55–8.

[100] Following the substitution of penal servitude for transportation in 1855, it was proposed to house all European prisoners in a single gaol in the Nilgiris. When this proved impractical, each province was required to make its own provision. MJP, nos 22–6, 4 September 1861, nos 121–2, 21 November 1861 (OIOC).

[101] Wiehe, *Journal*, pp. 3–6, 12–15.

[102] NWP CJP, no. 131, 11 April 1845 (OIOC).

[103] Wiehe, *Journal*, p. 23; Howell, *Note*, p. 32.

[104] Mary Frances Billington, *Woman in India*, 1895, reprint New Delhi: Amarko Book Agency, 1973, pp. 240–1.

[105] *Indian Jail Conference* (1877), p. 104.

for murdering their starving children during famines such as that of 1876–8 in Madras and Bombay. In the late nineteenth century as many as 80 per cent of women prisoners may have been gaoled for infanticide.[106] Women convicts were assigned separate quarters within the prison compound, walled off from other prison buildings (Figs 1 and 2), though the actual extent of their segregation varied, and instances of sexual contact with male prisoners or guards suggest that this was sometimes ineffectual.[107] In 1866 Carpenter reported that conditions for women prisoners in the Bombay Presidency were appalling: they were confined to a 'dismal ward', slept six or eight to a cell, were left 'utterly uncared for', under the superintendence of male warders and 'without any means of improvement'. She thought their accommodation better in Madras and especially at Alipur.[108] Conditions may have improved subsequently. In Madras gaol in the early 1890s the thirty-three women prisoners (out of a total of 870 prisoners) were under the charge of a European matron, a 'native' wardress and a convict warder from the weaver caste. They were allowed to keep their babies with them until they were two years old and, apart from some weaving and carpet-making, were employed in pounding grain for other inmates. Although corporal punishment and solitary confinement were prohibited, women were subject to certain gender-specific sanctions, such as having their hair shaved (in India a sign of widowhood but regarded by some colonial officials as a legitimate assault on their 'vanity'), though this was said not to happen in Madras.[109]

THE POLITICAL PRISON

From the 1890s, and especially after 1919, India's prisons entered a new and more overtly political phase. Of course the prison always had been in some sense 'political'. It had from the outset been instrumental in maintaining colonial authority and in punishing those who directly or indirectly threatened British power. But from the 1890s the colonial state began to be confronted by political movements that openly sought to end British rule and establish India's national sovereignty. Just as imprisonment constituted one of the principal means by which the colonial state sought to contain nationalist opposition, so nationalist 'gaol-going' became one of the main vehicles of anti-colonial defiance. In what has widely

[106] Ibid., p. 243; Padma Anagol, 'The Emergence of the Female Criminal in India: Infanticide and survival under the Raj', *History Workshop Journal*, 53 (2002), pp. 73–93.
[107] Mouat, *Report*, p. 63.
[108] Carpenter, *Six Months*, vol. 1, pp. 71, 103–5, 115, 202.
[109] Billington, *Woman*, pp. 244–7; *Indian Jail Conference* (1877), p. 104.

been seen as a 'new chapter' in India's prison history,[110] middle-class involvement in political activity and prison life created new tensions, making issues of class at times as central to the early twentieth century as questions of caste and religion had been to the nineteenth (though issues of caste and class were seldom entirely distinct). Political prisoners sought to distance themselves from the 'criminal' population of the gaols, and yet, over issues like diet, dress and work regimes, became embroiled in similar areas of dispute.

One can date the advent of the 'political prison' to the 1890s.[111] During this decade the British began to encounter a new, more militant form of Indian nationalism. In Maharashtra, B.G. Tilak organised popular festivals to mobilise Hindu support and in openly criticising the British administration seemed to countenance the use of force to achieve *swaraj* (self-government or independence). When Tilak appeared to be the inspiration behind the assassination of the plague commissioner, W.C. Rand, in Pune in 1897, he was tried and imprisoned for several months. Tilak was convicted on more serious charges in 1908, and, in a significant use of the spatial geography of internal exile, was sent to Mandalay gaol for six years.[112]

The partition of Bengal in 1905 generated a new wave of protest in that province and elsewhere. Apart from public demonstrations and boycotts in support of the Swadeshi campaign, the movement included terrorist attacks and assassinations. The state responded by sending Bengali terrorists to the notorious Cellular Gaol at Port Blair and sentencing others to long terms of rigorous imprisonment. Those convicted were exposed to the harshest punishments the state could muster—including arduous physical labour, solitary confinement, whippings and beatings for defiance of gaol regulations, punitive diets (or forced feeding when they went on hunger strike) and denial of access to books, newspapers and writing materials. For middle-class men, generally from high-caste *bhadralok* ('respectable') families, the ordeal of the prison proved hard to endure; some did not survive.[113]

---

[110]   C. Venkatesan, 'History of Prison Administration in the Madras Presidency, 1919–39', PhD thesis, University of Madras, 1981, p. 1.

[111]   Or even earlier, with the transportation from Bombay to Aden of the rebel Phadke in 1880: V.S. Joshi, *Vasudeo Balvant Phadke: First Indian rebel against British rule*, Bombay: D.S. Marathe, 1959.

[112]   See S.L. Karandikar, *Lokmanya Bal Gangadhar Tilak: The Hercules and Prometheus of modern India*, Pune: author, n.d.

[113]   Over 10,000 prisoners were sent to the Andamans between 1905 and 1920, a third of them from Burma: *Indian Jails Committee* (1919–20), p. 288. The experiences of political prisoners are described in many sources, including V.D. Savarkar, *The Story of My Transportation for Life*,

By the 1900s the prison figured prominently in an increasingly articulate and forceful public discourse of colonial oppression. Plays and novels were written depicting the horrors of gaol life. Tilak wrote an account of his 1897–8 imprisonment, one of the first of many hundreds of prison diaries and autobiographies to appear in India over the following fifty years.[114] Through the press and legislatures Indians began to demand investigation into prison conditions, asking about the treatment of political prisoners, calling for their freedom to perform religious observances, or demanding a voice in how the gaols were run. In 1914 the Government of India was forced to concede a demand in the Imperial Legislative Council for a committee of inquiry into gaol conditions (though it was anxious to steer discussion away from such contentious issues as capital punishment, flogging and the treatment of political prisoners).[115]

In the period up to and immediately following the world war the Indian prison system was pulled in several different directions. There was a continuing impetus for reform—to bring the colonial prison in line with recent reforms in Britain following the report of the Gladstone Committee in 1895.[116] The principal outcome (and the last major review of British Indian prisons) was the Indian Jails Committee of 1919-20, the first such enquiry to include Indian members. For the first time too members of the committee visited penal institutions abroad—in Britain, the United States, Japan, the Philippines and Hong Kong—and toured India. Its report began by acknowledging that while previous investigations had focused on prison discipline and health, the question of prisoners' reform and rehabilitation had been largely neglected. With an average daily population that had now risen to around 100,000 prisoners (twice the 1836 figure), the committee favoured increasing reliance on central, rather than district, gaols where prisoners could be more effectively supervised. It also focused attention on the one-third or more of Indian prisoners now said to be 'habitual' criminals, and the question of whether there should be special treatment for political prisoners (it said not, on the grounds that crime is crime whatever the

---

Bombay: Sadbhakti, 1950; Jogesh Chandra Chatterji, *In Search of Freedom*, Calcutta: K.L. Mukhopadhyay, 1967.

[114] *Dnyan Prakash*, 12 September 1898, Bombay Native Newspaper Reports (OIOC). For a discussion of this literature, see David Arnold, 'The Self and the Cell: Indian prison narratives as life histories' in David Arnold and Stuart Blackburn (eds), *Telling Lives in India: Biography, autobiography, and life history*, New Delhi: Permanent Black, 2004, pp. 29–53.

[115] Home (Jails), nos 32–45, October 1914 (NAI).

[116] See Sean McConville, 'The Victorian Prison: England, 1865–1965' in Morris and Rothman, *Oxford History*, chapter 5.

specific offence). But on several issues, like the use of convict warders, the committee remained equivocal.[117]

Barely had the committee reported than political events intervened. In 1921–2 M.K. Gandhi led the first of several India-wide *satyagrahas* in which activists belonging to the Indian National Congress courted imprisonment to express their defiance of colonial rule—in the belief that by 'swamping' the gaols they would help paralyse the administration and hasten *swaraj*, but also for the sake of self-imposed suffering, and because under such a 'satanic' regime it was wrong to be free. For Gandhi gaol-going was a religious duty: in his nationalist rhetoric prison became 'the temple of swaraj'.[118] When his allies, the Ali Brothers, were gaoled in September 1921, Gandhi confidently declared: 'This imprisonment may safely be regarded as a preliminary to the establishment of *swaraj*.'[119] Despite the opportune release of large numbers of prisoners, Indian gaols were flooded with thousands of political activists—more than 16,000 of them between mid-1921 and early 1922. This seriously alarmed the colonial authorities but did not bring about the anticipated administrative collapse.[120] Civil disobedience in 1930–3 and 1940–1 produced further upsurges in gaol populations.[121] The participation of women, many of them upper or middle class and of high-caste status, in gaol-going added to the dilemmas of the colonial authorities and to the force of nationalist propaganda. At the height of the Civil Disobedience Movement in February 1932, 954 out of 17,818 Congress protestors in Indian gaols were women.[122]

Apart from the symbolic significance and propaganda value of courting arrest and imprisonment, gaol-going helped to build discipline among the nationalist

---

[117] *Indian Jails Committee* (1919–20).

[118] *Young India*, 3 November 1921; *Swaraj*, 12 August 1921, Bombay NNR (OIOC).

[119] *Young India*, 22 September 1921.

[120] Judith M. Brown, *Gandhi's Rise to Power: Indian politics, 1915–1922*, Cambridge University Press, 1972, p. 318.

[121] In 1931, at a time of widespread political unrest, there were reported to be almost 134,000 prisoners in British India, ranging from 15,808 in Madras and 13,450 in Bombay (respectively 33.8 and 56.5 per 100,000 of the population) to 23,039 in Punjab (97.7) and 7,189 in the North-West Frontier Province (296.3). Even in the relatively low-key Individual Civil Disobedience Movement of 1940–1, 25,000 nationalists were gaoled: Ujjwal Kumar Singh, *Political Prisoners in India*, New Delhi: Oxford University Press, 1998, p. 169.

[122] Suruchi Thapar-Bjorkert, 'Gender, Nationalism and the Colonial Jail: A study of women activists in Uttar Pradesh', *Women's History Review*, 7, 4 (1998), p. 588. For the experiences of Nehru's two sisters, see Krishna Nehru Hutheesing, *Nehru's Letters to His Sister*, London: Faber & Faber, 1963, p. 12; Vijaya Lakshmi Pandit, *The Scope of Happiness: A personal memoir*, London: Weidenfeld and Nicolson, 1979, chapter 15.

ranks and, through the creation of prison 'schools', helped educate young activists in nationalist ideas and incorporate them into wider political networks (it later did the same for India's communists). But imprisonment was not only the goal of many nationalists: it was also central to the containing strategy of the colonial authorities, especially after the Amritsar massacre of April 1919, in which hundreds of protestors were killed or wounded, had demonstrated the perils of using crude military might against unarmed protestors. Imprisonment was not the only response of the colonial authorities. Armed with *lathis* (metal-tipped staves) and canes, and restricting arrests as far as possible to the nationalist leadership, the police were frequently deployed to intimidate and disperse demonstrators rather than arrest them. In the Quit India Movement of August 1942 the British went further and used the army and police to fire on protestors and saboteurs, as well as employing punishment by whipping and collective fines.[123] Even so, prison—or detention without trial—was the principal fate of most leading Congress and left-wing politicians of the period, some of whom, like Jawaharlal Nehru, India's first prime minister, spent several years in gaol.[124]

This paradoxical function of the prison—both to support and to combat political agitation—had far-reaching consequences. One was that, despite the efforts of the 1919–20 Indian Jails Committee, attention was deflected away from the reform and rehabilitation of ordinary prisoners to the demands of political prisoners. A second consequence was that the colonial prison became far more an object of sustained public hostility and informed criticism than it had been previously. Newspapers, debates in the legislatures, resolutions at political meetings, all dwelt on the 'barbarities' practised within prison walls, thereby reversing the claims the colonial authorities had once made for the superiority of their regime over its Indian predecessors. With the arrival of large numbers of mainly middle-class prisoners, demands grew for political prisoners to be afforded a completely different status from ordinary prisoners and to be given concessions over diet, clothing, work regimes, access to newspapers and books, and accommodation that acknowledged their distinctive nature. This gave expression to a strong sense of class difference: many prisoners, women and men, expressed their fury and dismay at being confined (or even held awaiting trial) alongside thieves, murderers and prostitutes. But it was not only against 'common criminals' that political prisoners compared themselves: they also viewed with equal indignation

---

[123] Francis G. Hutchins, *India's Revolution: Gandhi and the Quit India Movement*, Cambridge, MA: Harvard University Press, 1973, pp. 230–2.

[124] See Jawaharlal Nehru, *An Autobiography*, London, 1936, chapter 13, and his 'Prison Diary' in vols 5 and 6 of *Selected Works of Jawaharlal Nehru*, New Delhi: Orient Longman, 1973–4.

the superior treatment given, on racial grounds, to European prisoners. As one south Indian Congressman protested: 'our racial serfdom is nowhere more evident than inside the jail.'[125]

It could be argued that such protests ran counter to Gandhi's philosophy, which had urged nationalists to obey all lawful prison regulations and accept as part of the *satyagrahi's* suffering, the humiliations and hardships prison imposed. But in practice nationalists, backed by influential and articulate support in the press and legislatures, conducted their protests within the prison, often to great effect. Gradually the government yielded, reclassifying them as 'A' or 'B' class prisoners according to their background and status, leaving ordinary prisoners marooned in a residual 'C' class. The administration allowed political prisoners to wear their own clothes, to receive a superior diet and, in most instances, to have access to newspapers and books. But protests and disputes still rumbled on—for instance, whether political prisoners in Madras should receive buttermilk, an issue finally resolved only when the Congress took ministerial office in that province in 1937.[126]

The Gandhians were not the only political activists to find themselves in gaol. Terrorists and others who advocated violence in order to attain national independence or build a revolutionary socialist society in India were also imprisoned, albeit in smaller numbers. Many revolutionaries were denied 'political' status and in the Andamans or in gaols on the Indian mainland were subjected to the full force of the penal regime. Those who survived these brutal ordeals often abandoned political activism on their release or turned to more moderate paths. The prison was not without its effect.[127]

DISPOSING OF CORPSES

Despite determined attempts to enhance the severity and seclusion of the colonial prison, what the fate of the revolutionaries, even more than that of the Gandhians, underscored was the continuing permeability of the prison. There are many ways in which this could be illustrated but perhaps one of the most striking

[125]   G. Vasudeviah, cited in Ventakesan, 'History', p. 148. The demand for equal treatment went back to the 1890s: *Dnyan Prakash*, 12 September 1898, Bombay NNR; also *Bharatwasi*, 15 September 1921, ibid. (OIOC).

[126]   Singh, *Political Prisoners*, chapter 3; for a provincial case study, see Ventakesan, 'History'.

[127]   See the memoirs of one leader of the Hindustan Socialist Republican Army, sentenced to fourteen years' RI [Rigorous Imprisonment] in 1932 but released in 1938: Corinne Friend (ed.), *Yashpal Looks Back: Selections from an autobiography*, New Delhi: Vikas, 1981.

(and one which leads us back to the significance of the body as a central site for the contestations that surrounded the prison) concerns the disposal of prisoners' bodies. The established position was that the bodies of those who were executed or died in prison were to be handed over to any relatives or friends who claimed them, unless there were 'grounds for supposing that the convict's funeral will be made the occasion for a demonstration'. If the bodies were unclaimed, they should be burnt or buried 'in the manner most consonant with the customs of the tribe or caste of the criminal'.[128]

This issue assumed new prominence in 1908 with the death in prison of a Bengali revolutionary, Kanny Lal Dutt. The authorities released his body on the condition that there would be no demonstration; but, once handed over, a procession carried the corpse through the streets of Calcutta to the burning *ghat* amid shouts of *Bande Mataram* (Hail to the Motherland). The cremation was delayed to allow Dutt, his head now resting on a pillow and garlanded with flowers, to be seen by onlookers and photographed, and for a passage from the *Bhagavad Gita* to be read over him. The Bengal government was relieved that worse had not happened, but, convinced of 'the evils of any such demonstration', resolved to tighten up the rules.[129]

In 1929, amid wide publicity, the British executed three revolutionaries, including the celebrated Bhagat Singh. Fearful of public demonstrations if the bodies were handed over to relatives, the authorities tried to dispose of them secretly. They were smuggled out of Lahore gaol in lorries in the middle of the night, and driven 65 miles to a burning *ghat* on the banks of the Sutlej to be cremated. Expecting something of the sort, relatives and friends, including Bhagat Singh's sister, had been watching all the roads out of Lahore and by daybreak had located the smouldering funeral pyres. A large crowd gathered and collected ash and burnt bones from the site: an annual fair was subsequently held there to commemorate the 'martyrs'. Rumours often circulated about how the British tortured, killed and inappropriately disposed of the bodies of the dead. In 1879, for instance, the curious rumour circulated that the rebel Vasudeo Balvant Phadke was to be burnt alive in the funnel of the steamship taking him to imprisonment in Aden.[130] In the case of the Punjabi revolutionaries in 1929, it was

---

[128] Hodge, *Bengal Jail Manual*, p. 81; Home (Jails), notes to 19–28, November 1908 (NAI). For earlier concerns about public executions and the attention they attracted, see Singha, *Despotism of Law*, pp. 239–45.

[129] Chief Sec., Bengal to Sec. Home, India, 14 November 1908, Home (Jails), nos 19–28, November 1908 (NAI).

[130] Joshi, *Phadke*, p. 127.

reported that their bodies had been hacked to pieces before the cremation, and had not received the proper funeral rites. The British denied this but were not widely believed.[131]

Gandhi did not die in prison as the British frequently feared he might. But following the Quit India Movement of August 1942, he was detained at the Aga Khan's palace near Pune for the rest of the war, along with his wife and close associates. When his long-serving secretary Mahadev Desai died, Gandhi asked that his body might be taken away for cremation by Desai's family and friends. Despite a sympathetic inspector-general of prisons, the Bombay government refused to countenance this request, or allow Gandhi out of confinement, and the body was cremated instead within the palace compound. An identical fate awaited Gandhi's wife Kasturba: when she died in February 1944, her body was burnt at the same spot, and her ashes laid alongside Desai's *samadhi*.[132]

CONCLUSION

The prison in British India had a complex and varied history. It was, first and foremost, a state institution, created for, and operated in the interests of maintaining, the colonial order. Along with the courts, the police and the army, it was one of the principal mechanisms of state control. That said, the colonial prison did not simply replicate the model of Britain's own prisons or obediently follow American precedents. In the eyes of the British, India's physical conditions and cultural values imposed their own constraints upon the prison. To some extent this perception of difference gave a degree of agency to Indians: prisoners could use arguments based on caste and custom, race and religion to contest the universalising ambitions of modern penology, and to carve out for themselves some degree of autonomy within, or influence over, the prison. The authorities were at times prepared to counter this and to use the 'prejudices' of caste, religion and

---

[131] Friend, *Yashpal*, pp. 218–19. The rumours might relate to the practice of carrying out post-mortems before bodies were released, a long-standing source of public resentment and one many nationalists shared. One lawyer remarked: 'I don't find any justification whatsoever for this unbridled right of the Government to deal with the corpse in this inhuman fashion. All the rights that may be vested in the Government over the person of a prisoner must cease with the death and the last marks of respect should be shown to the dead.' Syama Charan, *My Conviction*, Muzaffarpur: Herculean Press, 1922, p. 82.

[132] Pyarelal and Sushila Nayar, *In Gandhiji's Mirror*, Delhi: Oxford University Press, 1991, pp. 58–62, 66–7.

custom to establish an even more punitive penal order—but mostly, for practical and political reasons, they did not.

The prison held an ambiguous status in colonial society. It was loathed and detested by most of those who knew or had heard of it. Unlike those Europeans who stressed its contribution to civilisation (though even among Europeans in India there were sceptics), few Indians of whatever class or background saw it as having any positive attributes. For them the prison was a highly visible symbol of oppression, but by the same token it was also an arena (in some respects a remarkably public arena) through which various causes could announce their claims and further their sentiments. In the nineteenth century the prison was taken as proof that the British were intent on destroying caste and imposing Christianity. In the early twentieth it showed the lengths to which they seemed prepared to go to suppress even legitimate, non-violent opposition. Prison became the ordeal through which nationalists strove to prove their moral mettle. That gaol-going became one of the principal tactics of the Indian nationalist movement was no accident. It was an affirmation of how central the prison had become in colonial policy, as in Indian consciousness.

BIBLIOGRAPHICAL NOTE

There now exists a substantial critical literature on the prison in colonial India as well as a number of earlier works of continuing utility. The political, legal and administrative context of the prison in late-eighteenth- and early-nineteenth-century India (though with particular emphasis on Bengal and northern India) is described in Tapas Kumar Banerjee, *Background to Indian Criminal Law*, Bombay: Orient Longman, 1963, especially chapter 6, and more critically discussed in Jörg Fisch, *Cheap Lives and Dear Limbs: The British transformation of the Bengal criminal law, 1769–1817*, Wiesbaden: Franz Steiner Verlag, 1983; and Radhika Singha, *A Despotism of Law: Crime and justice in early colonial India*, Delhi: Oxford University Press, 1998: chapter 6 of Singha's book includes extensive discussion of the Prison Discipline Committee of 1836–8. A further interpretative essay, in part reflecting on the Foucauldian paradigm, is David Arnold, 'The Colonial Prison: Power, knowledge and penology in nineteenth-century India' in David Arnold and David Hardiman (eds), *Subaltern Studies VIII*, Delhi: Oxford University Press, 1994, pp. 148–87. Clare Anderson's *Legible Bodies: Race, criminality and colonialism in South Asia*, Oxford: Berg, 2004, addresses a number of important issues relating to prisons and prisoners in India, including *godena* and convict dress. Several articles investigate aspects of the nineteenth-century prison and colonial penal practices, notably Anand A. Yang, 'Disciplining "Natives": Prisons and prisoners in early nineteenth century India', *South Asia*, 10, 2 (1987), pp. 29–45; Satadru Sen, 'The Female Jails of Colonial India', *Indian Economic and Social History Review*, 39, 2 (2002), pp. 417–38, and 'A Separate Punishment: Juvenile offenders in colonial India', *Journal of Asian Studies*, 63, 1 (2004), pp. 81–104. On the treatment of political prisoners under the British (and subsequently), see Ujjwal Kumar Singh, *Political Prisoners in India*, New Delhi: Oxford University Press, 1998. Prisoners' accounts of their own experiences are touched upon in several of the works cited here, but see also David Arnold, 'The Self and the Cell: Indian prison narratives as life histories' in David Arnold and Stuart Blackburn (eds), *Telling Lives in India: Biography, autobiography, and life history*, New Delhi: Permanent Black, 2004, pp. 29–53.

SEPOYS, SERVANTS AND SETTLERS: CONVICT TRANSPORTATION IN THE INDIAN OCEAN, 1787-1945[1]

Clare Anderson

Banishment and exile were common punishments in early modern Europe. Though not subject to confinement or direct corporal interventions *per se*, criminals were sent away from their communities and localities to an uncertain fate. Physical displacement was central to this type of punishment, for it effected permanent social rupture. With the acquisition of colonies overseas, banishment took on a new character. The dynamics of empire building assured not only the removal of European convicts from home but their subsequent transportation overseas and exploitation as cheap labour. Convicted offenders were sent to distant, unknown lands where they were employed either on public works projects or hired out to free settlers. Often Europeans worked in tandem with other forms of migrant or coerced labour, like indentured servants or slaves. Though it never entirely replaced imprisonment, transportation was an important supplement to local penal practices. It solved periodic crises of overcrowding, notably during times of economic hardship when prison populations tended to rise.

There is a clear association between European colonisation and forced labour. From the mid-sixteenth century the Portuguese used *degredados* to populate new colonies in Goa and coastal West Africa, including the Azores, Madeira, Principe,

[1] Research for this essay was funded by the British Academy South-East Asian Committee and the Economic and Social Research Council, to whom I am very grateful. Abbreviations are as follows: OIOC = Oriental and India Office Collections (BJC/BJP = Bengal Judicial Consultations/Proceedings; BomJP = Bombay Judicial Proceedings; IJP/IPP = India Judicial/Public Proceedings); NA = National Archives (GB); NAI = National Archives of India; NAM = National Archives of Mauritius; PP = Parliamentary Papers; TNSA = Tamil Nadu State Archives. I would like to thank the other contributors to this volume for their comments and suggestions on earlier versions of this piece. All errors are of course mine.

São Tomé and Cape Verde.[2] During the same period the Spanish transported convicts to Cuba and North Africa. German convicts were sold as galley slaves to Italian city states.[3] Though no comprehensive figures were compiled at the time, historians have calculated that during the seventeenth and eighteenth centuries between 30,000 and 50,000 offenders were transported from Britain to the American colonies, joining the large number of indentured servants already there. Indeed, perhaps three quarters of all European migrants in the period to 1776 were bonded labourers of some kind.[4] With the American Revolution the colonies were closed off to the reception of convicts. The British then undertook a penal experiment in West Africa, viewing convict labour as an ideal means of colonising a region where free settlers were unwilling to go. In 1782, 350 felons were sent to the Gold Coast; in 1785 only seven were still alive. With critics arguing that transportation was effectively a death sentence, later plans to export convicts for the development of indigo and rice plantations (to replace the interrupted supply from America) were abandoned.[5] The southern hemisphere became the next destination for convict workers. Some 160,000 men and women were shipped from Britain to penal settlements in New South Wales, Van Diemen's Land and Western Australia (1787–1868).[6] The French too shipped tens of thousands of convicts to colonies in New Caledonia (1790–1900) and French Guiana (1795–1809, 1852–1946).[7]

The judicial authorities used banishment as a punishment in pre-colonial India. High-caste Brahmins, for instance, could not be flogged or executed and so were exiled. Other forms of largely discretionary punishment included public shaming, mutilation and hanging, as well as confinement.[8] Though unconnected to

---

[2] Timothy J. Coates, *Convicts and Orphans: Forced and state-sponsored colonizers in the Portuguese empire, 1550–1755*, Stanford University Press, 2001.

[3] David Eltis, 'Europeans and the Rise and Fall of African Slavery in the Americas: An interpretation', *American Historical Review*, 98, 5 (1993), pp. 1407–11.

[4] Gwenda Morgan and Peter Rushton, *Eighteenth-Century Criminal Transportation: The formation of the criminal Atlantic*, Basingstoke: Palgrave Macmillan, 2004, pp. 12, 37–8.

[5] Philip J. Curtin, *The Image of Africa: British ideas and action, 1780–1850*, Madison, WI: University of Wisconsin Press, 1972, pp. 88–95.

[6] Lucy Frost and Hamish Maxwell-Stewart (eds), *Chain Letters: Narrating convict lives*, Melbourne University Press, 2001; Stephen Nicholas (ed.), *Convict Workers: Reinterpreting Australia's past*, Cambridge University Press, 1988.

[7] Alice Bullard, *Exile to Paradise: Savagery and civilization in Paris and the South Pacific*, Stanford University Press, 2000; Peter Redfield, *Space in the Tropics: From convicts to rockets in French Guiana*, Berkeley, CA: University of California Press, 2000.

[8] Tapas Kumar Banerjee, *Background to Indian Criminal Law*, Calcutta: R. Cambray and Co., 1990; Sumit Guha, 'An Indian Penal Régime: Maharashtra in the eighteenth century', *Past and Present*,

the application of civil or criminal law, forced labour—or *begari*—remained common into the early colonial period. Private individuals and government pressed local communities into portaging duties.[9] Given the sustained metropolitan experience, the precedent of *begari*, and continued East India Company expansion into South East Asia, it is not surprising that the British introduced overseas transportation into their package of legal reforms in the subcontinent. From the late eighteenth to mid-twentieth centuries the courts sentenced thousands of convicts to various terms of transportation. They were sent to penal settlements across the Malay Peninsula, Burma, Mauritius and the Andaman Islands.[10] During the early years of settlement, Company officials stressed continually the public advantages of convict labour in building roads and basic infrastructure. Convicts were relatively cheap, controllable and easily replaced. For this reason the settlements themselves drove supply, and periodic interruptions to it—usually as it was directed elsewhere—were greeted with indignation. The convict system had the added boon on the mainland of emptying Indian gaols of offenders sentenced to long terms (the majority for life), so relieving the presidencies of the cost of their maintenance. As a supplement to sentences of imprisonment, transportation also had enormous symbolic appeal. The prospect of a voyage across the *kala pani*—or black water—struck at the heart of the cultural fears of caste Hindus because the close living associated with the transportation ship was polluting. Moreover, during the years following the settlement of new territories, for all castes and religions, transportation represented a terrifying journey to unknown, distant lands.

There was an extensive pan-imperial trade in convicts across the empire during the British colonial period, and the geographical reach of transportation was

---

147 (1995), pp. 101–26; Radhika Singha, *A Despotism of Law: Crime and justice in early colonial India*, New Delhi: Oxford University Press, 1998.

[9] Banerjee, *Background*, pp. 98–101. See also Frederick John Shore, *Notes on Indian Affairs, vol. II*, London: John W. Parker, 1837, pp. 307–45.

[10] Clare Anderson, *Convicts in the Indian Ocean: Transportation from South Asia to Mauritius, 1815–53*, Basingstoke: Macmillan, 2000; Clare Anderson, 'The Politics of Convict Space: Indian penal settlements and the Andaman Islands' in Alison Bashford and Carolyn Strange (eds), *Isolation: Places and practices of exclusion*, London: Routledge, 2003, pp. 40–55; Clare Anderson, *Legible Bodies: Race, criminality and colonialism in South Asia*, Oxford: Berg, 2004; L.P. Mathur, *Kala Pani: History of Andaman and Nicobar Islands with a study of India's freedom struggle*, New Delhi: Eastern Book Company, 1992; Satadru Sen, *Disciplining Punishment: Colonialism and convict society in the Andaman Islands*, New Delhi: Oxford University Press, 2000; C.M. Turnbull, 'Convicts in the Straits Settlements, 1826–67', *Journal of the Malaysia Branch of the Royal Asiatic Society*, 43, 1 (1970), pp. 87–103; Anand A. Yang, 'Indian Convict Workers in Southeast Asia in the Late Eighteenth and Early Nineteenth Centuries', *Journal of World History*, 14, 2 (2003), pp. 179–208.

wide. Numerically the South Asian convict stream was by far the most significant, with perhaps as many as 80,000 convicts transported overseas during the period 1787–1943.[11] The East India Company shipped 2,000 Indian convicts to Benkulen (1787–1825), at least 300 more to its first abortive Andaman Islands settlement (1793–6), and about 1,500 to Mauritius (1815–37). When the Dutch retook Benkulen in 1825 the British transferred the convicts to Penang (Prince of Wales Island), which was already a penal settlement. During the period 1790–1860 at least 20,000 convicts were transported from India to Penang, Malacca and Singapore (known as the Straits Settlements after 1823). Approximately 5–7,000 convicts were shipped to Arakan and the Tenasserim Provinces (Burma) during the period 1828–62. Finally, the Andamans received about 50,000 convicts between 1858 and 1943, when the transportation system came to an end with the Japanese occupation of the Islands.[12]

During the first half of the nineteenth century other convict migrant streams were not insignificant. The authorities transported a few thousand convicts from Ceylon to Mauritius and South East Asia (1815–68), and from Mauritius and the Cape Colony to Robben Island (1814–96).[13] Further, three or four hundred non-Anglo-Celtic convicts were transported from Canada, the Cape and the West Indies to New South Wales and Van Diemen's Land.[14] About a hundred convicts were sentenced to transportation in Mauritius and sent to the Australian

---

[11] A lack of systematically recorded figures means that calculations are somewhat tentative. These are based upon dispersed records in the Bengal, Bombay and Madras judicial proceedings series, which include convict ship indents, and Andaman Islands annual reports.

[12] Rabin Roychowdhury, *Black Days in Andaman and Nicobar Islands*, New Delhi: Manas Publications, 2004.

[13] Anderson, *Convicts in the Indian Ocean*, pp. 25, 43, 98, 106; M.A. Durand Appuhamy, *The Kandyans' Last Stand Against the British*, Colombo: Gunasena and Co., 1995; Harriet Deacon, 'The British Prison on Robben Island 1800–1896' in Harriet Deacon (ed.), *The Island: A history of Robben Island 1488–1900*, Cape Town: David Philip, 1997.

[14] Ian Duffield, 'From Slave Colonies to Penal Colonies: The West Indians transported to Australia', *Slavery and Abolition*, 7, 1 (1986), pp. 25–45; Ian Duffield, 'The Life and Death of "Black" John Goff: Aspects of the black convict contribution to resistance patterns during the transportation era in Eastern Australia', *Australian Journal of Politics and History*, 33, 1 (1987), pp. 30–44; Ian Duffield, '"Stated This Offence": high-density convict micro-narratives' in Lucy Frost and Hamish Maxwell-Stewart (eds), *Chain Letters: Narrating convict lives*, Melbourne University Press: 2001, pp. 119–36; Leslie C. Duly, '"Hottentots to Hobart and Sydney": The Cape Supreme Court's use of transportation, 1828–38', *Australian Journal of Politics and History*, 25, 1 (1979), pp. 39–50; V.C. Malherbe, 'Khoikhoi and the Question of Convict Transportation from the Cape Colony, 1820–1842', *South African Historical Journal*, 17 (1985), pp. 19–39; Cassandra Pybus and Hamish Maxwell-Stewart, *American Citizens, British Slaves: Yankee political prisoners in an Australian penal colony 1839–1850*, Melbourne University Press: 2002.

settlements (1825–45).[15] Simultaneous to transportation from South to South East Asia, from the 1830s to 1860s the colonial authorities in the Straits Settlements and Burma shipped several thousand convicts to mainland Indian gaols. These Chinese and Malay prisoners ended up in district prisons across Bengal and Madras presidencies, though those sent to Bombay were imprisoned in a special reformatory centre in the summer capital, Mahabaleshwar (1834–64).

Given this criss-cross trade in convicts it is clear that transportation was not simply bound up with labour demands. Its widespread appeal as a penal sanction—more severe than local imprisonment but less harsh than capital punishment—was also closely associated with the display of colonial strength that the permanent removal of social undesirables surely represented. This was especially important in potentially fragile colonies, where whole communities must have felt the social and economic impact of transportation. While transportation constituted one element of colonial law and order in a general sense, it is also worth noting that indigenous communities like the South African Khoisan and Xhosa involved in frontier skirmishes, rebellious slaves like the Baptist War rebels in Jamaica (1831–2), and recalcitrant Indian and Chinese indentured workers in Mauritius (1825–45), all fell under the purview of the colonial courts in this respect. Some of the first Indian convicts transported to South East Asia were polygar rebels from the Malabar coast.[16] *Adivasi* (tribal) communities like the kols, bhils and sandals, who resisted colonial incursions into land and revenue extraction during the period 1830–55, were all affected by overseas transportation.[17] The first convicts shipped to the Andamans were mutineer-rebels involved in the widespread north Indian uprisings of 1857–8. They were followed by Wahabis, Manipuris, Kukas and, in the early twentieth century, Mapilahs and nationalist agitators.[18] State prisoners too were deported overseas. The Mughal Emperor of Delhi and his entourage were sent to Rangoon in the aftermath of 1857–8. King Thibaw and Queen Supayalat were imprisoned in Benares gaol at the end of the third Anglo-Burmese war (1885).

Though we know something of the context in which African, Indian and Chinese convicts were shipped to Australia, we know relatively little about their fate in what were predominantly white settler colonies. Sustained scholarly

---

[15]   Clare Anderson, 'Unfree Labour and its Discontents: Transportation from Mauritius to Australia, 1825–1845', *Australian Studies*, 13, 1 (1998), pp. 116–33.

[16]   Yang, 'Indian Convict Workers', p. 13.

[17]   See also Anderson, *Convicts in the Indian Ocean*, pp. 28–32.

[18]   Aggarwal, *The Heroes*, pp. 32–7; N. Iqbal Singh, *The Andaman Story*, New Delhi: Vikas, 1978, pp. 176–204; Mathur, *Kala Pani*, pp. 73–6.

investigation will surely illuminate further their experiences. We are on firmer ground with Indian penal settlements. Despite their disparate geography and *longue durée*, they shared certain features. First, convicts' productive capacities were absolutely central to their operation, and the settlements were entirely organised around labour. Second, convicts shaped the nature and operation of penal settlements in remarkably similar ways, whether through outright resistance or more subtle forms of negotiation. Third, transportation was a strongly gendered process, and metropolitan thinking about the type of punishment and work appropriate for women, particularly in relation to the demarcation of public and private spheres, was relatively uniform, and paid little heed to the local context. The complex inter-relationships that characterised penal settlements thus shared many features that transcended their geographical boundaries. It is also clear that transportation did not replace altogether, but co-existed with, other repressive colonial practices. During this period the British both expanded and developed the prison. Historians have drawn further parallels between the prison in South Asia and the asylum, the workhouse and the lock-hospital.[19] This essay will also explore the relationship between penal transportation and other forms of repression, notably co-existent corporal interventions like penal tattooing and the forced settlement and sometimes overseas shipment of the so-called 'criminal tribes'.

REGULATING TRANSPORTATION
IN THE EARLY NINETEENTH CENTURY

The transportation of Indian convicts overseas was first mooted in the legal reforms of Hastings and Cornwallis. In 1773 the East India Company ordered that every prisoner sentenced to hard labour or life imprisonment should instead be transported to Benkulen. Shortly after the resumption of transportation from Britain to New South Wales, in 1789 the Company gave permission to a free settler to transport twenty life prisoners to Penang for his own profit—on condition that he issued rations and treated them well. It was not long before Penang became a Company penal settlement. Life prisoners and those sentenced to mutilation were transported there to work on public works projects. In 1793 the Company tried to settle the Andaman Islands as a penal colony. It directed that all life convicts be transported there to work on land clearance, cultivation and

---

[19]   Philippa Levine, *Prostitution, Race and Politics: Policing venereal disease in the British Empire*, London: Routledge, 2003; J. Mills, *Madness, Cannabis and Colonialism: The 'native-only' lunatic asylums of British India, 1857–1900*, London: Macmillan, 2000.

other projects.[20] Three hundred convicts were transported,[21] but after outbreaks of disease, within three years the settlement was abandoned. The surviving convicts were sent to Benkulen and the free settlers were taken back to Bengal.

The Company issued the first regulations on transportation a few years later. Regulation IV (1797) directed the commutation to transportation of all sentences of imprisonment for seven years or more. Regulation II (1799) extended transportation to escaped prisoners. Regulation LIII (1803) directed that punishments of mutilation be commuted to imprisonment or transportation.[22] Regulation VIII (1808) made all cases of dacoity (gang robbery) not liable to the death penalty punishable with life transportation. Attempted murder could also be punished through transportation. Regulation IX (1808) codified the law of contumacy so that if notorious suspects did not surrender themselves within two months of being asked to do so, they were liable to transportation for life. It was later discovered that this regulation contained a legal loophole, as those apprehended after the two month period prescribed by the proclamation could be tried only for contumacy, and not for a specific offence. Thus they could only be transported for life, not sentenced to death as they would have been if convicted of the specific crime. This was amended by Regulation V (1822).[23]

Despite this flurry of legislative activity, it was not long before transportation began to fall from favour. Delays in implementing sentences led to a number of high-profile escapes. Other convicts returned to India, bringing news of the settlements and so diminishing public dread of the punishment. The Company also increasingly viewed transportation as an expensive penal option. The building of a new gaol just outside Calcutta, Alipur, at the same time reduced the pressure on the district gaols.[24] Subsequently, in 1811 all the transportation regulations were repealed and all those under life sentences were sent to Alipur gaol instead.[25] In 1813, however, the Company performed an abrupt *volte-face*. It reintroduced transportation as a penal option after the ever-spiralling cost and potential security

---

[20] OIOC P.128.7 (BJP 20 December 1793): H. Barlow, Register Nizamat Adalat, to E. Hay, Secretary to Government Bengal, 20 November 1793.

[21] OIOC P.128.12 (25 July 1794): J. Duncan, Resident Benares, to G.M. Barlow, Secretary to Government Bengal, 10 July 1794.

[22] Jörg Fisch, *Cheap Lives and Dear Limbs: The British transformation of the Bengal criminal law, 1769–1817*, Wiesbaden: Franz Steiner Verlag, 1983, pp. 53, 61, 72.

[23] PP 1824 XXIII. Regulation V (Bengal) 1808: A Regulation for amending certain provisions of Regulation IX, 13 June 1822.

[24] Banerjee, *Background*, pp. 93–4, 362.

[25] Resolution of the Government at Fort William, 10 December 1811, cited in Banerjee, *Background*, pp. 94–5.

problems in Alipur gaol became clear.[26] In 1816 a regulation for the transportation of convicts to Mauritius, and their employment or transfer elsewhere was passed.[27] Regulation XVII (1817) followed, making burglary, theft and robbery punishable by transportation for life, if they included wounding or maiming, or were combined with robbery by open violence. It also made convicts who escaped from life transportation liable to execution, and those who escaped from a term sentence liable to re-transportation. Life transportation was also extended as a penalty for arson, robbery by open violence, attempted or actual burglary or theft, and robbery accompanied by attempted murder or serious injury.[28] Regulations in the Bombay and Madras presidencies largely followed those in Bengal. The main difference was that in Bombay, sentences of transportation passed by the provincial courts could only be for life, but if passed by the Supreme Court, for life or a term of years.[29] In all three presidencies convicts were sentenced to transportation generally and not to a particular destination. That was decided on the basis of current overseas demand.

Before 1834 the East India Company had a monopoly over long distance trade routes, so most convicts were shipped to penal settlements on its Chinese fleet. If there were no Company ships available, private trading vessels were tendered. In 1834 the Company lost its monopoly on trade routes and so most convicts were transported on such ships. The cost of transportation depended on a variety of factors, notably the availability of ships and the length of the voyage. Bengal or Madras to Benkulen cost about 60 rupees per convict, to the Straits between 35 and 40 rupees, to Burma around 30 rupees, and to Mauritius about 60 to 75 rupees. Shipping links from Bombay were rather erratic, and transportation journeys relatively long. Transportation to Burma or the Straits cost about 75 to 80 rupees per convict, and Mauritius between 50 to 100 rupees a head. Until the 1840s regulations were somewhat piecemeal, and with discipline sometimes lax there were a number of violent outbreaks on board transportation ships. Death rates, on the other hand, were extremely low, mainly because vulnerable prisoners usually died while awaiting their transportation in mainland gaols.[30]

---

[26] Clause Third, Section II, Regulation IX, 1813, cited in Fisch, *Cheap Lives*, p. 78.

[27] PP 1819 XIII. Papers relating to East India Affairs: Viz. Regulations Passed by the Governments of Bengal, Fort St George and Bombay, in the Year 1816: Regulation XV, 18 May 1816.

[28] PP 1819 XIII. Regulation XVII (Bengal) 1817: a regulation to provide for the more effectual administration of criminal justice in certain cases, 16 September 1817. See also Fisch, *Cheap Lives*, pp. 73, 95.

[29] OIOC P.401.32 (BomJP 21 September 1836): Memorandum by Secretary to Government (J.P. Willoughby), 10 August 1836.

[30] Clare Anderson, "'The Ferringees are Flying—The Ship is Ours!': The convict middle passage

1. Chetoo, an incorrigible convict of the fifth class, Singapore. [J.F.A. McNair, *Prisoners Their Own Warders*, 1899]

Prisoners in India displayed an often sophisticated understanding of the process of transportation. Despite colonial claims about the total social breach that transportation represented, there is little doubt that overseas news gradually permeated Indian prisons. In 1828 life prisoners were given the right to petition for commutation of their sentence to transportation. Shortly afterwards a group of over a hundred petitioners withdrew their applications when they were informed that their destination was not Singapore, as they had expected, but the new settlement in Tenasserim, about which nothing was known.[31] With continued transportation a necessary feature of the system, inevitably penal settlements did not remain isolated for long. There were frequent shipping links between South East Asia and the Indian mainland and convicts and their scribes took advantage of this in their prodigious letter writing. Indeed, lost contact between convicts and their families frequently led to petitions from the latter requesting news and information. It is also worth noting that at the expiration of their sentence, convicts in the Straits and Burma (and later on the Andamans) were free to return to India if their families agreed to support them. Despite the grinding poverty experienced by many, they rarely refused.[32]

Between 1789 and 1849 life convicts from Bengal and Madras were tattooed on the forehead with their name, crime and date of sentence, a process known as *godna*. These inscriptions were supposed to serve as a penal mark and as a surveillance strategy, though in practice they were more transient signs. Although women were exempted from many corporal interventions such as flogging, they were also made subject to *godna*. As such it was a means of emasculating the 'native criminal' through the gendering of penal space. The Bombay Presidency had always refused to sanction what it referred to as a 'barbarous' practice, highlighting the challenge it posed to Britain's claim to be a civilising presence. In 1847 the Government of India decided that if penal tattooing was not in force in Bombay then it ought to be abolished elsewhere. Changing colonial sensibilities were effectively incompatible with the permanent marking of convicts, and *godna* was abolished in 1849.[33] No doubt later on the presence or absence of penal tattoos was a useful means of distinguishing new from old transportation convicts.

---

in colonial South and Southeast Asia, 1790–1860', *Indian Economic and Social History Review*, 41, 3 (2005), pp. 143–86.

[31] Anderson, 'The Politics', p. 44.

[32] An assertion based on extensive documentation of correspondence recorded in the TNSA judicial proceedings series.

[33] Anderson, *Legible Bodies*, chapter 2.

INDIAN PENAL SETTLEMENTS IN SOUTH EAST ASIA

Convict labour was particularly valuable in recently acquired East India Company territory where workers were willing to engage only for relatively high wages. Convicts were employed at hard labour, clearing land, digging ditches and building basic infrastructure. As penal settlements became bigger, they also became more socially complex, and convicts were given various privileges and exemptions from hard labour on the basis of time served and good behaviour. The types of classificatory systems established—penal hierarchies that divided convicts into 'classes'—would have been unthinkable on the Indian mainland at the time. However, in South East Asia they were necessary to counter potential resistance by large numbers of mostly life convicts shipped to relatively isolated places, and almost exclusively worked at some distance from their barracks. Permanent prison buildings were not constructed for some years; and in new penal settlements convicts either lived in old military barracks or in temporary camps near public works. Even with the construction of more secure accommodation, the potential for convict rebellion or resistance was never far from administrators' minds. Each penal settlement operated through the promise of both punishment and reward, and convicts were able to rise up through the ranks until they enjoyed a degree of freedom that frequently surprised outsiders. Early rules were framed in Benkulen in 1800.[34] In 1820 the *Bencoolen Regulation for the Better Management of the Bengal Convicts* divided convicts into three classes, according to the length of time they had spent in the settlement and their subsequent behaviour. Deserving convicts were removed from hard labour and employed as artificers or in the salt works, with a monthly cash gratuity. They also enjoyed a certain freedom of movement.[35] The *Bencoolen Regulation* was adapted for the Straits Settlements in 1825.[36] In turn it formed the basis for the more complex *Butterworth Rules*, adopted in the Settlements in 1845 and then

---

[34] OIOC P.129.32 (BJC 1 January 1807): Rules for the management of convicts in Bencoolen, 18 June 1800; A regulation for the management of the convicts transported from Bengal to Fort Marlborough, 5 August 1806.

[35] OIOC P.134.48 (BJC 20 February 1821): Bencoolen Regulation for the Better Management of the Bengal Convicts, 5 October 1820.

[36] OIOC P.136.66 (BJC 19 May 1825): Minute on the Management of Convicts at Prince of Wales Island, 8 March 1825; OIOC P.137.37 (BJC 12 January 1826): J. Crawford, Resident Councillor Singapore, to W.B. Bayley, Secretary to Government Bengal, 20 April 1825; OIOC P.142.37 (BJC 17 September 1845): Regulations for Convict Management Singapore, 23 June 1825 (revised 1 December 1825).

extended to Burma.[37] While sixth class 'incorrigible' convicts were consigned to the chain gang, first class convicts became overseers (*tindals*) of their fellow transportees, thus blurring the distinction between prisoner and warder. This in itself had important implications for convict discipline, and there were frequent complaints about brutality and corruption. A convict's goal was the acquisition of a ticket-of-leave. Once in possession of the necessary papers, he or she could live outside the 'lines' and engage in paid employment.

Once the immediate needs of newly settled territories had been met, and land cleared and basic amenities established, convict occupations grew in nature and scale. In addition to land clearance and the building and repairing of roads and bridges, convicts worked as sawyers, potters, weavers, brass founders, brick and tile makers, blacksmiths, boatmen, cart drivers and grass cutters. The elderly and infirm were put to work as gardeners, watchmen and herdsmen, some in newly established botanical gardens. As in mainland prisons, others of appropriate caste contributed to the self-sufficiency of these penal institutions and worked as *mehtars*, *dhobis* and barbers.[38] Transported convicts were also engaged in experimental colonial revenue-raising schemes. In the Burmese settlements this included mining; in Mauritius, silk production and cotton, sugar and coffee cultivation.[39] Convicts were also used in British diplomatic and military efforts. A few were transferred from Mauritius to Madagascar during British economic and social negotiations in the region in the 1820s.[40] They were also employed as soldier-bearers during the Naning War in Malaya (1831–2).[41] A few dozen Eurasian convicts were sent to Indian penal settlements too, though they were not in practice put to hard labour. Rather they were employed as servants to Europeans,

---

[37] OIOC P.142.37: W.J. Butterworth, Governor of Singapore, to A. Turnbull, Under Secretary to Government Bengal, 26 February 1845.

[38] For a contemporary summary of the convict system in Benkulen and the Straits Settlements, see J.F.A. McNair, *Prisoners Their Own Warders: A record of the convict prison at Singapore in the Straits Settlements established 1825, discontinued 1873, together with a cursory history of the convict establishments at Bencoolen, Penang and Malacca from the year 1797*, Westminster: Archibald Constable and Co., 1899.

[39] OIOC P.141.18 (BJC 5 December 1837): E.A. Blundell, Commissioner Tenasserim Provinces, to R.D. Mangles, Secretary to Government Bengal, 17 September 1836; OIOC P.141.66 (BJC 9 July 1842): Blundell to G.A. Bushby, Secretary to Government of India, 22 June 1842; Anderson, *Convicts in the Indian Ocean*, pp. 46–8.

[40] Anderson, *Convicts in the Indian Ocean*, pp. 48–9.

[41] Emrys Chew, 'The Naning War, 1831–1832: Colonial authority and Malay resistance in the early period of British expansion', *Modern Asian Studies*, 32, 2 (1998), p. 382.

or worked as clerks or overseers in the settlements.[42] As Arnold puts it, '[t]he European body maintained its privileged status even in confinement.'[43]

Convict women made up only a tiny proportion of the total number of convicts sent to the settlements. Just six were transported to Mauritius. In Singapore in 1824 there were just twenty-four female convicts out of a total of almost 1,500.[44] As in India, women were kept at 'domestic' work in the barracks, notably cleaning, grinding grain and sewing. This employment in what was traditionally low-caste labour was always a potential flashpoint in colonial relations, and also produced a distinction that reflected metropolitan views on the appropriate visibility of women in the public and private spheres. When the Prison Discipline Committee reported on the penal settlements in 1838, male and female convicts were living together in the convict 'lines'. It was not till the 1840s that the settlements began to develop separate accommodation for women. This had little practical impact and convict men and women continued to live together into the 1840s.[45] There is no doubt that these imbalanced sex ratios had an impact on colonial gender relations. In 1856 Inspector-General of Prisons, F.J. Mouat, inspected Indian convict accommodation in Sandoway Gaol, and reported that several of the women had young children. 'If all that I heard regarding this female ward be true,' he said, 'it is little better than a brothel, and a scandal to the prison.'[46] He later claimed that he had been told (by whom we do not know) that the gaol *subadar* and *darogah* had contracted syphilis, apparently after intercourse with one of the women still in confinement. Further, he alleged that 'a quantity of gold and other expensive personal ornaments' were taken from women before his inspection. Mouat described this jewellery as 'most probably the price of concubinage'.[47] Shortly afterwards he recommended that the transportation of women cease altogether, though female convicts continued to be shipped overseas.

As well as being employed on various public works projects, officials put male convicts to work in a private capacity too, particularly as servants. They claimed

---

[42] Anderson, *Legible Bodies*, pp. 119–22.

[43] Arnold, 'The Colonial Prison', p. 170.

[44] Anderson, *Legible Bodies*, p. 37.

[45] OIOC P.142.37 (BJP 17 September 1845): Butterworth to Turnbull, 26 February 1845, enc. Report A: Present System of Management and Discipline of Convicts at Singapore, Superintendent, D.A. Stevenson, 9 January 1845.

[46] F.J. Mouat, *Reports on Jails Visited and Inspected in Bengal, Bihar and Arracan*, Calcutta: F. Carbery, Military Orphan Press, 1856, pp. 188–9.

[47] OIOC P.145.22 (BJP 31 July 1856): Mouat to C.J. Buckland, Secretary to Government Bengal, 24 May 1856.

that free labour was hard to come by, though their actions no doubt reflected a certain cultural and linguistic familiarity with their Indian charge. As one commentator argued for the Burmese settlements, employing Indian convicts saved them the trouble of learning the local language or teaching their servants the duties of a European household.[48] There is evidence that convict women forced the hand of colonial administrators in relation to work, and in South East Asia refused to take service outside the convict 'lines'.[49] The private employment of convicts—except in an official capacity such as groom—was unacceptable to officials on the mainland though, and if they found out about it, they expressed strong disapproval.[50] Nevertheless, there is no doubt that in some places there was a strong demand for convict workers from all quarters. After the abolition of the slave trade in 1807, Mauritius, for instance, faced an acute shortage of workers on its sugar plantations. In this context, in the 1810s several hundred Indian convicts were allocated to the island's labour hungry planters, in direct contravention of government orders.[51]

In contrast to the ambivalence and inconsistency of the Indian authorities on the issue of reform during the early nineteenth century, the language of rehabilitation was strongly in evidence in the operation of Indian penal settlements. This was partly because officials expressed the view that transportation was a punishment that ideally cut convicts off from their former communities, and hence supposedly criminal influences. Rather than expressing a strong commitment to such penological ideals, these notions became a rhetorical means of convincing the Indian presidencies to keep up convict supply. In 1817, for instance, Mauritian Governor Farquhar wrote that the convicts' moral character and habits had been improved to such an extent that they could no longer be considered a danger to the community. This reformation was of course predicated on the transformation of convicts into a useful labour force, with the penal and economic imperatives of transportation effectively inseparable.[52] Formerly Farquhar had

[48] John Furnivall, 'The Fashioning of Leviathan', *Journal of the Burma Research Society*, 29, 1 (1939), p. 41.

[49] OIOC P.136.31 (BJC 26 August 1824): Minute of W.E. Phillips on the mode of treatment of convicts transported to Prince of Wales Island, 15 April 1824.

[50] OIOC P.140.52 (BJC 22 Sept 1834): J.J. Harvey, Assistant Commissioner Arakan, to C. Macsween, Secretary to Government Bengal, 1 September 1834; Macsween to F. Dickinson, Superintendent Arakan, 22 September 1834.

[51] Anderson, *Convicts in the Indian Ocean*, pp. 62–6; Clare Anderson, 'The Bel Ombre Rebellion: Indian convicts in Mauritius, 1815–53' in Gwyn Campbell (ed.), *Abolition and its Aftermath in Indian Ocean Africa and Asia*, London: Routledge, 2005, pp. 50–66.

[52] Anderson, *Convicts in the Indian Ocean*, pp. 57–8.

been Lieutenant-Governor of Penang and so had long experience of the Indian convict system. Stamford Raffles too held appointments in Penang, Benkulen and Singapore. Twenty years later the Governor of the Straits Settlements, H.G. Bonham, wrote that reformation could be effected only through offering convicts hope. 'If on the other hand no such stimulus is given and the men are led to believe that they will, notwithstanding they have behaved well for a series of years, find themselves in exactly the same condition as on their arrival,' he wrote, 'it must induce a recklessness of disposition which independent of other considerations in my opinion in these remote stations it is most desirable by all proper means to repress.' This form of management, he argued, was a far more effective spur to good behaviour and tool of reform than severe punishment.[53] Indeed, in one early experiment in penal rehabilitation that also had the idea of permanent colonial migration and settlement in mind, after 1806 the authorities gave ticket-of-leave convicts in Benkulen, land, seeds and livestock. Their families were given the right of inheritance.[54]

As in India, such incentives were accompanied by the threat of severe punishment for misdemeanours. Everyday forms of resistance were a feature of all the penal settlements. J.F.A. McNair, erstwhile Superintendent of Convicts in the Straits, claimed that convicts caused sores and feigned rheumatism and paralysis in order to avoid work. One man had even pretended to be blind for some years to evade the labour gang.[55] In 1832 the Surveyor-General of Mauritius wrote that convicts continually stated themselves to be ill when they were not.[56] Prisoners were particularly quick to express their discontent when officials tried to make changes to the labour regime. Individual convicts deserted or even committed suicide. One convict in Mauritius, Topar Jaut, had been given a medical certificate exempting him from work but was nevertheless sent back to stone-breaking. His overseer reported that the man had said: 'sir I wold sooner dye than live for I am an old man not able to work.'[57] In 1818 a group of seventy-five transportation convicts in Mauritius transferred from road to plantation labour deserted *en masse*, claiming that their working conditions had deteriorated. There was a violent confrontation on the plantation which resulted in the biggest criminal

---

[53] TNSA JP vol. 326B: H.G. Bonham, Resident Councillor Singapore, to H. Chamier, Secretary to Government Madras, 21 April 1837.

[54] OIOC P.129.32 (BJC 1 January 1807): A regulation for the management of the convicts transported from Bengal to Fort Marlborough, 5 August 1806.

[55] McNair, *Prisoners Their Own Warders*, pp. 152–5.

[56] Anderson, *Convicts in the Indian Ocean*, pp. 68–9.

[57] Anderson, *Convicts in the Indian Ocean*, chapter 4 (quote p. 83).

2. Andamans flogging triangle. [Robert Heindl, *Meine Reise nach den Strafkolonien, mit vielen Originalaufnahmen*, Berlin and Vienna: Ullstein and Co., 1913]

trial in the territory of the British colonial period.[58] A further difficulty faced by prison administrators was the easy access that prisoners had to tools like crow bars and pick axes, which they used in sporadic attacks against European over- seers. During the 1840s a new administration tightened up the prison regime in the Tenasserim Provinces, restricting convicts' mobility and making greater demands on their labour. This led to a massive rise in convict escapes. The com- missioner wrote that prisoners used to a certain degree of liberty and light work naturally felt incarceration inside the prison walls and increased road labour in irons most severely.[59] In one violent protest, 120 convicts at work in Moulmein turned their working implements against their guards.[60]

Convicts engaging in such resistance could be moved down the hierarchy of punishment as well as up, losing as well as gaining privileges. Convicts were placed in heavy fetters or the stocks, or put to severe forms of labour like stone- breaking. From the moment they embarked on transportation ships they were also made subject to the often arbitrary punishment of flogging.[61] Although only a small percentage of convicts were ever beaten in this way, as convicts were al- ways punished in front of their working parties, large numbers of convicts would have witnessed what was a carefully orchestrated spectacle. Its threat therefore loomed large, with the infliction of up to one hundred stripes of the rattan an agonising punishment which could result in severe infections from which con- victs sometimes died.[62] Other punishments included imprisonment in local gaols or, in extreme cases, execution.[63] A number of convicts were also re-transported between penal settlements; a couple were even sent from Mauritius to Van Die- men's Land.[64] This serves to underline the relationship between penal settlements

---

[58] Anderson, 'The Bel Ombre Rebellion'.

[59] OIOC P.142.51 (BJC 22 July 1846): H.M. Durand, Commissioner Tenasserim Provinces, to Halliday, 21 May 1846.

[60] OIOC P.142.62 (BJC 10 March 1847): J.R. Colvin, Commissioner Tenasserim Provinces, to Halliday, 22 February 1847. For Mauritius, see also Anderson, *Convicts in the Indian Ocean*, pp. 61–2.

[61] Anderson, '"The Ferringees are Flying"', pp. 167–71.

[62] OIOC P.144.20 (BJC 8 April 1852): Minute by the Governor of Bengal, 31 March 1852; A.P. Phayre, Commissioner of Arakan, to Grant, 18 February 1852; History of the case of a prisoner named Mohcum Sing who died from the effects of flogging, J. Kearney, Sub-Assistant Surgeon, 28 January 1852.

[63] For more details of secondary punishments in Indian penal settlements, see Clare Anderson, 'The Execution of Rughobursing: The political economy of convict transportation and penal labour in early colonial Mauritius', *Studies in History*, 19, 2 (2003), pp. 185–97.

[64] Anderson, *Convicts in the Indian Ocean*, pp. 75–9; Angus Calder, *Gods, Mongrels and Demons: 101 brief but essential lives*, London: Bloomsbury, 2003, pp. 7–10.

and other spaces of confinement or punishment like the flogging triangle, the gaol, the gallows and the guillotine.[65] Moreover, and remembering the penal tattoo inscribed on the forehead of each life convict, such corporal interventions reveal the reality of a somewhat uncertain and unsteady coalescence of penal strategies during this period.

Despite the weapons available to the colonial armoury, the penal regimes in place in the convict settlements often seemed relatively sympathetic, and as such did not always meet with the approval of the Indian authorities. The Prison Discipline Committee found 'glaring defects' at Singapore, for instance, particularly in relation to the employment of convicts as peons or servants. Such occupations, it maintained, were not hard labour at all.[66] At the end of 1837 the Madras judicial authorities decided that because, in their eyes, sentences of hard labour were not being enforced properly, they would remove the presidency's convicts from the island and ship them to Tenasserim.[67] The Resident Councillor countered the claims about the absence of hard labour with some force. First, he argued, there was no remunerative indoor labour to which convicts could be put, as the Prison Discipline Committee had suggested. Second, he noted that convicts were excused from hard labour only once they had, through good behaviour, progressed up the penal ladder. The Bengal authorities backed him up, further underlining the need for incentives in the peculiar circumstances of overseas penal settlements.[68] The Madras authorities subsequently conceded the point and decided to resume transportation to Singapore.[69] The great contemporary advocate of penal labour at the time, F.J. Mouat, was, on the other hand, most impressed by the nature of convict work in the settlements. He visited the Straits in 1851 and later wrote, 'there exists in no other country a more remarkable example of the successful industrial training of convicts.' Indeed, he noted, Singapore's St Andrew's cathedral, entirely built with convict labour, was 'one of the finest specimens of ecclesiastical architecture which I had seen in the East.'[70]

From time to time contemporaries in South East Asia attempted to calculate the value of convict labour. Their approximations were entirely dependent on

---

[65]   During the early nineteenth century convict (and slave) lepers in Mauritius were also subject to transfer to Ile Curieuse (Seychelles) and Diego Garcia. Anderson, *Convicts in the Indian Ocean*, p. 42.

[66]   OIOC P.141.1 (BJC 13 September 1836): C.E. Trevelyan, Officiating Secretary Prison Discipline Committee, to Mangles, 30 June 1836.

[67]   TNSA JP vol. 326B: Bonham to Chamier, 21 April 1837.

[68]   Ibid.: H.G. Bonham, Resident Councillor Singapore, to J.P. Grant, Secretary Prison Discipline Committee, 5 April 1836; Mangles to Trevelyan, 13 September 1836.

[69]   Ibid.: Chamier to Mangles, 17 October 1837.

[70]   Mouat, 'On Prison Ethics and Prison Labour', p. 232.

changing local considerations, particularly with regard to the relationship be-tween convict and other forms of labour. In the early years of settlement, officials maintained that notwithstanding the cost of rations, accommodation and super-vision, a convict workforce was far cheaper than hired free labour. In Arakan and Tenasserim, for instance, the prohibitive cost of local labour was the rationale behind the first request for Indian convicts.[71] It was later said that free labourers could not be found at any price. In 1845 the Principal Assistant Commissioner of Arakan wrote that because there was so much land awaiting cultivation, local communities would hire themselves out only at very high wages. Migrant la-bourers from Chittagong came only for the harvest, and returned home at the start of the rains.[72] Similarly the Governor of the Straits Settlements, W.J. But-terworth, noted in 1847 that it was very difficult to determine the actual value of convict labour, and it was far greater than appeared from simple calculations alone.[73]

When the labour supply eased, or settlements began to flourish, doubts started to emerge about the productivity of convict workers, and transportation fell from favour. As Indian indentured labourers began to arrive in Mauritius during the second half of the 1830s, for instance, questions were raised about the value of Indian convicts. As a result of the changing labour relations on the island which favoured indentured workers over convict ones, it was argued that convicts were far less productive than their new counterparts. Transportation from India to Mauritius thus ceased in 1837, though the penal settlement itself was not broken up till 1853. By the 1840s merchant interests in the increasingly economically dynamic port of Singapore also began to feel some anxiety about accommodat-ing a penal settlement.[74] This was at least in part because of the strong public presence of convict labour gangs—indeed the rationale of the system demanded their widespread dispersal across the Straits. In early calls for the cessation of transportation to the island, in 1851 the *Singapore Free Press* wrote of the Straits as 'a common sewer'; three years later it lamented that 'the very dregs of the popu-lation' were transported there.[75]

---

[71] OIOC P.138.56 (BJC 10 January 1828): Extract of a letter from the Civil Commissioner in the Tenasserim Provinces, 14 December 1827.

[72] OIOC P.142.46 (BJC 15 April 1846): A.P. Phayre, Principal Assistant Commissioner Arakan, to D. Williams, in charge current duties Commissioner's Office Kyaukpyu, 10 December 1845.

[73] OIOC P.142.60 (BJC 27 January 1847): Butterworth to A.R. Young, Under Secretary to Gov-ernment Bengal, 9 December 1846.

[74] For instance: OIOC P.142.42 (BJC 7 January 1846): Butterworth to Turnbull, 24 September 1845; Turnbull to Butterworth, 7 January 1846.

[75] C.M. Turnbull, *A History of Singapore, 1819–1988*, Oxford University Press, 1996, p. 55.

The situation in Burma was quite different. Still relatively undeveloped and with a relatively small number of free European settlers, the demand for convicts remained high during this period. The long-term impact of transportation on Burma has however been questioned. John Furnivall, writing long after the abolition of the settlements there in 1862, claimed that the 'common sense policy' of importing convicts during the early years of British settlement was a 'bad guide for empire builders'. Convict labour, he claimed, drove out free labour because the latter was unable to compete with a constant supply of cheap labour. Moreover, free labourers would not accept the sort of work that came to be associated with convicts. Therefore, convicts both diminished the supply of free labour and raised the rate of wages. Moreover, outdoor labour became stigmatised. Furnivall claimed that in the long term, the penal settlement created an immense barrier between the British and the Burmese. This was, he argued, still in place on the eve of the Second World War.[76]

While the importance of convict labour to the economic development of South East Asia and Mauritius is unquestionable, it is also important to recognise the significance of convicts' social impact in these regions. Convicts worked side by side with slaves and local prisoners. Given the wide dispersal of convict working parties and their relative freedom of movement—at least once they had served any probationary period of hard labour in place at the time—it is not surprising that convicts struck up relationships of all kinds with local communities. It is important to stress the permeability of these early penal settlements. Convicts were involved in petty production and the buying and selling of a wide range of goods. They also participated in religious festivals like the *Muharrum*, and indulged in leisure activities with local social groups. There is little sense that local communities stigmatised convicts. This was perhaps in part related to convicts' self-projected identities. In Mauritius, for instance, convicts were often described as *sepoys* transported for rebelling against the British. Such an image was no doubt compounded by their wearing of military uniforms, which was common amongst north Indian hill workers at the time. In the Straits Settlements convicts called themselves *kumpanee ke naukur*, or (East India) Company servants.[77] Anand Yang argues that this self-appellation was probably connected to the relatively recent emergence of the concept of 'prisoner', and the relationship between distance and work in the more common military title *naukur*.[78] Imbalanced convict sex ratios meant that male convicts forged affective relationships

[76] Furnivall, 'The Fashioning of Leviathan', p. 43.

[77] Anderson, *Legible Bodies*, pp. 105–6.

[78] Yang, 'Indian Convict Workers', pp. 3–4.

with local women.[79] There is no question that there are large numbers of convict descendents in South East Asia and Mauritius. Despite the general pardons extended to all life convicts during the 1850s, '60s and '70s, few returned to India. Indeed, Rajesh Rai has established a clear connection between the convict warder system and continued Indian employment in the Singaporean prison service into the 1970s.[80] It is also clear that convict transportation paved the way for more substantial labour streams constituted through the later Indian indentured migration.[81]

THE MUTINY-REBELLION OF 1857–8 AND THE ANDAMAN ISLANDS

As the mutiny-rebellion spread across north India during 1857–8, shock waves of all kinds followed in its wake. One of these was a fractured penal policy, for during the course of the uprising, dozens of gaols in the North West Provinces, Bengal and the Panjab were destroyed or broken open and some 20,000 prisoners set free.[82] The question of what to do with these recaptured prisoners, as well as others convicted of mutiny-related offences, greatly exercised colonial minds. At the same time the merchant community in the Straits indicated its unwillingness to accept mutineer-rebels. In Singapore a rumour spread that the 3,000 Indian convicts in the settlement were planning an uprising. In a number of public petitions and meetings, Europeans questioned the loyalty of the Indian garrison and lamented the dangers posed by the apparent freedoms still conferred on the convicts.[83] Several families were apparently sent aboard ships in the harbour for safety. The press reported the existence of a 'feverish anxiety' which had led to women fainting in church.[84] The local press reported:

---

[79] For Mauritius, see Anderson, *Convicts in the Indian Ocean*, chapter 5; Yang, 'Indian Convict Workers', p. 4.

[80] Rajesh Rai, 'Sepoys, Convicts and the "Bazaar" Contingent: The emergence and exclusion of "Hindustani" pioneers at the Singapore frontier', *Journal of Southeast Asian Studies*, 35, 1 (2004), pp. 1–19.

[81] PP 1875 XXIV Mauritius (Treatment of Immigrants): Report of the Royal Commissioners appointed to inquire into the treatment of immigrants in Mauritius, p. 27.

[82] OIOC P.206.62 (IJP 27 August 1860): statements showing the number of prisoners who escaped from the gaols of the North West Provinces, Bengal and Panjab during the mutiny of 1857, and who are still at large.

[83] OIOC P.188.47 (IPP 2 October 1857): petition of M.F. Davidson, C. Spottiswoode and eleven others, 4 August 1857; memorial of the Christian Inhabitants of Campong Bencoolen, and the adjoining Campongs (A. Poons, A. Simonides, W. Woodford and twenty-seven others), 21 August 1857.

[84] OIOC P.188.47 (IPP 2 October 1857): Blundell to C. Beadon, Secretary to Government of India, 28 August 1857; 'The panic', n.d.

We are no longer an infant colony—that stage has been passed when convict labour is either desirable or necessary. But the treatment of the convicts reflects strongly upon a system which holds out greater privileges than are conferred on nearly all the lower classes of natives. Either let the flow of convicts cease, or place them under a proper system, with a large body of European Troops to keep them down. We would rather dispense with their services altogether, and return to the various Presidencies their offscourings.[85]

The settlement refused to accept any more Indian convicts, though it remained a destination for convicts from Ceylon into the 1860s. The penal settlement was broken up in 1873.[86] Officials in the penal settlements in Burma were similarly nervous about the transportation of mutineer-rebels. Commissioner A. Fytche wrote of the extreme agitation and 'unsteadiness' of the Indian convicts in Moulmein. He feared that they would combine in rebellion with Indian gaol peons, police and possibly the free Muslims of the town. When a batch of fifty mutineer-rebel convicts arrived in July 1857, he refused to land them.[87] The mutiny-rebellion thus marked the end of transportation to Arakan and eventually the Tenasserim Provinces too.

Before the mutiny-rebellion the British had floated the idea of resettling the Andaman Islands, using convicts as a means to fulfil their longer term aim of productive colonial expansion, notably the protection of shipping and trade routes in the region. The impact of the uprising, however, urged the establishment of a place for the exile of political offenders. The trajectory of proposed settlement in the Andamans therefore changed, and the committee already set up to consider the suitability of the Islands for settlement was ordered instead to report on where a penal settlement should be best located. Several thousand mutineer-rebels were transported there; ordinary offenders subsequently trod in their footsteps. The long-term vision of the British with respect to the Andamans might perhaps be found in the report of a surgeon visitor to the islands in 1859. The Islands, he wrote, might become a source of riches, 'a new outlet for the knowledge, civilisation, commerce, and Christianity of our country'. 'The punishment of a section of Bengal convicts is', he continued, 'but a small object compared with the attainment of a great end.'[88]

---

[85] OIOC P.188.47 (IPP 2 October 1857): 'The panic', n.d.

[86] Turnbull, 'Convicts in the Straits', pp. 93, 103.

[87] OIOC P.146.12D (BJP 28 January 1858): A. Fytche, Officiating Commissioner Tenasserim and Martaban Provinces, to E. Lushington, Officiating Assistant Secretary to Government Bengal, 22 July 1857.

[88] OIOC P.206.61 (IJP 29 July 1859): G.G. Brown's report on the sanitary state of the Andamans, March 1859.

The character of the convict colony established in the Andaman Islands in 1858 was very different to the earlier penal settlements in neighbouring South East Asia and across the Indian Ocean in Mauritius. To a large degree this was because the British first settled the Islands as a penal colony, unlike other areas of South East Asia which received convicts after they came under colonial control. Equally, in the Andamans the convicts remained almost entirely separate from the often hostile indigenous communities that bordered the penal colony. Indeed, during the early years of settlement the landscape and population of the Islands provided a sort of natural prison. In the absence of secure places of confinement or sufficient personnel, the threats posed by the unknown jungle, sea and inhabitants comprised the convict guard.[89] Though one mutineer-rebel escaped from the penal colony and lived with a tribal community for over a year,[90] during the early years of settlement, convicts who came across the local population were more likely to be killed than welcomed. Despite these differences, the Straits, Mauritius, Burma and the Andamans shared certain features. Like their South East Asian neighbours, Andamans' officials were keen to promote economy and self-sufficiency.

Superintendent J.P. Walker arrived in the Andamans with the first batch of two hundred mutineer-rebels in March 1858. Formerly he had been in charge of Agra Gaol and so had considerable experience of convict management. The first convicts were followed by thousands more: 3,697 during the first eighteen months alone.[91] With nothing but ruins left of the settlement abandoned sixty years earlier, Walker lost no time in putting the convicts to clearing Chatham Island in the mouth of the harbour—felling trees, digging ground and so on.[92] The convicts lived in tents, and Walker organised them in military fashion, a type of discipline that of course had much in common with the systems developed for penal labour more generally.[93] Military-style barracks for convicts were constructed later on. The convicts formed section gangs of twenty-five men,

[89] Anderson, 'The Politics', p. 44.
[90] M.V. Portman, *A History of Our Relations with the Andamanese, vol. I*, Calcutta: Superintendent Government Printing, 1899, pp. 279–88.
[91] OIOC P.206.62 (IJP 6 January 1860): J.C. Haughton, Superintendent Port Blair, to W. Grey, Secretary to Government of India, 13 November 1859.
[92] The following details are taken from OIOC P.188.53 (IJP 7 May 1858): J.P. Walker, superintendent Port Blair, to Beadon, 6 April 1858. The report is also at NAI Home (Judicial), 7 May 1858, nos 24–46. For extracts from the original correspondence, see also Portman, *A History of Our Relations*, chapter 8.
[93] Douglas M. Peers, 'Sepoys, Soldiers and the Lash: Race, caste and army discipline in India, 1820–50', *Journal of Imperial and Commonwealth History*, 23, 2 (1995), pp. 211–47.

each under a convict section gangsman. Four sections made a subdivision, and these were placed under a convict subdivision gangsman. Four subdivisions constituted a division, over which a convict division gangsman, a free overseer and a native doctor were placed in charge. As Chatham was cleared, convicts were sent to the relatively remote north side of Phoenix Bay, followed by nearby Ross Island. Other areas gradually came under colonial control.

From the very inception of the settlement, Walker divided convicts up according to class and status. The *bania* system that he developed for the provisioning of convicts, for instance, was in practice almost entirely staffed by former sepoys.[94] Gangsmen too were selected from the 'political' convicts, Walker noting that they were superior to free gaol overseers he had seen in mainland prisons.[95] Presumably their familiarity with military discipline was a boon to the management of convicts. Faced with ceaseless convict escapes and the threat of a convict uprising never far from his mind, Walker also relied heavily on the type of corporal punishments associated with the army.[96] He adopted a policy of flogging all convicts who returned from escape bids with thirty stripes with a rattan cane.[97] An administrator later posted to the Islands claimed that the 'worst characters' were taken to the beach handcuffed in pairs and then secured to the ground with an iron bar through their fetters. They did whatever work they could manage there.[98] Notoriously, just two months after settlement, Walker conducted the mass hanging of eighty-one convicts who had tried to escape.[99] Although his actions reflected the imperatives of the extreme circumstances of the colony, the mainland authorities were not impressed. Walker showed little remorse, retorting to criticism that convict management in the Andamans was a quite different matter to India.[100]

The social complexities of the penal colony increased further after it was opened up to ordinary offenders—male and female—after the mutiny-rebellion. By the 1870s a class system based on that developed in the Straits and Burma had

[94]   OIOC P.206.61 (IJP 29 July 1859): G.G. Brown's report on the sanitary state of the Andamans, n.d. March 1859.
[95]   OIOC P.206.61 (IJP 20 September 1859): Mouat to Rivers Thompson, Junior Secretary to Government Bengal, 3 September 1859; Walker to Grey, 10 September 1859.
[96]   Peers, 'Sepoys, Soldiers and the Lash'.
[97]   OIOC P.206.60 (IJP 12 November 1858): Walker to Beadon, 4 September 1858.
[98]   Portman, *A History of Our Relations, vol. I*, p. 257.
[99]   NAI Home (Judicial) 28 May 1858: Walker to Beadon, 1 May 1858; NAI Home (Judicial) 30 July 1858: Walker to Beadon, 7 May 1858; NAI Home (Judicial) 16 July 1858: Walker to Beadon, 12 June 1858.
[100] OIOC P.206.60 (IJP 17 September 1858): Walker to Beadon, 7 August 1858.

developed. Convicts were divided into groups on the basis of behaviour and time served, and given the opportunity to rise to 'self-supporter' status—the equivalent of the South East Asian ticket-of-leave. The differences between convicts were, as in South East Asia, expressed through their uniforms.[101] By this time too the nature of the work performed by convicts had undergone a radical shift. The Andamans administration strove towards self-sufficiency and as well as performing the hard labour associated with land clearance and development, convicts worked as tailors, milkmen, shopkeepers, as well as taking on the operational roles of clerks, book keepers and servants. Indeed, a number of commentators noted the deep irony of employing convicted murderers (for most Andaman convicts had been convicted for serious offences) as nannies or of entrusting them with the tools of the barber's trade—cut-throat razors.[102] In a recent study of the penal colony in the Andaman Islands during the second half of the nineteenth century, Satadru Sen has linked the issue of convict labour to broader attempts to mould Indians into rational, useful and orderly political subjects. In so doing he reveals its fundamental contradiction, for work was supposed to both demean *and* reform the prisoner.[103]

As in the South East Asian and Mauritian settlements, convicts in the Andaman Islands were not always compliant with the penal regime. Go-slows at work, the destruction of tools and attacks on overseers are all well–documented in the Andaman archive. In the most extraordinary incident of its kind, Panjabi convict Shere Ali assassinated the viceroy of India, Lord Mayo, when he visited the Islands in 1872.[104] Despite its seeming hopelessness, convicts also continued to escape. In one case, two Sikh convicts got as far as London, having been picked up at sea a hundred miles west of the Andamans by a Norwegian vessel. The men were placed in the Stranger's Home for Asiatic Seamen in the East End, and apparently visited Crystal Palace before being identified and sent back to the Andamans where they were lodged at Viper Island, by then a place of confinement for especially notorious convicts. One of them escaped twice more before disappearing from the historical record altogether.[105]

---

[101] Anderson, *Legible Bodies*, chapter 4.

[102] Martin Wynne, *On Honourable Terms: The memoirs of some Indian Police Officers 1915–1948*, London: British Association for Cemeteries in South Asia, 1985, p. 157; Robert Heindl, *Meine Reise nach den Strafkolonien, mit vielen Originalaufnahmen*, Berlin and Vienna: Ullstein and Co., 1913, facing p. 369.

[103] Sen, *Disciplining Punishment*, chapter 3.

[104] Sen, *Disciplining Punishment*, pp. 67–9 passim.

[105] Anderson, *Legible Bodies*, p. 153; *The Times*, 26 December 1873.

In 1858 Walker had championed the introduction of women into the penal colony as a means of assuring social and political stability. His family emigration scheme ran into difficulties though, mainly because convicts' wives were unwilling to travel to the Islands, and it was only with the introduction of female convicts that women began to arrive—albeit in much smaller numbers than men. As in India and its early penal settlements, work categories in the colony were gendered, and by the end of the century women worked the looms of the Islands' Female Factory.[106] Sen argues that it was only with the social diversification of the colony that convict labour more generally was divided into two types—punitive and rehabilitative—and there was a shift from labour as pure punishment towards skilled, reformative work.[107] Of course the nature of work in the colony during the early months and years of colonial settlement did not so much reflect a particular penal strategy as the overwhelming need to provide basic infrastructure for a fragile settlement.

Although transportation was supposed to exclude convicts from their former social and kin networks, it is clear that it did not. Letters were exchanged between the mainland and the Islands with a perhaps surprising regularity.[108] The detailed knowledge that many Indians had about their convict relatives and the Andaman Islands is astonishing. There is even evidence that convicts received visitors from the mainland, much to the consternation of the Government of India, which by the first decade of the twentieth century feared an investigative journalist might slip in.[109] The spread of knowledge about convict settlements had an important impact on penal policy. The 1877 Prison Conference reported that because of the large number of ex-convicts who had returned from the Andamans to India, transportation had lost its deterrent effect. 'Port Blair', they noted, 'is now a haven where prisoners would be.'[110] Eleven years later the Jail Management Committee made the same point.[111] Another report of 1890 argued that convicts saw

[106] Satadru Sen, 'Rationing Sex: Female convicts in the Andamans', *South Asia*, 30, 1 (1999), pp. 29–59.

[107] S.N. Aggarwal, *The Heroes of Cellular Jail*, Patiala, Panjab: Publication Bureau Punjabi University, 1995, pp. 79–87; Sen, *Disciplining Punishment*, chapter 3.

[108] NAI Home (Port Blair) A Proceedings, February 1876, nos 53–5: Note of C.A. Barwell, 18 November 1875.

[109] NAI Home (Port Blair) A Proceedings, October 1904, nos 60–1: W.R.H. Merk to H.H. Risley, 2 July 1904; Risley to Merk, 27 October 1904.

[110] NAI Home (Judicial) A Proceedings, September 1877, nos 68–88: Report of the Prison Conference (1877).

[111] NAI Home (Jails) A Proceedings, December 1889, nos 1–47: Report of the Committee on Jail Management in India (1888).

transportation as preferable to imprisonment on the mainland. It recommended the introduction of a 'penal stage' when convicts were first transported.[112]

These reports were the spur to the construction of a cellular gaol in Port Blair, built between 1896 and 1906. The gaol was an imposing Benthamite structure with a central watchtower overlooking seven wings. Life convicts were to be confined there for six months and then put to hard labour for four and a half years. After this they received an allowance and were eligible to become overseers. After ten years they earned a ticket to become a self-supporter, when they could send for their family or marry, and keep cattle. However, they were not free and could not leave the colony. Only after twenty to twenty-five years in the Andamans did the individual earn absolute release. Women were obliged to remain in the Female Factory unless employed as a domestic servant or married and living with her husband. She was eligible for outside employment and marriage after five years, but could not earn absolute release for twenty. Yet this last ditch attempt to reinvigorate the fear of transportation was always doomed to fail. Two years before the cellular gaol was finished, one Andamans official wrote that penal settlements could only ever exist for a short time. Eventually, he wrote, the terror of distance and the unknown disappear and transportation loses its effect. This had been the case in Australia, Singapore and New Caledonia, and he predicted would also occur in the Andamans.[113]

Shortly after the cellular gaol was completed the Andamans became an attractive destination for 'political' offenders whom the British wished to remove from the mainland. The authorities in India transported about five hundred in total, not including the 535 Tharrawaddy rebels whom the British transported from Burma in 1934. These convicts were middle-class men who had been convicted of conspiracy or sedition against the British.[114] The Indian Jails Committee of 1919–20 recommended the general abolition of transportation to the Andaman Islands, proposing that in future only especially dangerous offenders be sent. In 1921, however, the Government of India decided to abandon the penal settlement altogether, and started the process of repatriating Andaman convicts to mainland gaols. However, provincial governments were unable to cope, so at the beginning of 1922 transportation for male, non-political convicts was renewed.

[112] NAI Home (Port Blair) A Proceedings, June 1890, nos 74–8: Report on the Andamans by Mr C.J. Lyall and Surgeon-Major A.S. Lethbridge.

[113] NAI Home (Port Blair) A Proceedings, July 1906, nos 38–40: W.R.H. Merk, 'Note on the Andamans', 15 September 1904.

[114] Iqbal Singh, *The Andaman Story*, pp. 218–19; U. Kumar Singh, *Political Prisoners in India*, New Delhi: Oxford University Press, 1998, pp. 50–9.

Given the difficulties associated with imprisoning political prisoners on the mainland, in 1932 the government decided to reintroduce their transportation too.[115]

Anti-colonial agitators were subject to a quite different penal regime to ordinary offenders. They were isolated from the mass of prisoners, remained in the cellular gaol for the whole term of their sentence, and were put to more penal forms of labour like coir pounding, oakum picking and oil grinding. At the heart of these punishments was humiliation and degradation.[116] A series of reports on their treatment later appeared in the Indian press.[117] Both the Lahore *Tribune* and *The Bengalee* of Calcutta published accounts of the Andamans.[118] A number of nationalists also published memoirs after their release, in which they described the inhumanity and many indignities of transportation. Middle-class and high-caste prisoners were unfamiliar with many aspects of prison life, especially common messing and communal bathing, and thus felt its many deprivations acutely.[119] At the same time many suffered further sanctions for continued protest through refusal to work and hunger-striking.[120] Such tactics ultimately proved effective though, for after a mass hunger-strike in 1937, all the political prisoners then in the cellular gaol were repatriated to India.[121]

By the time the Japanese invaded the Andaman Islands in 1943 the British had fled. Two of the wings of the cellular gaol were destroyed either during the war or by a massive earthquake that shook the Islands in 1941. The Japanese invasion was of course the precursor to independence. Since then the Islands have been associated mainly with the relatively small number of nationalist convicts, and have thus become a prominent symbol of colonial defeat.[122] One historian writes that the Andamans have been 'sanctified by the dust of Martyrs' feet and their sweat and blood'.[123] A large proportion of the Islands' population today

---

[115] Mathur, *Kala Pani*, pp. 102–9.

[116] Sen, *Disciplining Punishment*, pp. 264–72.

[117] Sen, *Disciplining Punishment*, p. 268; Mathur, *Kala Pani*, p. 82.

[118] Iqbal Singh, *The Andaman Story*, pp. 193–5.

[119] B.K. Ghose, *The Tale of My Exile*, Pondicherry: Arya Office, 1922; Bhai Parmanand, *The Story of My Life*, New Delhi: S. Chand and Co., 1982; V.D. Savarkar, *The Story of My Transportation for Life*, Bombay: Sadbhakti Publications, 1950; B. Kumar Sinha, *In Andamans: The Indian Bastille*, New Delhi: People's Publishing House, 1988 [1st ed. 1939].

[120] Iqbal Singh, *The Andaman Story*, chapters 20, 21; Mathur, *Kala Pani*, chapters 8, 9.

[121] Mathur, *Kala Pani*, p. 122.

[122] B.L. Chak, *Green Islands in the Sea*, New Delhi: Publications Division, Ministry of Information and Broadcasting, Government of India, 1967 (Preface by Indira Gandhi).

[123] Aggarwal, *The Heroes*, pp. 20–6.

are 'local-born', that is, the descendents of Indian convicts. They have few of the caste strictures regarding marriage and other forms of social communication associated with communities on the mainland, and Hindus, Muslims and Christians celebrate festivals like *diwali*. They speak a form of creolised Andaman Hindi, which has its roots in the Andamans as a multi-lingual convict society.[124]

OVERLAPPING SPACES OF CONFINEMENT: RESETTLING THE CRIMINAL TRIBES

During the nineteenth century itinerant communities across the empire became associated with criminal activity. In Australia and New Zealand persons of no fixed abode—many of whom were indigenous to the continent—were both blamed for social disorder and seen as a threat to progress.[125] In the white settler societies of British colonial Africa vagrancy legislation was also bound up with fears of sexual danger.[126] As Florence Bernault illustrates in this volume, elsewhere in Africa, laws on vagrancy were very much part of the attempt to control the casual labour pool.[127] In India too the government passed legislation designed to both criminalise and control particular communities, though its targets were on the whole socially excluded groups considered hereditary criminals. In 1871 the first of three Criminal Tribes Acts came into force, its roots lying in earlier associations between non-settled communities, vagrancy and criminality.[128] Criminal tribes legislation comprised surveillance measures against communities—usually itinerant or displaced tribal groups—considered to be made up of hereditary criminals. Rachel J. Tolen describes this 'criminality' as a way of life resistant to wage labour and changing modes of production.[129] The Criminal

[124] G.K. Ghosh, *Tourism Perspective in Andaman and Nicobar Islands*, New Delhi: A.P.H. Publishing, 1998, pp. 87–8, 111–15.

[125] S. Davies, "'Ragged, Dirty ... Infamous and Obscene": The "vagrant" in late nineteenth-century Melbourne' in D. Philips and S. Davies (eds), *A Nation of Rogues? Crime, law and punishment in colonial Australia*, Melbourne University Press, 1994, pp. 141–57; M. Fairburn, 'Vagrants, "Folk Devils" and Nineteenth-Century New Zealand as a Bondless Society', *Historical Studies*, 21, 85 (1985), pp. 502–25.

[126] Jeremy Martens, 'Polygamy, Sexual Danger, and the Creation of Vagrancy Legislation in Colonial Natal', *Journal of Imperial and Commonwealth History*, 31, 3 (2003), pp. 24–45.

[127] Justin Willis, 'Thieves, Drunkards and Vagrants: Defining crime in colonial Mombassa, 1902–32' in David M. Anderson and David Killingray (eds), *Policing the Empire: Government, authority and control, 1830–1940*, Manchester University Press: 1991, pp. 219–35.

[128] Singha, *A Despotism of Law*, p. 44.

[129] Rachel J. Tolen, 'Colonizing and Transforming the Criminal Tribesmen: The Salvation Army in British India', *American Ethnologist*, 18, 1 (1991), p. 112. For the earlier period in South India,

Tribes Acts were first implemented in the North West Provinces, Awadh and the Panjab. They were gradually extended across India and by 1947 an extraordinary thirteen million people were classified under them. The disciplinary measures put in place included compulsory registration and a pass system. Of interest here are the reformatory and agricultural settlements that were set up to resettle 'offenders' and restrict their mobility, for the form they assumed was based on the Indian penal settlement.

As Tolen argues, the criminal tribes legislation 'encoded social relations in spatial geography'. Some of the reformatory settlements were controlled by the government. Other bodies responsible for their supervision were the London Missionary Society, the American Baptist Mission and the Salvation Army, the latter being particularly influential. The Salvation Army took over its first reformatory in 1908 on the invitation of the government of the United Provinces. Its aim was the transformation of entire communities into disciplined social bodies—indeed the motto of William Booth, the founder of the Army, was 'get into their skins!' Clothing, ornamentation and personal habits were targeted for change, and a rigid sense of time-discipline underlay both the daily roll call and the pass system. According to Tolen, it was labour that was the most important disciplinary practice. Factories, workshops and industrial schools were all set up as a means of overcoming caste—the demands of caste were of course seen as the spur to criminal behaviour—and thus of transforming born criminals into productive labourers. Commissioner Booth-Tucker termed this approach 'criminocurology'.[130]

The relationship between labour and reform was further tested in South India, for in 1913 the police authorities in the Madras Presidency proposed the use of criminal tribes in private enterprise. Though the government still favoured agricultural settlements, under the police scheme, the need for workers was established in particular areas, and then communities included in the Criminal Tribes Acts were targeted for employment in these areas. Subsequently, factories were declared criminal tribes settlements and a captive workforce created. Government policy shifted in 1916 when formal industrial settlements—for instance in the vicinity of textile mills—were set up. The criminal tribes in turn were forcibly settled and put to work. In 1916 the Madras Inspector-General of Prisons

---

see also R. Ahuja, 'The Origins of Colonial Labour Policy in Late Eighteenth-Century Madras', *International Review of Social History*, 44, 2 (1999), pp. 159–95.

[130] Tolen, 'Colonizing and Transforming', pp. 113–20.

likened conditions to slavery. The 1919–20 All-India Jails Commission referred to the settlements as 'novel kinds of jails'.[131]

There were material overlaps in the spaces of confinement of colonial India too. From the end of 1863 hundreds of indigenous Andamans tribals were forced into the Andaman Homes. This was a bid to 'civilise the savage' and so put an end to anti-colonial hostilities.[132] A number of criminal tribesmen and women were resettled in the Andaman Islands too. Missionaries were already active in the colony. The St John's Ambulance Brigade—like the Salvation Army, a religious organisation—trained convicts in elementary anatomy, physiology and sanitation and basic first aid.[133] Missionaries first took one of the so-called criminal tribes from Chotanagpur to the Andamans in 1906. They were followed by a group of Karen labourers from Burma, settled by the American Baptist Mission in 1925. Between 1926 and 1928 over five hundred Bhantus from the United Provinces were also resettled on the Islands. The imagined cultural geography of the Andamans is such that these groups now strongly associate themselves with political transportation to the Islands, and represent themselves as freedom fighters against British rule.[134]

CONCLUSION

What is perhaps most striking about penal transportation in the Indian Ocean from the late eighteenth to mid-twentieth centuries is the extent to which its operation departed from the changing thrust of penal thinking and practice in metropolitan Britain. Indeed, during the mid-nineteenth century, transportation from Britain (and the colonies) to Australia had fallen from favour. Yet it was at this precise historical moment that transportation from India to the Andaman Islands took off, and it was only much later—with the Second World War and the move to independence—that the penal colony was finally abolished. The

---

131 Meena Radhakrishna, 'The Criminal Tribes Act in the Madras Presidency: Implications for itinerant trading communities', *Indian Economic and Social History Review*, 26, 3 (1989), pp. 283–90.

132 Satadru Sen, 'Policing the Savage: Segregation, labor and state medicine in the Andamans', *Journal of Asian Studies*, 58, 3 (1999), pp. 753–73; Sita Venkateswar, *Development and Ethnocide: Colonial practices in the Andaman Islands*, Copenhagen: International Work Group for Indigenous Affairs, 2004, pp. 86–112. See also Andaman Homes' superintendent Portman's account in *A History of Our Relations*.

133 H.L. Adam, *Oriental Crime*, London: T. Werner Laurie, 1909, pp. 364–6.

134 S.K. Bhattacharyya et al., *All India Anthropometric Survey: Andamans*, Calcutta: Anthropological Survey of India, 1993; Ghosh, *Tourism Perspective*, pp. 90–2, 95–6; Mathur, *Kala Pani*, pp. 261–2.

reason for such a sharp breach perhaps lies in differing metropolitan/colonial perspectives on punishment more generally. At the same time there is no doubt that there was a distinctly cultural element to transportation in the South Asian context, and discourses about the pervasiveness of caste and the social death constituted by overseas transportation remained strong into the twentieth century.

It is clear that by the middle of the nineteenth century the gaol authorities in Britain were moving away from the association between imprisonment and productive labour. Given the exigencies of the colonial economy in South East Asia and the Andamans—and indeed elsewhere across the empire—this relationship remained central to modes of punishment.[135] Far from marking a change in the epistemology of punishment, therefore, the opening up of the Andaman Islands as a penal colony in the wake of the mutiny-rebellion of 1857–8 simply continued the association between transportation and productive labour. Punitive work was only properly introduced as a special sanction in the wake of the transportation of political offenders to the Islands after 1900. The penal colony then took on a different role, as a distant space of confinement for nationalist agitators whose presence on the mainland was considered threatening or undesirable. In independent India, the Andamans were solely associated with this later history and, though the cellular gaol continued to be used as a local prison, transportation was not revived. The political economy of the penal colony thus assured its abandonment, but the gaol remains central to modes of punishment across the postcolonial Indian Ocean world.

BIBLIOGRAPHICAL NOTE

The historiography of convict transportation has grown substantially in recent years. For the early-modern Portuguese empire, see Timothy J. Coates, *Convicts and Orphans: Forced and state-sponsored colonizers in the Portuguese empire, 1550– 1755*, Stanford University Press, 2001, and Maria Augusta Lima Cruz, 'Exiles and Renegades in Early Sixteenth Century Portuguese India', *Indian Economic and Social History Review*, 23, 3 (1986), pp. 249–62. Two major new publications on France are Alice Bullard, *Exile to Paradise: Savagery and civilization in Paris and*

---

[135] *Prison Discipline in the Colonies: Digest and summary of information respecting prisons in the colonies*, London: Eyre and Spottiswoode, 1867; *Prison Discipline in the Colonies: Further correspondence respecting discipline and management of prisons in Her Majesty's colonial possessions*, London: Eyre and Spottiswoode, 1868.

the South Pacific, Stanford University Press, 2000, and Peter Redfield, *Space in the Tropics: From convicts to rockets in French Guiana*, Berkeley, CA: University of California Press, 2000.

There is a reasonably well-developed literature on transportation from Britain to the Americas during the eighteenth century. Early accounts include Abbot Emerson Smith, *Colonists in Bondage: White servitude and convict labor in America 1607–1776*, Chapel Hill, NC: University of North Carolina Press, 1947. See also Roger A. Ekirch, *Bound for America: The transportation of British convicts to the colonies, 1718–1775*, Oxford: Clarendon, 1987, and Bob Reece, *The Origins of Irish Convict Transportation to New South Wales*, Basingstoke: Palgrave, 2001. Economic analyses of the value of convict labour can be found in two articles by Farley Grubb: 'The Trans-Atlantic Market for British Convict Labour', *Journal of Economic History*, 60, 1 (2000), pp. 94–122, and 'The Market Evaluation of Criminality: Evidence from the auction of British convict labor in America, 1767–1775', *American Economic Review*, 91, 1 (2001), pp. 295–304. A recent cultural history of American convict transportation is Gwenda Morgan and Peter Rushton, *Eighteenth-Century Criminal Transportation: The formation of the criminal Atlantic*, Basingstoke: Palgrave Macmillan, 2004.

The historiography of convict Australia is vast. Three publications worth a special mention are the methodologically groundbreaking collections edited by Ian Duffield and James Bradley (eds), *Representing Convicts: New perspectives on convict forced labour migration*, London: Leicester University Press, 1997; Stephen Nicholas, *Convict Workers: Reinterpreting Australia's past*, Cambridge University Press, 1988, and Lucy Frost and Hamish Maxwell-Stewart (eds), *Chain Letters: Narrating convict lives*, Melbourne University Press, 2001.

There are a number of publications that reveal the global scope of British colonial convict transportation to Australia, though no research monograph as yet. On the West Indies, see Ian Duffield's 'From Slave Colonies to Penal Colonies: The West Indians transported to Australia', *Slavery and Abolition*, 7, 1 (1986), pp. 25–45. Of use for the African context is Leslie C. Duly, '"Hottentots to Hobart and Sydney": The Cape Supreme Court's use of transportation, 1828–38', *Australian Journal of Politics and History*, 25, 1 (1979), pp. 39–50 and V.C. Malherbe, 'Khoikhoi and the Question of Convict Transportation from the Cape Colony, 1820–1842', *South African Historical Journal*, 17 (1985), pp. 19–39. Transportation from Mauritius is described by Clare Anderson in 'Unfree Labour and its Discontents: Transportation from Mauritius to Australia, 1825–1845', *Australian Studies*, 13, 1 (1998), pp. 116–33. For North America, see Cassandra Pybus and Hamish Maxwell-Stewart, *American Citizens, British Slaves: Yankee political prisoners in an Australian penal colony,*

1839–1850, Melbourne University Press, 2002. Harriet Deacon's collection discusses the local use of Robben Island as a penal settlement: *The Island: A history of Robben Island, 1488–1900*, Cape Town: David Philip, 1997.

There has been no systematic study of the use of sentences of transportation by Indian courts from the late eighteenth to mid-twentieth centuries. Useful references can, however, be found in Tapas Kumar Banerjee, *Background to Indian Criminal Law*, Calcutta: R. Cambray and Co., 1990, Jörg Fisch, *Cheap Lives and Dear Limbs: The British transformation of the Bengal criminal law, 1769–1817*, Wiesbaden: Franz Steiner Verlag, 1983, and Radhika Singha, *A Despotism of Law: Crime and justice in early colonial India*, New Delhi: Oxford University Press, 1998.

Research on Indian penal settlements in South East Asia, especially Burma, is patchy. The best overview on the Straits Settlements remains C.M. Turnbull, 'Convicts in the Straits Settlements, 1826–67', *Journal of the Malaysia Branch of the Royal Asiatic Society*, 43, 1 (1970), pp. 87–103. More recent work includes Rajesh Rai, 'Sepoys, Convicts and the "Bazaar" Contingent: The emergence and exclusion of "Hindustani" pioneers at the Singapore frontier', *Journal of Southeast Asian Studies*, 35, 1 (2004), pp. 1–19 and Anand A. Yang, 'Indian Convict Workers in Southeast Asia in the Late Eighteenth and Early Nineteenth Centuries', *Journal of World History*, 14, 2 (2003), pp. 179–208. The memoir of erstwhile superintendent J.F.A. McNair is an invaluable published source: *Prisoners Their Own Warders: A record of the convict prison at Singapore in the Straits Settlements established 1825, discontinued 1873, together with a cursory history of the convict establishments at Bencoolen, Penang and Malacca from the year 1797*, Westminster: Archibald Constable and Co., 1899.

On the Indian convicts transported to Mauritius, see Clare Anderson's *Convicts in the Indian Ocean: Transportation from South Asia to Mauritius, 1815–53*, Basingstoke: Macmillan, 2000; 'The Bel Ombre Rebellion: Indian convicts in Mauritius, 1815–53' in Gwyn Campbell (ed.), *Abolition and its Aftermath in Indian Ocean Africa and Asia*, London: Routledge, 2005, pp. 50–66; and 'The Execution of Rughobursing: The political economy of convict transportation and penal labour in early colonial Mauritius', *Studies in History*, 19, 2 (2003), pp. 185–97.

There are also several thematic studies of South East Asian and Indian Ocean penal settlements. On the spatial dynamics of transportation, see Clare Anderson, 'The Politics of Convict Space: Indian penal settlements and the Andaman Islands' in Alison Bashford and Carolyn Strange (eds), *Isolation: Places and practices of exclusion*, London: Routledge, 2003, pp. 40–55. On corporal interventions relating to the practice of transportation, see Clare Anderson, *Legible Bodies: Race, criminality and colonialism in South Asia*, Oxford: Berg, 2004. On convict shipment, see Clare Anderson, '"The Ferringees are Flying – the Ship is Ours!": The convict middle passage in colonial South and Southeast Asia, 1790–1860', *Indian Economic and Social History Review*, 41, 3 (2005), pp. 143–86.

There has been very little research on convict transportation from Ceylon to South East Asia. One notable exception that deals with its background is M.A. Durand Appuhamy, *The Kandyans' Last Stand against the British*, Colombo: M.D. Gunasena and Co., 1995.

There is a more extensive literature on the Andaman Islands, though most of it is focussed on the experiences of 'political' convicts. Such nationalist readings include S.N. Aggarwal, *The Heroes of Cellular Jail*, Patiala, Panjab: Publication Bureau Punjabi University, 1995; N. Iqbal Singh, *The Andaman Story*, New Delhi: Vikas, 1978; and L.P. Mathur, *Kala Pani: History of Andaman and Nicobar Islands with a study of India's freedom struggle*, New Delhi: Eastern Book Company, 1992. Nationalist memoirs of time served in the settlement's cellular gaol at the beginning of the twentieth century available in English are: B.K. Ghose, *The Tale of My Exile*, Pondicherry: Arya Office, 1922; Bhai Parmanand, *The Story of My Life*, New Delhi: S. Chand and Co., 1982; V.D. Savarkar, *The Story of My Transportation for Life*, Bombay: Sadbhakti Publications, 1950; and B. Kumar Sinha, *In Andamans: The Indian Bastille*, New Delhi: People's Publishing House, 1988 [1st edition 1939].

Satadru Sen has provided a welcome counter to this approach by focusing on colonial mechanisms of control during the nineteenth century. See *Disciplining Punishment: Colonialism and convict society in the Andaman Islands*, New Delhi: Oxford University Press, 2000, and 'Rationing Sex: Female convicts in the Andamans', *South Asia*, 30, 1 (1999), pp. 29–59. Sen also deals with the relationship between the Andamans convict settlement and tribal communities in 'Policing the Savage: Segregation, labor and state medicine in the Andamans', *Journal of Asian Studies*, 58, 3 (1999), pp. 753–73, as does Sita Venkateswar, *Development and Ethnocide: Colonial practices in the Andaman Islands*, Copenhagen: International Work Group for Indigenous Affairs, 2004. See also superintendent of Andaman Homes, M.V. Portman's two-volume account *A History of Our Relations with the Andamanese*, Calcutta: Superintendent Government Printing, 1899. For German readers, Robert Heindl's *Meine Reise nach den Strafkolonien, mit vielen Originalaufnahmen*, Berlin and Vienna: Ullstein and Co., 1913, is an extensively illustrated and fascinating account of a global tour of prisons and penal settlements during the first decade of the twentieth century, including the Andamans. Finally, Rabin Roychowdhury's account of the Japanese occupation of the Islands, *Black Days in Andaman and Nicobar Islands*, New Delhi: Manas Publications, 2004, provides details of Britain's abandonment of the penal settlement in 1943.

There is a very large literature indeed on the Criminal Tribes Acts: David Arnold, *Police Power and Colonial Rule, Madras 1859–1947*, Oxford University Press, 1986, pp. 138–47; Crispin Bates, 'Race, Caste and Tribe in Central India: The early origins of Indian anthropometry' in Peter Robb (ed.), *The Concept of Race in South Asia*, New Delhi: Oxford University Press, 1995, pp. 219–57; Mark Brown, 'Race, Science and the Construction of Native Criminality in Colonial India', *Theoretical Criminology*, 5, 3 (2001), pp. 345–68; Stewart Gordon, 'Bhils and the Idea of a Criminal Tribe in Nineteenth-Century India' in Anand A. Yang (ed.), *Crime and Criminality in British India*, Tuscon, AZ: University of Arizona Press, 1985, pp. 128–39; Andrew Major, 'State and Criminal Tribes in Colonial Punjab: Surveillance, control and reclamation of the "dangerous classes"', *Modern Asian Studies*, 33 (1999), pp. 657–88; Sanjay Nigam, 'Disciplining and Policing the "Criminals by Birth", Part 1: The making of a colonial stereotype – The criminal tribes and castes of North India', *Indian Economic and Social History Review*, 27, 2 (1990), pp. 131–64; Sanjay Nigam, 'Disciplining and Policing the "Criminals by Birth", Part 2: The development of a disciplinary system, 1871–1900', *Indian Economic and Social History Review*, 27, 3 (1990), pp. 257–87; Meena Radhakrishna, 'The Criminal Tribes Act in the Madras Presidency: Implications for itinerant trading communities', *Indian Economic and Social History Review*, 26, 3 (1989), pp. 271–95; Meena Radhakrishna, 'Surveillance and Settlements under the Criminal Tribes Act in Madras', *Indian Economic and Social History Review*, 29, 2 (1992), pp. 171–98; Meena Radhakrishna, 'Colonial Construction of a "Criminal Tribe": The itinerant trading communities of Madras Presidency' in Neera Chandhoke (ed.), *Mapping Histories: Essays presented to Ravinder Kumar*, Tulika, 2000, pp. 128–60; Rachel J. Tolen, 'Colonizing and Transforming the Criminal Tribesmen: The Salvation Army in British India', *American Ethnologist*, 18, 1 (1991), pp. 106–25; Anand A. Yang, 'Dangerous Castes and Tribes: The Criminal Tribes Act and the Magahiya Doms of northeast India' in Yang (ed.), *Crime and Criminality*, pp. 108–27.

Studies of other repressive cultures of confinement include David Arnold, 'European Orphans and Vagrants in India in the Nineteenth Century', *Journal of Imperial and Commonwealth History*, 7, 2 (1979), pp. 104–27; Harald Fischer-Tiné, '"White Women Degrading Themselves to the Lowest Depths": European networks of prostitution and colonial anxieties in British India and Ceylon ca. 1880–1914', *Indian Economic and Social History Review*, 40, 2 (2003), pp. 165–92; Philippa Levine, *Prostitution, Race and Politics: Policing venereal disease in the British Empire*, London: Routledge, 2003; and James H. Mills, *Madness, Cannabis and Colonialism: The 'native only' lunatic asylums of colonial India, 1857–1900*, Basingstoke: Macmillan, 2000.

SOUTH EAST ASIA:
REFORM AND THE COLONIAL PRISON

Ian Brown

In the early months of 1942—the opening phase of the Pacific War—the British were driven from Burma by the Japanese forces advancing towards India. One of the very final acts of the retreating colonial administration as it abandoned Rangoon, Burma's capital, was to throw open the prisons and give the inmates their freedom.[1] In other words, as the institutions of British rule were being dismantled or disintegrated, the prison was kept functioning right to the last. In fact the prison had also been present from the very beginning of British rule. One of the early tasks of the new administration in the territory of Tenasserim, which became a British possession on the conclusion of the first Anglo-Burmese war (1824–6), was to construct a gaol in each district.[2] Among the first buildings

Much of the source material for this chapter was located and collected by Thet Thet Wintin. In addition, her own research on the history of the prison in pre-colonial Burma, a doctoral thesis for the University of London, has informed the discussion here on the indigenous South East Asian prison before colonial rule. I am delighted to acknowledge both these invaluable contributions. I also wish to thank James Warren in Bangkok, Jasper van de Kerkhof in Leiden and François Guillemot in Paris for their help with Thai, Dutch and French sources, as well as the staff of the Oriental and India Office Collections in London, the National Archives Department in Yangon, the National Archives of the United States at College Park, Maryland and the Library of Congress, Washington, DC. I also wish to acknowledge the excellent comments of Clare Anderson, David Arnold and Robert Taylor on an earlier draft. I remain responsible for all errors.

[1] S. Woodburn Kirby, *The War against Japan: Volume II: India's most dangerous hour*, London: HMSO, 1958, pp. 93–94; Leslie Glass, *The Changing of Kings: Memories of Burma 1934–1949*, London: Peter Owen, 1985, p. 138. The release of prisoners onto the streets was intended to make it more difficult for the incoming Japanese to impose order. But there was also a humanitarian concern. With the European and Indian gaol staff abandoning their posts, the inmates simply could not be left locked in to face starvation or, possibly, an outbreak of fire. For the same reasons, the inmates of the asylum were also set free. It might be added that, as a further final evacuation measure, a party was sent to the Rangoon Zoo to shoot all the dangerous animals, the keepers having fled.

[2] J.S. Furnivall, 'The Fashioning of Leviathan: The beginnings of British rule in Burma', *Journal of the Burma Research Society*, 29, 1 (1939), pp. 36–7.

erected by the British in Rangoon after seizing lower Burma in the second Anglo-Burmese war (1852–3) was the gaol.[3] Burma was far from unusual in this respect. As French rule was imposed through Indochina—Cochin China in the 1860s, Annam and Tonkin in the mid-1880s—'camps of confinement were constructed ... prior to virtually any other colonial institution'.[4] Across South East Asia, and elsewhere, colonial rule so often began with the construction of a gaol.

But despite this long presence, and of course despite the fact that the prison might well be seen as having had a crucial importance in maintaining the social and political order in colonial South East Asia, it has attracted surprisingly little interest from historians of the region. Even the notorious reputations of many of the most prominent prisons in South East Asia—the names alone can be power-fully evocative, Changi, Insein, the 'Bangkok Hilton' [Bang Kwang], Poulo Con-dore, Bilibid—appear to have sparked relatively little serious historical inquiry. Certainly no secondary literature exists to compare with that on the history of the prison in India, Africa or Latin America, for example.[5]

This circumstance has determined the ambitions of this chapter in two im-portant respects. First, rather than aiming to cover the whole of South East Asia, giving roughly equal attention to each of the main territories, it focuses on the history of the prison in British-held Burma, with significant discussion too of the Philippines under American administration, that is from 1898. Reference to the history of the prison in the rest of South East Asia—French Indochina, Siam (which retained its political independence), the Malay States and the Straits Set-tlements, and the Netherlands East Indies—in this period is made only briefly, for comparative purposes. Second, the history of the prison in colonial Burma pre-sented here has been constructed through research in the records of the Burma prison administration, principally the administration's published annual reports. The use of official sources to construct the history of a prison system raises a number of methodological issues that are important far beyond Burma, and which therefore should be spelt out in some detail.

One issue might be anticipated but is in fact of lesser importance. The official record did not, as could be expected, invariably provide a sanitised account. As will be demonstrated below, the published reports produced by colonial Bur-ma's prison administration were often sharply critical of prison conditions and

---

[3] B.R. Pearn, *A History of Rangoon*, Rangoon: American Baptist Mission Press, 1939, p. 202.

[4] Peter Zinoman, *The Colonial Bastille: A history of imprisonment in Vietnam, 1862–1940*, Berkeley, CA: University of California Press, 2001, p. 29.

[5] The literature on South East Asia is reviewed in the bibliographical note at the end of this essay.

practices. Indeed, on a number of occasions in the early 1920s the reports—that appeared over the name of the inspector-general of prisons—even questioned the very idea of the prison, arguing that convicts were unlikely to be reformed and rehabilitated behind prison walls. A more serious methodological issue is that prison administration records would pay little attention to, or ignore completely, aspects of the prison that are regarded by historians as being particularly important. Thus the annual reports on prison administration in colonial Burma rarely record directly the prison experience of inmates, and certainly not from the perspective of the inmates themselves. They make little attempt to catch the daily realities, to look beyond the formal hierarchies and see where the real authority lay within a prison population—to see who really ran the prison. These aspects and perspectives might be explored through the written recollections or memoirs of prisoners, where they exist, although here too there are methodological concerns. Since the authors of such narratives were, by definition, highly literate and reflective, almost certainly their prison experience and their understandings of the daily realities of prison would differ significantly from those of the vast mass of inmates. Where the authors had been political prisoners, as was commonly the case, the understanding could be entirely different. Nationalists would regard time inside the colonial prison as an opportunity for political education, for learning the techniques of political agitation, and for building comradeship and party organisation. The colonial prison conferred legitimacy on nationalists sent there. This was far from the understanding held by the common criminal doing time. But these methodological issues need not disturb the historian of Burma's prisons: there were comparatively few political prisoners in colonial Burma and, apparently, no substantial legacy of prison memoirs.[6]

The final methodological problem with the use of official sources is the most important, and indeed introduces a major argument in this chapter. Each prison administration report produced in colonial South East Asia, and elsewhere, contained a vast body of detailed factual information, including, notably, statistical data. An annual report on prison administration in British Burma could include a statistical appendix running to a hundred pages or more. The colonial Burma reports record, for example, the number of convicts held in the Mandalay gaol who died of tuberculosis in 1905 (two: and eight were admitted to the prison hospital with the disease); the proportion of prisoners released from Burma's

---

[6] In contrast there are a very substantial number of first-person accounts of imprisonment in colonial Indochina, by political prisoners. For a brief introduction, and discussion of problems in using that material, see Zinoman, *The Colonial Bastille*, pp. 9–12.

gaols during 1935 who had gained weight during their time inside (59.6 per cent); the number of convict inmates in Insein in 1922 who were punished by the prison authorities for possession of prohibited articles (437); the number of 'native' prisoners in Rangoon Gaol in 1894 who received between twenty-six and thirty strokes of the rattan cane, on a single occasion, for breaches of prison discipline (fourteen). It might easily be assumed that such an extraordinary grasp of detail translated into a comparable command of the prison itself, that an administration that collected and assembled such a vast body of data on the inmate population of its prisons would thereby control it down to the smallest particular. But that was not the case. The annual reports on prison administration in British Burma project authority, discipline and order—the colonial prison as an instrument of immense power—but the daily realities inside the colonial prison were often ill disciplined, arbitrary and negotiated.

BEFORE THE COLONIAL PRISON

In the indigenous states of South East Asia before colonial rule the punishment of crime took many different forms. Death was imposed for murder and treason, of course, but also, for example, for highway robbery and arson in Burma, stealing from a monastery in Siam, theft of royal property in the Malay world, and adultery with the wife of a high-ranking Malay.[7] The act of execution itself also took many different forms. In the Malay world and Java the high born were executed by the thrust of a *kris*, the traditional dagger, to the heart. A European visitor to Siam in the 1850s reported that Siamese 'nobles' were executed by being 'put into a sack, and beaten to death in a public place'.[8] The common born condemned to death, he continued, were usually beheaded.[9] Some forms of execution involved terrifying cruelty. That same European visitor to Siam recorded, '[t]he penalty for melting an idol of gold or silver, stolen from a temple, is to be burnt alive.'[10]

---

[7] Anthony Reid, *Southeast Asia in the Age of Commerce 1450–1680. Volume 1: The lands below the winds*, New Haven, CT: Yale University Press, 1988, pp. 140–1.

[8] Sir John Bowring, *The Kingdom and People of Siam*, Kuala Lumpur: Oxford University Press, 1969 [first published 1857], volume 1, p. 181.

[9] For an extraordinary eyewitness account of a public beheading in Siam around 1900, see P.A. Thompson, *Lotus Land: Being an account of the country and the people of southern Siam*, London: T. Werner Laurie, 1906, pp. 265–9. Thompson also reported, however, that 'the death sentence is rarely passed in Siam, and still less often carried out'.

[10] Bowring, *The Kingdom and People of Siam*, volume 1, p. 182. A little more detail was provided by another European, resident in Siam almost two hundred years before the visit by Sir John Bowing: 'Those who are convicted of stealing anything that is devoted to the service of the king

Elsewhere across the region there are reports of the condemned being impaled on a stake, dismembered while still alive, shackled into some excruciatingly painful position until life drained away, and of being killed—trampled to death or torn apart and eaten—by an animal.[11] With regard to the last, a seventeenth-century Dutch account of Siam recorded that the punishment for adultery was to 'be thrown in front of an elephant in order to be put to death by that terrible monster'.[12] Eighteenth-century accounts of Java reported condemned criminals being thrown to tigers to be killed.[13] In earlier periods buffaloes, crocodiles, elephants and snakes had acted as the executioner.

Other forms of punishment in pre-colonial South East Asia included mutilation or amputation, tattooing and whipping—further violence against the body. The severing of hands and limbs for theft was found across the region, and not only in the region's Islamic states. A French resident in Siam in the late seventeenth century recorded that small-time thieves, when caught, had the ends of their fingers cut off, and were then released.[14] Amputation was also the punishment for those convicted of producing counterfeit coin, with a range of increasingly severe cuts to match the extent of involvement in the crime—a schedule described by the European visitor to Siam in the 1850s: 'the man who blows the bellows is punished by having his right-hand fingers chopped off; he who forms the coin has his right hand cut off; he who impressed the King's mark will lose his right arm.'[15] The same observer also reported the branding of offenders: 'Adulterers are punished by marking with a hot iron on the cheeks, and the forehead is sometimes branded for other crimes.'[16] Henry Gouger, a British merchant held in a Burmese prison for two years in the mid-1820s, later recounted that his gaolers, formerly condemned men who had been pardoned on condition that they became the prison's torturers and executioners, each had a ring-shape

---

or to the decoration of a pagoda are bound to a large pole and roasted alive over a slow fire': Nicolas Gervaise, *The Natural and Political History of the Kingdom of Siam*, translated and edited by John Villiers, Bangkok: White Lotus, 1989 [original published in 1688], p. 77. According to Gervaise, this punishment was also imposed on monks caught *in flagrante delicto* with a woman.

[11] Reid, *Southeast Asia in the Age of Commerce*, p. 141.

[12] Jeremias van Vliet, 'Description of the Kingdom of Siam (1638)' in Chris Baker, Dhiravat na Pombejra, Alfons van der Kraan, David K. Wyatt, *Van Vliet's Siam*, Chiang Mai: Silkworm Books, 2005, p. 155.

[13] Peter Boomgaard, *Frontiers of Fear: Tigers and people in the Malay world, 1600–1950*, New Haven, CT: Yale University Press, 2001, pp. 149–50.

[14] Gervaise, *The Natural and Political History of the Kingdom of Siam*, p. 77.

[15] Bowring, *The Kingdom and People of Siam*, volume 1, p. 181.

[16] Ibid., p. 182.

tattooed on each cheek and their criminal character—'murderer', 'thief', 'horse-stealer'—tattooed across their chest, to make undetected escape impossible.[17] And criminals were flogged. John Crawfurd, who undertook a mission to Siam in the early 1820s, reported that the kingdom's penal code made provision for a 'liberal and indiscriminate application ... of the bamboo for the punishment of all offences. Petty larcenies are punished by thirty blows; higher degrees of theft, by ninety blows, and an imprisonment ...; robbery, with ninety blows and imprisonment, with hard labour for life'.[18]

There were forms of punishment that sought the public shaming of the offender. In mid-nineteenth-century Siam:

> The convict, loaded with chains, and wearing the *cangue*, is marched through the principal streets of the town, preceded by cymbals and accompanied by police-officers; he is compelled to cry without ceasing, in a loud voice, 'My crime is—[so and so]. Be warned by my example.' When his voice is weak or silent, he is beaten with swords. He is thus escorted for three successive days through the town on foot, and three times in a boat round the city, subjected to the same conditions.[19]

A punishment still more degrading, it would appear, was to be sent out to cut grass for the royal elephants, perhaps for the rest of one's days.[20] There were still further forms of punishment in pre-colonial South East Asia. Criminals were fined, banished to remote parts of the realm, sent into servitude or forced to labour for the state.[21] And finally, criminals were imprisoned.[22]

Imprisonment for a specified length of time—time for crime—is, of course, by far the most prevalent form of judicial punishment in the modern world. But it is not difficult to understand why in pre-colonial South East Asia it was just one among many, and almost certainly a minor one at that. Perhaps it was partly

---

[17] *Two Years Imprisonment in Burma (1824–26): A personal narrative of Henry Gouger*, Bangkok: White Lotus, 2003 [first published 1860], pp. 144–5.

[18] John Crawfurd, *Journal of an Embassy to the Courts of Siam and Cochin China*, Kuala Lumpur: Oxford University Press, 1967 [first published 1828], p. 395. It should be noted, however, that Anthony Reid argues that '[e]xcept in Vietnam ... there was little use of lesser forms of corporal punishment' in pre-colonial South East Asia: Reid, *Southeast Asia in the Age of Commerce*, p. 141.

[19] Bowring, *The Kingdom and People of Siam*, volume 1, p. 182. A cangue was a collar of wood, fastened around the neck.

[20] H.G. Quaritch Wales, *Ancient Siamese Government and Administration*, London: Bernard Quaritch, 1934, p. 193.

[21] Reid, *Southeast Asia in the Age of Commerce*, pp. 141–3; van Vliet, 'Description of the Kingdom of Siam (1638)', p. 155; Quaritch Wales, *Ancient Siamese Government and Administration*, p. 195.

[22] Quaritch Wales, *Ancient Siamese Government and Administration*, p. 193; Crawfurd, *Journal of an Embassy to the Courts of Siam and Cochin China*, p. 395.

a matter of cost—although the state appears to have provided little or nothing to feed its prisoners, or indeed meet any of their basic needs.[23] Perhaps it was the obvious difficulty in holding criminals securely in crude wooden buildings with just a thin outer fence, even if inmates spent much of the time fettered at the ankles, bound to fixed poles, held in the stocks, or chained to the wall.[24] It was simply more practical to flog, fine, mutilate, tattoo, banish or execute. But a further consideration may have been more important. In pre-colonial South East Asia criminals were not to be reformed and rehabilitated but to be punished and deterred. Rehabilitation almost certainly demands a period of confinement: but punishment and deterrence could be secured equally effectively—or ineffectively—by non-custodial sentences. In other words, the limited aims of the pre-colonial state in its treatment of the criminal—to punish and deter—could be met without the use of imprisonment. The prison was unnecessary. It was not even needed in order to take notorious criminals out of circulation, and thereby protect society from further attack. That could be achieved just as easily by banishment and execution, of course, but also by mutilation and tattooing, in that the physical marking of a criminal made him instantly identifiable in society—a hand had been severed, the word 'murderer' was branded across the forehead—and thus shunned. A man sentenced to banishment, death, amputation or tattooing was, in that sense, being excluded—confined without being held in prison.

The function of confinement in pre-colonial South East Asia was therefore only rarely to punish the convicted criminal through imprisonment itself. Rather it was to detain the suspect while his alleged crime was being investigated, during the trial and, if convicted, until the sentence—exile, flogging, execution, amputation—was carried out: and integral to those processes, to investigate, interrogate and punish.

By all Western accounts, the indigenous prison in pre-colonial South East Asia was a place of unspeakable squalor and cruelty. And indeed, to punish and deter, the prison had to terrify. A notably vivid Western account is Henry Gouger's *Narrative of a Two Years' Imprisonment in Burmah*. Two passages catch the essence:

[23] Henry Gouger, held in a Burmese prison in the 1820s, reported that although it was said that a basket of rice was allowed by the king to each prisoner each month, 'we never saw any sign of rations during our long incarceration'. He concluded that the king's rice rations, if they existed, must have been taken by the guards. Prisoners were fed, Gouger explained, by their relatives and friends, who brought food to the prison. Failing that, the inmates relied upon the charity of strangers, who donated food in order to make merit. *Two Years Imprisonment in Burma*, pp. 159–60.

[24] Gouger's volume includes illustrations, first, of the exterior of the prison at Ava, that make clear the weakness of the structure, and second, of the prison's interior, showing the inmates bound and shackled: *Two Years Imprisonment in Burma*, between pages 24 and 25.

Before me, stretched on the floor, lay forty or fifty hapless wretches, whose crimes or misfortunes had brought them into this place of torment. They were all nearly naked, and the half-famished features and skeleton frames of many of them too plainly told the story of their protracted sufferings. Very few were without chains, and some had one or both feet in the stocks besides. A sight of such squalid wretchedness can hardly be imagined ... the stench was absolutely indescribable ... [p]utrid remains of cast-away animal and vegetable stuff ... the exudation from the bodies of a crowd of never-washed convicts, encouraged by the thermometer at 100°, in a den almost without ventilation ... the place was teeming with creeping vermin ...[25]

As a matter of course he [a young man accused of robbery] denied the crime; but denial was assumed to be obstinacy, and the usual mode of overcoming obstinacy was by some manner of torture. By order of the Myo-serai [assistant to the governor of the city], therefore, he was made to sit upon a low stool, his legs were bound together by a cord above the knees, and two poles inserted between them by the executioners, one of whom took the command of each pole, the ground forming the fulcrum. With these the legs were forced upwards and downwards and asunder, and underwent a peculiar kind of grinding ... [e]very moment I expected to hear the thigh-bone snap ... [the next day the young man] was tied by the wrists behind his back, the rope which bound them being drawn up by a pulley just high enough to allow his toes to touch the ground, and in this manner he was left until he should become more reasonable.[26]

Perhaps these accounts should be regarded with a little caution. Imprisoned by the Burmese during the first Anglo-Burmese war—he was accused of being a British spy—Gouger could not be expected to have provided a forgiving account of his experiences: and his Western audience would have been eager to hear the worst. But more important, as Gouger himself made clear, individual prisoners could secure better conditions and escape brutal treatment by bribing the gaol staff—who indeed encouraged bribes.[27] But then perhaps not many prisoners had the resources—of wealth or friends—to buy a less harsh regime.

THE COLONIAL PRISON

As noted at the beginning of this chapter, one of the first tasks undertaken by the Western administrations that were established in South East Asia in the nineteenth century was to construct prisons. The colonial prison—more broadly, contemporary European penological thinking and practice—immediately

---

[25]   *Two Years Imprisonment in Burma*, pp. 148–9.

[26]   Ibid., pp. 161–2.

[27]   Ibid., for example pp. 170–1.

brought major breaks with the past. It ended many of the most brutal forms of punishment—amputation, mutilation, execution by being burnt alive, impaled, or trampled to death by an elephant—and established the custodial sentence as the dominant judicial punishment. But there were also continuities between the modern prison and its indigenous predecessor, certainly in the first stages of colonial administration. There was a clear continuity in the physical structure of the early colonial prison. The gaols built by the newly established British administration in Tenasserim in the 1830s were ordinary wooden constructions behind a wooden outer fence.[28] There was little to distinguish them, in physical structure, from the Burmese prison at Ava in which Henry Gouger had been held in the 1820s. The first British gaol at Rangoon, built in the 1850s, was also a wooden construction.[29] Even in the mid-1860s all but three of the gaols in British Burma were constructed of bamboo and grass—not even wood.[30] Such weak structures could confine prisoners securely—and this was a much more serious issue now that the custodial sentence was the principal form of judicial punishment—only by near-constant use of fetters and chains, as in the indigenous prison. This in turn determined the prisoners' regime—in work, exercise, bathing, discipline and sleep. It was only with the construction of brick and iron prisons, in Burma from the final decades of the nineteenth century—monumental institutions on the Pentonville model—that a decisive break with the past could begin. Even so, there were a number of indigenous penological practices that, in Burma at least, had resonance right through the colonial period.

Across colonial South East Asia, the decades from the late nineteenth century saw the near constant construction of new prisons and an almost inexorable rise in the number of prisoners. In Indochina, the year in which the first territory—the eastern provinces of Cochin China—was ceded to the French, that is 1862, also saw the establishment of the penal colony (*bagne*) on Poulo Condore, an archipelago some 180 kilometres off the coast of southern Vietnam, and a start made on the construction of a main gaol in Saigon.[31] The Saigon Central Prison—known in Vietnamese as *Kham Lon*, the Big Gaol—was completed in late 1863. It originally had capacity for 400. The subsequent addition of further accommodation increased the capacity to 800 by 1930, although the actual number of inmates at any time was almost certainly much higher. Following

---

[28] Furnivall, 'The Fashioning of Leviathan', pp. 36–7.

[29] Pearn, *A History of Rangoon*, p. 202.

[30] *Report on the Prison Administration of Burma* [henceforth *RPAB*, although the title varied in the first two decades of the colonial prison administration], 1877, p. 38.

[31] Zinoman, *The Colonial Bastille*, pp. 29, 52, 61–3.

the extension of French rule to central and northern Vietnam—Annam and Tonkin—in the mid-1880s, a second central prison was constructed, this time on the outskirts of Hanoi's French quarter. Completed in 1898, the Hanoi Central Prison—known in Vietnamese as *Hoa Lo*, the Oven, and known to Americans of the Vietnam War years as the 'Hanoi Hilton'—originally had capacity for 460, later increased to 600. But again the actual number of inmates far exceeded the official capacity: the daily average in 1933 was no less than 1,430—severe overcrowding indeed. The construction of the Hanoi Central Prison came near the beginning of a major phase of prison building, involving the construction of larger institutions, which lasted some two decades. The pace slowed in the 1920s but increased again in the early 1930s in response to a strong upsurge in anti-colonial political activity. In early 1933 the prison provision across French Indochina consisted of ten penitentiaries, five central prisons and 89 provincial prisons.

In British Burma the original wooden structure of the Rangoon Central Gaol from the 1850s was dismantled and a far more secure and imposing masonry and iron construction rose on the same site.[32] This rebuilding proceeded in a piecemeal manner over several decades but appears to have been completed in the 1880s. Towards the end of that decade it was reported that the Rangoon Central Gaol held nearly four thousand prisoners[33]—an astounding figure. British Burma's second main prison, the Insein Central Gaol, in the northern reaches of Rangoon, took its first inmates in 1892.[34] In 1920 there were seven central gaols and twenty-four district gaols in British Burma—although the province's prison administration was dominated by Rangoon and Insein, each holding over two thousand prisoners.[35] The main prison in the colonial Philippines was Bilibid, built by the Spanish regime in the mid-1860s and located on the outskirts of Manila.[36] In the early 1900s—the Philippines now under American administration—Bilibid held almost four and a half thousand prisoners on average,

---

[32] *RPAB*, 1875, p. 46; *RPAB*, 1880, p. 11.

[33] *RPAB*, 1888, Resolution, p. 2. In 1887 the Government of India instructed that, in principle, the Rangoon Gaol should hold no more than two thousand inmates.

[34] *RPAB*, 1892, Resolution, p. 1.

[35] *RPAB*, 1920, pp. 20–3.

[36] This brief reference draws on Michael Salman, '"Nothing without Labor": Penology, discipline, and independence in the Philippines under United States colonial rule, 1898–1914' in Vicente L. Rafael (ed.), *Discrepant Histories: Translocal essays on Filipino cultures*, Philadelphia, PA: Temple University Press, 1995, pp. 116–22; John Lewis Gillin, *Taming the Criminal: Adventures in penology*, New York: Macmillan, 1931, pp. 36–65; and Greg Bankoff, *Crime, Society, and the State in the Nineteenth-Century Philippines*, Quezon City: Ateneo de Manila University Press, 1996, p. 159.

far in excess of its official capacity. In 1925 that figure was down to just under two and a half thousand. Even so, Bilibid still accounted for roughly two out of every five inmates in the Philippines—those convicted of serious crimes. The other important institution, holding over fifteen hundred convicts in 1925, was Iwahig Penal Colony on the island of Palawan, on the western extremity of the central Philippines. Under the Spanish, Palawan had been one of a number of far distant provinces to which political detainees, violent criminals and those simply seen as socially undesirable had been exiled. The incoming American administration re-established it as a penal colony in 1904, intended principally for first offenders sentenced to long terms who had been well behaved and industrious when held in Bilibid. The provincial gaols, numbering over fifty in the late 1920s and holding, in total, well over a thousand prisoners were a further important component of the prison system of the American Philippines. The main prison in the Federated Malay States was Pudoh Gaol on the outskirts of Kuala Lumpur, constructed from 1891.[37] Compared to, for example, Insein, Rangoon or Bilibid, this was a modest structure. When it was completed in 1896 Pudoh had accommodation for just 520 prisoners and even then 'was never overcrowded'. In Singapore, a British possession from 1819, the first prison buildings were no more than attap-sheds, enclosed by a high wall, in which were held convicts transported from India.[38] Gradually the sheds and huts were replaced by permanent structures, though the process was not completed until 1860. A new prison on a new site, the Pearl's Hill Gaol, was completed in 1882. A cellular gaol 'on the most approved English model at the time', Pearl's Hill held only local convicts, the transportation of Indian convicts to Singapore having now ended. A second main prison, Changi, at the eastern extremity of the island, was built in 1936.[39] Again, compared to Insein or Rangoon, this was a modest structure, intended to hold just 600 prisoners—although in February 1942, during the first weeks

---

[37] This brief reference was constructed from *Annual Report of the State of Selangor* [title varies], various years 1890–7.

[38] Roland St J. Braddell, 'Crime: Its punishment and prevention' in Walter Makepeace, Gilbert E. Brooke, and Roland St J. Braddell (eds), *One Hundred Years of Singapore*, London: John Murray, 1921, vol. 1, pp. 282–90. The number of Indian convicts held in Singapore in these years was commonly well over a thousand. They were supervised by warders selected from their own ranks, and in a young settlement, in which labour was scarce and expensive, their work in draining swamps, laying roads, and in the construction of buildings and bridges was greatly important to government and to the port's commercial interests. See also J.F.A. McNair, *Prisoners Their Own Warders*, Westminster: Archibald Constable, 1899, and the paper by Clare Anderson in this volume.

[39] Dhoraisingam S. Samuel, *Singapore's Heritage through Places of Historical Interest*, Singapore: Elixir Consultancy Service, 1991, pp. 298–9.

of the Japanese war-time occupation of Singapore, it held some three and a half thousand. In Siam, which maintained its political independence throughout the colonial age in South East Asia, the indigenous administration matched the prison building programmes taking place in its colonial neighbours. In Bangkok's early decades—it was founded in 1782—convicts were held in a stockade in the palace quarter of the city.[40] In the late nineteenth century a second gaol was constructed, in front of the newly established Ministry of Justice. And then, in 1893, after the return to Bangkok of a delegation of Siamese officials sent to Singapore to study the colony's prison system, a further gaol, the Bangkok Central Prison, was built. Bang Kwang Prison, located north of Bangkok in Nonthaburi, was completed in 1930. It held the long-term prisoners.

Driving the schedule of prison construction that was sustained across South East Asia from the middle of the nineteenth century through to the 1930s was, of course, the rise in prison populations. The prison population of French Indochina on 31 December 1913 was 18,340: but 29,871 on the same day in 1941.[41] In Siam the prison convict population on 31 March 1919 was 19,021, and on the same day in 1938, 27,760.[42] The daily average number held in the gaols of British Burma was 12,517 in 1900 but 18,206 in 1940.[43] In the American-ruled Philippines the prison population on 30 June 1907 was 5,456: and on 31 December 1933 it was 8,664.[44] That the colonial regimes in South East Asia—and the modern Siamese administration—sent such large numbers to prison, far more surely than were confined in the pre-colonial period, was of course largely a reflection of the fact that the custodial sentence was now a more important form of punishment for convicted criminals. But precisely why prison populations rose so markedly under colonial rule is less clear. The rise may simply have reflected a relentless increase in crime, fed by the social dislocation and economic hardship that marked the lives of many under colonial rule. But it may also have followed broader definitions of criminality that saw, for example, vagrants and fare-dodgers as criminals—and sent them to prison. And most important, it reflected the vastly increased capacity of the modern state to detect and arrest. The same relentlessly

---

[40] Steve Van Beek, *Bangkok Then and Now*, Nonthaburi: AB Publications, 1999, pp. 96–8.

[41] Zinoman, *The Colonial Bastille*, p. 48.

[42] *Statistical Yearbook Thailand*, BE 2480 [1937/38] and 2481 [1938/39], p. 380.

[43] *RPAB*, 1900, p. 1; *RPAB*, 1940, p. 1.

[44] *Eighth Annual Report of the Philippine Commission to the Secretary of War, 1907*, Washington, DC: Government Printing Office, 1908, part 3, pp. 172, 174; *Annual Report of the Governor General of the Philippine Islands, 1933*, Washington, DC: United States Government Printing Office, 1935, p. 69.

extending reach that enabled the state to tax more effectively, to register land ownership comprehensively, and to count and categorise an entire population, also sent far more people to prison. A remarkable number of lives were thus marked by colonial imprisonment.[45] The discussion now turns to the nature of that prison experience, first in colonial Burma.

PRISON CONDITIONS IN COLONIAL BURMA

In a number of important respects, physical conditions in Burma's prisons were substantially better in the 1930s, the final full decade of British rule, than they had been in, say, the 1880s or 1890s. For example, the prisons were less unhealthy, as was reflected in a much lower death rate—10.82 deaths per thousand of the average daily prison population in 1935, against 28.24 in 1890.[46] This decline in mortality came in large part from a major reduction in deaths from dysentery and diarrhoea. Of the 319 deaths that occurred among the inmates of Burma's prisons in 1890, 108, almost exactly one third, were reported as 'deaths from bowel-complaints'.[47] Of the 200 convict deaths in 1935, just seventeen, roughly one twelfth, were attributed to dysentery and diarrhoea.[48] These figures indicate a substantial improvement in standards of hygiene in the province's prisons over this period, specifically in the preparation of food, the provision of drinking water and the disposal of human waste.

The reduction in deaths from dysentery was secured in part by the institution of measures to contain the disease when and where it was found in the prison population. Wherever possible—and at the beginning of the twentieth century, most Burma gaols had isolation wards—prisoners with dysentery were quarantined: the faeces of dysentery patients were incinerated: and the hospital bedding

---

[45] The figures quoted earlier in the paragraph for the daily average number of prisoners in a particular year, or the number on a specific date, while impressively large, considerably understate the scale of imprisonment. For example, the daily average number held in the gaols of British Burma in 1920 was 14,607. But the total number spending time in prison during that year was 57,501 [*RPAB*, 1920, p. 23]. Taking the population of Burma in 1920 as 13.2 million, roughly one person in every 230 spent at least some time in gaol during that year. Since the population figure includes women and children, of course, the proportion of Burma's adult males that served time during the year was considerably higher—perhaps one in, say, 120. I have taken the first part of this statistical procedure, as well as the phrasing of this paragraph's final sentence, from Peter Zinoman, *The Colonial Bastille*, p. 63.

[46] *RPAB*, 1935, pp. 18–19; *RPAB*, 1890, p. 18.

[47] *RPAB*, 1890, pp. 18–19.

[48] *RPAB*, 1935, pp. 52, 54–5.

and clothing used by dysentery cases were distinctively marked and thoroughly disinfected after each use.[49] But the single most effective intervention by the colonial prison administration was improvement in the quality of drinking water. Burma's prisons took their water from a local river or from wells, frequently sunk within the walls of the prison itself. From 1891 regular analysis of the drinking water was carried out at each prison by the government chemist.[50] Where the water was found to be contaminated, an alternative source was located, although these were not always easy to bring into use. Further measures followed. In order to prevent the contamination of drinking water from handling, in the mid-1900s water-chatties were replaced in most of Burma's prisons by water-drums that had taps and lids that could be locked.[51] The annual report for 1918 noted that prison standing orders required that all drinking water be boiled.[52] And finally, from the close of the 1920s, chlorine was introduced into the water supply at Burma's prisons, an intervention that appears to have had an immediate impact in reducing further the incidence of dysentery and deaths from that disease.[53]

There were also substantial steps taken by the prison authorities with regard to smallpox, cholera, plague and malaria. And if those interventions had a less dramatic impact than the measures taken to reduce the incidence of dysentery, this was essentially because those diseases had rarely threatened the prison population on the same scale. From the first decade of the twentieth century, and possibly earlier, each healthy prisoner was vaccinated against smallpox on admission to gaol, whether they had been previously vaccinated or not.[54] Whenever plague broke out in a town or district—Henzada in 1916—every inmate in the local prison was inoculated.[55] Furthermore, convicts would earn remission on their sentence for catching and killing rats within the prison[56]—presumably on the basis of a day's remission for a specified number of rats. And finally, in the mid-1900s it was reported that in most of the prisons in which malaria was prevalent, inmates were being given regular doses of quinine.[57] Mortality from these diseases was therefore low. Of the 200 convicts who died in Burma's prisons in

[49] *RPAB*, 1905, p. 10.
[50] *RPAB*, 1892, Resolution, p. 5; Report, p. 29.
[51] *RPAB*, 1905, p. 9.
[52] *RPAB*, 1918, p. 9.
[53] *RPAB*, 1933, p. 23.
[54] *RPAB*, 1925, p. 15; *RPAB*, 1905, p. 9.
[55] *RPAB*, 1916, p. 13.
[56] *RPAB*, 1912, p. 17.
[57] *RPAB*, 1904, p. 13.

1935, just five lost their lives to malaria, and a further five to plague.[58] There was a single death from cholera.

But there were two diseases against which the prison administration in colonial Burma had only limited success: and as mortality from dysentery fell, these emerged as the principal killers in Burma's prisons. The first was pneumonia, which accounted for twenty-four (of 200) convict deaths in 1935. The second was tuberculosis, which was markedly more deadly. In 1935 it accounted for sixty-three convict deaths, that is for almost one death in three among Burma's convict population. And yet the prison authorities had long given attention to the treatment of prisoners with tuberculosis, and to measures to reduce the infection of other inmates. The annual report for 1905 noted that 'every precaution' was being taken to prevent the spread of the disease within the prison.[59] Tuberculosis prisoners were regularly exposed to the open air, and were held in separate wards, where this was possible: moreover, great care was taken to destroy their sputa and to disinfect the clothing and bedding allocated for their sole use. By the early 1920s a special tuberculosis ward had been opened in the prison at Myingyan, south-west of Mandalay, a location chosen, presumably, because the air there was less oppressive than in the delta. The annual prison administration report for 1922 noted, perhaps with a little pride, that while tuberculosis inmates had access to that special facility, there was as yet no specialist TB hospital in Burma for the general public.[60] Later in the 1920s plans were advanced for the construction of dedicated tuberculosis and leper prisons—apparently two separate institutions—at Meiktila, again where the air was less oppressive. But the plans fell victim to the financial cuts forced on the Burma government at the beginning of the 1930s by the depression crisis.[61] That still left the tuberculosis ward at Myingyan, which had beds for fifty inmate patients.[62] But despite these initiatives, in the mid-1930s, as noted earlier, tuberculosis was the single most important cause of death in Burma's prisons. Part of the explanation may lie in the argument that since a substantial proportion of new inmates had contracted tuberculosis outside, its presence in Burma's prisons was being constantly renewed.

On a number of occasions in the 1920s and 1930s, by which point the improvements in prison death and disease rates had taken firm hold, the senior prison administration claimed that conditions for inmates were better than conditions

[58] *RPAB*, 1935, pp. 19–20, 54–5.
[59] *RPAB*, 1905, p. 11.
[60] *RPAB*, 1922, p. 13.
[61] *RPAB*, 1931, p. 1.
[62] *RPAB*, 1935, p. 20.

for the general population outside. Noted immediately above was the comment in 1922 that while prisoners with tuberculosis could be sent to the special ward at Myingyan, there was no specialist TB hospital in the province for the general public. The annual report for 1939 made the point that the death rate in Burma's prisons was less than half that for Burma's population as a whole, suggesting, perhaps, that life prospects were far more favourable inside than outside.[63] Then again, the annual report for 1924 claimed that

prolonged stay in jail improves a prisoner's health ... his bodily ailments receive greater attention inside than outside the jail. While in prison, he is well fed, well clothed and better looked after than he would be as a free man. The sanitary defects to be found in his home are nowhere to be seen in any jail.[64]

The 1921 report had made much the same point but with greater bite—perhaps bitterness.

The fortunate convict is generally overhauled; vaccinated; inoculated it may be against plague, cholera, typhoid; treated for scabies, ... syphilis, malaria; thoroughly examined for hookworm and tubercle; and he usually leaves jail a healthier man than when he came in. Little wonder that some critics hold that our jail system fails to deter.[65]

For a substantial proportion of the inmates of Burma's gaols—the vagrants, hunted-down dacoits, the scavenging thieves, beggars, drug addicts and alcoholics—it is indeed quite possible that their health was better, and perhaps their life expectancy greater, inside the prison. But then such is almost inevitably the case where the prison draws its inmates from a population in which poverty is widespread, social support limited and access to medical treatment non-existent.

In other respects too prison conditions had improved over the decades of colonial administration. In the 1930s the inmates held in Burma's gaols were subject to far less physical restraint, worked a less brutal labour regime, and faced far less violent prison discipline than had been the case in the final decades of the nineteenth century. In the mid-1860s all prisoners were held in chains at night, to keep down the number of escapes but perhaps also in order to maintain control with limited gaolers.[66] Lying in double rows, each inmate was shackled to

[63] *RPAB*, 1939, p. 19. Of course the comparison is invalid, since the two age groups that account for a high proportion of the mortality in a general population—infants and the elderly—are either entirely absent or poorly represented in a prison population.

[64] *RPAB*, 1924, p. 20.

[65] *RPAB*, 1921, p. 14. The argument—'a stay in jail improves the health of the prisoner'—was repeated in *RPAB*, 1931, p. 15.

[66] *RPAB*, 1872, p. 51.

1. On the treadmill at the Rangoon Central Gaol. [Wellcome Library, London]

chains that ran the length of the prison ward and were securely fixed to the end walls, an arrangement closely similar to the night-time security found in Burma's pre-colonial prison. However, in 1867 use of the night-chain was discontinued in prisons with a secure outer wall, and the following year it was abandoned in every prison in British Burma.[67] Each inmate now slept in a separate berth. But they were still restrained with fetters. Thus the annual report for 1882 noted that even prisoners serving short sentences, and 'irrespective of physique or of character', were generally shackled.[68] But then, through the 1880s and 1890s the use of fetters for safe custody fell markedly, presumably as secure outer walls and main gates were completed at each prison in the province.[69] In 1896 it was reported that no prisoner serving less than five years, except 'notoriously danger-ous characters', was now being put in irons for safe custody: and then in 1902 it was noted that as a rule fetters were seldom used within Burma's prisons 'for

[67] *RPAB*, 1867, pp. 50–2, 75–6; *RPAB*, 1868, p. 32.
[68] *RPAB*, 1882, p. 37.
[69] *RPAB*, 1894, p. 34.

safeguarding'.[70] As for the prison labour regime, that most brutal instrument, the treadmill, was in use at both the Moulmein and Rangoon prisons in 1900,[71] but was then dismantled, possibly later in the decade.

Perhaps most dramatic here was the sharp reduction in, and eventually the near elimination of, the flogging of inmates for breaches of prison discipline. Flogging was very common in colonial Burma's prisons in the 1860s and 1870s, partly because it was seen as 'a good punishment for Burmese prisoners'—a racial categorisation that deemed the Burmese to be distinctively fearful of flogging—but also because alternative punishments, for example reduced diet or solitary confinement, were seen as either ineffective or impractical.[72] In 1878 corporal punishment was inflicted on 2,953 occasions.[73] In some gaols the flogging was wildly excessive. At Ma-ubin, on average each inmate was being flogged for an offence against prison discipline once every three-to-four months, it was reported in 1877.[74] In 1880 it was noted that Moulmein and Akyab were flogging inmates on a far greater scale than any other gaol in British Burma.[75] During that year a special inquiry—carried out just at the Moulmein and Akyab gaols apparently—found that prisoners caught in possession of tobacco or opium, both forbidden articles, were usually flogged.[76] At Moulmein it was also the practice to flog prisoners who were judged to have shown too little interest in their reading and writing lessons. The Chief Commissioner, the head of the colonial administration in Burma, openly denounced the near indiscriminate flogging of inmates. '[It] cannot be too strongly condemned, and must once and for all be put a stop

---

[70] *RPAB*, 1896, p. 28; *RPAB*, 1902, p. 13. Fetters were then still used when inmates were sent to work outside the prison walls, and as punishment for breaches of prison discipline. Indeed the annual report for 1900 noted that the most common punishment imposed for major prison offences was to put the offender into fetters or handcuffs: *RPAB*, 1900, p. 4. The use of fetters as a punishment for breaches of discipline was abolished in Burma's prisons only towards the end of the 1930s: *RPAB*, 1937, p. 20.

[71] *RPAB*, 1900, p. 5.

[72] *RPAB*, 1869, pp. 67, 69.

[73] *RPAB*, 1878, p. 11.

[74] *RPAB*, 1877, Resolution, p. 6.

[75] *RPAB*, 1880, Resolution, pp. 4–5.

[76] The Chief Commissioner, in his resolution on the 1880 report, was sufficiently open to add that prisoners were in fact obtaining illicit tobacco and opium through the free warder staff—staff often living outside the prison walls, and certainly able to move without restriction between the prison and the outside world—who carried messages to, and brought in articles from, the prisoners' families and friends: *RPAB*, 1880, Resolution, p. 4. In effect, the prison staff—as a group, not necessarily the same individuals—was both complicit in the offence and flogging the inmates when the latter were caught.

to', he insisted in 1877.[77] Three years later the Chief Commissioner directed that inmates found in possession of forbidden articles or held to be failing the prison labour regime should no longer be flogged but must be punished in some other way.[78] In 1882 floggings for breaches of prison discipline were down to 456.[79] And they continued to fall through the remaining decades of British rule, despite the increases in the prison population. The rattan was used on 313 occasions in 1902, and then eighty-two in 1925.[80] In 1931, nineteen inmates were whipped in the gaols of British Burma for breaches of discipline, and in 1940, just seven.[81]

The improvement in conditions in Burma's prisons by the 1930s should not obscure the fact that even in that final decade of British colonial administration, the inmates' experience of prison was harsh, and commonly brutal, violent and degrading. Senior officials may well have held that Burma's criminals were leaving the province's gaols in better physical shape than on admission, and then questioned whether such a regime could possibly deter crime, but few of the inmates could have seen their experience of prison as other than severe and intimidating.

That perspective—the prison experience through the eyes of a prisoner—was caught in the novel *The Victim* by the Burmese author Ludu U Hla. Half the novel is devoted to the years spent by its central character, Tun Myint, as an inmate of the Rangoon Gaol. Those were the first years of Burma's independence—Tun Myint was transferred to the prison in Rangoon on 29 February 1948, British rule had ended on 4 January 1948—but it is unlikely that the inmates' regime had changed greatly from the final years of colonial administration. Though a work of fiction, *The Victim* is strongly autobiographical. Ludu U Hla was himself held in the Rangoon Gaol, as a political prisoner, between 1953 and 1956: his account of Tun Myint's time inside, in the first person singular, is compellingly detailed and immediate: and on no point of detail or broad impression does the account collide with the factual sources. It is difficult to convey the timbre of Ludu U Hla's account from a brief passage—some details will be noted later in

---

[77] *RPAB*, 1877, Resolution, p. 6.

[78] *RPAB*, 1880, Resolution, p. 4.

[79] *RPAB*, 1882, p. 12.

[80] *RPAB*, 1902, p. 5; *RPAB*, 1925, p. 6.

[81] *RPAB*, 1931, p. 5; *RPAB*, 1940, p. 8. Of the seven inmates whipped in 1940, five had committed assault, one had refused to work, and one had deliberately harmed himself in order to avoid prison labour: cf. J.S. Furnivall [*Colonial Policy and Practice: A comparative study of Burma and Netherlands India*, New York University Press, 1956, p. 268]: 'In Burma whipping ... is a regular feature of jail discipline ...'

the chapter—but a central theme is the constant bargaining by prisoners with low-level gaol staff for less brutal treatment, in exchange for money-bribes, grovelling servility or sexual compliance. The Tun Myint/Ludu U Hla experience of the Rangoon Gaol was certainly severe and intimidating. In the rice shed

the hand-mill became so heavy that even two men found it a strain to work it. No rest was permitted during working hours however great one's fatigue. They had to keep on milling so that there was a continuous sound of rice coming through. As this had to be kept up without a break from six to eleven in the morning, then again from twelve to four, altogether nine full hours, it demanded every ounce of stamina and perseverance. As for a soft fellow like me, I would have found it hard to turn the mill even ten times. Anyone unpopular with the *tansee* [a grade of convict officer] was forced to do it by himself, and if he should be unequal to the task, he would be beaten up in the rice shed 'for failing to do the regulation work'.[82]

An official account of the inmates' daily routine, around 1910, was as follows:

At 5.15 a.m., the day commences, the prisoners rise from their wooden beds in the dormitories and *chota hazri* is served in the form of four ounces of rice porridge. In double file they are marched to the work places, where all manner of work is undertaken, including carpentry, carving, coach building (on a small scale), blacksmithy work, tailoring, weaving, wickerwork, wheat-grinding, coir [fibre from the outer husk of the coconut, used to make rope and matting] work, shell cleaning, mat making, leather work, netting money bags, net making, oil pressing, paddy grinding, rope making, skin curing, brickmaking, laterite quarrying, delon making, soorki pounding, stone-breaking, gardening, and paddy cultivation. At 9 o'clock work ceases for an hour, and the prisoners return to their dormitories and are given breakfast. This consists of 1lb. 12ozs of cooked rice, six ounces of cooked beans, and six ounces of anti-scorbutic [to prevent scurvy] vegetables which are grown in the gardens attached to the gaol. This 2½ lbs. of cooked food is just about as much as most prisoners can manage to demolish. When the food has been eaten, the convicts are taken to the water tanks in the yard to drink their fill. At 10 o'clock a return is made to the work-shops and labour is resumed until 4 p.m. Dinner, which is similar to breakfast, is then doled out, and when it has been eaten the prisoners are marched in squads to the bathing trough. At 6.30 the wards are locked up for the night. Sunday is free from work, and the convicts are kept in the compounds of their dormitories the whole of the day, where they are made to wash their clothes and clean their fetters.[83]

---

[82] Ludu U Hla, *The Victim*, translated by Than Tun and Kathleen Forbes, Mandalay: Ludu U Hla, 1976, p. 200.

[83] E.P. Frenchman, 'Prisons' in Arnold Wright, H.A. Cartwright, O. Breakspear (eds), *Twentieth Century Impressions of Burma: Its history, people, commerce, industries and resources*, London: Lloyd's Greater Britain Publishing, 1910, p. 255.

2. Inside the Mandalay Gaol. [Noel F. Singer, *Burmah: A photographic journey 1855-1925*, Stirling: Kiscadale, 1993]

Burma's inmates, drawn from an overwhelmingly agricultural background, but with large numbers coming into prison off the streets of Rangoon, often struggled to adjust to the strict regimentation and precise time-discipline of the colonial prison. In part the difficulty was that, with few exceptions, they did not possess the relevant practical skills and experience for the prison workshop—in the words of the annual report for 1870, 'they have to be taught a trade before they can [do] anything'.[84] But in addition they may well have been ill-equipped temperamentally or psychologically by their rural origins for the mechanically repetitive, industrial-world regime of the prison.[85]

---

[84] *RPAB*, 1870, Resolution, p. xvii: see also *RPAB*, 1871, Resolution, p. iv.

[85] Perhaps this is the point to note that there were few suicides among the inmates of colonial Burma's prisons—at most two or three in any year, and frequently none. This might be attributed to the lack of privacy in the mainly communal prison, an argument perhaps encouraged by the fact that inmates who did commit suicide often had to show considerable inventiveness: 'an under-trial prisoner [at Insein] committed suicide by jumping off a mango tree in the under-trial enclosure' [*RPAB*, 1940, p. 28]. On the other hand, given the ease with which illicit articles such as opium and tobacco circulated within colonial Burma's prisons, poison could surely have been obtained by or for those determined to end their life. It would obviously be unsafe to infer from the low suicide rate that there was little despair or desperation in the prisons of British Burma. For Burmese-Buddhist mental attitudes to imprisonment, focusing on the prison

RUNNING COLONIAL BURMA'S GAOLS

But crucial in determining the inmates' experience in prison was the character and competence of the gaol staff with whom the prisoners had near constant, day-in day-out, contact. Senior in this regard were the warders. In the gaols of British Burma the warders were Indians, recruited mainly from the United Provinces.[86] Until 1937, Burma was a province of British India, and Indians, often familiar with British administrative practice and able to communicate with British officials if not in English then through military Hindi, had long been coming into the province in large numbers and taking up jobs in the government sector, including the police and the prison service. In the mid-1920s there were roughly one thousand Indian warders working in Burma's gaols.[87] Several attempts were made around this time to appoint locals—in 1926 Burman warders were employed at the Tharrawaddy and Mandalay gaols 'as an experimental measure'— but with little success.[88] It was said that Burmans were refusing to come forward because the wages were far too low and the hours too long. But it is also quite possible that Burmans were simply reluctant to seek work in a sector where Indian domination was complete, in part because the entrenched Indian warders would not have welcomed Burman interlopers.

The senior prison administration had a low opinion of its Indian warders. The 1872 annual report declared bluntly that many warders '[are] morally worse than the prisoners themselves, and give more trouble'.[89] The 1923 report was more restrained but still highly dismissive: the province's Indian warders 'are by no means brilliant in character or intelligence'.[90] The critical factor here was the low warder pay, partly because it meant that the position could attract only the truly incompetent and suspect but also because it encouraged the warders to add to their wages by all manner of illicit dealings. They brought opium and

---

experiences of members of the post-1988 democracy movement but with a substantial historical dimension, see Gustaaf Houtman, *Mental Culture in Burmese Crisis Politics: Aung San Suu Kyi and the National League for Democracy*, Tokyo: Institute for the Study of Languages and Cultures of Asia and Africa, Tokyo University of Foreign Studies, 1999, part 2.

[86]   *RPAB*, 1923, p. 18.

[87]   Alexander Paterson, *Report on the Prevention of Crime and the Treatment of the Criminal in the Province of Burma*, Rangoon: Government Printing and Stationery, 1926, p. 55.

[88]   *RPAB*, 1926, p. 10; *RPAB*, 1919, p. 17; *RPAB*, 1925, p. 26.

[89]   *RPAB*, 1872, p. 51.

[90]   *RPAB*, 1923, p. 18.

3. Indian guards at the Rangoon Central Gaol, 1910s. [Frank and Frances Carpenter Collection, Library of Congress, Washington, DC]

tobacco into the gaols for sale to the prisoners, they ran extortion rackets inside the gaols, they helped inmates to escape.[91] In 1880, with a total warder staff in the gaols of British Burma of 282, warders were punished for serious offences and failures on no less than 328 occasions.[92] They were possibly more criminal than the inmates.

And of course there were the issues of race and language. The Indian warders did not speak Burmese, the language of the large majority of inmates.[93] Thus their orders were presumably often unclear to the prisoners, and the social understanding between the two was surely limited. Interestingly, from 1914 the gaolers, the rank above warder and occupied by Burmans, Indians, and Anglo-Indians, were required to pass a test in colloquial Hindi.[94] This suggests the administration was more concerned that the senior gaol staff, including warders, were able to communicate effectively with each other in Hindi than that those ranks could communicate with the Burmese inmates. The divide between warder and inmate was reinforced by a province-wide Burmese hostility towards the Indian presence, a hostility that became markedly more prominent from the 1920s, and would erupt into large-scale rioting in Rangoon in 1930 and 1938. Alexander Paterson, a Commissioner of Prisons for England and Wales, on an official visit to Burma from late 1925, observed that the Burmese instinctively regarded the Indian as inferior, and reported that '[t]he youngest prisoners may be seen openly flouting the control of their Indian warders'.[95] Effective discipline could not exist in Burma's prisons when 'those in authority are openly despised'.

On occasion Burmese resentment exploded into violence. On 24 June 1930 a riot occurred within the Rangoon Central Gaol.[96] Although order was restored after little more than an hour, the riot left dead thirty-four inmates, one warder and one lorry driver attached to the gaol. It was the most serious prison disturbance in Burma under British administration. The riot was apparently precipitated by the determination of a new superintendent, appointed just three weeks earlier, to clamp down on the poor discipline, corruption and brutality then said to be rife at Rangoon. The inmates would have resented the passing of a lax regime, in which illicit articles and small luxuries had been widely available

---

[91] *RPAB*, 1880, Resolution, p. 3; *RPAB*, 1867, p. 57.

[92] *RPAB*, 1880, Resolution, pp. 2–3.

[93] *RPAB*, 1908, pp. 7–8.

[94] *RPAB*, 1914, p. 7.

[95] Paterson, *Report on the Prevention of Crime*, p. 55.

[96] The following draws on James Warren, 'The Rangoon Jail Riot of 1930 and the Prison Administration of British Burma', *South East Asia Research*, 10, 1 (2002), pp. 5–29.

and light work duties easily negotiated. But there was also resistance from prison staff who had been doing well from various scams. Indeed there is one suggestion that the riot was instigated by two senior Rangoon gaolers in an attempt to bring down the superintendent. But at the same time, there was clearly a racial dimension. The new superintendent was an Indian, Major J. C. Bharucha, I.M.S.: the principal aim of the riot, according to the official enquiry, was to murder him. Less than a month earlier Rangoon town had seen severe rioting between Burmese and Indian labourers that left several hundred dead, almost all Indians. In the immediate aftermath, according to a contemporary British observer, '[t]he Burmese proletariat walked with a lighter step. They had shown the Indians their place ... they had been taught a lesson!'[97] Perhaps the Burmese convicts held in the Rangoon Central Gaol were now set on teaching that lesson to the Indian officers who stood over them. And finally, the context within which the gaol riot erupted—an Indian staff of about 125 faced a largely Burmese convict population of roughly two thousand—was, beyond doubt, racially charged.

This was certainly not the only occasion on which racial resentment exploded in violence. In July 1934 the chief gaoler at the Insein Central Gaol, an Indian, was attacked and wounded by four inmates serving life-terms.[98] But at the same time it is evident that Burma's prisons did not become a racial war zone. Rather, the Burmese inmate's contempt appears to have been channelled principally into distancing the Indian warder from much of his immediate existence, a process encouraged by the inability of the inmate and warder to communicate effectively in a common language. In the daily routines of the Burmese inmate, the Indian warder's presence was diminished. And into that space moved the other tier of prison staff who had close, day-in day-out contact with the inmates.

These were the staff appointed from within the prison population itself—the convict warders, overseers and nightwatchmen. Using inmates to assist in the running of Burma's prisons helped to reduce costs. But inmates were also seen to bring a number of advantages to the work. For example, confined to the gaol, convict staff, in contrast to the paid staff, were unable to act as a link with the outside world, bringing in opium and tobacco and carrying messages and conspiracies between the inmates and their families and friends beyond the walls.[99] Convict staff were best positioned to keep senior prison officers informed as to what was going on within the inmate population, not least because they too

---

[97] Maurice Collis, *Trials in Burma*, London: Faber and Faber, 1953, p. 164.
[98] Warren, 'The Rangoon Jail Riot of 1930', p. 21.
[99] *RPAB*, 1896, p. 29.

were Burmese, unlike the paid warders.[100] And often the convict officers were
more intelligent and effective in maintaining discipline than the paid warders,
the poor quality Indians.[101] The annual report for 1925 was forthright: 'convict
officers are an absolute necessity in the running of our jails.'[102]

But there were also a number of severe criticisms. It was said at different times
that Burman convict warders tended to sympathise with their fellow prisoners,
not with the established prison officers: that through fear of certain tough inmates they would often turn a blind eye to breaches of prison regulations and
more serious, criminal, activities: that they showed favouritism to some inmates
but were quite willing to set up those they disliked: that they participated in, and
often instigated, the illicit dealings that were rife within the gaol population.[103] It
was reported that convict staff had stolen from prisoners, and had assaulted and
terrorised those in their charge.[104] They were party to gaol escapes.[105] In 1892
convict warders took a leading part in a serious riot at the Akyab Gaol, in which
the European gaoler was murdered, and six prisoners were killed or wounded by
gunshot, as order was restored.[106] In the mid-1920s, Alexander Paterson, the visiting Prison Commissioner, was understandably scathing: 'The system of convict
officers, overseers and night watchmen ... is cheap and nasty. It has led in the past
to bullying, immorality and corruption ...'[107]

An 'absolute necessity' in the running of the gaols, but at the same time a major
cause of the intimidation, corruption and violence that was rife within them, the
convict staff clearly occupied a pivotal position in the prisons of colonial Burma.
From the perspective of the inmates, shaped by their daily experience, the convict
staff ran the gaols.[108] Their position was not always unchallenged. Prison orders
permitted the appointment only of casual prisoners, and not habituals, as convict warders, overseers and nightwatchmen. This meant that casuals—first-time
offenders, those convicted of less serious crimes—would frequently find them-

---

[100] *RPAB*, 1923, p. 8.

[101] *RPAB*, 1922, p. 6.

[102] *RPAB*, 1925, p. 7.

[103] *RPAB*, 1881, p. 20; *RPAB*, 1886, p. 11; *RPAB*, 1913, p. 6.

[104] *RPAB*, 1914, p. 4; *RPAB*, 1911, p. 6. In 1920 there were thirty reported assaults by convict of-
       ficers on inmates at the Rangoon Central Gaol: *RPAB*, 1920, p. 4.

[105] *RPAB*, 1908, p. 4.

[106] *RPAB*, 1892, Resolution, p. 3; pp. 10–12.

[107] Paterson, *Report on the Prevention of Crime*, p. 56.

[108] This point is strongly evident in Ludu U Hla's narrative. A convict officer tells Tun Myint: 'I
       am as powerful as a prince in this prison. I have the power and influence to do what I like to
       anybody, whether good or ill.' Ludu U Hla, *The Victim*, p. 226.

selves in charge of Burma's toughest criminals. Predictably the toughs would soon dominate the convict staff, through bullying, intimidation and, more subtly, by threatening serious trouble that could cause the responsible convict warder or nightwatchman to be disciplined or removed from his post.[109] But even these cir-cumstances confirm the pivotal position of the convict staff in the running of the gaol, in the sense that it was the convict staff, even if under duress, who presided over the prison's daily routine in all its mundane detail. They were pivotal not simply because of their close physical proximity to the prisoners but principally because, unlike the Indian warders or the European gaolers, they were able to communicate effectively with them. In the prisons of colonial Burma, only the convict warders, overseers and nightwatchmen really knew what was being said and done within the inmate population.

In the report produced at the end of his official visit to Burma in the mid-1920s, Alexander Paterson was highly critical of the arrangement by which at twenty-seven of the thirty-one gaols in the province, the smaller gaols, the posi-tion of superintendent was a part-time post, held as a supplementary responsibil-ity by the civil surgeon in the area.

[The part-time prison superintendents] sign their names upon a hurried series of forms, they hear applications from, and administer justice among, prisoners whose language is usually a closed book to them. They are compelled to accept from the Chief Jailor and his subordinate jailors, not only their interpretation of all that a prisoner says, but also their account of all that happens in the jail itself. Their conception of a jail rarely goes further than supposing all is well if the prison is clean, and the prisoners quiet, the accounts cor-rect, and there are no escapes.[110]

Paterson's observation was compelling but surely too narrowly applied. It was not only the part-time prison superintendents but also the chief gaolers, subordinate gaolers and warders who were forced to depend on others—the various grades of convict officers—to interpret what was being said and to explain what was happening.

Clearly the convict staff abused their pivotal knowledge and understanding. As noted above, they stole from inmates, assaulted them, and terrorised prisoners into handing over money and personal items. There were also cases of homo-sexual rape.[111] At Mandalay Gaol in 1915, three convict officers, together with

---

[109] *RPAB*, 1905, p. 5; *RPAB*, 1919, pp. 5–6.

[110] Paterson, *Report on the Prevention of Crime*, pp. 53–4.

[111] Ludu U Hla's *The Victim* suggests that homosexuality was rife in the Rangoon Gaol. Tun Myint, an attractive young man, is relentlessly pursued by a convict officer, with threats of vio-

two habituals, raped a newly admitted prisoner. 'Nine other convict officers ... were present in the ward at the time but were not on duty, and one convict night watchman, who was on duty ... took no notice of what was occurring. ... The chief culprit in the case, ... a convict warder, was reported as having a great deal of influence over the prisoners.'[112] But it is also critical to recognise that the convict staff could abuse their position in ways that advantaged the inmate population. Where convict warders were dealing in opium and tobacco, prisoners found escape from reality or relief from pain and boredom. When favour was shown, labour tasks were lightened. By turning a blind eye to infractions of petty rules, prison existence was made less tiresome. Inmates were helped over the wall.

In the final analysis, the prison in colonial Burma was a weakly run, poorly disciplined institution. The image unfailingly projected in the annual reports on prison administration in the province—the immense detail, the precise accounts, the numerous statistical appendices—was of complete command. The reality was that the prison hierarchy had only a limited grip on what took place within the gaol. In the absence of disciplined command—inevitable when the warder establishment faced a racially hostile prison population whose language it could not fathom—the inmates were left open to assault and extortion or, alternatively, were able to secure protection and leniency. The absence of firm command also implied that the prison hierarchy did not possess the leverage to reform and rehabilitate inmates—if indeed that were its aim.

PERCEPTION AND PURPOSE IN BURMA

In British Burma the prison population was strikingly high. In the mid-1910s the average daily inmate population as a proportion of the total population of the province was just under 140 per 100,000.[113] The comparable figures for the United Provinces and Bengal were a little over fifty and just under thirty respectively.

---

lent reprisal if he failed to respond. Eventually, drugged with marijuana put into his food, he complies. Sex was an important currency within the prison. As was explained to Tun Myint: 'There's a trade in human bodies in the prison. Whenever a handsome young boy turns up here, an old hand befriends him and looks after him, in order to make the boy feel attached to him. Then later on someone who wants a wife can buy the boy from the older man, and thus gains the right to treat him as his marriage partner.'
'So he's trying to buy me from you like that.'
'He asked me to sell you for fifty rupees, and tried to bait me with a cushy job if I fell for the offer.'
Ludu U Hla, *The Victim*, pp. 192–3.

[112] *RPAB*, 1915, p. 6.
[113] Calculated from *RPAB*, 1915, Statement A.

In other words, an inhabitant of Burma was almost three times more likely to be sent to prison than an inhabitant of the United Provinces, and almost five times more likely than an individual in Bengal. British officials in Rangoon would frequently assert, 'Burma ... is by far the most criminal nation of the Eastern Empire [British India].'[114] Perhaps there was a subliminal argument here—that the Burmese were by far the most criminal race in British India. But taken at face value, the assertion was simply a further statement of the observation that the prison population in British Burma was high, and made no attempt to explain why this should have been so. In fact the reasons were highly complex. They may well have included a weakening in social discipline across much of rural Burma under the impact of rapid economic change, a decline in Burmese religious authority, and the imposition by the British of definitions of criminal behaviour that did not always accord with established Burmese belief and practice—the British locked up Burmese for behaviour that the latter did not regard as wrong. But some insight may be gained by examining the composition of the inmate population: who were the inmates, why had they been sent to prison, and how long would they spend inside?

The vast majority of the inmates were male. Of the 19,736 convicts held in the gaols of Burma during 1925, just 510, or less than 3 per cent, were female.[115] Only a relatively small part of the prison population served a substantial sentence. Of the total of 21,322 inmates held in 1915, to select a year at random, just 1,941, or a little over 9 per cent, had been sentenced to terms of imprisonment of two years or more.[116] In contrast, 8,054 inmates, almost 38 per cent of the total, were serving sentences of three months or less: indeed 3,853 inmates, or 18 per cent—almost one in five of those held in the gaols of Burma during 1915—had been sentenced to less than one month. The most commonly committed offences that sent Burmese to prison in this period were theft, housebreaking, and vagrancy—here called 'bad livelihood'. Thus, of the 19,736 held during 1925, 5,324 (27 per cent) were in for theft, 1,992 (10 per cent) for housebreaking and 1,063 (5 per cent) had been picked up as vagrants.[117] In contrast, just 320 were held for murder or attempted murder, of which eighty-three had been sentenced to transportation for life and 145 would hang, and 349 had been convicted of dacoity—gang robbery.

---

[114] *RPAB*, 1894, p. 2.

[115] *RPAB*, 1925, p. 183.

[116] *RPAB*, 1920, Resolution, p. 6. To this figure might be added the 704 who had been sentenced to transportation, either for a term of years or for life, and the 163 who had been sentenced to hang.

[117] *RPAB*, 1925, Statement D [pp. 176–83].

In other words, the prisons of colonial Burma were filled with men serving relatively short sentences, often a matter of a few weeks, for relatively modest crimes, or simply for being destitute. Thus the Rangoon Central Gaol took, in the words of the annual report for 1916, '[a] large proportion of the diseased and submerged lower tenth of Rangoon's population'.[118] There was not much that could be done to rehabilitate such inmates. Small-time thieves could only be put out of circulation for a few weeks, and given a shock that might deter: down-and-outs were merely being shovelled off the streets.

Given the composition of the inmate population, and given too the poor quality of the prison's paid subordinate staff—a point considered earlier—it is perhaps surprising that the senior prison administration in colonial Burma made frequent reference to the reform and rehabilitation of the inmate. It is true that in his resolution on the annual report for 1868, the Chief Commissioner for British Burma stated bluntly, 'prisoners are sent to Gaol primarily to be punished.'[119] But just one year later the Inspector-General of Prisons was providing a progressive perspective on the purposes of the prison. He acknowledged that with respect to 'the three great objects of imprisonment ... intimidation, instruction, and amendment', the Burma administration was still struggling with the first, with the construction of 'a system as will deter from crime'.[120] But the Inspector-General was confident that, in time, 'the utopian doctrine that a long residence in gaol may be conducive to a man's improvement in knowledge and in virtue', as he put it, would receive the same attention in Burma as it was already receiving 'in almost every part of the world'. And indeed in time reform and rehabilitation came to the fore in the thinking of the Burma prison administration. '[T]he main object of penal institutions', stated the 1932 annual report, '[is] to return the offender to society a normal man as far as it lies in our power.'[121]

Reality never came close to matching this rhetoric. For example, the provision of basic instruction for the inmates of Burma's prisons, clearly an important element in reform and rehabilitation, remained extremely thin right through to the end of the colonial period. Compulsory instruction was adopted into the Burma prison rules at the end of the 1870s.[122] In 1878 no classes had taken place in nine of Burma's prisons, and at the remaining seven it was only at Bassein

---

[118] *RPAB*, 1916, p. 11. A census of Rangoon inmates conducted in August 1914 revealed that one in six was a known drug taker—opium, morphine and cocaine: *RPAB*, 1914, p. 11.

[119] *RPAB*, 1868, Resolution, p. xvii.

[120] *RPAB*, 1869, pp. 78–9.

[121] *RPAB*, 1932, p. 21.

[122] *RPAB*, 1879, Resolution, pp. 3–4.

that inmates had been taught in significant numbers.[123] The following year there were no classes in four prisons. The annual report for 1881 noted that just one quarter of inmates was attending classes on a daily basis.[124] Even thirty years later the Mandalay Gaol had just begun 'to have reading and writing taught to illerate [*sic*] prisoners who wish to learn'.[125] In these years the instructors were appointed from among the prisoners themselves. But in the mid-1920s trained paid teachers were engaged for five of the province's central prisons.[126] Attendance at classes was compulsory for one year for prisoners aged under twenty-five, voluntary for the others, and inmates were given instruction in reading, writing, simple arithmetic, elementary geography, history and health. Each inmate was in class for forty-five minutes each day. This scheme had been introduced simply as an experiment, but the annual report for 1928 noted the administration's intention to extend such primary education to all the province's large prisons.[127] The world economic crisis then hit Burma, and included in the cuts in government expenditure that followed was the dismissal of the paid teachers from the five central prison schools, their work being transferred to convicts with at least some education—a return to old ways.[128] The cut was not restored during that decade, even as provincial finances improved, and consequently at the end of the 1930s there was only one paid teacher in the entire Burma prison system—at the juvenile gaol at Meiktila.[129]

The failure of colonial Burma's prison administration to translate its rhetoric of reform and rehabilitation into practice can perhaps be adequately explained just in terms of a shortage of funds. But there may have been a further, very striking factor. On a number of occasions in the 1910s and in the 1920s, the senior administration expressed serious doubt whether the prison—not simply the prison in Burma but the prison as an institution—was a truly effective instrument to reform the behaviour of the criminal and to rehabilitate him back into society. Doubt surfaced in the annual report for 1918. While prison, and in particular the remission system, gave 'a man a chance of reforming himself by good behaviour', the Inspector-General argued,

[123] *RPAB*, 1878, Resolution, p. 4.
[124] *RPAB*, 1881, Resolution, p. 4.
[125] *RPAB*, 1910, p. 2.
[126] *RPAB*, 1926, p. 3.
[127] *RPAB*, 1928, p. 3.
[128] *RPAB*, 1932, p. 2. That said, in the mid-1930s all the central prisons in Burma with the exception of Akyab now provided classes for prisoners—but, again, taught by convict teachers: *RPAB*, 1935, p. 3.
[129] *RPAB*, 1939, p. 24.

it is doubtful how far the prisoner who learns, to his own benefit, how to obey the artificial jail code of behaviour, really fits himself for the responsibilities of freedom. To some extent the qualities of honesty, industry, and discipline may be developed in jail, and so far the system may be, to a limited extent, truly reformatory. But mostly these qualities are not developed in jail.[130]

Honesty, industry and discipline were more likely to flourish, he continued, among men conditionally released from prison to work outside on specific projects—the Inspector-General noted the recruitment of 1,523 prisoners into the 148th (Burma) Jail Labour Corps, sent to Mesopotamia at the beginning of 1918—or among those sent to agricultural colonies, such as that established by the prison administration in the American Philippines, or to such institutions as the George Junior Republics in the United States.

The effectiveness of the prison—'a comparatively modern method ... and [therefore] ... still on trial'—was questioned more aggressively still in an extraordinary extended passage in the *Report on the Prison Administration of Burma* for 1922.[131] The Inspector-General, Major H.H.G. Knapp, opened with the fundamental question, relevant of course far beyond Burma: 'With what object do we put men into prison?' Major Knapp outlined the standard points. But his position was that, with respect to many of them, the prison was a failing institution. It did not deter crime—after all, Burma's prison population and the province's crime figures both continued to soar. Neither did it reform and rehabilitate.

we must, I fear, admit that our jails are not, and probably cannot be made, reformatories ... it is too much to expect a man to be fit for freedom after he has been shut up for a term of years ... [and we should] explore fully every alternative to jail, such as the probation system [and] release on condition of good behaviour ... The direction of prison reform should have as its aim the closing of jails rather than the building of more of these costly institutions.[132]

This final sentence was indeed extraordinary.

There was a further prominent critical voice at this time. In November 1925 one of the Commissioners of Prisons for England and Wales, the most senior rank in the metropolitan prison administration, arrived in Rangoon to advise on gaol conditions in Burma. The commissioner, Alexander Paterson, was to be the most influential figure in prison administration and thinking in England in the

---

[130] *RPAB*, 1918, p. 16.
[131] *RPAB*, 1922, pp. 14–16.
[132] Ibid. , pp. 15–16.

decades between the world wars, his guiding aim being to create more humane, less rigidly oppressive conditions for convicts, that would thus encourage their reform and rehabilitation.[133] In the early 1920s Paterson's progressive perspective was already long-established and well-known, and it is inconceivable that the Burma prison administration, and in particular the then Inspector-General, Major P.K. Tarapore, was unaware of the line he was likely to take in his examination of gaol conditions in the province. Indeed Major Tarapore, who appears to have engineered the invitation to Paterson, almost certainly did so because he could confidently anticipate that the commissioner's views on the capacity of prison to reform and rehabilitate chimed with those of himself, his immediate predecessors, and perhaps many of his senior colleagues.

Paterson remained in the province for four months. His *Report on the Prevention of Crime and the Treatment of the Criminal in the Province of Burma*, published by the Burma government in 1926, contained a brief but crucial section marked 'The Object of a Prison'.

No one visiting the great jails of Burma, studying first the 2,600 first offenders at Rangoon, and then the 2,500 habitual prisoners at Insein, can forbear from asking the simple question—what is the good of it all? What purpose has been served by dragging all these men from earning a livelihood with their wives and families (as the majority of them were doing) and enforcing upon them this highly artificial life within walls, where they do very little work and cost the Province over 20 lakhs [two million rupees] every year? What effect has it on them or the world outside? Can no more effective and less expensive way be found to meet the end for which prisons were designed?[134]

And later:

The main criticism of the jails of Burma ... is that there are too many people in them ... There has been little clear thinking on the subject of prisons, their purpose, their method

---

[133] Basic accounts of Alexander Paterson's career and achievements can be found in: *Dictionary of National Biography: Supplement 1941–1950*, Oxford University Press, 1959, pp. 658–61; *The Times*, 10 November 1947 [obituary]; and Rupert Cross, *Punishment, Prison and the Public: An assessment of penal reform in twentieth century England by an armchair penologist*, London: Stevens, 1971, pp. 29–37. For a detailed, scholarly assessment, see W.J. Forsythe, *Penal Discipline, Reformatory Projects and the English Prison Commission 1895–1939*, University of Exeter Press, 1990, *passim*. And for the voice of the man himself, see S.K. Ruck (ed.), *Paterson on Prisons: Being the collected papers of Sir Alexander Paterson M.C., M.A.*, London: Frederick Muller, 1951. Two of Paterson's most oft-quoted aphorisms are: 'Men come to prison as a punishment not for punishment'; and 'It is impossible to train men for freedom in a condition of captivity.'

[134] Alexander Paterson, *Report on the Prevention of Crime and the Treatment of the Criminal in the Province of Burma*, Rangoon: Government Printing and Stationery, 1926, p. 46.

and their effect, among the general community. They are accepted as necessary and convenient evils, with a hope that they are not too expensive ... Committal to prison is the refuge for a community that will not take the trouble to think of any other way of dealing with a troublesome person.[135]

Paterson proposed three measures that would, he suggested, roughly halve Burma's prison population. The first two were modest in both nature and potential impact—the introduction of a probation scheme, applied principally to first offenders, and the creation of residential schools for young offenders aged fourteen to eighteen. But his third was more radical. Paterson proposed that normally no convict should be held in prison for more than two years.

It is very doubtful whether after two years any good is done to a man by further detention in the circumstances of jail-life. He will get used to it, relapse into the half-light of a monotonous regime, lose count of time and space, and become daily more fitted to be a prisoner than a free man.[136]

It followed that the prison should focus on the initial reform of the convicted criminal, instilling in him discipline and the habit of hard work.[137] At the end of two years, which should see the completion of that initial reform of character, convicts—of course only those sentenced to more than two years—would be 'at the disposition of the state'. First offenders, except those convicted of murder or dacoity, would be organised into labour gangs and, under the direction of the Public Works Department, be put to work on road construction or the clearing of forest for cultivation. They would be joined by wives and families, live in temporary structures close to the work site, and be paid the wage of free labour. There would be no guards. Idle workers would be returned to gaol. In contrast, habitual offenders, again except those convicted of murder or dacoity, would be sent to an island settlement—Paterson identified Cocos Island and the island of Pyinzalu, on the southern edge of the delta, as possible sites. There they would be free within the limits of the settlement, would again be joined by wives and families, and would be expected to be self-supporting, perhaps from the processing of the coconuts that grew locally in abundance. Finally, Paterson proposed that murderers and dacoits would not be subject to the initial two years of imprisonment but rather, on conviction, would be sent immediately to the penal colony in the Andaman Islands. They too would be joined by wives and families.

---

[135] Ibid., pp. 61–2.
[136] Ibid., pp. 62–3.
[137] Ibid., pp. 63–7.

Paterson's case against the prison, more accurately against long-term imprisonment, was compelling. And his proposed alternative, whatever the practical difficulties it might involve, was a coherent response to the failings he had identified. Although Paterson was not, of course, part of colonial Burma's prison administration, but a senior figure from the imperial centre, in a number of crucial respects his report was clearly integral to the thinking of the Burma prison administration in the 1920s. Thus his founding proposition—that the criminal was unlikely to be reformed and rehabilitated within the walls of a prison—had been argued on a number of occasions by successive Inspectors-General of Prisons, Burma, in the years before Paterson had arrived in the province. Indeed, as was noted above, it had been Major Tarapore, the then Inspector-General, who almost certainly had instigated the invitation to Paterson, because the Burma prison administration anticipated, correctly, that he would provide a kindred authoritative voice. It should also be noted that the prison commissioner's report was firmly anchored in its Burma context. In other words, although his ideas had clearly been profoundly shaped by his considerable experience in the prison administration in England, he was not simply using the Burma trip and his Burma report as a platform for an established agenda. Thus, as noted earlier, he gave strong emphasis in his report to the tensions between the Burmese inmates and the Indian warders, a critical dynamic in the running of the province's prisons, but one rarely mentioned in the annual reports. And his proposed alternative to long-term imprisonment, the use of convict labour to construct roads and clear forests, made much of the argument that the future prosperity of Burma, a labour-short economy, depended largely on improvements in communications and continued expansion in the cultivated area.

The Burma government rejected Paterson's core recommendation that no individual should spend more than two years in a walled gaol[138]—although perhaps few governments, then or since, would have embraced such a radical approach. It also rejected his recommendations that murderers and dacoits be sent to the Andaman Islands (the Indian authorities having in effect abolished transportation to the Andamans) and that habitual criminals be sent to the province's own island settlement (possible sites, including the Cocos Islands, having proved to be impractical). But other Paterson initiatives were taken up, or indeed were already being pursued. In the late 1920s two camp gaols, each located at a government-owned stone quarry, were established, the first at Alon in the Lower Chindwin District (north-west of Mandalay) and the second at Mokpalin in Thaton District

---

[138] Resolution by the Governor in Council on Paterson, *Report on the Prevention of Crime*, p. 4.

(east of Rangoon).[139] In the mid-1930s the two camp gaols—temporary structures—held one-eighth of Burma's convict population.[140] In June 1931 a combined Borstal and Senior Training School, under a superintendent brought out from England, was opened at Thayetmyo in central Burma.[141] And through this period from the mid-1920s to the end of the 1930s, the prison administration's annual reports—the public record of its measures and thinking—continued to emphasise the core importance of the reform and rehabilitation of the convicted criminal, although the argument that they were unlikely to be achieved within the walls of a prison, prominent in the first half of the 1920s, was no longer pursued. The focus now was on making the conventional prison work.[142] Thus the report for 1938 pointed to greater understanding and subtlety in the treatment of the convict held in gaol:

The practical problems of prison administration ... will be solved not by brute force and by the administration of more and more punishments but by the newer type of intelligence, knowledge of human nature, courage and willingness to take the inmates of penal institutions into confidence in order to help them to overcome their difficulties.[143]

PERCEPTION AND PURPOSE IN THE PHILIPPINES

A progressive rhetoric of reform and rehabilitation was also used by the prison administration in the American-ruled Philippines, indeed more insistently and to greater practical effect than was the case in British Burma. Perhaps important here was the fact that the Philippines administration clearly regarded the disciplines of criminology and penology as exact sciences. Senior prison officials enthusiastically held that the causes of criminal behaviour and the penal

---

[139] *RPAB*, 1928, p. 6.

[140] *RPAB*, 1935, p. 2.

[141] *RPAB*, 1931, p. 1.

[142] One aspect of this was recognition that, for the individual, prison had to have time to work. It was frequently argued in annual reports in the 1930s—for example *RPAB*, 1935, p. 4—that a sentence of just a few months, let alone a few days, was too brief to have an impact in deterring or reforming. It followed that minor offences, for example, travelling by train without a ticket, should be punished not by a week or so in gaol but in some other way, perhaps flogging. Paterson, of course, had focused not on a minimum effective term but the maximum, to argue that more than two years in prison did harm rather than good to the convict's chances of reform and rehabilitation.

[143] *RPAB*, 1938, p. 28. However, brute force still had its place. At the beginning of that decade a special block had been created at the Moulmein Gaol to receive and discipline the province's most disruptive inmates—the bullies and 'bad hats': *RPAB*, 1931, p. 5.

procedures that would reform and rehabilitate the criminal could be—indeed were now being—exposed by rigorous scientific inquiry. Thus the 1924 report of the Governor General, the section concerned with the Bureau of Prisons, characterised the Philippine prison as a 'laboratory'—an interesting choice of word—in which

human nature is analyzed in its physical, intellectual, and ethical sides and the minds of the so-called social outcasts are awakened and molded through the application of such reformatory agencies, namely, labor, education, and religion, with the result that even the once habitual offenders are thoroughly trained and rehabilitated and exhibit upon their discharge an average standard of virtue and turn out to be useful citizens.[144]

Senior officials in the prison administration undertook fact-finding tours of gaols in the United States. They attended and addressed annual meetings of the American Prison Association: in August 1925 the Assistant Director of Prisons, Manuel A. Alzate, attended the Ninth International Prison Congress, held in London.[145] The Philippines prison administration projected itself as being at the forefront of modern penological thinking, its prisons among the best in the world. Every opportunity was taken in the administration's publications to parade the highly laudatory comments of visitors to the Philippines and to its prisons.[146]

There seems little doubt that conditions in the main prison in Manila, Bilibid, improved substantially under American rule, and that in many respects the administration of the gaol in that period was highly progressive. In October 1916 the Director of Prisons, Waller H. Dade, addressed the Annual Congress of the American Prison Association, held in Buffalo.

---

[144] *Annual Report of the Governor General Philippine Islands, 1924,* Washington, DC: Government Printing Office, 1926, p. 161.

[145] *Annual Report of the Governor General of the Philippine Islands, 1925,* Washington, DC: United States Government Printing Office, 1927, pp. 298–9.

[146] The *Annual Report of the Governor General of the Philippine Islands* for 1927 [Washington, DC: United States Government Printing Office, 1928, p. 232] reported the comment of Congressman M.G. Maas after a visit to Bilibid: 'Best discipline and spirit have yet seen in a prison'. A Mr Paul R. Clark was reported as commenting: 'I came from a prison city but your prison is far superior to ours.' The *Philippines Prisons Review* for November 1927 [3, 11, p. 14] reported the words of Geoffrey J. Fose, a visitor from Australia that the Philippines prison system 'is splendid and it is a great pity that it is not more extensively adopted in other parts of the world'. It would appear that Bilibid was a considerable attraction for visitors to Manila in the 1920s, not least among American tourists reaching the Philippines by ocean liner [*Annual Report of the Governor General Philippine Islands, 1924,* Washington, DC: Government Printing Office, 1926, p. 165].

[I cannot] think that lecturing to men on what they should do and then entombing them like wild beasts in cold and cheerless cells, to be gnawed to distraction by their own reflections, will ever bring the end we seek. But take for a moment the opposite and give them well lighted and well ventilated dormitories where they can talk with a fellow human; where they can discuss what they have read and heard during the day; a library with up-to-date reading matter, for can you conceive of their not wishing to keep abreast of the affairs of the world? Give them an abundance of good, wholesome food, cooked and served in a manner that would prove appetizing if served on your table or mine.[147]

The new American prison administration undertook a major reconstruction of Bilibid. Many of the existing buildings, erected under the Spanish, were re-fitted: the dark and airless dungeons that had occupied the lower part of the prison's central building were converted into storerooms.[148] Moreover, new buildings, modern constructions more open to light and air, were erected on the prison site—dormitories, workshops, a central kitchen, guards quarters. In 1909 an 'exceedingly well equipped' hospital, located within the prison's walls, was opened.[149] The previous year a water-distilling plant and electric light had been installed.[150]

But more interesting was the range and nature of the daily routine imposed by the American administration in the prison, intended to reform and rehabilitate inmates. Some elements might be anticipated. Thus prisoners were given some basic schooling, at least in reading, writing and the elements of arithmetic. In the late 1920s every inmate of Bilibid under thirty years of age attended two periods of schooling a day.[151] The classes were taught by fellow prisoners who had some education, supervised by a civilian superintendent. Bilibid also contained extensive workshops in which the inmates could learn a craft or industrial skill (and which, through the sale of workshop products, secured profits for the Bureau of Prisons). Again the presence of such facilities might have been expected in a large-scale modern prison in late-colonial South East Asia. But in terms of the range of crafts and skills pursued there, and the quality and sophistication of the articles produced, Bilibid was almost certainly without rival in the region. In

[147] Waller H. Dade, 'Prison System of the Philippines' [Read at the Annual Congress of the American Prison Association, Buffalo, 7–12 October 1916], National Archives of the United States at College Park, RG 350, 6281-16.

[148] John Lewis Gillin, *Taming the Criminal: Adventures in penology*, New York: Macmillan, 1931, p. 37.

[149] *Report of the Philippine Commission to the Secretary of War, 1909*, Washington, DC: Government Printing Office, 1910, p. 195.

[150] *Report of the Philippine Commission to the Secretary of War, 1908*, Washington, DC: Government Printing Office, 1909, part 2, p. 793.

[151] Gillin, *Taming the Criminal*, p. 44.

the late 1920s it produced carts, carriages and wagons; service uniforms, prison garb and civilian clothes; embroidery-work and lace; hammocks; and shoes.[152] There was a car repair shop, a foundry, smithy, wheelwright shop, upholsterers, shoe-repairers and a general machine shop. But most prominent, the Industrial Division of Bilibid Prison produced high quality furniture, crafted from Philippine hardwoods, and wicker, rattan and bamboo pieces. Indeed orders for Bilibid furniture were received from across the world—although, with such strong demand, customers often had to wait many months for their orders to be met—and the furniture won numerous medals at international expositions. The Bureau of Prisons published glossy catalogues of the full range of Bilibid products.

Two innovations introduced into the Bilibid regime by the American administration were quite striking. The first was the prisoners' court. Initiated in 1915, the court was composed of prisoners—as first constituted, the court president, judges, prosecuting and defence counsels, and sheriffs.[153] It tried relatively minor breaches of prison discipline, including stealing, loafing, fighting, disobeying orders, neglect of duty, hiding food and refusal to work. As far as prison circumstances would permit, the court's procedures were those of 'regularly established' courts in the world outside, for example, in the calling of witnesses. The sentences imposed involved loss of privileges, from forfeiting a meal to loss of remission for good behaviour. The findings of the court were reviewed by the Director of Prisons. In only a modest fraction—248 cases from a total of 2,848 heard in 1917—were they modified. Second, the American prison administration, in its own words in the mid-1920s, spared no effort 'in making the life of the prisoners as pleasant as possible by providing ... instructive and reformative amusements'.[154] Thus prisoners were given opportunities to play, for example, baseball and volleyball. In January 1927 the Bilibid baseball team took on opponents from the San Marcelino Shoe Factory, the USS *Preble*, and from Camp Nichols, a local

[152] Ibid., pp. 38–42.

[153] *Report of the Philippine Commission to the Secretary of War, 1915*, Washington, DC: Government Printing Office, 1916, p. 230; *Report of the Governor General Philippine Islands, 1921*, Washington, DC: Government Printing Office, 1922, p. 154; *Report of the Governor General of the Philippine Islands to the Secretary of War, 1917*, Washington, DC: Government Printing Office, 1918, p. 137.

[154] *Annual Report of the Governor General Philippine Islands, 1924*, Washington, DC: Government Printing Office, 1926, p. 164. A more revealing statement of this argument appeared in the report for 1931: 'It is one of the essentials of prison administration that the inmates should be given the boon of wholesome recreation. It would be a basic fault to permit the inmates to brood, to be possessed of a sullen spirit that might flare up into open acts of insubordination': *Annual Report of the Governor General of the Philippine Islands, 1931*, Washington, DC: United States Government Printing Office, 1932, p. 235.

4. Retreat at Bilibid Prison, Manila, with the prison band in attendance. [United States National Archives and Records Administration, College Park, Maryland]

army-camp.[155] Radio broadcasts could be heard nightly: and each inmate was allowed to listen to a radio entertainment show once a week. Each Saturday and Sunday silent films were shown, provided to the prison free of charge by the Universal Film Exchange Company. The films projected were selected with a view to instructing and reforming the inmates. On the big holidays—Fourth of July, Christmas, Rizal Day, New Year—theatrical troupes, magicians and singers performed in the prison. And finally, Bilibid had its own orchestra, which provided concerts each Saturday and Sunday, and a prison band, which, each day at five o'clock, played at the 'retreat'—the final assembly of all inmates, before they filed away to their dormitories. The retreat would usually draw a good crowd of visitors, who would watch the performance—not simply the musical performance by the band but a routine of gymnastic exercises performed by a selected, trained group of inmates—from a gallery built on the roof of the prison's main tower.[156] It was a central factor in Bilibid's reputation as a tourist attraction.

But despite the progressive elements in its regime, Bilibid clearly remained a conventional prison. The more striking institution within the Philippine system in this period was, therefore, the Iwahig Penal Colony on the island of Palawan,

[155] *Philippine Prisons Review*, 3, 1 (1927), pp. 34–5. The Bilibid inmates won one, and lost two.
[156] Gillin, *Taming the Criminal*, pp. 45–6.

established in the first years of American administration, in 1904.[157] Iwahig was innovative in two main respects. Convicted criminals were not sentenced to serve their term in the colony: it was not the case that the courts simply exiled to Iwahig those convicted of the most serious crimes, or the completely incorrigible, as a still more brutal alternative to being sent to prison. Rather, Iwahig took long-term convicts who had already served a substantial part of their sentence in Bilibid, during which time they had clearly demonstrated their trustworthiness. In the late 1920s the detailed requirements were: first offenders sentenced to from twelve years to life, who had served at least one fifth of their sentence and who, by good conduct, had been promoted to first class convict and were close to promotion to the highest, or 'trusty', class. There were similarities here to the proposals that Alexander Paterson would put to the Burma administration in the mid-1920s. Thus convicts, except murderers and dacoits, would spend a limited time—two years—in prison, sufficient to instil discipline and industriousness. Further confinement would simply institutionalise the individual, Paterson would argue, making long-term rehabilitation more difficult. At the end of two years they would be 'at the disposition of the state', and either be put to work on road construction or the clearing of forest for cultivation, or be sent to a self-supporting island settlement.

The second innovation was that the Iwahig Penal Colony was run principally by the convicts themselves—it was a self-governing republic. Taking as its model the George Junior Republic, 'a reformatory school for delinquent and wayward children' in upstate New York, the convicts at Iwahig elected most of the settlement's officials, provided the men for the local police force, and ran the colony's judicial system. They participated in a vigorous internal economy—raising cattle, rearing poultry, cutting the forests, fishing, and cultivating tapioca, rice and corn. The colony had astonishingly few non-convict officials—in the late 1920s just the superintendent and his two assistants, one doctor and one nurse, the bandmaster, three teachers, eight foremen, the farming instructor, two chaplains, the cashier and two others, twenty-three in total—and a number of these were ex-Iwahig convicts. There were no guards. And none of these officials, with the exception of the superintendent, possessed a weapon. The Iwahig Penal Colony was no modest operation. In 1928 it occupied over 100,000 acres, and had around 2,000 residents, a figure that included the families of selected convicts.

[157] The following draws principally on Gillin, *Taming the Criminal*, pp. 54–61; Michael Salman, "'Nothing without Labor": Penology, discipline, and independence in the Philippines under United States colonial rule, 1898-1914' in Vincent L. Rafael (ed.), *Discrepant Histories: Translocal essays on Filipino cultures*, Philadelphia, PA: Temple University Press, 1995, pp. 119–22.

After visiting the penal colony in 1914, the Episcopal Bishop of the Philippines declared that Iwahig was, to his knowledge, the most 'successful experiment in the treatment of criminals in the world'.[158] While falling short of the bishop's enthusiasm, the present discussion of the Philippine prison administration's progressive vision may also have been too benevolent, reflecting the largely uncritical character of the published official sources that have been used.[159] There is clearly a darker narrative to be written. Thus there were occasions when the authorities lost control of the prison. A riot at Bilibid in December 1904 left nineteen inmates dead and forty wounded, and the first years at Iwahig were devastated by disease, mutinies and escapes.[160] There were scandals. In November 1906 Dr Richard P. Strong, the director of the Bureau of Laboratories in Manila, inoculated twenty-four inmates at Bilibid against cholera infection, as part of a scientific trial. Dr Strong failed to explain to the inmates what he was doing, and their permission was not sought. Moreover the cholera vaccine used in the trial had been contaminated with a virulent strain of bubonic plague, and thirteen of the prisoners died as a result.[161] There were also long-term failings in the Philippine prison system. Despite the transfer of large numbers of convicts to Iwahig, Bilibid remained seriously overcrowded throughout the American period.[162]

---

[158] Quoted in Salman, '"Nothing without Labor"', p. 121. Iwahig's remarkable, progressive approach was widely recognised: see, for example, 'Uncle Sam has a Siberia. It's not like the Czar's. In the Philippine Islands is a penal colony where nearly fifteen hundred life prisoners work out their existence—a remarkable place graphically described', *The World Magazine*, 8 January 1911.

[159] The annual reports on prison administration in the American Philippines were far briefer, less detailed and less critical than the reports for British Burma.

[160] Salman, '"Nothing without Labor"', pp. 117, 119.

[161] For a superb study of the Strong case, that pays due attention to its scientific, racial and political contexts, see Kristine A. Campbell, 'Knots in the Fabric: Richard Pearson Strong and the Bilibid Prison vaccine trials, 1905–1906', *Bulletin of the History of Medicine*, 68, 4 (1994), pp. 600–38.

[162] Gillin, in *Taming the Criminal* [p. 52], was notably critical of the crowded dormitories. By this point a further increase in capacity was not possible. Located in a densely built quarter of the city, Bilibid was restricted to its original, seventeen-acre site. However, just before the outbreak of the Pacific War, a new prison was constructed at Muntinlupa, a short distance south of Manila. Bilibid's inmates were transferred to the new institution and the old prison was closed—at least briefly, until filled with American and Filipino prisoners of war. Charles Brown, *Bars from Bilibid Prison*, San Antonio, TX: The Naylor Company, 1947, p. 6. Interesting to note, in other parts of the region too, this period saw the relocation of the main prison away from a densely built quarter of the capital towards the less visible, less populated outskirts—the construction of Bang Kwang outside Bangkok (1930) and Changi at the eastern extremity of Singapore (1936). The closing of Rangoon Central Gaol, occupying 'a large expanse of valuable land in the residential quarter of the town', was seriously discussed from at least the turn of the century [*RPAB*, 1904, Resolution, p. 1: see also *RPAB*, 1922, p. 1] but never carried out until long after the

And that may have contributed to, apparently, a persistently high death rate at Bilibid.[163] Finally, the Iwahig Penal Colony can be seen not as a striking penal innovation but as part of a 'carcereal continuum' that also included the plantation and the mission school, an 'interpretive metaphor' for the American colonial presence in the Philippines.[164]

And yet the progressive ambitions of the Philippine prison administration—if not always its achievements—remain clear. A further piece of evidence will sustain the point. In December 1924, the Director of Prisons, Ramon Victorio, addressed staff and students of the College of Law of the University of the Philippines. The progressive vision was clear: 'The Bilibid Prison believes and practises the idea that it is a reformatory rather than a penitentiary, an institution to reclaim and refit men and women from a life of crime to a life of usefulness.'[165] But more interestingly, the Director of Prisons, a Filipino, embedded those beliefs and practices in his country's aspirations for political independence. '"The actual condition of a nation's prison is the best barometer of its civilisation"', he quoted:[166] the establishment of a progressive prison administration was important evidence that Filipinos had the capacity for self-government. There is a significant general argument here, to which the discussion will shortly return.

PERCEPTION AND PURPOSE IN THE NETHERLANDS EAST INDIES AND FRENCH INDOCHINA

The rhetoric of reform and rehabilitation was heard elsewhere in late-colonial South East Asia, if less loudly. In the Netherlands East Indies, the early years of the twentieth century saw the exposure, and attempted suppression, of serious abuses in the prison system: and then from about 1920 a number of progressive ideas

---

British had left. One further disadvantage of the densely populated location, according to the 1921 report, was that prohibited articles—notably tobacco—were constantly being thrown over the wall into the prison compound where they were picked up by the inmates [*RPAB*, 1921, p. 4].

[163] In 1930 the death rate at Bilibid, per thousand of the average daily population, was 91.3, and in 1931, 54.3: *Annual Report of the Governor General of the Philippine Islands, 1931*, Washington, DC: United States Government Printing Office, 1932, p. 234. As was noted in an earlier discussion, in British Burma's prisons in 1935 the death rate was 10.82 per thousand of the average daily prison population.

[164] This is the approach employed by Michael Salman: '"Nothing without Labor"'.

[165] 'Insular Prison System in the Philippines' in Ramon Victorio, *Prison Reform in the Philippines*, Manila: n.p., 1927, p. 19.

[166] Ibid., p. 17.

and practices were introduced into the administration.[167] One important innovation was the division of convicts into a number of categories—corrigible and
incorrigible, juveniles, the insane—and the establishment of different forms of
penal regime in different forms of institution. This period saw the establishment
of a juvenile prison at Tanah Tinggi, with a regime adopted from the British Borstal: in the final stage of their sentence the inmates were lodged in cottages outside the prison. For long-term convicts a penal colony was created on the island
of Noesa Kambangan: there the inmates had considerable freedom of movement,
and were instructed in the cultivation of rubber. There were major architectural
innovations, reflecting modern thinking and practice—separate spaces for work,
eating and recreation, and the allocation of prisoners to single sleeping-cells.
Vocational training and prison workshops—turning out, for example, shoes and
uniforms—were established. Prison staff received training. Prisons were regularly
inspected and prisoners were medically examined each month. The use of the
rattan in punishment for breaches of prison discipline was discontinued, except
where the alternative, solitary confinement with hard labour, was not available
to the authorities. There may have been a further progressive measure—a reduction in the average daily prison population through the 1920s, from roughly
56,000 in 1921 to some 46,000 in 1927. It would appear that many of these
innovations—the classification of prisoners, the creation of different forms of
penal institution, the combination of individual cells and communal space, the
establishment of a prison for juveniles, the training of gaol staff—were being
introduced in the Netherlands East Indies long before they were introduced in
the Netherlands itself.[168] Reform and rehabilitation were also prominent in the
thinking of the prison administrations of British Malaya.[169]

---

[167] The following draws on Anne Marie Christien Bruinink-Darlang, *Het penitentiair stelsel in Ne-
derlands-Indië van 1905 tot 1940* [The penal system of the Netherlands East Indies from 1905
till 1940], Alblasserdam: Kanters, 1986 [English summary, pp. 411–17].

[168] It is interesting to note that John Furnivall, a scholar-official in Burma's colonial administration,
judged the prison system—and, more broadly, the administration of the law—in the Netherlands East Indies as markedly superior to that of British Burma: *Colonial Policy and Practice: A
comparative study of Burma and Netherlands India*, New York University Press, 1956, pp. 267–9.

[169] Two references, from the late 1940s, sustain this point. 'We believe that the purely retributive
system of imprisoning offenders as a punishment has not proved its effectiveness, and that the
energetic and enthusiastic implementation of correct methods of reformative treatment is the
only existing hope that society has of re-educating offenders to the stage where they can again
take their place in the community as responsible citizens': *Report of the Singapore Prison Enquiry
Commission, 1948*, Singapore: Government Printing Office, 1948, p. 25. 'The fundamental question is whether the prisoner is merely to be punished or reformed, and the test of the degree
of civilisation of a country and the long-term value of its penal system depends upon whether

The thinking in French Indochina was, apparently, radically different. In a fine study of the history of imprisonment in colonial Vietnam, Peter Zinoman argues,

one of the most remarkable aspects of the prison system in French Indochina was its utter failure to deploy disciplinary practices. Indochinese prisons never employed cellular or panoptic architecture and held the vast majority of inmates in undifferentiated, over-crowded and unlit communal rooms. On questions of rehabilitation, behavioural modification, and the reformative effects of mandatory labour, the archive of colonial penal discourse is virtually silent.[170]

Zinoman identifies four factors that discouraged the deployment of disciplinary practices—an ambition to reform and rehabilitate the criminal—in the prison administration of French Indochina.[171] The first was the persisting influence in the colonial prison of indigenous, Sino-Vietnamese, carceral traditions: thus the 'native' prison guards persisted in seeing the inmates mainly as opportunities for extortion rather than failed individuals who, with their intervention, could be reformed. Second, the prison in French Indochina had evolved directly from the prisoner-of-war camps first established by the French in the 1860s, the beginning of the conquest, 'an institution that was repressive, not corrective'. Third, 'the essentially racist orientation of the colonial state', together with an increasing belief in French criminology in the nineteenth century that some offenders were innately incorrigible, encouraged the view that non-European criminals were simply beyond reform and rehabilitation—and thus that attempts to reform them were futile. And finally, the 'tight-fisted' French colonial administration refused to provide the resources necessary to create a prison system that would indeed reform. Peter Zinoman further argues that, in this respect, the prison administration in French Indochina was far from unusual in the colonial world—quite the reverse. He notes Anand Yang 'finding neither a "voice of humanitarianism" nor a discourse "about reformation or rehabilitation"' as he worked his way through British Indian penal documents.[172] He cites John Furnivall to indicate that the prison in British Burma 'rarely embodied modern disciplinary technologies'.

---

greater emphasis is laid upon punishment or rehabilitation': O. V. Garratt, *Report on the Prisons of the Federation of Malaya for the Year 1949*, Kuala Lumpur: Government Press, 1950, pp. 12–13.

[170] Peter Zinoman, *The Colonial Bastille: A history of imprisonment in Vietnam, 1862-1940*, Berkeley, CA: University of California Press, 2001, p. 16. Later statements of the argument are less uncompromising: 'While disciplinary power never dominated the workings of the colonial prison system in Indochina, it would be an overstatement to deny its existence there altogether' [pp. 35–6].

[171] Zinoman, *The Colonial Bastille*, pp. 16–17.

[172] Ibid., p. 37.

However, this chapter has established that this was not the case. A humanitarian awareness, and a concern to reform and rehabilitate, is present—on occasions, strongly present—in the records of prison administration in the American Philippines and British Burma. This was not mere rhetoric. The building of the self-governing republic at Iwahig, the establishment of the Bilibid band, the creation of separate sleeping, work, eating and recreation spaces in the prisons of the Netherlands East Indies, the establishment of a separate gaol for juveniles at Meiktila, were practical measures that sought, ultimately, to reform and rehabilitate the criminal. If they failed, that is to be explained more in terms of the failure of the prison as an institution to reform and rehabilitate, than any weakness in the measures taken here. And when reform and rehabilitation were 'mere' rhetoric, nevertheless the concerns were deeply felt—as when the Inspector-General of Prisons, Burma, publicly declared that the province's gaols did not, and probably never would, reform their inmates, and called for an exploration of every alternative to imprisonment.

Thus there were important differences in the perception and purpose of the prison in the different territories of colonial South East Asia. And to a marked degree those differences of purpose reflected differences in the broader relationship between coloniser and colonised. The issues here are hugely complex but two considerations may have been influential. The first, taking the phrase from Peter Zinoman, was 'the essentially racist orientation of the colonial state'. While it is clearly difficult to characterise the specific nuances and intensity of racial beliefs in any given colonial context, it is surely possible to distinguish between racial perspectives that confirmed that 'native' criminals were incorrigible (apparently the orientation of French rule in Indochina) and those which entertained the prospect of the 'native' criminal's reform and rehabilitation (the American Philippines and British Burma). The second was political circumstance. Where the prospect of independence was fiercely resisted by the colonial state—Vietnam—the prison became a battleground, used by the colonial authorities to suppress political dissent, and seen by nationalists as providing opportunities for political education and organisation, and as conferring further legitimacy on their struggle. But where a colony was clearly moving towards independence (the Philippines from the 1910s, with Filipinos themselves then becoming increasingly prominent in government), a progressive prison administration could become a mark of modernity.

BIBLIOGRAPHICAL NOTE

The prison in colonial South East Asia has attracted far less attention from historians than the richness and importance of the subject would demand. A striking example of what can be achieved is Peter Zinoman, *The Colonial Bastille: A history of imprisonment in Vietnam, 1862–1940*, Berkeley, CA: University of California Press, 2001. Zinoman makes close use of the vast body of first-person accounts of political imprisonment under the French that were published in northern Vietnam after 1954, and one of his central themes is that the French colonial prison played a critical role in shaping Vietnamese anti-colonial political identity and organisation. There is less focus, therefore, on the prison experiences and perceptions of the 'common criminal'. Parts of Peter Zinoman's evidence and argument have also appeared in: 'The History of the Modern Prison and the Case of Indochina' in Vicente L. Rafael (ed.), *Figures of Criminality in Indonesia, the Philippines, and colonial Vietnam*, Ithaca, NY: Cornell University, Southeast Asia Program, 1999, pp. 152–74; and 'Colonial Prisons and Anti-Colonial Resistance in French Indochina: The Thai Nguyen Rebellion, 1917', *Modern Asian Studies*, 34, 1 (2000), pp. 57–98. For the Philippines under Spanish rule, there is an extensive discussion of the prison system in Greg Bankoff, *Crime, Society, and the State in the Nineteenth-Century Philippines*, Quezon City: Ateneo de Manila University Press, 1996, chapter 6. For the Philippines under American rule, there is a brief discussion in Michael Salman, '"Nothing without Labor": Penology, discipline, and independence in the Philippines under United States colonial rule, 1898–1914' in Vicente L. Rafael (ed.), *Discrepant Histories: Translocal essays on Filipino cultures*, Philadelphia, PA: Temple University Press, 1995, pp. 113–29. For an earlier, more detailed account of the Philippine prison system under American administration, see John Lewis Gillin, *Taming the Criminal: Adventures in penology*, New York: Macmillan, 1931, chapter 2. See also Alfredo M. Bunye, 'The Philippine Prison System', unpublished Doctor of Civil Laws thesis, University of Santo Tomas, Manila, 1952. A detailed account of the prison system in the Netherlands East Indies over the final decades of Dutch rule is provided by Anne Marie Christien Bruinink-Darlang, *Het penitentiair stelsel in Nederlands-Indie van 1905 tot 1940* [The penal system of the Netherlands East Indies from 1905 till 1940], Alblasserdam: Kanters, 1986: this includes an extended summary in English.

Clare Anderson, *Legible Bodies: Race, criminality and colonialism in South Asia*, Oxford: Berg, 2004, includes substantial discussion on the British penal settlements in Burma and the Straits Settlements in the first half of the nineteenth century. For Singapore, see also Anoma Pieris, 'Hidden Hands and Divided Landscapes: Penal labor and colonial citizenship in Singapore and the Straits Settlements, 1825–1873', unpublished PhD thesis, University of California, Berkeley, 2003. J.F.A. McNair, *Prisoners Their Own Warders: A record of the convict prison at Singapore in the Straits Settlements established 1825*, Westminster: Archibald Constable, 1899, remains a valuable account. Further relevant references can be found in Clare Anderson's essay in this volume. Thet Thet Wintin, 'The Prison in Pre-Colonial Burma', unpublished PhD thesis, University of London, 2006, is a pioneering study of confinement in South East Asia before the modern period.

Finally, a classic first-hand account of imprisonment in pre-colonial Burma has recently been republished: *Two Years Imprisonment in Burma (1824–26): A personal narrative of Henry Gouger*, Bangkok: White Lotus, 2002. A vivid fictional, but strongly autobiographical, account of imprisonment in the Rangoon Central Gaol in the early years of Burmese independence is found in Ludu U Hla, *The Victim*, translated by Than Tun and Kathleen Forbes, Mandalay: Ludu U Hla, 1976. And, as noted above, Zinoman, *The Colonial Bastille*, pays particular attention to the large number of prison memoirs from colonial Vietnam.

THE PROMISE OF REPENTANCE: THE PRISON IN MODERN CHINA

Frank Dikötter

CONFINEMENT BEFORE THE PRISON

Punishment, as noted in the introduction, was not based on the custodial sentence in most traditional penal systems. In late imperial China the majority of criminals found guilty by county magistrates were sentenced to fines, beatings, penal servitude, exile and death; imprisonment *per se* was not used as a legal penalty.[1] Spaces of confinement, however, existed in the form of gaols, which were used for the incarceration of suspects awaiting trial, criminals sentenced to penal servitude, convicts on their journey to exile, and prisoners awaiting execution. Gaols were generally located in county capitals inside the magistrate's *yamen* (the name of a government office in imperial China). Imperial regulations required that male and female inmates be confined in separate quarters, while the compound often had two or three levels for the separation of different categories of criminals. Suspects awaiting trial were secured with manacles and shackles and confined to the inner gaol (*lijian*), while criminals waiting to begin their sentences of exile or penal servitude were linked by chains and incarcerated in the outer gaol (*waijian*). A 'dark gaol' (*anjian*) also existed for bandits and murderers

---

[1] Useful studies on the judicial system in imperial China include Derk Bodde and Clarence Morris, *Law in Imperial China: Exemplified by 190 Ch'ing dynasty cases (translated from the Hsing-an hui-lan), with historical, social and juridical commentaries*, Cambridge, MA: Harvard University Press, 1967, and, in alphabetical order, Mark A. Allee, *Law and Local Society in Late Imperial China: Northern Taiwan in the nineteenth century*, Stanford University Press, 1994; Kathryn Bernhardt and Philip C. Huang (eds), *Civil Law in Qing and Republican China*, Stanford University Press, 1994; Ch'ü T'ung-tsu, *Law and Society in Traditional China*, Paris: Mouton, 1965; G.A. Hayden, *Crime and Punishment in Medieval Chinese Drama: Three Judge Pao plays*, Cambridge, MA: Council on East Asian Studies, 1978; Geoffrey MacCormack, *Traditional Chinese Penal Law*, Edinburgh University Press, 1990; Brian E. McKnight, *Law and Order in Sung China*, Cambridge University Press, 1992.

who had been sentenced to death. The penal code outlined the duties of care of the magistrate over his prisoners, who should be supplied with regular food, warm clothes and straw mats. Offenders should be protected from abuse, bribery and maltreatment, while sick prisoners should be given medical treatment. In cases of illness or death, a special report had to be filed by the magistrate, including details of the illness, its treatment and, in the case of death, an examination of the corpse. Benevolence and compassion were to guide the actions of a magistrate: as a seventeenth-century manual for magistrates emphasised, failure to provide people with a proper education was the underlying cause of crime. Social transformation through the influence of virtue lay at the heart of good governance, it was thought, and criminals should be treated with commiseration.

Despite published imperial regulations and proclaimed moral duties, imperial gaols were as much open to abuse, torture, corruption and starvation as their counterparts in Europe. Overcrowding in particular was a major source of death and disease in the penal system during the Qing (1644–1911). In the eighteenth century, constant demographic growth led to deteriorating social and economic conditions, and the imperial government responded to intensifying unrest and crime by expanding the system of banishment. Similar to the transportation of convicts in France and England during the same period, exile was perceived to be a more benevolent form of punishment than the death penalty. It was also believed to have a rehabilitative potential: convicts could expiate their crimes in a process of self-renewal (*zixin*). However, the opportunity for rehabilitation was limited to a small number of officials who benefited from privileged legal treatment; once they had demonstrated an appropriate degree of repentance, they could be registered as civilians.[2] In general, as exile expanded under the Qing, the existing gaols used for overnight accommodation became seriously congested. As demographic growth, economic competition and social mobility generated new problems of law and order, the number of prisoners awaiting execution under the Qing must also have increased substantially, although research in this field is patchy.

While research into the conditions of county gaols is beyond the scope of this chapter, places of confinement must have come under intense pressure during the eighteenth and nineteenth centuries. Even a cursory reading of reported judicial cases indicates that county gaols were beset with problems, ranging from high rates of disease to official corruption and maltreatment of prisoners. Discontent

---

[2] Joanna Waley-Cohen, *Exile in Mid-Ch'ing China: Banishment to Xinjiang, 1758–1820*, New Haven, CT: Yale University Press, 1991, pp. 64, 85 and 122.

with the existing legal order was expressed in organised trends of thought. Already in the eighteenth century, statecraft officials such as Chen Hongmou had emphasised the rehabilitation of criminals, proposing that a sense of self-respect and repentance be encouraged while the physical discomforts of punishment like the cangue should be reduced.[3] Compilations of statecraft essays appeared throughout the nineteenth century, as scholars like Wei Yuan, Lin Zexu, Gong Zizhen and Bao Shichen not only encouraged learning from European powers, but also advocated legal reform and practical scholarship. They criticised the corruption and malfunctions of the existing judicial system and highlighted the need to use punishments in order to educate people in ethical norms (*mingxing bijiao*): they considered the law to be an auxiliary to moral considerations. As Joseph Cheng has observed, many of the legal reforms discussed during the late Qing had their origin in statecraft compilations: the multiplication of regulations and precedents, the abuses of the guards, the excessive severity of existing punishments, the frequent escape of those sentenced to penal servitude, trial procedures and prison conditions were all discussed in great detail throughout the nineteenth century, while the deteriorating gaol conditions were deplored in memorials submitted by censors.[4]

Both statecraft scholarship and evidential research were instrumental in undermining confidence in the existing regime of punishments: foreign criticism of the use of corporal punishment and the existing conditions of local gaols would reinforce these negative perceptions and constitute an additional spur to change. As in Europe until the last third of the eighteenth century, no other penalties were envisaged despite the continuous dissatisfaction with the existing judicial system. A viable substitute would appear for the first time in all its splendour to Qing envoys sent abroad in the 1860s: moral education and reformative punishment seemed to be summed up in the very modern prison. When the first Qing envoys to Europe visited Pentonville Prison they were full of admiration: confinement appeared to be a desirable alternative to banishment, as prisons, it seemed, could more effectively induce repentance (*huiguo*) and self-renewal (*zixin*). Guo Songtao, for instance, recorded with approval how in a rigorous penal system even relatively small misdemeanours committed by children and

---

[3] Fu-mei Chang Chen, 'Local Control of Convicted Thieves in Eighteenth-Century China' in Frederic Wakeman and Carolyn Grant (eds), *Conflict and Control in Late Imperial China*, Berkeley, CA: University of California Press, 1975, p. 140.

[4] Joseph Kai Huan Cheng, 'Chinese Law in Transition: The late Ch'ing law reform, 1901–1911', doctoral dissertation, Brown University, 1976, pp. 38–9.

women were punished by a term in prison.[5] During his visit to Philadelphia, Li Gui—to take another example—had an opportunity to visit the local prison. As he wandered through the gardens landscaped with trees and flowers, entered the central building and paced the long corridors lined with clean and airy cells, Philadelphia prison appeared to him as a fortress of perfection entirely dedicated to the rehabilitation of its temporary inhabitants.[6] Scholars working independently of the government also advocated legal reform. Wang Tao, one of the founders of modern journalism in China, believed that offenders needed not only education but also vocational training, two needs addressed by the prison.[7] Even when he openly favoured the radical adoption of political innovations from foreign countries, like constitutional government, he believed that the roots of these institutions could be traced back to the Confucian classics and a long-lost Golden Age. Modernity, in his opinion, was a means to reinvigorate tradition:

[In England] there has never been such cruelty as torturing and beating an offender with bamboos and clubs so that his blood and flesh spread all over. In prison the convict is supplied with food and clothing, so that he will not be hungry or cold. He is taught to work and not allowed to become idle. He is visited every seven days by preachers to make him repent and live a new life. He is never maltreated by those in charge of the prison. The excellence of the prison system is what China has never had since the Golden Age.[8]

However, as in other countries, prison reform only became a government priority with the advent of a radically new vision of political order. An ideology of legal equality and national sovereignty with political legitimacy openly vested in the people rather than in the emperor appeared only after 1895, eventually leading to the collapse of the imperial system and the emergence of a republican regime in 1911.

LEGAL REFORM DURING THE LATE QING

The Treaty of Shimonoseki that ended the Sino-Japanese War of 1894–5 was followed by an outpouring of patriotic agitation, as memoranda protesting against

---

[5] Guo Songtao, *Lundun yu Bali riji* (London and Paris diary), Beijing: Yuelu shushe, 1985, pp. 151–5 and 305–6.

[6] Li Gui, *Huanyou diqiu xinlu* (New records of my travels around the world), Beijing: Yuelu shushe, 1985, pp. 243–9.

[7] Wang Tao, *Manyou suilu* (Travel notes), Beijing: Yuelu shushe, 1985, pp. 149, 243–8.

[8] Wang Tao, 'A Note on the British Government' in Teng Ssu-yü and J.K. Fairbank (eds), *China's Response to the West: A documentary survey 1839–1923*, Cambridge, MA: Harvard University Press, 1982, p. 140, with a few stylistical changes.

the terms of the agreement or requesting reform were sent to the throne. Some reform-minded scholars also proposed to strengthen the country in its confrontation with foreign powers through a wide range of economic, administrative, military and educational reforms. In search of wealth and power, they articulated for the first time a distinctly nationalist agenda of reform in which all people in China were represented as an organic unit to be mobilised, educated and disciplined in a national fight for survival. In contrast to their precursors, reformers promoted an alternative body of knowledge that derived its legitimacy independently of the official examination system: while drawing on a number of indigenous strains of knowledge, including evidential research, statecraft scholarship and New Text Confucianism, they also actively appropriated foreign ideas, ranging from the sociological work of Herbert Spencer to the political thought of John Stuart Mill. Foreign knowledge was used to advance a new vision of political order in which power was vested in the nation: whether a constitutional government or a democratic republic, thinkers after 1895 envisaged a radical transformation of the imperial system in the face of increased foreign aggression. Evolutionary theories, which disseminated slogans about the 'survival of the fittest', further undergirded a message of change, as the reformers claimed that a struggle for the 'survival of the race' (*baozhong*) in a context of international competition was the inescapable consequence of more profound evolutionary forces. Yan Fu, for instance, closely associated national wealth with penal reform in an annotated presentation of Montesquieu's *L'Esprit des Lois*, published between 1904 and 1909: he deplored the 'cruel and inhumane' practice of extracting confessions under torture and praised the merits of a modern prison system based on moral education (*jiaohua*).[9] Within a new vision of the body politic, prison conditions emerged for some reformers as a yardstick to measure a country's degree of political progress: old-style gaols were condemned as barbaric places of arbitrary oppression, while the modern prison was seen as an enlightened place of scientific management and fruitful repentance.

Although the Reform Movement was brought to an abrupt end by the Empress Dowager in 1898, the revision of the legal system was part of the New Policies (*xinzheng*) initiated by the Qing in the wake of the Boxer Rebellion (1900). A further impetus to legal reform came during the treaty revisions signed with foreign powers, as Britain, the United States and Japan supported legal reforms in their treaties of 1902 and 1903, including the abolition of corporal punishment

---

[9]   Yan Fu, 'Mengdesijiu fayi – anyu' (Montesquieu's *The Spirit of Laws*: Some comments) in *Yan Fu ji* (Collected writings of Yan Fu), Beijing: Zhonghua shuju, 1986, vol. 4, p. 954.

and the introduction of a modern prison system. In these treaties the Qing expressed their desire to undertake legal reform in exchange for a promise by foreign powers that they would relinquish extraterritorial rights. Article XII was crucial in providing an incentive for the Qing government to overhaul its judicial system:

China having expressed a strong desire to reform her judicial system and to bring it into accord with that of Western nations, Great Britain agrees to give her every assistance to such reform, and she will also be prepared to relinquish extraterritorial rights when she is satisfied that the state of the Chinese laws, the arrangement for their administration and other considerations warrant her in so doing.[10]

Spurred on by foreign powers and high-ranking officials anxious to obtain the abolition of extraterritoriality, legal reform progressed remarkably fast. After 1905 traditional penalties such as dismemberment of the body, beheading of the corpse, the public display of heads and tattooing were abolished, while beating with the bamboo was gradually replaced by fines. As a draft for the new criminal code was completed in 1908, punishments were further limited to the death penalty, imprisonment or fines. This profound transformation of the regime of punishment entailed an overhaul of the existing detention system: not only should old gaols be reformed in line with modern penal principles current in Europe, but their number had to be drastically increased in order to accommodate a rising tide of inmates, as the custodial sentence became the most common form of punishment next to fines.

Appointed in 1904 by the Qing as the co-director of the Bureau of Legal Codification (*Falüguan*), Shen Jiaben (1840–1913) was particularly influential in laying the foundations of a modern penal system. He combined the principle of *ganhua*—claimed to have been dominant during the first three dynasties (before 221 BC)—with the idea of the modern prison, represented as a school in which criminals could be rehabilitated. The character *hua* appeared in other composite terms which were current during the late Qing: *jiaohua* was a 'civilising process' by which individuals were transformed through the inculcation of ethical norms in education, while *jinhua*, or 'transformation forwards', was a term used to translate the Darwinian notion of 'evolution', entailing a directional process of evolution forwards. *Ganhua* referred to moral reformation by an emotional appeal to the feelings of a criminal. The protean term *ganhua*—the core value of the penal system in modern China—anticipated repentance and moral reformation:

[10]   Cheng, 'Chinese Law in Transition', p. 74.

to affect (*gandong*) a criminal and obtain change (*zhuanhua*) by exemplary words or acts, to admonish and guide by providing a model, to 'change by persuasion'. Shen expressed his conviction, which would be shared by many prison reformers and judicial administrators in the following decades, that most offenders were open to change by education, and that social order could be gradually improved by the correction of offenders. From being a place of retribution, the prison should become a 'place of change by persuasion' (*ganhua zhi di*) in which 'evil is changed to good' (*gai e wei shan*).

Like many reformers in the late nineteenth century, Shen Jiaben placed prison reform within an evolutionary framework of 'international competition' (*guoji jingzheng*) in which a country's penal system was thought to reflect a measure of 'civilisation or barbarity' (*wenming yeman*). Not only could extraterritoriality be reclaimed by the elimination of traditional county gaols—represented as backward, 'uncivilised' and inhumane—but moral parity with the most 'advanced' nations around the globe could be achieved by their replacement with modern, 'scientific' institutions of confinement in which criminal elements would be transformed into moral citizens. Four concerns were to guide prison reform, namely the construction of model prisons, the training of prison staff, the promulgation of prison rules and the collection of criminal statistics. Deciding to concentrate scarce financial resources on a few model institutions from which a beneficial and transformative influence could gradually spread, he believed that new prisons should be built following the most advanced international standards: model prisons should first be established in major cities and provincial capitals before eventually reaching down to the county level. Discipline, education and hygiene were the three main items in the training of staff, who should be rigorously trained in special schools dedicated to penological matters. The best rules and regulations would be compiled from foreign countries in drafting a prison constitution to be adopted at all administrative levels, while science would guide the collection of statistical material, which should include details of the causes of crime; the nationality, address, status, profession and educational background of criminals; and other vital statistics.[11]

An edict on prison reform was passed by the Qing in 1907, endorsing most of the penal principles which Shen Jiaben had presented in his earlier memorials.

[11] Shen Jiaben, 'Zou shixing gailiang jianyu yi zhuyi sishi zhe' (Memorial on four important matters on the implementation of prison reform), *Qingmo choubei lixian dang'an shiliao* (Archival documents on constitutional reform in the late Qing), Beijing: Zhonghua shuju, 1979, vol. 2, pp. 831–2; see also Shen Jiaben, 'Zou qing shixing gailiang jianyu zhe' (Memorial request to improve prisons), *Dongfang zazhi*, 4, 7 (July 1907), pp. 354–7.

The Board of Justice ruled that provincial capitals and treaty ports should have one model prison each, built on either the fan-shaped or the cruciform model. The Board also endorsed the need for both single and shared cell systems, supported the study of law and penology, and gave equal weight to both punishment and reformation. John Howard, the eighteenth-century prison reformer, was given pride of place in the Board's recommendations, while Japan was also praised as an example to be emulated.[12] In addition to Shen Jiaben's views, Zhang Zhidong and Liu Kunyi's proposal for the detention and reformation of paupers and vagrants was included in the establishment of separate training centres for criminals (*fanzui xiyisuo*) and for vagrants (*minren xiyisuo*). Punishment and reformation (*ganhua*) were given equal weight in the new penal system. While John Howard, icon of prison reform on the other side of the world, was consecrated as a global figure of penal modernity in China, official delegations headed by leading government representatives were sent to international conferences on penal administration, including the Eighth International Penitentiary Congress in Washington in 1910: as ideas and people increasingly crossed boundaries, the late Qing became more intertwined with the global movement for prison reform.

CHINA'S FIRST MODEL PRISON

The movement for prison reform that appeared at the end of the Qing gathered momentum after the fall of the empire in 1911: Beijing No. 1 Prison, one of the first model prisons built in China to the highest international standards, took its first inmates in 1912. Built on a double fan-shaped plan with cell blocks radiating from two central towers, Beijing's model penitentiary was based on Pentonville Prison: guards were able to see five different rows of cells. Most cells appeared well ventilated and lit, and all windows were to be open for part of the day; while most of Beijing still lived in darkness at night, the prison was lit by electricity with one bulb for every two cells.[13] Each inmate was given a wooden bed, a cotton-wadded quilt, a hay mattress and a pillow. The prisoners were required to stay silent, not only during work but also when they were in their cells. Sidney Gamble observed that, although experience in many countries proved that a rule requiring silence not only failed to prevent men from communicating with each other but was also practically inefficient, it was rigidly applied in modern prisons in Beijing: 'They are allowed to talk about the necessary details of their work, but

[12] Fabu, 'Zou yifu shixing gailiang jianyu zhe' (Memorial on the improvement of prisons), *Dongfang zazhi*, 4, 12 (December 1907), pp. 558–62.

[13] Sidney D. Gamble, *Peking: A social survey*, London: Oxford University Press, 1921, pp. 310–14.

1. The model prison of Beijing. [Sidney D. Gamble, *Peking: A social survey*, London: Oxford University Press, 1921]

are not supposed to communicate about anything else, and in visiting a prison one is struck with the silence.'[14]

In an emphasis on reformation and vocational training, workshops were placed across the ends of the cell buildings: these included carpentry, weaving, typesetting, printing and bookbinding, tailoring, stonemasonry and work with metal, leather and bamboo, with twenty-five to forty prisoners to each trade. Some limited land inside the prison compound was available for cultivation. Prisoners worked for ten hours in the winter and twelve in the summer; the pay depended on the quality and amount of work performed. Part of the earnings were allowed to be spent, the remainder being deposited with the Ministry of Justice and paid on release. According to one foreign visitor, 'anyone who visits the model industrial prison in Peking comes away impressed with the ability of Chinese officials to establish and manage industrial institutions.'[15]

Prisoners were graded according to conduct and work: good behaviour could lead to extra privileges or even to conditional release. Many prisons in republican

[14]   Ibid., p. 318.
[15]   Andrew H. Woods, 'The Menace of Insanity to Popular Government', *Zhonghua yixue zazhi*, 7, 4 (December 1921), p. 203.

2. Watchtower of the model prison in Nanjing (Jiangsu Number One Prison). [Zhu Shen (ed.), *Jingwai gailiang ge jianyu baogao luyao* (Essential record of the improvement of various prisons in the capital and the provinces), Beijing: Sifabu jianyusi, 1919]

China used four different forms to mark achievements in behaviour (*xingzhuang*), work (*zuoye*), moral teaching (*jiaohui*) and basic education (*jiaoyu*). Behaviour was further divided into obedience, words and deeds, sensibility, thrift and hygiene, while labour included marks for learning, meticulousness, diligence, economy in the use of materials and care for machinery. Each form allocated a certain number of points, the total of which was calculated monthly and divided to obtain an average figure locating the prisoner on a scale of excellence: that single figure had the power to add or remove a variety of privileges which shaped the prisoner's life. In Beijing No. 1 Prison, inmates who broke the rules were punished by reproach, loss of pay for work, and deprivation of the privileges of receiving visitors, writing letters, reading, using personal belongings and taking exercise. More serious offences resulted in rationing of food, solitary confinement for up to a maximum of seven days or confinement in a dark room for up to seventy-two hours. Baths were taken twice a week in summer, once a week in spring and only once every ten days in winter. Underclothes had to be changed every ten days in winter and twice a week in summer, while pillowcases and bedclothes were also regularly washed according to prison regulations. A doctor trained in modern medicine looked after the prisoners' health needs, assisted by a well-equipped dispensary and a small hospital with two nurses. A special physical examination was given to all prisoners on entering and leaving the prison, while outdoor exercise, including marching around the courtyard for half an hour, was taken daily. Prisoners under eighteen years of age were given school work equivalent to that of ordinary primary schools, which amounted to one or two hours a day. In an emphasis on *ganhua*, religious and moral lectures were given to all the prisoners, either in the prison lecture room or during the noon rest in the workshops. While lectures were given in chapels in England, in the No. 1 Prison the lecture theatre resembled a public lecture hall, with portraits of the five great teachers on the wall behind the lecturer's platform. These were Confucius, Laozi, Mohammed, Jesus and John Howard (1726–90), the English prison reformer.

EXPANSION OF THE PRISON SYSTEM

Prison reform was by no means confined to the capital, although an evaluation of new prisons outside Beijing in the early republican period is complicated by the relative dearth of reliable source material.[16] Significant geographical differences existed in the spread of prison reform, so that there were inequalities between the coastal regions and the hinterland. Most provinces along the coast and in the north-east could boast two or three new prisons by 1927. Fengtian province was exceptional, since it acquired over a dozen new prisons in the early republican period, while Shandong and Hebei, including Beijing, could also claim half a dozen new penal institutions. Shanxi too was a vigorous promoter of prison reform, having constructed five model prisons within the first decade of the republic. Jiangsu and Anhui had three to five model prisons, while most provinces in inner China could only afford to build one or two. Hunan province only started building new ones after the Guomindang came to power in 1927. Guangdong had no officially sponsored model prisons, although there were local efforts to achieve prison reform. The remote provinces of Qinghai, Xinjiang and Xining only set up new prisons during the Second World War after the central government was forced by the Japanese invasion to take refuge in the hinterland. Suiyuan, Chahar and Ningxia, on the other hand, were listed as having a new prison in the provincial capital by that time.

While many so-called new prisons were no more than slightly modified county gaols that dated back to the imperial period, in particular in the countryside,

---

[16] See Frank Dikötter, *Crime, Punishment and the Prison in Modern China*, London: Hurst and New York: Columbia University Press, 2002.

it would be wrong to dismiss the movement towards prison reform as a mere exercise in self-promotion, lacking any real depth and restricted in actual practice to two or three unrepresentative prisons copied from foreign models. Even foreigners who supported extraterritoriality and were prone to regard the entire judicial system as desperately inadequate were impressed by some of the new prisons emerging in early republican China. A correspondent of the *North China Herald* reported his visit in 1914 to the model prison of Jinan, the capital of Shandong province, in unusually positive terms. Erected under the governor Sun Baoqi the preceding year, the buildings were inspired by European models and included a court-house, a detention house and an 'industrial prison'. Inmates looked well-fed and well-dressed, and were growing their own vegetables and learning a trade in large rooms reserved for carpet-weaving, yarn-spinning or silk-making. Three rows converged on a small central court where guards could see the whole length of each line of cells, which were described as lofty, well-ventilated and lit at night by electricity. The prisoners did not wear uniform and were unfettered, contrary to the situation in traditional gaols.[17]

Dozens of similar model institutions were built across the country, as county magistrates, city mayors, provincial governors and central governments, with varying degrees of success, actively pursued an extensive programme of prison reform: by the 1930s over 25,000 prisoners were detained on any one day in about sixty modern prisons, not counting detention houses and county gaols (this was comparable to the prison population of a large European country like France or England). Based on various statistical estimates which have been analysed elsewhere,[18] it can be hypothesised that new prisons held some 40 per cent of the entire prison population. The prison population for the 1930s can thus be estimated at 75–90,000, an extremely low figure in relation to the overall population, which was probably over 450 million, although no census was carried out in the republican era. Taking the higher figure of 90,000 prisoners, the ratio of imprisonment in republican China was around twenty per 100,000 of the population.

Despite the relatively low rate of imprisonment, congestion was the worst problem of the penal system. Many old county gaols were built before the introduction of the custodial sentence and new prisons rapidly exceeded their official capacity. Gradually throughout the republican period the prison population increased, and the building of new prisons always seemed to lag behind

---

[17] 'A Chinese Model Prison', *North China Herald*, 19 September 1914, p. 898.
[18] Dikötter, *Crime, Punishment and the Prison*.

the ever-rising tide of criminal convictions. Collective pardons were one way of solving the problem of congestion. Continuing a long-standing political tradition of granting pardons to demonstrate their benevolence,[19] most governments in republican China released a large number of inmates. Release on parole and on bail were two further methods widely used to lessen the prison population. In the 1930s the Ministry of Justice repeatedly ordered prison authorities to discharge conditionally prisoners on parole more liberally to reduce overcrowding. Frequently, however, wealthy prisoners were the ones to be released, for instance by commuting a prison sentence into a fee. In Beijing it was reported in September 1930 that prisoners who could afford to buy their freedom were released, and two of them, both being leaders of drug-smuggling rings, apparently accepted the offer, paying an additional $5,000.[20]

Those who lingered in prison tended to be overwhelming illiterate, male and poor. A detailed analysis of the social and economic background of sentenced criminals shows that the unemployed were the largest social category behind bars, followed by workers, farmers and merchants. Economic disparities were even greater: fewer than 7 per cent of prisoners in 1929 had property of any substance, and the great majority had no possessions at all. However, the most significant factor of social differentiation was education: only 0.5 per cent of men and women had a higher education, while just over 10 per cent had received a standard education.[21] Literacy, rather than wealth or occupation, was a key determinant in a moral universe that viewed the lack of education as a prime cause of crime: a strong link thus existed between the penal philosophy of reformation, which represented illiteracy as immorality, and the actual penal regime, which predominantly targeted socially marginalised groups of young, poor and unemployed men. This observation was also made by contemporary criminologists.[22]

If the poor constituted the overwhelming majority of the captive population, most prisoners were also male: incarceration was a gendered experience in which women represented a minority, typically 5 to 7 per cent. Special rules applied to female prisoners, and those over seven months pregnant or having given birth

---

[19] Brian E. McKnight, *The Quality of Mercy: Amnesties and traditional Chinese justice*, Honolulu, HI: University Press of Hawaii, 1981.

[20] 'Peking Prisoners and Freedom', *North China Herald*, 2 September 1930, p. 348.

[21] Sifa xingzhengbu (ed.), *Sifa tongji (1929 niandu)* (Judicial statistics: 1929), Nanjing: Sifa xingzhengbu, 1931, pp. 320–33.

[22] See, for instance, Wang Long, *Jiangsu diyi jianyufan diaocha zhi jingguo ji qi jieguo zhi fenxi* (Process and analysis of the results of an investigation into Jiangsu No. 1 Prison's inmates), Nanjing: Tongjiju, 1935.

less than a month earlier were exempted from detention. Convicted criminals and suspects on trial may have been imprisoned together in local prisons which did not have the means to separate different categories of prisoner, but women were always segregated from men. If a special building was not built for female prisoners, they were locked up in single cells, although they did share the workspace with male prisoners and often performed similar tasks, for instance sewing or making paste and matchboxes. Women were also allowed to take small children into custody, and both could become sick and die as a result, although in some cases they were released by compassionate prison directors.

All the evidence shows that the prison population was dominated by the socially vulnerable, since criminals with any status, connections or wealth managed to negotiate their way out, while social élites could often avoid the judicial process altogether. Prison was, above all, punishment for the poor. But the poor were not passive, as is evidenced by numerous riots and escapes which periodically rocked the penal system. Overcrowding, poor food, lack of medical care, brutal treatment from guards—these were some of the vectors transmitting tensions that broke out into violence. Violence, in turn, was often used specifically in order to escape: escapes were a regular feature of life in modern prisons and county gaols, as prisoners seized every opportunity—be it a natural catastrophe or a military skirmish—to abscond. Most attempts happened when prison security collapsed during such disturbances as summer floods, although poor conditions in gaol also generated violence and mass break-outs. However, not all prisoners chose to escape, even given the opportunity. In February 1927 a prisoner in a Jiangsu county gaol called for medical help, luring the official on duty and a guard into the cell; they were tied up and locked in. The prisoners made their way to the workshop, where they piled up tables to scale the prison wall. Fifteen prisoners scrambled to escape in the confusion, but others refused to leave their cells and waited for authority to be restored.[23] Even model prisons had their reputation compromised by escape attempts. In August 1927 Jiangsu No. 1 Prison was forced to ask for police reinforcements in the middle of one night when dozens of prisoners ran amok, a group of prisoners even finding a room with guns and ammunition. They could be forced back to their cells only after one of the leaders was shot in a set-to with the guards. Overcrowding after

---

[23]   Number Two National Archives, Nanjing, 7/1082, 'Jiangsu Wujiang, Jiangdu, Jingjiang, Gaoyou, Jinshan dengxian jianfan tuotao youguan wenjian' (Documents relative to the escape of prisoners from Wujiang, Jiangdu, Jingjiang, Gaoyou, Jinshan and other county gaols in Jiangsu province), 1929–39, pp. 1–13.

the Guomindang occupation of Nanjing was explicitly blamed for the unrest by the acting director.[24]

Violence and the fear of it also marked relationships between the prisoners themselves. Where ledgers detailing the prisoners' punishments have survived, they reveal an atmosphere of latent aggression: in one of the court gaols in Shanghai, prisoners were reprimanded, deprived of visits or restrained by handcuffs or leg-irons for a set number of hours for quarrelling, shouting and exchanging insults; 'mutual fights' (*huxiang ouda*) were frequently mentioned.[25] A major threat for new arrivals, especially in country gaols, came from their fellow inmates. Informal cell bosses (*laotou* or *pengtou*) could bully, blackmail or use other methods to put pressure on new prisoners.[26] Guards themselves were violent: not only did they often come from the same social and economic background as the prisoners, but many were illiterate and received no special training, thus undermining the penal principles of reformation: guards cared less about the prisoners' 'moral self-renewal' than about supplementing their income and maintaining their own security. Corruption was widespread and bribes were common, as even in high-security prisons, strong links were forged between inmates and guards, on the basis of similar interests or a shared dialect and common place of origin. The boundaries of most prisons were thus porous, as guards colluded with prisoners, money, food and drugs moved in and out of confinement, and, more generally, the social hierarchies in the wider society were replicated inside the prison, undermining the very notion of equality to create social exclusion: society colonised the prison. What emerged in the penitentiary—far away from the control of the central government—was what Carlos Aguirre has called a customary order, understood not so much as a disciplinary regime aimed at the redemption, rehabilitation and industriousness of the inmates, but at the pragmatic maintenance of a tacit compromise between prisoners and authorities which avoided major eruptions of violence and unrest.[27] The capillarity of the prison, created by a network of discrete links between prisoners and guards, allowed society to invest and ultimately subvert the penitentiary project.

[24] Jiangsu Provincial Archives, Nanjing, 1047/41jianzheng/696, 'Diyi er jianyu baodong deng qingxing' (Riots and other problems in Jiangsu No. 1 and No. 2 Prisons), 1927.

[25] Shanghai Municipal Archives, Q177/1/640, 'Chengfabu' (Registry of punishments), 1946.

[26] Number Two National Archives, Nanjing, 7/2166, 'Zhejiang gaoyuan banli exing renfan ji zengshe kanshousuo de chengwen' (Petition of the Zhejiang High Court on the problem of evil prisoners and the expansion of gaols), 23 May 1935.

[27] Carlos Aguirrre, *The Criminals of Lima and Their Worlds: The prison experience, 1850–1935*, Durham, NC: Duke University Press, 2005, pp. 154–5.

The greatest threat to prisoners, however, was disease. The various prison files indicate an annual death rate of about 10 per cent during the early republican period, although seasonal fluctuations were caused by hunger and cold during the winter and by epidemics resulting from heat and humidity during the summer. Death rates were high even among suspects awaiting trial, as many died of tuberculosis and other diseases caused or aggravated by poor diet and inadequate living conditions. Death rates were roughly halved in new prisons in the 1930s due to government action. About 3 to 5 per cent of prisoners died in the early 1930s, the most common cause being TB, closely followed by dysentery and other gastro-intestinal disorders. Cholera—no doubt because of the many measures taken against it by the Ministry of Health after 1927—only claimed a few lives. Perhaps the worst penal institution in republican China, the infamous Jiangsu No. 2 Prison at Caohejing, accounted for one of every five deaths in custody in 1931, over 1,400 inmates being cramped into its cells.[28] Death rates were not necessarily higher in the county gaols. In a few cases these could benefit from generous private donations and receive government subsidies to implement reforms, showing that the prison system was not necessarily a two-tier one in which county gaols inevitably lagged behind the model prisons of provincial capitals. Liaoning No. 1 Prison, notorious for its appalling management, reported 245 deaths in 1930. In comparison, the thirty-two county gaols scattered over the province, usually perceived as far less modernised than the large prisons, reported an average of two to three deaths, although some of these smaller institutions could hold well over 100 prisoners.[29]

While prisoners may have been despised as the great unwashed, they could articulate their grievances in the form of complaints, generally written by groups or even committees. Rather than focusing on a specific instance, prisoners tried to cast their net as widely as possible, presumably in the hope that one accusation would stick. Many complaints were looked into either by the high court or by the ministry, and the reports and documents these investigations produced, including interrogations of prisoners and guards and detailed inspection of prison accounts, could run to hundreds of pages. Of course the archives do not reveal the fate of those prisoners who made written complaints, nor do they say much about the hidden deals within the judicial administration which prejudiced impartial investigations into allegations of serious misconduct. But however imperfect,

---

[28] Sifa xingzhengbu (ed.), *Sifa tongji (1931 niandu)*, pp. 672–5.

[29] Liaoning Provincial Archives, Shenyang, JC17/661, 'Benchu zhuansong shijiu nian xinjiu jiansuo renfan siwang zhengshu chengbao Sifa xingzhengbu' (This office presents to the Ministry of Justice the certificates of all deaths in custody in old and new prisons for 1930), 1930.

the records produced during judicial investigations gave the semblance of im-partiality—and also testify to the ability of prisoners to turn the regulations against the administration. Moreover, while complaint procedures were open to manipulation, the relative absence of accusations of physical torture suggests that the system suffered from problems common to prisons generally rather than from any tendency of the Guomindang to abuse power. The insufficiency of food, medical care, vocational training, basic education and family visits were the most frequent causes of collective discontent. Finally, even in small county gaols the language of modernity was appropriated by prisoners determined to exercise their rights against the local authorities: almost all complaints showed a high awareness of prison rules and human rights (*renquan*). Modern communi-cation techniques were even used: in Guanyun county, a list of allegations was telegraphed in 1929 to the provincial high court by prisoners who claimed to have been forced into making payments to prison staff.[30] While these examples illustrate how prisoners contributed to shaping life inside the prison, it would be wrong to portray ordinary life behind bars as a struggle between prisoners on the one hand and oppressive guards on the other. As noted above, both groups often came from a similar background and colluded in the creation of a customary order which had little to do with repentance or industry but with the mainte-nance of a semblance of peace. This customary order not only replicated but also consolidated the social hierarchy found outside the prison walls: vast disparities in status and pay existed within the penal hierarchy, as foreign-educated prison directors following international trends in penal thought had little in common with illiterate guards eking out a living on the ground, while huge differences separated educated political prisoners, who could command special privileges, and ordinary farmers without the necessary links to fend off powerful cell bosses or violent prisoners.

PENOLOGY AND THE EXEMPLARY SOCIETY

As the above section shows, despite the considerable hopes invested in prison reform, many new prisons never quite lived up to their promise, as proclaimed ideals failed to be matched by institutional practices. The continued reliance on physical punishments and the high death-rate among prisoners contradicted

[30] Jiangsu Provincial Archives, Nanjing, 1047/41baogao/860, 'Guanyun guanyuyuan beikong ji diaocha ge jiansuo deng juan' (Documents on the investigation of a complaint made against Guanyun county gaol personnel), July 1930.

the ambitious proposals of prison reformers. Rhetoric and reality remained far apart, as overcrowding and underfunding impeded the implementation of a reformative programme based on the notion of *ganhua*. As the criminologist Yan Jingyue noted after spending the summer of 1926 conducting a survey among the inmates, the educational programme offered by Beijing No. 1 Prison was insufficient to tackle the various needs of a largely illiterate prison population, while it also failed to keep released convicts from re-entering their previous life of crime. Recidivists formed a large proportion of the inmates, as seasoned offenders and habitual criminals were undeterred by serving a term in prison.[31] The reformative project fared no better in other model prisons, and the harsh reality of penal life was often far removed from the high standards and aspirations embodied in the rules and regulations regularly published and revised in the republican period. The constant lack of adequate financial resources, poor strategies of personnel recruitment, lack of control over prison guards, and widespread corruption inside the penal system meant that the authorities who actually operated the prisons had widespread discretion in dealing with prisoners and were often detached from the main goals of prison reform which were formulated by the state: a history of the prison shows not so much the 'disciplinary power' of the modern state but on the contrary the many limits of the government in controlling the very institutions it set up: prisons were run by a customary order established by guards and prisoners on the ground rather than by a panopticon project on paper.

The failure to narrow the gap between institutional realities and proclaimed goals marred the prison reform movement in republican China. However, unlike other countries, the idea of reformation was rarely condemned. While the emphasis on reformation migrated from the world of prisons to juvenile reformatories in Europe, where young people were still viewed as malleable and thus open to moral transformation, belief in the perfectibility of human nature and faith in the capacity of institutions to reform depraved minds continued to hold sway in republican China, where even critics of the prison never questioned the educative mission of punishment. While penology was at first restricted to the legal institutions set up during the late Qing, it developed rapidly during the 1920s and 30s: lawyers, judges, magistrates, prison officers, procurators and sociologists were the vectors of new knowledge, as they participated in international conferences and introduced important innovations from abroad in talks, lectures, articles and

---

[31] Yan Jingyue, *Beijing fanzui zhi shehui fenxi* (Sociological analysis of crime in Beijing), Beijing: Yanjing daxue shehuixuexi, 1928, p. 35.

books. Many of the penal principles they advanced were disseminated by less notable writers, particularly in the form of simple textbooks used for the preparation of examinations in law and politics. Participation in international meetings and contributions to periodicals, which were important for the discussion and dissemination of penal innovations, were also seen to be significant.

Whether government authorities or professional penologists, all considered correct behaviour as of paramount importance in the moral education of subjects, and they viewed the emulation of models as a fundamental pedagogical strategy. Just as the sages were upheld as models of virtuous behaviour to be emulated by the people in imperial China, models pervaded the institutional landscape of republican China: model schools, model villages and model cities were all devised to encourage correct moral behaviour and promote standards to be emulated by the rest of the country. Administrative culture in republican China was marked by the expectation of model behaviour, as benevolent rule was seen to have a transformative effect on the rest of society. The promotion of strict rules of behaviour for every possible social situation was part of this 'exemplary society', in the words of Børge Bakken.[32] Slogans appeared on prison walls enjoining prisoners to behave correctly, while rules of proper deportment were propagated to the rest of the population in mass campaigns like the New Life Movement: lack of national unity and social cohesion was believed to be a moral and spiritual problem as much as a political one.

Inherent in the prescriptive culture of modern China was a system of rewards and punishments. In imperial China ledgers of merit and demerit promoted good deeds while discouraging incorrect behaviour. These moral account books listed all the good and bad deeds and had a point system whereby readers could precisely evaluate their own moral conduct.[33] The progressive stage system used in republican prisons was also based on inducements whereby the prisoner could gain certain privileges or even conditional release when adhering to the standards of good conduct. Intricate point systems were used to evaluate a prisoner's progress, including points for good behaviour and hard work. In 1923 the prisoners of Shenyang Model Prison were divided into four classes, each wearing either a red, yellow, blue or white cross as a mark of his behaviour. According to the prison authorities, 'one can know the moral character of a prisoner by merely

---

[32] Børge Bakken, *The Exemplary Society: Human improvement, social control, and the dangers of modernity in China*, Oxford University Press, 2000; see also Harald Bøckman, 'China's Development and Model Thinking', *Forum for Development Studies*, 1 (1998), pp. 7–38.

[33] Cynthia J. Brokaw, *The Ledgers of Merit and Demerit: Social change and moral order in late imperial China*, Princeton University Press, 1991.

looking at the mark which is pinned on his coat.'[34] Prison administrators them-selves were enmeshed in an administrative culture that revolved around the con-stant evaluation and monitoring of government officials. Evaluation encouraged virtuous behaviour, promoted the exemplary norm and welded the individual to the collectivity. In prisons, detailed knowledge of individuals was produced in ef-forts to measure and quantify repentance: knowledge enabled a moral judgement to be reached on each criminal.

Although penology was marked by divergent approaches, opposed political opinions and varied values, a certain unity of outlook existed, since it attracted modernising élites who shared a nationalist view, expressed faith in the educa-tive mission of the prison and believed in the fundamental malleability of human nature. Penologists chose the reformative model of imprisonment from an in-ternational repertoire of diverse and often contradictory systems. This model was part of a widespread voluntarist worldview embraced by modernising élites who believed that the potential of every citizen should be developed in order to build a powerful nation. While these ideas, in retrospect, may seem hopelessly naive, successive governments in the republican era were also keen to participate fully in international penal conferences and to apply international standards to their prison system. In August 1934, to take but one example, China adopted the minimum standards for the treatment of prisoners set by a penal commission of the League of Nations, which included the principles of separation of different categories, the provision of adequate clothing and bedding, minimum standards in food and vocational training, the protection of prisoners' health and the mini-mum use of corporal punishment: in an age of undemocratic regimes in Italy, Germany and the Soviet Union, full acceptance of these standards put China firmly among the more progressive countries in penal matters.[35]

ALTERNATIVES TO THE PRISON

Even opponents of the prison rarely contemplated the abandonment of the custodial sentence, arguing instead for even more regulations, more resources and, often, yet more prisons. Where critical voices appeared, they were generally sympathetic to the Soviet Union, seeing in labour camps a superior system that

[34] Commission on Extraterritoriality, *Chinese Prisons (with plans and illustrations)*, Beijing: Commis-sion on Extraterritoriality, 1925, p. 51.

[35] League of Nations Archives, Geneva, R3753, 'Correspondance with Governments (Unification of criminal law and cooperation in the suppression of crime)', 1932–4; see also Sifayuan (ed.), *Sifayuan gongzuo baogao* (Report on the work of the Judicial Yuan), Nanjing: Sifayuan, 1935, p. 7.

3. Making match boxes in the model prison of Beijing. [Sidney D. Gamble, *Peking: A social survey*, London: Oxford University Press, 1921]

punished more humanely and effectively—as we shall see below the labour camps would be embraced by the communists. The Guomindang repeatedly envisaged agricultural work as an alternative to the prison and made plans to transport prisoners to agricultural colonies in various remote parts of the country. In 1929, Chen Fumin, an adviser to the Ministry of Justice, produced a detailed plan for using prisoners in reclamation schemes, hoping that agricultural colonies would ease the problem of overcrowding. Inspired by favourable reports on labour camps in Siberia, the use of forced labour in exile (*liuxing*) was also contemplated by Luo Wen'gan, while a formal proposal to use *liuxing* was made at the first session of the Fifth Party Congress in November 1935.[36] Such plans had little practical success during the Nanjing decade, although the idea was revived after 1937 as Japan pushed the Guomindang back into the hinterland. In October 1941, for instance, a special camp was set up more than 200 miles from Pingwu in the inhospitable

[36] Li Jianhua, *Fanzui shehuixue* (Criminal sociology), Shanghai: Huiwentang xinji shuju, 1937, pp. 229–30.

north-west of Sichuan province. Prisoners were expected to build their own houses, reclaim and cultivate acres of wasteland, and receive two healthy meals a day out of the colony's agricultural production. However, during the first couple of years prisoners and guards only found vast expanses of inhospitable wasteland that did not yield enough even for their own sustenance, and shortage of funds obliged the camp leader to request the neighbouring authorities repeatedly for equipment and food. It was planned to build fifteen 'peasant sheds' (*nongshe*) as temporary accommodation for a few dozen prisoners to enable them to survive in the cold winter in an environment far removed from even the basic amenities of peasant villages, but by the end of the first year only two were completed.[37] Many of the prisoners sent to the colony were too old or sick to work in the fields, and there were constant security problems. Prisoners were difficult to supervise in the open, and some eventually escaped only to die in the camp's harsh natural surroundings. Local courts which sent prisoners to the colony failed to keep up their required monthly payments, and prisoners therefore went hungry and cold.[38] Despite these initial problems, the authorities continued the Pingwu experiment, which eventually had 150 prisoners working in 1946. Of these, a hundred were engaged in farming, growing maize, rice, potatoes and vegetables, and raising pigs.[39]

Other agricultural colonies were established in a number of provinces, a resolution being passed at the third plenum of the Third National Political Council of the Guomindang in September 1944 requesting the government to expand convict labour on state-owned wasteland in the interior provinces. The Ministry of Justice asked different high courts to locate suitable tracts of wasteland and negotiate with the provincial governments for their acquisition. The plan immediately encountered practical difficulties. In Gansu province, sufficient wasteland was found to the west of the river, but its cultivation was impeded by lack of water and communications. The soil was barren and infertile, and made worse by a recent drought. In Shaanxi province existing wasteland had already been turned over to the military, while other suitable plots were privately owned and could not easily be transferred to the provincial government. The response from the Yunnan High Court was more positive: Simao (just north of the southern part of the province known as Xishuangbanna) was identified as a potential site

---

[37] Number Two National Archives, Nanjing, 7/1934, 'Sichuan jianfan yiken shixiang de wenshu' (Documents on the reclamation of wasteland by prisoners in Sichuan province), 1942–3.

[38] Ibid.

[39] National Historical Archives, Taipei, 151/2300, 'Sichuan jiansuo waiyi jianfan yiken qingxing' (Conditions of reclamation of wasteland by prisoners at the convict colony of Sichuan), 1947.

and an investigation team was sent to visit the region. They found that although the soil was fertile, malaria flourished in this hot and humid subtropical region. There was no public transport, and reaching Simao from Kunming took twenty days on horseback. Considering the threat of malaria and the exorbitant costs of transportation, this plan too was finally abandoned.[40]

Some county gaols also pursued agricultural work after 1945, lured by a vision of economic self-sufficiency and moral reformation through uplifting contact with the soil. In Xinchang county, Zhejiang province, wasteland behind the gaol was cultivated by two prisoners in 1948, an innovation that attracted the central government's attention, although a much bigger project was hampered by underfunding.[41] Agricultural colonies, the only serious alternative to prisons envisaged during the entire republican period, were never developed in any systematic way, mainly because of practical administrative difficulties. Although extraterritoriality had been relinquished by all foreign powers by 1943 and the prison system itself had suffered severe damage, at no point was any other form of punishment advanced as a suitable alternative to the reformative prison. It would take a ruthless one-party state to force millions into labour camps in the remote countryside after 1949.

PHYSICAL PUNISHMENT

The reintroduction of corporal punishment was briefly considered after the fall of the empire in 1911: as the ideal of *ganhua* seemed ineffectual in curbing crime, a measure of pain was thought to be a necessary corrective that might instil some fear in the criminal mind. Liang Qichao, one of the leading reformers during the late Qing, was among an influential minority who supported corporal punishment. Just before he resigned as Minister of Justice, he submitted a plan for judicial reform to Yuan Shikai in March 1914 which included a proposal to restore punishments such as flogging and exile in order to reduce prison congestion.[42] In the wake of his proposal, the bamboo (*chixing*) was legally brought back into use as a form of corporal punishment by Yuan Shikai from November 1914 to

[40] National Historical Archives, Taipei, 151/2077, 'Ge jiansuo huangdi kaiken qingxing' (On the reclamation of wasteland by various prisons), 1945.
[41] National Historical Archives, Taipei, 151/2386, 'Ge jiansuo xiujian jianshe kaiken huangdi deng shixiang' (Various prisons repair prison buildings, reclaim wasteland and other matters), 1948.
[42] Liang Qichao, 'Chengqing gailiang sifa wen' (Proposal on the improvement of judicial administration), *Yinbingshi wenji* (Complete works of Liang Qichao), Shanghai: Zhonghua shuju, 1941, vol. 31, pp. 28–33.

September 1916, and sentenced criminals were given a set number of blows ranging from thirty to 120. The bamboo was reserved for petty crimes, including theft and cheating, and only applied to criminals sentenced to terms of three months or less. Within the walls of the prison, corporal punishment was generally banned except for the bamboo (*zhangze*), which was also reinstated by Yuan Shikai on 19 March 1914. A special regulation allowed the director to prescribe any number of blows under forty in accordance with the severity of the offence; singled out in particular were 'stubborn prisoners who do not straighten their ways and purposely resist'.[43]

While there is little evidence that a 'punishment of the body' was replaced by a 'punishment of the soul', as corporal punishments and petty deprivations, besides ritual humiliations such as the shaving of new convicts, remained part and parcel of the new penal regime, hunger, disease and death being daily realities which further degraded the bodies of prisoners, it is remarkable that penal authorities were reluctant to officially use flogging as an instrument of control inside the prison—except, as noted above, under Yuan Shikai. By seeking the complete elimination of corporal punishment in China, prison reformers embraced standards of penal treatment that were still highly contentious in other parts of the world, including Europe. The foreign community in Shanghai, for instance, applauded the resurrection of the bamboo under Yuan Shikai, seen as a 'courageous' and 'efficacious' measure which, according to the *North China Herald*, should serve as an example to the Mixed Court in Shanghai.[44] Worried about the appearance of 'habitual criminals' in the treaty ports and calling for penal colonies to hold them indefinitely under an open-ended sentence, the journal reported favourably on the ability of the lash to instil fear of the law in criminal elements, stating, 'the primary object of penal laws is not the punishment or the reform of the criminal, but the protection of the community.'[45] Corporal punishment was repeatedly proposed by the British-controlled Municipal Council in Shanghai: in 1906, 1914 and again in 1922 it lobbied for its reintroduction, despite clear indications that the Consular Body was not prepared to consider the proposal 'under any circumstances'. Among the arguments advanced by the Council was that the 'healthy routine and regularity of food supply has no terrors for the criminal classes'. In 1928 the Commissioner of Police observed that, while the policy of sentencing a large number of persons to death might have

43 Yu Shaosong (ed.), *(Gaiding) sifa ligui* (Revision of judicial laws and regulations), Beijing: Sifabu zanshiting, 1922, pp. 1384–5.

44 'Corporal Punishment in China', *North China Herald*, 9 January 1915, p. 110.

45 'The Professional Criminal', *North China Herald*, 30 May 1914, p. 684.

some deterrent effect, every sentence for a crime of violence should include a number of strokes with the cat-o'-nine-tails: this punitive tool had been introduced with complete success in Hong Kong and was used against pimps in London and hooligans in Australia.[46] The Council again approved the proposal, although one member wisely wrote in the margin that 'we have tried a number of times to get the Chinese to do this but without success': the Consular Body again quashed the proposal.[47]

In a striking reversal of roles common to a global movement of prison reform in which international emulation and national innovation were widely perceived to be symbolic indicators of a country's position on a scale of civilisation, local authorities in China not only found themselves resisting calls for the resumption of corporal punishment by foreign communities, but also actively sought to protect their nationals from physical punishment inflicted by foreign powers in the concessions. Chinese officials invoked the debates of the Municipal Council to lobby the Ministry of Justice for increased penal reform: in 1913, for instance, representations were made to the ministry by the Director of Judicial Administration of Jiangsu and the Shanghai Chinese Chamber of Commerce, as the foreign Mixed Court in Shanghai proposed the resumption of the lash in view of the great number of 'loafers' in Shanghai and the increasing problem of prison congestion. It was argued that the ministry should prevent this trend by building a new prison for Shanghai: besides the reformation of criminals, the prison would also contribute to the restoration of judicial power in the future.[48] The elimination of corporal punishment and physical torture of prisoners thus became a mark of success in international comparisons between governments, as prison authorities acted within a global frame of reference in which emulation led to ever shifting standards and expectations, each trying to be more 'modern' than the other.

POLITICAL PRISONERS

A small number of camps for political dissidents was established in the republican era, although their importance has been blown out of all proportion by the

[46] On flogging and the use of the cat-o'-nine-tails in Hong Kong, see Frank Dikötter, '"A Paradise for Rascals": Colonialism, punishment and the prison in Hong Kong (1841–1898)', *Crime, History and Societies*, 8, 1 (summer 2004), pp. 49–63.

[47] Shanghai Municipal Archives, U1/3/1913, 'Crimes of Violence: Corporal punishment', 1922–8.

[48] 'A New Shanghai Prison', *North China Herald*, 15 March 1913, p. 761.

official historiography in the People's Republic of China.[49] This imbalance has been aggravated by the publication of prison memoirs, largely written by political dissidents who not only belonged to a privileged élite accustomed to social recognition, but also received preferential treatment in prison: for instance, Chen Duxiu was merely confined to his house after his first arrest under Yuan Shikai (he spent his time fathering a baby) while imprisonment under Jiang Jieshi allowed him to write and publish a number of books from the relative comfort of his cell. Political prisoners were not only appalled at not being treated with the respect they considered their due—despite the better treatment they often received in prison—but also contributed to casting prisons in a highly negative light in the literary imagination. Accounts of imprisonment invariably represented prisons as the epitome of ruthless political oppression and arbitrary brutality against which leaders of the revolutionary movement demonstrated their relentless bravery and unremitting spirit of sacrifice. Heroes and martyrs of the opposition stood valiantly in the face of cruel oppression. These views were further disseminated by foreign observers sympathetic to the revolutionary movement, describing prisons as 'medieval torture chambers'.[50] As Bruce Adams has critically observed of Russia—a country in many ways comparable to China—political radicals had little in common with the poor farmers and uneducated delinquents who found their way into prison.[51] Not only did political prisoners replicate a privileged viewpoint, but they never amounted to more than a fraction of the general prison population.

The use of imprisonment to silence dissent and penalise opposition was reflected by the appearance of a new penal institution called *fanxingyuan*, or 'place for self-examination'. The first of these was established in Hangzhou in 1928, followed by fifteen others in most provinces under Guomindang control. They

---

[49] Xue Meiqing (ed.), *Zhongguo jianyushi* (The history of prisons in China), Beijing: Qunzhong chubanshe, 1986; Xue Meiqing and Cong Jinpeng, *Tianjin jianyu shi* (History of Tianjin prison), Tianjin: Tianjin renmin chubanshe, 1999; Zhu Decheng (ed.), *Hubei jindai jianyu* (Modern prisons in Hubei), Wuhan: Hubei sheng laogai gongzuo guanliju, 1987; Gu Xiaoyan, *Zhongguo de jianyu* (China's prisons), Shenyang: Jilin renmin chubanshe, 1988; Liang Minli, *Jianming Zhongguo jianyu shi* (Concise history of prisons in China), Beijing: Qunzhong chubanshe, 1994; Wang Lirong, *Zhongguo jianyu shi* (History of prisons in China), Chongqing: Sichuan daxue chubanshe, 1996.

[50] *China Today*, an organ of the American Friends of the Chinese People, regularly denounced the prisons of the Guomindang; see, for instance, 'White Terror', *China Today*, 1, 3 (December 1934), p. 43.

[51] Bruce F. Adams, *The Politics of Punishment: Prison reform in Russia, 1863–1917*, DeKalb, IL: Northern Illinois University Press, 1996, pp. 5–7.

were generally small and run along the lines followed by model prisons, except that the curriculum aimed to denounce the 'evils of communism' and enable offenders to 'become aware' (*juewu*) of the error of their ways, gain basic education and acquire vocational training. Contemporaries observed that 'innocent small fry' usually ended up in the political reformatories, including middle-school students who had dabbled in Marxism or petty government workers who had been denounced by personal enemies.[52] More important communist leaders ended up in military prisons, for instance the Wusong-Shanghai Garrison Headquarters, also called Longhua Prison in Shanghai, where they were generally treated better than ordinary prisoners. As Gregor Benton notes in his history of the New Fourth Army, which was left behind in south China to survive in desperate conditions after Mao Zedong started the Long March, the prisoners who turned their cells into studies to catch up on the latest learning were sometimes better off than the southern guerrillas, who lived in the mountains where life was dangerous and books were scarce.[53] Unlike the mixture of grit, gravel and coal dust served in the notorious Caohejing prison for common offenders, the rice in Longhua Prison was unhusked but edible, unlimited in quantity and accompanied by cabbage soup. Prisoners were allowed books and magazines to read and could communicate with each other through small holes high in the cell walls. Study sessions were even organised on the different struggles within the Chinese Communist Party (CCP). Wang Fanxi studied economics and philosophy to kill time—he was released on parole after serving two-thirds of his sentence.[54]

A small number of camps to hold opponents to the regime, called 'concentration camps' (*jizhongying*) in communist literature, appeared during the Second World War, the most infamous coming under the auspices of the Sino-American Cooperation Organisation (SACO, *Zhong Mei tezhong jishuhezuo suo*), set up in Chongqing under a secret agreement signed by the United States with Jiang Jieshi in 1941 and allowing American specialists to help train secret agents under Dai Li, the powerful head of Special Services. The main SACO prison, popularly known as the White House (*Bai gongguan*), had a dozen communal cells in which up to twenty prisoners were packed like sardines. Although the White House became a poignant symbol of repression in communist mythology after all but a few of the inmates were killed when the camp was abandoned following the

---

[52]   Graham Peck, *Two Kinds of Time*, Boston, MA: Houghton Mifflin, 1950, p. 140.

[53]   Gregor Benton, *Mountain Fires: The Red Army's three-year war in south China, 1934–1938*, Berkeley, CA: University of California Press, 1992, p. 476.

[54]   Wang Fan-hsi, *Memoirs of a Chinese Revolutionary*, translated and with an introduction by Gregor Benton, New York: Columbia University Press, 1991, pp. 164–70.

end of the civil war,[55] the number of prisoners remained relatively low at about 200, a figure which pales into insignificance when compared with the millions of ordinary people executed in waves of communist terror before and after 1949, as the next section briefly shows.

COMMUNIST LABOUR CAMPS

The prison was also adopted by the CCP, which replicated to a very large extent the penal philosophy of reformation as well as the more general penal terminology created by the prison reformers since the late Qing. But there were crucial differences. The primary function of prisons during the Jiangxi Soviet (1924–33), when the communists secured control over a region far away from the Guomindang-controlled cities, was the incapacitation of political enemies, although poor security and inadequate sanitation subverted even this relatively straightforward goal from the very start. Scarce resources also limited the scope of imprisonment, and prisons were gradually forced to take on a productive purpose: the high costs of incarceration, it was thought, could be reduced by putting prisoners to work. As a result of the United Front policy during the Yan'an period (1934–44), when the CCP became ensconced in the north after fleeing the Jiangxi Soviet, the emphasis was finally shifted towards the reformative function of prisons: education should be primary and punishment secondary, as prisoners should be 'reformed' (*zixin*) to become disciplined members of a communist society.[56] A more fundamental difference was the overt rejection of the legal codes developed since the late Qing. The rule of law was scorned as a bourgeois concept and would be replaced by party decrees for decades to come: revolution justified terror, and opposition to the one-party state was sufficient to warrant the label of counter-revolutionary. The notion of equality before the law, strongly promoted by various republican regimes, was also brushed aside in an insistence on arbitrary factors such as party rank, social status and willingness to confess and collaborate: as in other communist regimes, rhetorical opposition to economic and social inequalities led to strong inequalities in the treatment of suspects. The most significant difference, however, was the sheer number of people incarcerated. In the base area of Shandong, the idea of using prisons (*jiansuo*) to confine convicts was already abandoned in the 1940s, as military instability, concrete

---

[55] Fu Boyong and Zhang Zhenglü, *Yuzhong douzheng jishi* (Veritable records of struggle in prison), Chongqing: Chongqing chubanshe, 1984, p. 47.

[56] Patricia E. Griffin, *The Chinese Communist Treatment of Counterrevolutionaries, 1924–1949*, Princeton University Press, 1976, pp. 109–16.

4. Corridor in new prison. [Ministry of Justice, *The Thirteen New Prisons of China*, Beijing: Ministry of Justice, 1918]

organisational problems and scarce resources during the war against Japan on the one hand, but also mounting numbers of prisoners during the civil war with the Guomindang after the Second World War on the other, led towards a system of mobile labour teams and camps dispersed throughout the countryside: by 1948 large labour camps containing up to 2,000 prisoners each were well established in Shandong, even before the appearance of several labour teams in the mines of Gongchangling and Benxi in Manchuria, developed with the help of Soviet advisers.[57]

If even before the proclamation of the People's Republic on 1 October 1949 anybody even remotely suspected of having collaborated with the Guomindang was declared a criminal by the communist party, millions more would be imprisoned during the purges of the 1950s. Jean-Luc Domenach's monumental study of labour camps in communist China estimates that the state terror unleashed by the party in the founding years of the People's Republic led to 4 to 6 million prisoners being held in labour camps, not including the execution of up to two million suspected of real or imaginary crimes against the party.[58] Taking into account the following decades, even the most conservative estimate of the number of deaths in PRC labour camps runs in the millions, although the upper estimate of 15 million is no doubt too high.[59] Comparisons with the concentration camps set up by Jiang Jieshi (Chiang Kai-shek) during the Second World War are thus meaningless: not only were political prisoners under the Guomindang counted in the hundreds or at most thousands in a country of half a billion people, as opposed to millions under the CCP, but all the evidence, including testimonies from former inmates who experienced imprisonment at the hands of both nationalists and communists, indicates that prison life after 1949 was a fate far worse and far more common than before. Most historians prefer to compare the PRC with the Soviet Union, all the more since Soviet law, the USSR Code and Russian advisors were influential in shaping the penal system in China in the 1950s. Although primary sources used by different authors examining the labour camps in China are disparate and tenuous at best, based generally on printed sources and interviews with former prisoners and judicial personnel, it is generally agreed that the percentage of the overall population imprisoned in the Soviet Union

---

[57] Frank Dikötter, 'The Emergence of Labour Camps in Shandong Province, 1942–1950', *China Quarterly*, 175 (September 2003), pp. 803–17.

[58] Jean-Luc Domenach, *L'archipel oublié*, Paris: Fayard, 1992, pp. 71–2.

[59] The figures are reviewed in Philip F. Williams and Yenna Wu, *The Great Wall of Confinement: The Chinese prison camp through contemporary fiction and reportage*, Berkeley, CA: University of California Press, 2004, pp. 189–90.

was higher than in the PRC. However, this key difference is explained by Jean-Luc Domenach by the fact that mass campaigns and mass organisations in the PRC already fulfilled punitive functions, as ordinary people became enmeshed in a widespread and intrusive network of surveillance which lowered the need for incarceration. Moreover, in contrast to Stalin, Mao Zedong fully intended to 'reform' each and every prisoner: where prisoners in the *gulag* were left with their own thoughts, a heavy emphasis on remoulding every aspect of a prisoner's morals, ideas and habits, ultimately leading to the birth of a 'new man', was at the heart of penal practice in the PRC. Rather than *gulag*, the Russian term used to describe the camp system in the Soviet Union, a number of writers thus prefer to use the term *laogai*, an abbreviation of *laodong gaizao*, meaning 'reform through labour', as forced labour is known in the official vocabulary of the communist party.

The emphasis on re-education is also evident in the second component of the concentration camp system, namely 're-education through labour' (*laodong jiaoyang*, abbreviated as *laojiao*): instituted in the mid-1950s, it allowed the legal system to be bypassed and local governments to remove undesirable elements without any limit placed on the length of time served by inmates. Where *laogai* inmates received specific sentences, *laojiao* prisoners were given an indeterminate sentence, some spending ten to twenty years in labour camps without ever appearing before a judge or being given the opportunity to contest the charges against them. However, as impressionistic studies based on prison memoirs and novels have shown, the treatment of both types of prisoner did not differ substantially:[60] labour camps were often located far away from the coastal cities in the deserts of Xinjiang, Gansu and Qinghai provinces or the frozen plains of Manchuria; malnourishment, poor sanitation and overcrowding frequently led to a range of debilitating diseases which spread to both *laogai* and *laojiao* prisoners; while all slept in cramped barracks infested with vermin, huddled together on wooden planks and were desperate for more than a diet of coarse grain and half-rotten vegetables. Death was so common during the Great Leap Forward that Zhang Xianliang, one of the most popular prison writers, was mistaken for a corpse when he slipped into a comatose state caused by a starvation diet: he was piled onto a cart high with corpses to be buried in a mass grave when somebody discovered that he was still breathing. The torture of both categories of prisoner was also widespread, many types of physical punishment such as 'hanging a chicken by its feet'—with an inmate's wrists tied behind his back and supporting

---

[60] See Williams and Wu, *The Great Wall of Confinement*, pp. 189–90.

the full weight of the body when suspended from the rafters of a building, arms being pulled out of the shoulder sockets—going straight back to imperial practice from which communist rhetoric was so keen to distance itself. While conditions improved somewhat after the death of Mao Zedong, physical abuse, inadequate nutrition and rampant disease, as well as the retention of ex-prisoners in the camp's vicinity, an emphasis on the 'remoulding' of prisoners and the use of heavy labour without regard for skills that could be used after release continue into the twenty-first century and indicate a stubborn unwillingness to overhaul an outmoded prison system that creates massive and systematic suffering for no reason. And today, as under Mao, a person can be sent to a camp for up to three years for 're-education through labour' by mere administrative order, to be mandated by a local government without any referral to whatever minimal legal procedures may exist: it can be renewed for up to ten years.

CONCLUSION

Prisons in republican China suffered from underfunding and overcrowding, while inmates were submitted to a degrading regime of institutional discipline marked by daily boredom at best and custodial death at worst: the same holds true for prisons in other countries today, including England and the United States. Disease, dearth and death were rampant in republican spaces of confinement, an observation which extends not only to the penal regimes of other countries between the two World Wars, but also to the poor and unemployed who eked out a miserable living outside the prison walls. Designed to replace 'feudal' and 'cruel' forms of physical punishment that were deemed to be incompatible with a modern mode of governance, the custodial sentence around the globe produced its own set of problems that penologists have not been able to solve to this day. Noting the tendency of human beings to become corrupt by power, the great liberal thinker Benjamin Constant already in the early nineteenth century feared the 'obscure dictatorship' exercised by guards over inmates:

Incarceration, of all forms of punishment, is the one which attracts the most frequent and easy abuse. Its apparent mildness compounds the problem .... If we consider the tendency we all have to abuse the slightest power; if we bear in mind that the best of us change suddenly when granted a discretionary power, that the only check on despotism is publicity, and that everything in the bosom of the prison is done in secrecy and obscurity, I cannot think of any imagination which should not be struck with terror.[61]

[61] Jacques-Guy Petit, *Ces peines obscures. La prison pénale en France (1780–1875)*, Paris: Fayard, 1990, p. 545.

Yet as this chapter has illustrated, an 'obscure dictatorship' was also held by powerful prisoners over weaker ones, as the social hierarchies found outside the prison were reinforced by a customary order inside the penitentiary in which those at the bottom of the social scale had everything to fear—whether from cell bosses or from influential guards.

Financial limitations further deflected the goal of reformative imprisonment. As in other countries, prison reform was only one task among many others set by the central government. Local, provincial and central authorities pursued a range of pressing issues in republican China, ranging from universal education to basic health care. Prison reform alone was a huge project that demanded vast administrative and financial resources that even developed countries did not command. While economic and institutional constraints impeded the actual implementation of various plans proposed by the central government, many local and regional authorities nonetheless strove to adhere to agreed prison rules, often using local human and financial resources when insufficient funds were provided by the Ministry of Justice. Prison reform, moreover, was deeply enmeshed with existing cultural values, economic systems, institutional frameworks, political configurations and competing individual aspirations. Conceived as a benevolent project which upheld the promise of repentance, it was inevitably transformed by these different factors, leading to accommodations and compromises that strayed away from the initial vision of rehabilitative incarceration. As elsewhere, benevolent intentions were subverted by practical constraints as the custodial sentence started to engender as many problems as it had been designed to solve. Moreover, as Émile Durkheim observed long ago, the core problem of the prison as a form of discipline resides in the lack of inclination of the majority of prisoners to participate in the process of 'reformation': in other institutional situations such as the school or the factory, the individual must to some extent share the goals of the disciplinary process for discipline to be effective. As the prisoner was robbed of a sense of self-respect which is so central to self-discipline, the prison did not produce 'disciplined subjects' but rather hardened recidivists.

Imprisonment in republican China was a new legal tool, but one that was used to pursue a traditional vision of an ordered and cohesive social body governed by virtue. Modernising élites viewed the reformation of criminals as an integral part of a much larger project of national regeneration in which social cohesion, economic development and state power could only be obtained by moulding obedient subjects. Based on the idea of reformation, the custodial sentence was, on the one hand, part of a global movement towards penal reform and, on the other, a local reconfiguration of a more traditional faith in the transformative capacity of education. In resonance with the Mencian view of human nature as inherently good and extremely malleable, the notion of reformation sustained the belief that criminals could achieve individual self-improvement with proper institutional guidance. Because the inculcation of correct behaviour was of paramount importance in the moral education of subjects, the emulation of models was a dominant pedagogical strategy. Model prisons were thus the microcosm of an exemplary society in which the emulation of models—whether in the school, the factory or the army—was seen as a mission of educative transformation, a project for social discipline and a strategy for national power. The conformity inherent in this worldview suited the political élites, in whose power it was to define models in the first place. It also corresponded to a particular social structure in which a highly educated élite viewed the rest of the population as backward, illiterate and superstitious. This strong élitist bias was expressed in a paternalistic approach that aimed to reform, correct, guide and educate the poor folk who had strayed on to the path of crime. The exemplary prison director was to act towards his prisoners as a caring father towards his obedient sons. Benevolent as well as punitive, like the state, he reformed while he punished.

Prisons in republican China were theoretically accountable to the public and practically scrutinised by a variety of competing groups, ranging from charitable associations and judicial inspectors to local journalists and foreign observers. China after 1949, on the other hand, became a hermetically closed universe in which information on labour camps was a state secret. Whatever safeguards had existed for prisoners were discarded in the name of the dictatorship of the proletariat. Sheer numbers also explain why the prison system of the republican period came to an abrupt end in 1949: the huge mass of people arrested by the CCP far outstripped the capacity of existing prisons. On the other hand, the communist regime, like its republican predecessors, continued to view human beings as profoundly malleable and open to moral transformation: the very notion of *ganhua* remained at the heart of the communist system of punishment. However, while the CCP shared with previous regimes faith in the power of institutions to mould obedient and socially responsible citizens, the worst problems of the reformative prison were further amplified as the communists transformed the penal system into a political tool: political factors superseded and eliminated legal ones under communist rule. While republican penologists had briefly envisaged the use of the indeterminate sentence and agricultural labour in the 1930s and '40s, these ideas were never fully implemented, as the result of administrative impediments and legal constraints. After 1949 they formed the backbone of the 'reform through labour' system, as tens of millions ended up in labour camps in the countryside for indeterminate periods until deemed by the party to have been re-educated.

BIBLIOGRAPHICAL NOTE

There is a growing body of work on the history of law and justice in imperial and modern China, but relatively few studies have specifically focused on the prison in the late nineteenth and twentieth century. Scholarship on the history of the prison produced in the People's Republic tends to be superficial and adapts a rather predictable analytical framework, but can be useful as an introduction to some of the main events and sources, for instance Xue Meiqing (ed.), *Zhongguo jianyushi* (The history of prisons in China), Beijing: Qunzhong chubanshe, 1986; Xue Meiqing and Cong Jinpeng, *Tianjin jianyu shi* (History of Tianjin prison), Tianjin: Tianjin renmin chubanshe, 1999; Zhu Decheng (ed.), *Hubei jindai jianyu* (Modern prisons in Hubei), Wuhan: Hubei sheng laogai gongzuo guanliju, 1987; Gu Xiaoyan, *Zhongguo de jianyu* (China's prisons), Shenyang: Jilin renmin chubanshe, 1988; Liang Minli, *Jianming Zhongguo jianyu shi* (Concise history of prisons in China), Beijing: Qunzhong chubanshe, 1994; Wang Lirong, *Zhongguo jianyu shi* (History of prisons in China), Chongqing: Sichuan daxue chubanshe, 1996. Marxist scholarship has been criticised in an interpretive essay by Michael Dutton, *Policing and Punishment in China: From patriarchy to 'the people'*, Cambridge University Press, 1992. The principal study of the prison in republican China is Frank Dikötter, *Crime, Punishment and the Prison in Modern China*, London: Hurst and New York: Columbia University Press, 2002, but the prison under communism has been approached by a number of authors, the key work being that of Jean-Luc Domenach, *L'archipel oublié*, Paris: Fayard, 1992, others including Frank Dikötter, 'The Emergence of Labour Camps in Shandong Province, 1942–1950', *China Quarterly*, 175 (September 2003), pp. 803–17; Frank Dikötter, 'Crime and Punishment in Post-Liberation China: The prisoners of a Beijing gaol in the 1950s', *China Quarterly*, 149 (March 1997), pp. 147–59; Patricia E. Griffin, *The Chinese Communist Treatment of Counterrevolutionaries, 1924–1949*, Princeton University Press, 1976; James D. Seymour and Richard Anderson, *New Ghosts, Old Ghosts: Prisons and labor reform camps in China*, Armonk, NY: Sharpe, 1997; Philip F. Williams and Yenna Wu, *The Great Wall of Confinement: The Chinese prison camp through contemporary fiction and reportage*, Berkeley, CA: University of California Press, 2004; and Harry Wu, *Laogai: The Chinese gulag*, Boulder, CO: Westview Press, 1992.

ENVISIONING THE COLONIAL PRISON

Clare Anderson and David Arnold

The modern prison is a paradox, presenting a recurrent tension between the seen and the unseen. In taking punishment away from the public gaze and confining prisoners behind high walls and in fortress-like buildings, the designers of the modern prison attached paramount importance to the need for seclusion. For the sake of punishment and reform they sought to cut prisoners off from the pleasures, rewards and consolations of the outside world and to make their invisibility and inaccessibility to relatives and friends a source of fear and deterrence. By sending prisoners to distant locations, by transporting them to penal settlements and colonies overseas, or by transferring them to even remoter outposts, the abstraction and seclusion of prisoners was made, in theory at least, even more complete.

And yet visibility in one form or another remained central to penal intent, as much in the colonised societies with which this chapter is largely concerned as in Europe and North America, where many of the ideas and practices of modern penology employed in the colonial world were first formulated.[1] If in the modern prison the external, public view were to be restricted or denied, the constant gaze of the inspectors and warders, and their power to effect discipline and reform through their almost omniscient powers of observation was emphasised.[2] Equally, if the power of the prison as a deterrent or reforming institution were to be impressed upon the public, if the prison were to satisfy those who ordered it into existence or were responsible for its financing and governance, if it were to

---

[1] This chapter will focus on British rule in South Asia and the Indian Ocean—territories with which the authors are most familiar—though it will also draw on illustrative material from elsewhere outside Europe and North America.

[2] Miran Bozovic, 'Introduction' to Jeremy Bentham, *The Panopticon Writings*, London: Verso, 1995, pp. 11–15.

impact on the conduct and morality of society at large, then it was necessary to produce some tangible signs of its abiding presence and transforming effect. Internally and externally, therefore, the prison relied on selected forms of visibility. Yet it also had to recognise that some forms of envisioning and representation, authorised or not, might actually work to qualify or subvert official purpose and disciplinary intent.

MAKING THE PRISON VISIBLE

Early prisons may have been relatively inconspicuous or lacking in any obvious architectural and functional distinctiveness: they might be a mere assemblage of huts or ramshackle and decaying buildings converted from other purposes. In the short term, military barracks, fortifications and warehouses were all pressed into use as gaols (figure 1). In early colonial India unenclosed gaols were sometimes situated in the middle of towns—or even public markets—a blurring of penal and public space that assisted their permeability and rendered them virtually invisible as distinct institutions. The fate of a single building might, over time, reflect the overlapping, multi-layered history of such colonial institutions and their collective disciplinary intent. One location in Mauritius was first used as a place for the confinement of prisoners of war (1810–15), then as the headquarters of

1. Original huts for convicts, Singapore. [J.F.A. McNair, *Prisoners their own Warders*, 1899]

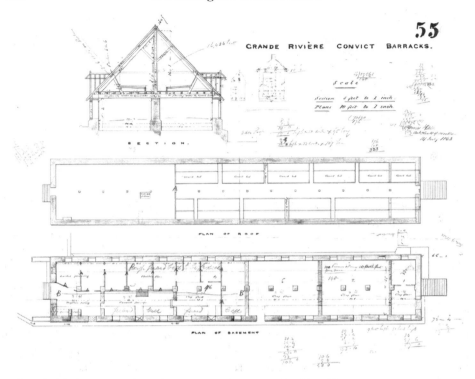

2. Grande Rivière convict barracks, Mauritius. [Ministry of Public Infrastructure, Mauritius].

the island's Indian penal settlement (1815–53) and finally as a 'vagrant depot' for runaway indentured labourers (1864–86)(figure 2).[3] In several Latin American countries, convicts might, through an imaginative switch in institutional roles, be housed in former convents. Cells designed for monastic contemplation thereby became cells suited to penal confinement.[4] But, in general, as extempore prisons proved unsuitable and anachronistic, as labouring on the public roads was gradually replaced (as in India) by a greater emphasis on intramural labour, or as the sight of convicts publicly in chains came to be seen as 'uncivilised' (or possibly to invite public sympathy rather than approbation), so the visibility of prisoners

---

[3] Vijayalakshmi Teelock (ed.), *The Vagrant Depot of Grand River, its Surroundings and Vagrancy in British Mauritius*, Port Louis, Mauritius: Aapravasi Ghat Trust Fund, 2004. For a fascinating account of the layout of another disciplinary institution, colonial settlements for Indian 'criminal tribes', see William J. Glover, 'Objects, Models, and Exemplary Works: Educating sentiment in colonial India', *Journal of Asian Studies*, 64, 3 (2005), pp. 539–66.

[4] As with the colonial convent of Guadalupe in Lima which became Guadalupe gaol (information from Carlos Aguirre).

3. Buenos Aires Penitentiary. [Archivo General de la Nación, Buenos Aires]

was diminished while that of the prison was enhanced. As in London and other Western capitals, the reformed and reconstructed prisons of the mid and late nineteenth century became highly visible urban structures. The earnest replication and diligent adaptation of layouts drawn from European and North American models—embodying a progressive move towards cellular accommodation as in the North West Provinces of India from the 1840s—further reflected the sense of the modern prison as the embodiment of orderliness and control.[5] In size and extent, gaols were often among the most imposing edifices the city could present, cathedrals of carceral power that towered over other buildings, sacred or secular, and commanded strategically important parts of the colonial townscape. Seen from street level, from maps and photographic panoramas, or latterly from the air, prisons were among the most visually imposing landmarks of the modern city (figure 3). The shifting cultural dynamics that shaped the prison's physical form and location were invariably intertwined with the changing spatial dynamics of punishment itself, and the relationship of both to (in)visibility.[6]

[5] For one example of the evolution of prison design, see James Semple Kerr, *Design for Convicts: An account of design for convict establishments in the Australian colonies during the transportation era*, Sydney: Library of Australian History, 1984. On African gaols, see Florence Bernault, 'The Politics of Enclosure in Colonial and Post-Colonial Africa' in Florence Bernault (ed.), *A History of Prison and Confinement in Africa*, Portsmouth, NH: Heinemann, 2003, pp. 16–26. For a castellated (military) prison in India at Secunderabad, see Jan Morris with Simon Winchester, *Stones of Empire: The buildings of the Raj*, Oxford University Press, 1983, p. 91.

[6] Harriet Deacon, 'Patterns of Exclusion on Robben Island, 1654–1992' in Alison Bashford and Carolyn Strange (eds), *Isolation: Places and practices of exclusion*, London: Routledge, 2003,

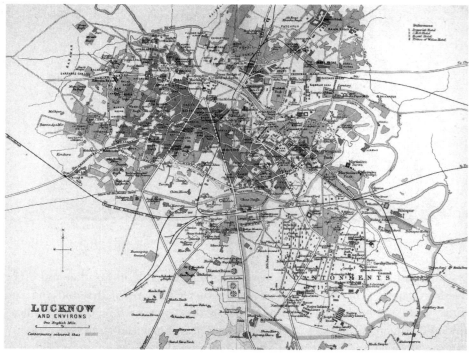

4. Town Plan of Lucknow, India, *c.* 1908. [*Imperial Gazetteer Atlas of India* (1909)]

In late-nineteenth- and early-twentieth-century South Asia, central and district gaols were frequently located, as if to state the obvious, on 'Jail Road', as in Lucknow and Lahore (figures 4 and 5). In Singapore the prison was the city's largest building complex, and shaped urban culture in important ways. It was situated off Bras Basah Road, which was known locally as *lau kau* (ankle chains).[7] By virtue of their visibility and disciplinary function, colonial prisons served not just as places of punishment and confinement but also as 'moral objects', whose commanding presence and evident purpose might be hoped to influence and 'educate' the colonial public.[8] In India they were often sited alongside other modern disciplinary institutions—lunatic asylums, reformatories, hospitals and

pp. 153–72; Anoma Pieris, 'Hidden Hands and Divided Landscapes: Penal labor and colonial citizenship in Singapore and the Straits Settlements, 1825–1873', PhD in Architecture, University of California, Berkeley, 2003.

[7] Anoma Pieris, 'On Dropping Bricks and Other Disconcerting Subjects: Unearthing convict histories in Singapore', *Fabrications*, 15, 2 (2005), p. 79.

[8] See also Glover, 'Objects, Models, and Exemplary Works'.

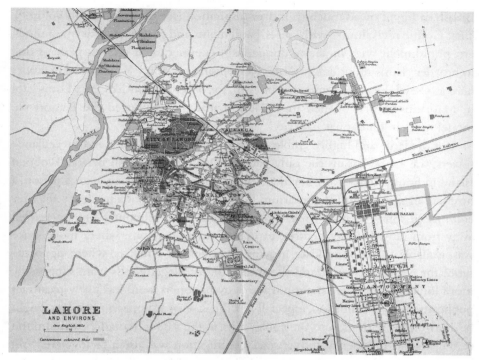

5. Town Plan of Lahore, India, *c.* 1908. [*Imperial Gazetteer Atlas of India* (1909)]

colleges—in a kind of institutional enclave, conveniently and strategically located between the old 'native' town, the civil lines and the military cantonment, each of which had some claim on its presence.

The location and disciplinary intent of penal institutions in British colonies reflected European and North American trends. Conversely, the architecture of the purpose-built prison often served to underline its distinctively colonial as much as its penal character. Unlike their *ad hoc* predecessors, prisons in India were often fortress-like, suggesting sternness and authority, sometimes, as in Britain, neo-classical, promising rationality and order, but seldom in a more whimsical, half-vernacular style like the Indo-Saracenic.[9] In turn, the prisons built by the

---

[9] On the architecture of British prisons, see John Pratt, 'The Disappearance of the Prison: An episode in the "civilizing process"' in Bashford and Strange (eds), *Isolation*, pp. 24–30. For the perceived appropriateness of different styles of imperial architecture, see Thomas R. Metcalf, *An Imperial Vision: Indian architecture and Britain's Raj*, London: Faber and Faber, 1989, and *Forging the Raj: Essays on British India in the heyday of empire*, Oxford University Press, 2005, chapters 6 and 10. Unfortunately Metcalf makes no reference to prison design.

British in Egypt owed much to Indian inspiration (see Gorman in this volume). That Gothic revivalism—with spires, battlements and gargoyles associating modern punishment with medieval dungeons[10]—never caught on was perhaps due to broader claims about colonialism as a civilising mission.[11] Yet colonial practices here as elsewhere were somewhat uneven, for other prisons like Port Louis gaol in Mauritius, which opened in 1834, anticipated or followed the Pentonville model in their 'functional austerity'.[12]

But the large and highly visible city gaol, with its high walls and surveillance towers, was by no means the only pattern. During the British period, Robben Island in South Africa constituted an entire carceral archipelago, with a prison, a hospital, an asylum and a leprosarium.[13] Moreover, there was a tendency for later colonial prisons—as in Burma, Mauritius and the Philippines—to be moved away from crowded city centres, to out-of-town locations, where more space was available to accommodate growing numbers of convicts, where opportunities for personal contact and the smuggling of illegal goods were supposedly more limited, and where demonstrations by prisoners were less likely to attract public attention. Health too, especially in the case of European prisoners, might be a reason for relocation to the cooler hills, in the case of India to Ootacumund in the Madras Presidency, though racial segregation was also a factor here.[14] Yet the relocation of prisons also reflected changing colonial sensibilities about the nature of punishment itself. Much to the chagrin of penal administrators in Britain, into the 1860s and beyond, colonial prisoners were often employed in outdoor work. This presented a stark contrast to Britain, where by the middle of the nineteenth century, prisoners were mainly punished through non-productive labour. Colonial prisons like Port Louis could not cope with the increased pressure on space such employment implied, so against a background of metropolitan pressure for change, new prisons were built in more spacious locations: in the Mauritian case, in the highlands at Beau Bassin, which opened in the 1880s. Indian prisons were better able to cope with changing international thinking in this respect, for the issue of indoor/outdoor labour had never been reconciled,

[10] Pratt, 'The Disappearance', pp. 24–5.
[11] This was also the case in Africa. See Bernault, 'The Politics of Enclosure', p. 17.
[12] Pratt, 'The Disappearance', p. 29. On architectural form in colonial Africa, see Bernault, 'The Politics of Enclosure', pp. 16–22.
[13] Deacon, 'The British Prison on Robben Island 1800–1896', and 'The Medical Institutions on Robben Island 1846–1931' in Deacon (ed.), *The Island*, pp. 33–56, 57–75.
[14] The segregation of white from black prisoners was also a key feature of colonial African prisons. See Bernault, 'The Politics of Enclosure', pp. 18–20.

and thus many presidency gaols had already been converted for the employment of at least some of the prisoners in indoor labour.[15] This perhaps explains why most Indian prisons remained at the heart of colonial cities. In contrast, there was no such crisis in late-nineteenth-century Africa, where prisons were always designed as collective gaols. Open courtyards housed prisoners viewed as incapable of enduring a cellular system.[16]

The envisioning of the prison was then about interior spaces as well as exterior perspectives. Although the prison was a prominent, often highly visible symbol of colonial rule, its interior, as a working institution, was often left open to the public imagination. In the era before photography, architectural drawings and prison plans tended to remain in the administrative sphere and were rarely published, even in specialist volumes or parliamentary reports, perhaps out of fear that making plans public would facilitate escapes.[17] Similarly, although the prison was a site of intensive medical observation and sanitary surveillance, as the enormous volume of statistical data, case notes and pioneering studies of diseases in nineteenth- and early-twentieth-century Indian gaols attests,[18] prisoners and their hospitals were rarely if ever sketched, photographed or otherwise represented in visual form.[19] The prison, it would seem, was mainly reported in

---

[15] F.J. Mouat, 'On Prison Ethics and Prison Labour', *Journal of the Royal Statistical Society*, 54, 2 (1891), p. 221.

[16] Bernault, 'The Politics of Enclosure', pp. 20–1.

[17] Though there are paintings of gaols in the Oriental and India Office's Judicial Proceedings series, few were published in official reports. For one rare example see F.J. Mouat, *Reports on Jails Visited and Inspected in Bengal, Bihar, and Arracan*, Calcutta: F. Carbery, Military Orphan Press, 1856, facing p. 6 (Alipur Jail). Colonial Office records in the National Archives (Kew) would yield rich dividends in relation to British colonies more generally. A good starting point for tracing debates on imprisonment is *Prison Discipline in the Colonies: Digest and summary of information respecting prisons in the colonies*, London: Eyre and Spottiswoode, 1867. For Colonial Office plans of Jamaican prisons, see Diana Paton, *No Bond but the Law: Punishment, race, and gender in Jamaican state formation, 1780–1870*, Durham, NC: Duke University Press, 2004, pp. 95–8. Archaeologists have used such plans to enormous effect in excavating the material culture of prison sites in colonial Australia. See, for instance, the collection in *Australasian Historical Archaeology*, 19 (2001), and *The Archaeology of Institutions of Reform*, special issue of the *International Journal of Historical Archaeology*, 5, 1 (2001).

[18] David Arnold, *Colonizing the Body: State medicine and epidemic disease in nineteenth-century India*, Berkeley, CA: University of California Press, 1993, chapter 2.

[19] One rare exception was the photographing of leper convicts in the Andamans during an 1877 experiment on the use of gurjun oil in the treatment of the condition. J. Dougall, *Report on the Treatment of Leprosy with Gurjun Oil*, pp. 4–5. (In an interesting example of the colonial circulation of penal and medical technologies, this printed report was found in a prisons department file in the Mauritius Archives).

6. Interior of the Let-Ma-Yoon Prison, Burma, *c.* 1825. [Henry Gouger, *Narrative of a Two Years' Imprisonment in Burmah*, London: John Murray, 1860]

written form, through the scrutiny and professional gaze of its superintendents and doctors (who in nineteenth-century India were often the same).

But if the interior of the prison and the fate of its inmates were seldom documented visually, it is worth noting that by contrast, drawings, sketches and engravings in the pre-photography era abound. In the main, these show the infliction of punishment, often in graphic detail. Perhaps these images were intended, by their often violent and gruesome content, to titillate a certain European public taste, but perhaps they also served to point out a moral contrast between the 'primitiveness' of some extra-European societies and those apparently happier nations where such cruel and arbitrary punishments were prohibited. Perhaps too, subliminally at least, they suggested that there were societies in Asia and Africa for which modern forms of punishment were too mild to be sufficiently punitive, or that righteous colonial retribution against rebels and outlaws required more than mere custodial sentencing (on the *longue durée* of flogging in colonial Africa, see Bernault in this volume). Whatever their import, the production, circulation and consumption of such images propagated both a sense of cultural distance and a continuing distraction between Western civilisation and 'native' savagery.[20]

[20] In this connection, see the many lurid and sensational images in Nicolas Bancel *et al.* (eds), *Images d'empire: Trente ans de photographies officielles sur l'Afrique française*, Paris: Association Connaissance de l' Histoire de l' Afrique Contemporaine, 1997, none of which relate directly to the prison.

7. Extracting the truth by torture in China, *c.* 1850. [British Library, London]

Pre-colonial images tend to show the inhumane conditions that existed in places of confinement and hence to illustrate the apparent primitivism of indigenous penal practices, or the distress and humiliation experienced by European captives in them (figure 6).[21] Some, as of Egypt, seem conversely to suggest the laxity and indiscipline of non-European gaols. In other cases, the production and circulation of such drawings and prints reflected and served to justify European claims to superiority over supposedly uncivilised places, such as China (figure 7). They also catered to a Western appetite for the sensational and cruel or for the exercise of domination over, and retribution against, supposedly 'inferior' cultures or races. Three-dimensional models of punishment by exotic 'others' featured prominently in metropolitan colonial exhibitions during the second half of the nineteenth century (figure 8). Periodicals like the *Illustrated London News* (founded in 1842) and *The Graphic* (1869) ran series of images that repeatedly placed indigenous bodies at the mercy of colonial ones. They published, for instance, line drawings of the execution of mutineers and rebels in 1857 in India and later of soldiers captured in the Afghan war and Sudanese rebels.[22]

[21] Linda Colley, *Captives: Britain, empire and the world, 1600–1850*, London: Cape, 2002, p. 290. Further images in this genre are the images of Europeans held captive during the Indian mutiny-rebellion of 1857–8. See C. A. Bayly (ed.), *The Raj: India and the British, 1600-1947*, London: National Portrait Gallery, 1990, p. 241.

[22] There is, of course, a long history to images of this kind, particularly depicting punishments inflicted on rebels and slaves, as in the Americas: for example, John Stedman, *Expedition to Surinam*, first published 1796, London: Folio Society, 1963, facing p. 6.

8. 'Death by a hundred cuts', China. [Chinese model in the possession of the Wellcome Trust: Wellcome Library, London]

VISUALISING PRISONERS

As we suggested above, under early colonial regimes, as in India, prisoners were highly visible as road gang labourers. One of the cartoons in G.F. Atkinson's satirical observations on social life in a post-mutiny upcountry station—'Curry and Rice'—shows a group of convicts in leg irons, accompanied by their well-fed overseer, saluting the local European magistrate. The implication of the drawing and the accompanying text seems to be that not only were convicts in road gangs a familiar sight, but that they were not worked particularly hard or greatly inconvenienced either by their irons or their overseers.[23] Although outdoor labour persisted—as Arnold shows in this volume—as new prisons were built and intramural labour gained in importance, convicts became more shadowy figures. Sketches of the penal settlement in the Andaman Islands appeared in various newspapers and periodicals in 1858, and again in 1872 when the convict Shere Ali murdered the viceroy, Lord Mayo. But removed from the context of a dramatic assassination in a picturesque location, drawings and paintings of life inside prisons were rare.[24]

Perhaps the contradiction between the orderliness suggested by modern prison architecture and design on the one hand, and the noisy, fetid reality of life within the prison walls was hard to reconcile. Unlike in Britain and North America, indigenous and local European élites remained for much of the period seemingly unconcerned about either crime as social consequence or gaol conditions (or had few formal means by which to express their concern). In consequence, there was no market for the satirical or other prints (like those of George Cruickshank) so popular in Britain. Like images of punishment more

---

[23] 'Our magistrate' in George Francis Atkinson, *'Curry and Rice': On forty plates; Or the ingredients of social life at 'Our Station' in India*, London: Day and Son, n.d. (1859).

[24] Andamans imagery has much in common with depictions of early-colonial Australia, where sketches of landscape and settlement presented a certain ordered progress to imperial expansion. There were also certain cultural alignments to be made in the production and consumption of images featuring white convicts juxtaposed with aborigines. See Robert Hughes, *The Fatal Shore: A history of the transportation of convicts to Australia, 1787–1868*, London: Collins Harvill, 1987, following p. 210, following p. 450. Of further interest in these respects are images of French Guiana and New Caledonia, where there were similarly reflexive spatial and cultural dynamics between landscape, indigenous communities and white settlers. See Alice Bullard, *Exile to Paradise: Savagery and civilisation in Paris and the South Pacific*, Stanford University Press, 2000; Peter Redfield, *Space in the Tropics: From convicts to rockets in French Guiana*, Berkeley, CA: University of California Press, 2000.

9. 'Convict', Singapore, *c.* 1848. [Frank S. Marryat, *Borneo and the Indian Archipelago*, 1848]

broadly, the few drawings of prisons that exist mainly harbour discursive meanings that equate colonial expansion with civilisation and progress. Sketches of the penal settlement in the Andamans, for instance, juxtapose pictures of orderly huts with indigenous communities dressed in European garb. Other pictures were a form of social critique. Engravings of gaol treadmills in colonial Jamaica, for instance, were central to debates about the abolition of apprenticeship, for the treadmill was depicted as a brutal weapon in the production of the colonial prison as a space of 'less eligibility' for the control of bonded labour.[25] Pictures of the flogging of convicts in colonial Australia too were a means through which the transportation system could be portrayed as a brutal institution contiguous to the slave trade.[26]

More commonly, outsiders—touring dignitaries, missionaries and clerics, penal reformers, or simply privileged travellers—visited prisons and provided their own word-pictures of the conditions they found and the state of the inmates. Such descriptions might serve specific purposes, either in conveying imperial images of foreign lands and peoples in the popular travelogues of the day, or in impressing upon their readers the need to give generously to missionary enterprises.[27] In the Straits Settlements (Singapore, Penang, Malacca) letters to the editors of the colonial press were another medium for descriptions (or criticisms) of prison life.[28] Only occasionally did such commentators record their impressions in visual form, and such images fall firmly into the category of the 'picturesque' that readers of travel writing were expected to enjoy (figure 9). Unpublished representations are more difficult to interrogate, for we do not know the productive intent of travellers such as Clementina Benthall, who recorded a scene from the penal settlement in Ramree Island (Arakan, Burma) (figure 10) in 1849, or the 1858 line drawing of Indian prisoners grinding corn by the Swedish artist Egron Lundgren.[29]

Coinciding with improved print technology, the advent of photography in the 1850s potentially opened up the exterior and interior of the colonial prison in unprecedented ways. For the first time photographs could be mass-produced in books and periodicals, although in the early years sketches drawn from

---

25 Paton, *No Bond but the Law*, pp. 105–9.

26 Hughes, *The Fatal Shore*, 'The rituals of the cat', following p. 450.

27 For example: James Backhouse, *A Narrative of a Visit to Mauritius and South Africa*, London: Hamilton, Adams and Co., 1844; Mary Carpenter, *Six Months in India*, vol. I, London: Longmans, Green and Co., 1868; Reginald Heber, *Narrative of a Journey through the Upper Provinces of India, from Calcutta to Bombay, 1824–1825*, vol. I, 3rd ed., London: John Murray, 1828; Frank S. Marryat, *Borneo and the Indian Archipelago, with Drawings of Costumes and Scenery*, London: Longman, Brown, Green and Longmans, 1848; W.H. Marshall, *Four Years in Burmah*, vol. II, London: Charles J. Skeet, 1860. A further genre for British and French convict settlements in Australia, New Caledonia and French Guiana were memoirs apparently (though not always) written by returned or escaped convicts. In turn these had their roots in the penny pamphlets of convict-era colonial America. See Gwenda Morgan and Peter Rushton, *Eighteenth-Century Criminal Transportation: The formation of the criminal Atlantic*, Basingstoke: Palgrave Macmillan, 2004, chapter 4.

28 Pieris, 'Hidden Hands and Divided Landscapes'; C.M. Turnbull, 'Convicts in the Straits Settlements, 1826–67', *Journal of the Malaysian Branch of the Royal Asiatic Society*, 43, 1 (1970), pp. 87–103.

29 Bayly (ed.), *The Raj*, p. 137.

10. Prisoners carrying water in Arakan, Burma, 1849. [Centre of South Asian Studies, University of Cambridge, Benthall Papers]

photographs were most commonly circulated. Perhaps surprisingly, photographs of the gaol and its prisoners were also enthusiastically sent and received in post-card form.[30] Yet the production and consumption of prison photographs followed an uncertain pattern. For India at least, remarkably few such images survive, and few if any appear in the administrative realm (the same was true of Egypt; see Gorman in this volume).[31] This was quite unlike republican China, or parts of Latin America, where large numbers of pictures of new model prisons and their wards—still new, freshly painted and largely untenanted except for carefully po-sitioned warders or visitors—accompanied official reports.[32] Extant photographs

[30] Peter Redfield reproduces a postcard of Kourou sawmill *c.*1900 in *Space in the Tropics*, p. 216. An amusing *carte postale* of a convict music band in the penal settlement at New Caledonia also features in the postcard albums held at the library of Kinloch Castle on the Isle of Rum. We thank George W. Randall for this information. The circulation of colonial postcards has received relatively little scholarly attention. For a fascinating exception (which however does not discuss prison postcards), see Saloni Mathur, 'Wanted Native Views: Collecting colonial postcards of India' in Antoinette Burton (ed.), *Gender, Sexuality and Colonial Modernities*, London: Routledge, 1999, pp. 95–115.

[31] And yet Egypt was the only nation to screen a prison film at one of the early-twentieth-century international penal congresses, in 1925 (with thanks to Tony Gorman).

[32] Frank Dikötter, *Crime, Punishment and the Prison in Modern China*, London: Hurst, 2002, illustra-tions between pp. 210–11; Carlos A. Aguirre, *The Criminals of Lima and Their Worlds: The prison experience, 1850–1935*, Durham, NC: Duke University Press, 2005, pp. 182, 185.

11. Prisoners oil-pressing, India, c. 1900. [H. L. Adam, *Oriental Crime*, 1909]

can mainly be related to either the development of Indian tourism or the production of orientalised popular accounts of India written for the home market. After Thomas Cook's first round-the-world tour in 1872, gaols such as the
old thug prison at Jabalpur were included in the itinerary of many European
travellers. 'The jail ought to be seen', noted one guide, 'for here are detained
in comfortable durance the last of that terrible tribe of murderous devotees
known as Thags.'[33] Other photographs appeared in other types of contemporary
literature.[34] Surviving images of Indian prisons and prisoners in the main are
reassuring—that prisoners are engaged in useful toil, require minimal coercion or
surveillance, and live in a clean, healthy and humane environment. These visual

---

[33] W.S. Caine, *Picturesque India: A handbook for European travellers*, London: Routledge, 1891, pp.
380–1. See also Piers Brendon, *Thomas Cook: 150 years of popular tourism*, London: Secker and
Warburg, 1991, pp. 159–60. A short tour from Calcutta to the Andamans, Nicobars and Rangoon was advertised in 1887 as 'a delightful three weeks' trip': *Cook's Indian Tours*, London:
Thomas Cook and Son, 1887.

[34] For instance, H.L. Adam, *The Indian Criminal*, London: J. Milne, 1909; H.L. Adam, *Oriental
Crime*, London: T. Werner Laurie, 1909. See also H.J.R. Twigg, *Monograph on the Art and Practice
of Carpet Making in the Bombay Presidency*, Bombay, 1907, plate 1.

confirmations of the success of the disciplinary regime show carefully posed photographs of prisoners diligently and apparently meekly going about the task assigned them—making carpets or *dhurries*, toiling in prison laundries, kitchens and workshops, or even exercising in the prison yard (figure 11).[35] In this sense, Indian photographs are closely related to those images presented in J.F.A. Mc-Nair's celebrated account of the penal settlements in the Straits—*Prisoners Their Own Warders*—which includes images of convict work gangs and impressive convict-built constructions, like St Andrew's cathedral.[36] Similar pictures were reproduced in accounts of personal visits or tours, like those of world-famous German criminologist Robert Heindl who visited penal settlements in New Caledonia, Egypt, the Andamans, Ceylon and Australia during his round-the-world trip (see also Anderson in this volume). We would speculate that like McNair's images, at least some of these were available in postcard form, for prints such as those of prisoners working the treadmill were also reproduced in other volumes, for example the popular Global Impressions series edited by ex-journalist Arnold Wright.[37]

There are also more brutal photographic images of punishment and execution. These reflected but also reinforced the purpose of earlier drawings, because although most were staged, they seemed to offer the promise of visual impartiality. Most famous perhaps are Felice Beato's carefully composed images of the execution of mutineer-rebels in 1857–8.[38] John Thomson's popular albums of *China and Its People* also included posed photographs of prisoners wearing the cangue (wooden punishment collar) (figure 12).[39] Such images underline the violence involved in the production of penal images. One extreme case was in 1886 Burma, when it emerged that a British official had kept groups of prisoners waiting before firing squads in repeatedly unsuccessful attempts to capture

[35] On China, see Dikötter, *Crime, Punishment and the Prison*, illustrations 2, 3, 5, 14, 22, 25 and 37. See also the photographs of the Robben Island leprosarium in Deacon, 'The Medical Institutions'. In what was perhaps an effort to portray the benevolence of the institution, the images include a striking print of the women's Christmas party.

[36] For examples of this style of representation in colonial Australia, see Kerr, *Design for Convicts*, plates 7, 11, 13 and 14.

[37] Robert Heindl, *Meine Reise nach den Strafkolonien, mit vielen Originalaufnahmen*, Berlin and Vienna: Ullstein and Co., 1913.

[38] Zahid Chaudhary, 'Phantasmagoric Aesthetics: Colonial violence and the management of perception', *Cultural Critique*, 59 (2005), pp. 63–119.

[39] J. Thomson, *The Straits of Malacca, Indo-China and China or Ten Years' Travels, Adventures and Residence Abroad*, London: Samson Low, Marston, Low and Searle, 1875. See also Stephen White, *John Thomson: A window to the Orient*, New York: Thames and Hudson, 1985.

12. The Cangue in China, 1874. [Wellcome Library, London]

the moment of execution.[40] More disturbing photographs reveal the brutality of the sexual abuse, beheading and quartering of Chinese prisoners, possibly in response to the Boxer Rebellion. Though strongly suggestive of a fierce response to native insurgency, their broader purpose is unclear, for we do not know who took them and for what purpose. It is unlikely such images would have found a popular publishing outlet.[41]

Towards the end of the nineteenth century photography became more than an illustrative device representing—and to a large extent exemplifying—the prison. It acquired a second, more evidently disciplinary, purpose. Gaol officials and ethnographers used photographs extensively to record in a 'scientific' fashion and with the 'stern fidelity' only photography was thought to allow, both the individual and collective characteristics of prisoners.[42] As such, prison photography supplemented more general state practices of identification and surveillance. In this it failed miserably, for as Anderson has argued elsewhere, the representational line between the 'individual' and the 'ethnographic' was often so blurred that photographs of prisoners lacking social markers of some kind were unreadable (figure 13).[43] The exception to this were collective photographs of convicts expressing their penal class, as in McNair's images of transportees in Singapore (see Anderson in this volume).

More readable images were those that anchored the prisoner socially, and it is here that Indian prison photography differs from the collective shots favoured in places like China. We see, for instance, the Brahmin undergoing rigorous imprisonment, and wearing his sacred thread, or the incarcerated criminal tribesman in his distinguishing garb (figure 14). Pictures of Robben Island similarly frame Xhosa prisoners of war in 'traditional' dress.[44] Without details of their provenance, or visual signifiers like the convict neck ticket or iron ring, it is difficult to distinguish many of these pictures from the more common ethnographic shots with which we are most familiar. This blurring of boundaries—between the

---

[40] Ray Desmond, *Victorian India in Focus: A selection of early photographs from the collection in the India Office Library and Records*, London: HMSO, 1982, pp. 65–6. Images of the crucifixion of Burmese dacoits by villagers are in the postcard albums at Kinloch Castle (with thanks to George W. Randall). See also Clare Anderson, *Legible Bodies: Race, criminality and colonialism in South Asia*, Oxford: Berg, 2004, p. 160.

[41] These gruesome photographs are in the Wellcome Library, London.

[42] The expression 'stern fidelity' was used by the Rev. Joseph Mullins in an address to the Photographic Society of Bengal in 1856. On the 'indexicality' of Indian photographs, see Anderson, *Legible Bodies*, pp. 141–2.

[43] Anderson, *Legible Bodies*, chapter 4.

[44] Harriet Deacon, 'Introduction' in Deacon (ed.), *The Island*, p. 3.

13. Madras convict, descriptive roll photograph. [Tamil Nadu State Archives]

penal and the ethnographic photograph—is reflected in the fact that pictures of prisoners fed into broader enquiries about the biological and cultural meaning of race in places like the Cape and Sierra Leone, and of course South East Asia, India and Ceylon. They also embodied the conflicts and ambivalences associated with anthropometric projects more generally.[45]

[45] Anderson, *Legible Bodies*, chapter 6; Harriet Deacon, 'The British Prison'; Elizabeth Edwards, *Raw Histories: Photographs, anthropology and museums*, Oxford: Berg, 2001, chapter 6.

Anthropometric photography for the purpose of prison discipline was itself a significant further development. By the end of the nineteenth century, copies of prisoners' photographs accompanied physical descriptions and measurements in gaol records, forming the basis of what came to be known as the Bertillon system of classification. This was supposed to facilitate the identification of escaped prisoners or habitual offenders. However, Bertillonage was not without its limitations and difficulties. Despite the assumption that the photograph represented a 'true' image of an individual, his or her appearance could change considerably over time (or be deliberately altered or disguised). At the same time the sheer number of records produced impeded their ordering as a readily accessible source of information.[46] There is the further question as to how far prisoners could themselves subvert or give a degree of personal agency to the images in which they were represented. The limitations of the technology demanded prisoners' compliance in measurement or long camera exposures. There is abundant evidence to suggest that prisoners refused to sit still or pulled faces while the picture was taken. Moreover, cultural sensitivities precluded the photographing of women, thus removing them completely from the purview of the colonial state in this respect.[47]

Late colonial representations of incarcerated nationalists are by their nature individuating images. The pictures of Gandhi which appeared in newspaper cartoons fed into the convention of the solitary prisoner in a barred prison cell. This reinforced wider discursive representations of the prison as a readily recognisable space of anti-colonial struggle and trope of unfreedom. Photographs of Jawaharlal Nehru in Naini Tal in the mid-1930s, or of Nelson Mandela and fellow ANC prisoners in Robben Island in the 1970s, suggest rather more humanised (and in some ways less fearsome) versions of the same basic elements—the barred cell and the labour yard, but also, as befits middle-class inmates, books, a desk on which to write, and the possibility of conversation with other prisoners.[48] And yet the colonial authorities had little control over the circulation of such images. At the end of the nineteenth century photographs of anti-colonial agitators began to appear in the vernacular press. Sympathisers, recognising their

[46] For these and related issues, see Anderson, *Legible Bodies*, chapter 5.

[47] Ibid., chapters 5 and 6. If photographs of Indian male prisoners were rare, pictures of females were almost non-existent. Exceptional images are of married convict women, pictured with their husbands in the Andamans. See Adam, *The Indian Criminal*, facing p. 215; Adam, *Oriental Crime*, facing p. 346.

[48] For Nehru, see photographs in *Selected Works of Jawaharlal Nehru*, vols 5 and 6, New Delhi: Orient Longman, 1973–4; and for Mandela, Nelson Mandela, *Long Walk to Freedom*, London: Abacus, 1995, following pp. 354 and 530.

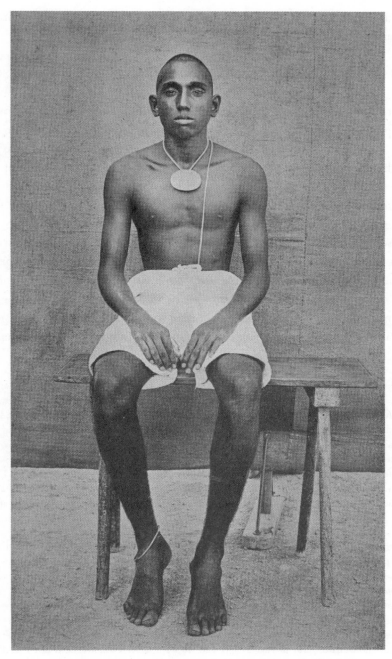

14. Brahmin undergoing a sentence of rigorous imprisonment. [H. L. Adam, *The Indian Criminal*, 1909]

potential appeal, also reproduced images of prisoners convicted of sedition on popular everyday items like matchboxes or handkerchiefs.[49]

SELF-REPRESENTATION AND POPULAR IMAGERY OF THE PRISON

If we turn from discussion of official representations of prisons and prisoners to those produced by prisoners or circulating among the outside population—such as the material culture of anti-colonial agitation described above—we might note that there appear to be relatively few visual images of the prison or fellow inmates produced by prisoners themselves, except, ironically, the photographs of prisoners taken by Indian transportation convicts who ran the gaol studios in Singapore.[50] Certainly, prisoners (especially educated prisoners or those with the resources to pay a scribe) wrote or otherwise recorded their impressions of prison life—witness the almost constant stream of letters home, prison petitions and the large volume of prison memoirs from around the globe.[51] But few inmates of colonial prisons in Asia or Africa had access to drawing materials, let alone photographic ones, or the skills needed to use them.[52] One fleeting glimpse of a Panjabi state prisoner's drawing of a ship and Singapore island is merely in the record of its destruction by officers who intercepted his mail.[53]

[49] Anderson, *Legible Bodies*, p. 161. Note also the subversion of Mau Mau rebel leader Dedan Kimathi, who when he learnt they had no picture of him, sent the British his photograph. David Anderson, *Histories of the Hanged: Testimonies from the Mau Mau Rebellion in Kenya*, London: Weidenfeld and Nicolson, 2005, opposite p. 278.

[50] Anderson, *Legible Bodies*, p. 193.

[51] Anderson, *Histories of the Hanged*; David Arnold, 'The Self and the Cell: Indian prison narratives as life histories' in David Arnold and Stuart Blackburn (eds), *Telling Lives in India: Biography, autobiography, and life history*, Bloomington, IN: Indiana University Press, 2004, pp. 29–53; P. Gready, 'Autobiography and the "Power of Writing": Political prison writing in the apartheid era', *Journal of Southern African Studies*, 19, 3 (1993), pp. 489–523; Mary Ross, 'The Prisonhouse of Language: Literary production and detention in Kenya' in Graeme Harper (ed.), *Colonial and Postcolonial Incarceration*, London: Continuum, 2001, pp. 176–86; Satadru Sen, 'Contexts, Representation and the Colonized Convict: Maulana Thanesari in the Andaman Islands', *Crime, History and Societies*, 8, 2 (2004), pp. 117–39; Peter Zinoman, *The Colonial Bastille: A history of imprisonment in Vietnam, 1862–1940*, Berkeley, CA: University of California Press, 2001, pp. 8–12.

[52] Colonial Australia appears unique among British colonies, for the survival of a relatively large number of convict sketches and paintings, probably because they were kept within convict-turned-settler families. This fact perhaps also explains the survival of sketches by *déportés* in New Caledonia: Bullard, *Exile to Paradise*, pp. 126, 195 and 204–5. Aguirre also discusses Peruvian prisoner artist Godnez in *The Criminals of Lima*, pp. 212–14.

[53] Nahar Singh, *Documents Relating to Bhai Maharaj Singh*, Gurdwara Karamsar, 1968, document 73.

There were, no doubt, ways in which prisoners modified their prison environment so as to assert their own individuality or to leave tangible traces—by the graffiti with which they marked prison cells or the tattoos with which they adorned their bodies (see Aguirre and Gorman in this volume). Some of these images represented a longing for freedom and for the outside world, or reflected more directly on their prison experience and status. Some tattoos may have been intended to recall a prisoner's faith, parents and sweethearts, but others may have been directed—as marks of defiance and bravado perhaps—at the observation of other prisoners and warders.[54] And yet even this most personal of corporal practices was investigated by prison administrators for what it might reveal of the social (or rather criminal) body.[55] Few prisoners were engaged in the sort of crafts or occupations that allowed for creative expression of other kinds. The Burmese wood carvers who fitted out the superintendent's bungalow on Ross Island in the Andamans, or convicts like Bawajee Rajaram and his convict draughtsmen, who drew up many of the architectural plans in the building of Singapore, were truly exceptional.[56] The gaol artefacts commonly shown at world exhibitions and fairs like the Colonial and Indian Exhibition of 1886 reveal more about the supposed relationship between the prison and 'modernity' than about prisoner creativity.[57] Prisoners were most commonly engaged in laborious work; those working in typesetting, carpet-making, pottery, brick-making and carpentry had

---

[54] For comparative literature on convict tattooing in Australian penal settlements, see: Hamish Maxwell-Stewart and Ian Duffield, 'Skin Deep Devotions: Religious tattoos and convict transportation to Australia' in Jane Caplan (ed.), *Written on the Body: The tattoo in European and North American history*, London: Reaktion, 2000, pp. 118–35. On Russia, see Abby M. Schrader, 'Branding the Other/Tattooing the Self: Bodily inscription among convicts in Russia and the Soviet Union' in Caplan (ed.), *Written on the Body*, pp. 174–92. A contemporary British survey is Amanda Wait, *Marked Men: Stories and pictures from the inside*, n.p.: Bar None Books, 2004. On contemporary Russian prison tattoo culture, see Alix Lambert, *Russian Prison Tattoos: Codes of authority, domination and struggle*, Atglen, PA: Schiffer, 2003; Sergey Vasiliev and Danzig Baldayev (eds), *Russian Criminal Tattoo Encyclopaedia*, London: FUEL, 2005; Danzig Baldayev et al., *Russian Criminal Tattoo Encyclopaedia, vol. II*, London: FUEL, 2006.

[55] See Gorman in this volume, as also Aguirre, *The Criminals of Lima*, pp. 166–7; Anderson, *Legible Bodies*, pp. 69–71; Jane Caplan, '"National Tattooing": Traditions of tattooing in nineteenth-century Europe' in Caplan (ed.), *Written on the Body*, pp. 156–73.

[56] Pieris, 'On Dropping Bricks', pp. 88–9. There are parallels here with convict architect Francis Greenaway in Australia.

[57] *Colonial and Indian Exhibition, 1886: Empire of India, special catalogue of exhibits by the Government of India and private exhibitors*, London: William Clowes and Sons, 1886, p. 42. At least two other extra-European countries—Japan and Australia—as well as America also presented penal exhibits on the nineteenth-century global stage. See Aram A. Yengoyan, 'Universalism and Utopianism: A review article', *Comparative Studies in Society and History*, 39, 4 (1997), p. 790.

little scope to leave anything but a productive mark. For instance, the flat-weave *dhurries* produced in Indian gaols between the 1880s and 1920s sometimes incorporated the date of manufacture and even words such as 'Lucknow Jail' into their design; but the range of images allowed to the weavers was limited. Prisoners were given patterns to follow or commissioned by the gaol superintendent (and his wife) to produce specific designs.[58]

But representations of the prison and prisoners were not confined to official sources and to images generated within the prison itself. Attempts were made publicly to make the unseen and largely unknown somehow accessible and meaningful to a wider audience. Much of this was, no doubt, by word of mouth and by rumour. But images of the prison and of prisoners also passed into the realms of popular culture, feeding into popular ballads, novels and plays. There is, for instance, an established Middle Eastern tradition of prison literature (*adab al-sujun*), in poetry and prose (see Gorman in this volume). In India too the gaol fed into vernacular and English literature which included missionary tracts.[59] These cultural forms created what Carlos Aguirre refers to in Latin America as 'a powerful imaginary'.

Representations of the prison were also produced through the visual images that accompanied popular broadsheets and ballads: see the image in the *corrido* c.1900 on the opening of the Mexico penitentiary, in Salvatore and Aguirre.[60] At times artists sought to invoke the prison less as an awesome abstraction than as the context for the travails of celebrated individuals, whose heroic exploits, social status, or political leadership had already earned them public acclaim or notoriety. One example of this concerns the Tarakeshwar murder case in 1873 Bengal, which found its way into the popular Kalighat style of painting. This episode involved the *mahant* or head of the Shiva temple at Tarakeshwar, who was prosecuted and imprisoned for adultery with a clerk's wife (Elokshi by name). She was violently attacked and murdered by her jealous husband, Nabin Chandra Banerjee, a clerk in the office of the Superintendent of Government Printing. This compelling mixture of religion, sexual intrigue and violence gave the Kalighat

---

[58] Steven Cohen, *The Unappreciated Dhurrie: A study of the traditional flatwoven carpets of India*, London: David Black, 1982, esp. p. 35.

[59] Anindita Mukhopadhyay, '*Jail Darpan*: The image of the jail in Bengali middle-class literature', *Studies in History*, 15, 1 (1999), pp. 109–44; A.L.O.E., *Beyond the Black Waters: A tale*, London: T. Nelson and Sons, 1890. Perhaps the most famous literary representations of the colonial gaol in English are Arthur Conan Doyle's *The Sign of Four* (representing the Andaman Islands) and (in translation) Franz Kafka's geographically unhinged *In the Penal Colony*.

[60] Salvatore and Aguirre, *The Birth of the Penitentiary*, following p. 159.

15. The *mahant* as a prison gardener, Kalighat painting *c.* 1880. [Victoria and Albert Museum, London]

painters a field day. Most of the images in this series from *c*.1880–90 show the evolving relationship between the *mahant* (Madhav Chandra Giri) and the comely Elokshi, but others show the *mahant* on trial and his arrival in gaol to serve his three-year term of rigorous imprisonment. A further illustration (figure 15) shows the *mahant* working in the prison garden. There is little about his dress and posture to suggest the hardship and humiliation of prison life, except that his figure is dwarfed by that of an armed and uniformed prison officer (who wears, perhaps incongruously, a hat, the universal marker of the European or *topiwallah* in Indian art and popular imagination). A final image shows the *mahant* straining to work a giant oil-press under a guard who stands over him with a whip and gun.[61]

CONCLUSIONS: THE POLITICS OF POSTCOLONIALITY

We have only touched on some of the issues relating to the architectural and spatial dynamics of the prison and its representation in the countries and colonies with which this volume is concerned, and there is scope for further research. Clearly, there was a certain unevenness to prison construction and design, and the meaning of penal imagery, especially photography, as an important technology that brought about further complexity and change. In some places like China, photographs of gaol buildings and inmates were commissioned and deployed by the authorities to support their interpretation of the prison as an effective, orderly and, not least, modern institution. In others, notably India, images of prisoners mainly fed into the exoticisation of Indian society more generally. Officials and their governments also represented formal structures and actual life inside the gaol in different ways. Some images, like those of industrial labour in the Straits penal settlements, presented a picture of the value of rehabilitation. Others like the Andamans sketches fell into the category of the picturesque, or framed prisoners through more familiar social tropes like 'caste' or 'tribe'. Conversely, the prison and associated penal practices fed an appetite for the sensational and the exotic in the colonial imagination, especially through scenes that displayed acts of retributive violence against inferior 'types' or 'races', or the barbarity of local modes of punishment.[62] However, even here the official view of the prison could be challenged and subverted in various ways, for visual images of the prison and

---

[61] W.G. Archer, *Kalighat Paintings*, London: HMSO, 1971, pp. 12–15 and figures 26–41. On the gendering of public space implied by this scandal, see Swati Chattopadhyay, *Representing Calcutta: Modernity, nationalism and the colonial uncanny*, London: Routledge, 2006, pp. 229–37.

[62] Perhaps the footage of French prisoners embarking for Devil's Island in Guiana that appeared as a British Pathe news item in 1933 might also be read in this way.

of prisoners conveyed a wide variety of messages and were open to a similarly wide variety of interpretations. For instance, as Anderson has shown elsewhere, it is impossible to unpick the meaning of the relationship that individual convicts had with their own photograph.[63]

The politics of the independent nation state have given an important further dynamic to the representation of colonial institutions like the prison. At one level these relate to the fact that the isolated landscapes that were appealing as penal settlements also hold enormous allure as tourist destinations, such that penal spaces like the Andaman Islands, or French Guiana, have been re-imagined as places of peace and beauty.[64] The social (re)production of societies founded as institutions of confinement is at the same time enormously complex and controversial.[65] As Casella and Fredericksen have argued, the imagination of penal space there must invoke a sense of difference from the imperial state in order for a de-colonised consciousness to emerge.[66] The cellular gaol museum in the Andamans, for example, is now a tourist attraction, framed around a politics of martyrdom that is dated from the mutiny-rebellion of 1857–8. It is also a place of pilgrimage for surviving anti-colonial activists.[67] Films like the Bollywood blockbuster *Kala Pani*, portraying the brutality of nationalist imprisonment in the cellular gaol, have enjoyed enormous success (on the cinematography of incarceration in the Middle East, see also Gorman in this volume). Robben Island too, inevitably perhaps, holds massive symbolic appeal in post-apartheid South Africa.[68] In postcolonial Congolese art, imprisonment and corporal punishment have been used as a visual device to express the politics of Belgian repression.[69] As such, prison images of all kinds belong both to the discursive realm of state power and penology, but also to far wider realms of imagination and representation. They move both within discourses of colonialism and beyond them.

---

[63] Anderson, *Legible Bodies*, p. 162.

[64] Clare Anderson, 'The Politics of Convict Space: Indian penal settlements and the Andamans' in Bashford and Strange (eds), *Isolation*, pp. 40–55.

[65] On prison heritage in Ireland and Australia, see Eleanor Conlin Casella, 'Prisoner of His Majesty: Postcoloniality and the archaeology of British penal transportation', *World Archaeology*, 37, 3 (2005), pp. 453–67. Also Harriet Deacon, 'Intangible Heritage in Conservation Management Planning: The case of Robben Island', *International Journal of Heritage Studies*, 10, 3 (2004), pp. 309–19.

[66] Eleanor Conlin Casella and Clayton Fredericksen, 'Legacy of the "Fatal Shore": The heritage and archaeology of confinement in post-colonial Australia', *Journal of Social Archaeology*, 4, 1 (2004), pp. 99–125.

[67] Anderson, 'The Politics of Convict Space'.

[68] Bernault, 'The Politics of Enclosure', pp. 10–11.

[69] Ibid., pp. 34–5.

INDEX